M A Y A N
ORACLES
FOR THE
MILLENNIUM

Other Avon Books by
R. T. Kaser

AFRICAN ORACLES IN 10 MINUTES
I CHING IN 10 MINUTES
RUNES IN 10 MINUTES
TAROT IN 10 MINUTES

MAYAN ORACLES FOR THE MILLENNIUM

R.T. KASER

AVON BOOKS ◆ NEW YORK

VISIT OUR WEBSITE AT
http://AvonBooks.com

All the glyphs and special symbols used in this book were rendered by the author using ALTSYS Fontographer V.4.0 for the Macintosh. Fonts "mayaGLYPH," "aztecGLYPH," "Lightning," and "RTKkards" copyright © 1995, 1996 by R.T. Kaser.

The "Mayan Tarot" illustrating Reading #11 is by Pittsburgh artist William B. Cox, based on a concept by R.T. Kaser, © copyright 1995, 1996 by R.T. Kaser and William B. Cox.

All Mayan dates for the 20th century were verified using the computer program MacMaya, copyright © 1992–1995 by Warren Anderson, Box 811, Wilson, Wyoming 83014. Used with permission.

The Lancandone chants and Mayan invocations that open the main sections of this book are excerpted and adapted from Alfred M. Tozzer; *A Maya Grammar*, Papers of the Peabody Museum of American Archeology and Ethnology, Harvard University, Volume 9, 1921. Reprinted courtesy of the Peabody Museum, Harvard University.

AVON BOOKS
A division of
The Hearst Corporation
1350 Avenue of the Americas
New York, New York 10019

Copyright © 1996 by Richard T. Kaser
Published by arrangement with the author
Library of Congress Catalog Card Number: 96-23251
ISBN: 0-380-78134-4

Library of Congress Cataloging in Publication Data:
Kaser, R. T.
     Mayan oracles for the millennium / by R.T. Kaser.
          p. cm.
Includes bibliographical references and index.
1. Oracles   2. Divination   3. Horoscopes   4. Mayas–Miscellanea   I. Title.
BF1751.K35 1996   96-23251
133.3—dc20   CIP

First Avon Books Trade Printing: December 1996

AVON TRADEMARK REG. U.S. PAT. OFF. AND IN OTHER COUNTRIES, MARCA REGISTRADA, HECHO EN U.S.A.

Printed in the U.S.A.

OPM   10   9   8   7   6   5   4   3   2   1

With Reverence for
The Great Spirit of Tobacco
and
to Chris Miller

ok-s-ik-ob ti yol itšil
Cause to enter the spirit within . . . .
—*Mayan Invocation*
at the End of the Katuns
The Prophecy of Chilam Balam*
Alfred Tozzer translation

*Excerpted and adapted from Tozzer's A Maya Grammar. See bibliography.

PREFACE

Welcome to the new millennium! . . . and to an ancient system
of timekeeping and destiny planning that's still timely
and relevant today.

When the Maya of Mexico invented their sacred calendar 2,600 years
ago, they had no idea we would be coming along later with our own calendar. They had no idea we would be celebrating the passage of our second thousand-year millennium at about this time. But as it turns out, as
we now reach our 21st century, the ancient Mayan calendar is reaching
a "millennium" of its own . . . the end of 5,200 cycles, the conclusion of
a "Creation Epoch," and the beginning of a new era.

In just a few minutes you will be using the signs and symbols from
the Maya's sacred calendar to determine the auspices for any day, compute your personal horoscope, ask any question on your mind, or start
keeping count of Mayan time yourself. But first, a little background . . .

Mysteries of Space and Time

It was at least 20,000 years ago when their ancestors came to North
America out of the Far East, via Siberia, and down from Alaska. Those
who eventually settled in Mexico took to farming beans, squash, a little
tobacco, and corn, a crop they developed from a weed. Like most farm-
ers, they took their signs and omens from the sky, which doubled for
them as both weather advisor and calendar planner.

They were the Maya. And by the time of Christ, they had computed the movement of the sun, moon, and planets with a precision
matched only by modern computers and current science. They were
obsessed with tracking the movements of the heavenly bodies. They
were obsessed with telling time. And not just because it helped them
scientifically forecast when it was the "right time" to plant and harvest
their crops . . .

"As above, so below," the Maya say. What went on in the sky was
seen by them to be a great, cosmic, and universal truth. "What applies
to everything else in the Universe must also apply to us." And they were
bound and determined to figure out what this Divine Plan was.

When the Maya looked up at the sky, they saw the sun rising and
setting. They saw the moon phasing. They saw the Zodiac turning—for

them, straight overhead. They gave the constellations names. And they told myths about the patterns they picked out in the stars. In this respect they were like the Babylonians, Mesopotamians, Arabs, Egyptians, Greeks, Romans, and Chinese—who all thought it wise to observe and learn from the stars.

The Maya learned many of the same lessons they did. You can tell time by watching the moon... but only to a certain point of precision. You can tell time by watching the sun... and a year is 365 days (or so) long. Furthermore you can predict things (like when the rains are coming) by making these observations. Why? Because there's pattern in the Universe.

The Maya discovered the fact that everything in the heavens cycles and recycles. Every phase of the moon repeats. Every so often the sun returns to a certain point on the horizon. And every five times it does, eight cycles of Venus will also be completed.

In fact, the more and more you look, the more and more it appears as if the Universe is a cycle within a cycle within a cycle within a cycle... or as one of the Hebrew Prophets described it, a wheel within a wheel within a wheel. And modern science has taken nothing away from this central observation.

The Maya were obsessed with time and its recurring cycles. For just as one might predict the seasons by their recurrence—and even recurring weather patterns might be foreseeable over a number of years—could one not also predict when conditions were right for the recurrence of social, political, and even more mundane human events?

This was the Maya's theory. And so they began recording dates... which over hundreds of years grew into vast chronologies... still standing today on the stones where they were carved as Mayan history lessons. On such-and-such a day, a King took office. On this date a ball game was played. And on another we had to sacrifice for rain.

With the precision of scientists collecting data to support their hypotheses, the Maya kept detailed record books (made from the bark of trees). Each hour, each day, each month, each century, each millennium, was counted and numbered and associated with a set of signs. Each date was double-checked with an entirely separate system to make sure no error had been made.

Over the centuries, these holy books, copied by hand and passed down from one sun-counter priest to the next, served both as perpetual almanacs and as "books of human fate." It was by consulting the signs for a person's birth date, that these *astronomers* also served their people as *astrologers* and diviners. One could "look up" today's date to find its horoscope. Or one could even count a handful of objects to determine the auspices surrounding a given question.

It is these ancient systems of timekeeping, astronomy, astrology, and divination that we are going to be using here.

Signs and Symbols

The primary signs and symbols you will be using look like this....

Mayan Day Signs

Sea Creature Air Night Corn Serpent Death Deer Rabbit Rain Dog

Monkey Broom Reed Jaguar Eagle Owl Earthquake Blade Storm Lord

They were used by the Maya as early as 600 B.C. Two thousand years later—as Europeans were about to arrive in North America—the same systems were still in use by the reigning Aztecs, who had redesigned the symbols to look like this....

Aztec Day Signs

Alligator Wind House Lizard Snake Death Deer Rabbit Rain Dog

Monkey Grass Reed Ocelot Eagle Vulture Earthquake Flint Storm Flower

In asking your questions, charting your horoscope, or tracking time, you will have the option of using either the original Mayan hieroglyphic signs or the stylized Aztec symbols—whichever you prefer.

Like our days of the week, these "Day Signs" were used by the ancient sun-counter priests (and are still used in some remote regions of Mexico and the Yucatán) to mark the passage of time. These symbols were (and are) also used as "Zodiac Signs" in Mayan and Aztec astrology, and—like our Tarot cards or Runes—as symbols for interpretation in fortune-telling.

Using a handful or two of dried soup beans, the cutout Maya Lightning Cards in the back of the book, or your finger to point at the diagram on page 11, you will be able to access these ancient signs and put them to work in your modern life. To get started, turn to Reading

#0—"Select Your Means." If you'd like to know more about the new millennium the Maya foresaw for us, read on . . .

Time Running Out?

Though we tend to think of time as a "line," on which the past, present, and future can be distinctly marked, the Maya saw time as a series of endless cycles. The largest cycle they identified began— are you ready for this?—41,341,050,000,000,000,000,000,000,000 years ago! . . . in other words, a long, long time before the Earth itself had formed and cooled. (Interestingly enough, the Egyptian hieroglyphs contain symbols of years numbering as high as 1,000,000,000,000,000,000.)

Like the Maya, we also sometimes view time as a recurring cycle, but on a much smaller scale. There are 24 hours in our day, and each hour repeats again tomorrow. There are seven days in a week that each repeat next week. And there are 12 months in a year that each repeat next year. But that's as far as our cyclical timekeeping goes. Though we count decades of 10 years, centuries of 100 years, and millennia of 1,000 years, we would never imagine a year when it might be 1968 again or a time when the 18th century would return.

But to the Mayan way of thinking, all time eventually cycles back to a point when it will repeat. As we ourselves now turn our calendar over on a new decade, new century, and new millennium—all at the same time—the Mayan calendar is primed to complete three cycles of its own: a *Katun*, a *Baktun*, and a *Creation Epoch*. The longest of these, the Creation Epoch, began on a day that we would call August 12, 3114 B.C.[1]. The Maya believed on that day the current Creation Epoch started. It was the fifth such epoch that the world has known.

In comparison, the Hebrew calendar traces the beginning of time to 3761 B.C. The Chinese calendar extends back to 2637 B.C. The ancient Greeks counted time starting in 776 B.C., the year of the first Olympiad. And the classical Romans dated their calendar back to 753 B.C., the mythical date when Rome was founded. The Christian calendar—which has, in its modern form, come into wide secular use the

---

[1]Other books may list a slightly different date for this. I have opted for using the system in which the year 1 A.D. is preceded by the year 1 B.C. (with no zero-year in between). Others may tell you it's 3113 B.C. because they are counting a Year Zero between 1 A.D. and 1 B.C. Both methods refer to the same day and are equally accurate. The August 12th date is accurate within about 24 hours, which is as close as the community of Mayan scholars has agreed and is consistent with other contemporary books on Mayan astrology.

world over—starts counting time with the birth of Christ, the year 1, ending B.C. dates (literally "before Christ") and beginning A.D. dates (Anno Domini, "in the year of the Lord"). In the faith of Islam, the calendar begins in our 622 A.D., the year when Mohammed left Mecca.... It's not really a question of which calendar is right or wrong, for time, as Einstein said, is relative. But in this book we will be correlating our calendar with the one the Maya invented in order to make use of their astrological and divinatory systems.

At this time we are living during the last 20-year period (called a Katun) of the Maya's Fifth Creation Epoch. When this Katun is completed, on December 21, 2012, three cycles in the Mayan calendar will all be completed at once:

the current Katun itself,

the current Baktun (20 Katuns), and

the current Creation Epoch (13 Baktuns).

You will not need to be too concerned with these larger periods of time as you use this book. But the symbols and numbers we will be working with are the basic units that literally "add up" to these larger periods.

If you'd like to get started, turn to Reading #0 now. It will tell you more about the symbols and how you will be able to access them to achieve the ends that bring you here. But if you want to know more about Mayan timekeeping before you start, read on....

Mayan Time Frames

At the crux of this system of timekeeping is the "day," known as a *Kin*. Each Kin was designated by using one of the Day Signs. For example, ▦ was the symbol for Sea Creature; ◼ for Air; and ▦ for Night. Or, using the Aztec glyphs: ⌇, ▨, and ▤ for Alligator, Wind, and House. And so on.

There were 20 such day symbols to denote the Kins. And after all the symbols had been used—and thus a 20-day period had passed—a *Uinal* (pronounced "Ve-nal") was said to have been completed. As a unit of time, the Uinal is roughly equivalent to our concept of "month."

Each Kin was also numbered, much as we assign a number to each day of our own months. But in their primary calendars and associated astrologies and divinations, the Maya did not number these days 1 to 20, as we would expect. Rather, they counted them from 1 to 13 and then started over again at 1, to create another period of time roughly equivalent to our concept of "week," but closer to the length of our "fortnight."

These two magical time periods—20 days and 13 days—were the principal units of Mayan and Aztec timekeeping. Most other units of time were established as factors (or multiples) of these basic units.

After the 20-Kin Uinal, the next largest period of time was the *Tzolkin*. A Tzolkin was equal to 13 Uinals of 20 Kins each—a period of time that equals 260 days. The Tzolkin was regarded as a high holy number of days, since—among other things—it approximates the period of time that a pregnant woman carries her child. Coincidentally, it also serves as a useful multiple for astronomical observations, since it can be used to compute just about everything from eclipse cycles of the sun and moon to the transit of Venus. It was the key by which the Mayan astronomers unlocked many of the mysteries of the Universe. And last but not least, it represents all the possible combinations of signs and numbers that can occur when one simultaneously counts through the 20 Day Signs, while numbering them 1 through 13.

It is this Tzolkin calendar—with its 260 combinations of signs and numbers—that will figure prominently in this book as we tell your fortune, chart your horoscope, and project the outlook for this (or any) day. But Mayan timekeeping did not stop there....

The next higher unit in both Mayan and Aztec time was the *Tun*, a 360-day period, at the end of which a stone (or *Tun*) was erected to commemorate the passing of eighteen 20-Kin Uinals—roughly the equivalent of a solar year.

Though the Maya knew that there should actually be 365 days in the year—and we will be using their 365-day calendar as well—they preferred the symmetry of the 360-day Tun and used it as the basic unit in all their higher calculations of time.

The Tun, in turn, became the basis for: the Katun, which equals 20 Tuns (7,200 days); the Baktun, which equals 20 Katuns (144,000 days); and the Creation Epoch, which equals 13 Baktuns (1,872,000 days). It is these latter three time periods that will time out together on December 21, 2012—an event to be accompanied, myth says, with a cataclysmic destruction of the Earth no less frightening than the Christian concept of Armageddon. According to these prophecies, earthquakes, volcanoes, hurricanes, and tidal waves all may herald the start of the Sixth Creation Epoch on December 22, 2012.

How the Book Works

Mayan Oracles has been designed to give you an informative, interesting, and entertaining experience with the Mayan and Aztec fortune-telling calendars.

You will be working with the actual signs and symbols that Mayan priests of old and their more recent Aztec followers used in their own calendars, astrologies, and divinations. The signs and symbols in this book were designed using authoritative sources, including facsimiles of the few surviving Mayan books. You will see the same symbols carved all over Mexico on the ancient ruins of these lost civilizations.

<u>**Asking Questions.**</u> When you are asking direct questions of these oracles (as in the first six Readings), you will be using a method of counting beans (or stones or crystals) that is based on a fortune-telling technique still used by practicing Mayan priests in the Yucatán. In this method, a handful of beans is counted out for each question that you ask. The number of beans in any count will determine which of the 20 Day Signs or 13 numbers is your answer. To find out what these symbols mean, you'll just turn to one of the Answer sections in the book and read your response from these oracles.

Or, at your option, you can make a set of Magic Lightning Cards (see the cutouts at the back of the book). Just mix up your cutouts and select one to get your sign. Or—even simpler—use your index finger and one of the book's preprinted diagrams to Point-n-Click your way to an answer. All these methods are described in Reading #0. In any of the book's 13 other Readings, you will have the option to use whichever method is most convenient and comfortable for you.

<u>**Daily Readings**</u>. You will also be learning how to convert dates from our calendar into Mayan or Aztec symbols, starting in Reading #7. This is another authentic means of using these calendars for divination—the result being that you will derive a general forecast for the day...a sort of daily horoscope, if you will.

There is an Almanac in the back of the book that will help you do this. But just as the priests of old had to do a little calculating when they referred to their own Almanacs, you, too, will need to do a little basic math. It's about as easy as counting on your fingers (and toes), but the book will walk you through it step by step. And you'll get the hang of it in no time.

The Almanac in this book has been painstakingly constructed, based on the directions contained in an ancient Mayan book, which is today known as *The Paris Codex*. *The Paris Codex* contains various formulas for assuring that any timekeeper of old could compute a calendar with accuracy. And it works: The dates noted in this Almanac have been checked against computer programs used by scholars who study these calendars for a living. So when you compute a date here, you can be fairly sure it's correct. The Almanac covers all dates from now until December 21, 2012—virtually every day "from here to eternity."

Chart Your Horoscope. Once you have learned how to convert dates from our calendar into Mayan and Aztec symbols, you will be able to do what the Mayan priests did for children at their birth. You will be able to turn to these signs to consider your fate and, as a result, learn how to control your own destiny. The Almanac also will permit you to compute the Mayan or Aztec signs for any birth date between 1909 and 2012. So you can do a workup for everyone in your family, if you like.

Your horoscope will consist of various signs and symbols that, taken together, will complete your "chart." To read your horoscope, you'll just turn to the back of the book, where you will find a complete profile of your work life, home life, love life, and financial prospects. I've also included ways to compute whether you are compatible with someone of another sign. (See Reading #13's Extra Credit section.) You will have the opportunity to keep your horoscope up-to-date by combining your signs with the signs for any given day, which will give you a personal forecast for every day from now until December 21, 2012.

How to Proceed

The best way to get started is to turn to Reading #0 and follow the easy, step-by-step instructions. You'll be asking a question of these oracles and getting an answer immediately. There are 13 of these self-contained Readings—and if you do them in order, you will be walked through everything there is to know and do with the book.

Once you get the hang of things, or any time you want to fly solo, or if you simply prefer to learn things in a "lecture format," turn to the Quick Reference Guide which will summarize everything you need to know from the other Readings in order to conduct consultations on your own.

Finding Your Answers. Whichever route you take, you will be asking your own questions every step of the way. Once you have counted your beans or computed a date, all you will have to do is look up your signs and read your answers. The answers will be found either within the Reading you are doing or at the back of the book in the Quick Reference Guide. Each Reading will tell you where to find the answer that relates to the question you just asked.

As part of the answers, you will pick up information about Mayan and Aztec mythology, culture, and tradition. The sections of the text dealing with the mythology are written in the classic Mayan literary style of recurring couplets, which tend to repeat what was just said. But most answers are in contemporary American language, expressed in modern American terms.

In constructing this book, I have relied heavily upon the work of anthropologists and other researchers who are still in the process of deciphering the Mayan hieroglyphs. These scholars have provided me with my understanding of how the calendar works and what is known of the meanings originally attached to the individual signs and symbols we will be interpreting here. But I have not hesitated to use my own intuition and knowledge of other divination systems in my reinterpretation of these symbols for the modern age . . . and neither should you.

Consistent with the Mayan tradition of assigning actual dates to the signs, my research for this book also included the analysis of several thousand dates from recent times. If the Maya were correct in believing that history repeats itself, our dates should theoretically work as well as theirs in being instructive and predictive. I was, in fact, quite astounded at how well recent dates fell into a pattern with the signs they accompanied.

I have included many of these current dates among the answers found in the Quick Reference Guide. I have also left space there for you to record your own dates—historical, political, or personal. If you do this over a period of time, you will effectively do what the Mayan priests of old did with their timekeeping systems: You will construct your own chronology and divination system that is precisely tuned to your own perception of what is important in your world.

I have also worked with an artist to develop a series of illustrations that may help you relate better to the hieroglyphs. These drawings—which are loosely based on one of only four surviving Mayan books—are found in Reading #11. Tarot card enthusiasts will note a striking resemblance to the images they are already familiar with.

And finally, I have given you the opportunity to take a 260-day vision quest, which is the traditional training period of a Mayan priest. If you follow this route (outlined in each Reading's Extra, Extra Credit section), you will be encouraged and guided in observing the signs that can be read directly from nature.

Should you find that things Mayan appeal to you, there is a bibliography at the back of the book. And should you wish to go on and study the Mayan glyphs and their meanings for yourself, you will be well prepared.

Why Does It Work?

As with all divination systems—including Tarot, I Ching, Runes, Nigerian Ifa, and every other system I have encountered—these Aztec and Mayan oracles tend to work in mysterious ways.

To the people who originally practiced these beliefs, the systems worked due to divine intervention. The gods determined the signs that came in answer to any specific question. The priests who read these signs were considered to possess divine and secret knowledge that allowed them to interpret the signs correctly in terms of their omens, auspices, or portents.

You are free here to believe whatever you please.

Should you take the answers you receive here as gospel truth? That, too, is up to you. But it was not my intent to dictate your destiny—in fact, that's something I firmly believe only you can do for yourself. Bring your own real issues and important questions to this book, use it as a way to stimulate and challenge your own creative thought . . . and you will not go wrong.

So without further ado, let's get on with it. . . . Cause to enter your spirit within.

R. T. Kaser
December 21, 1995 (8 Dog)
First Day of Winter
New Moon

CONTENTS

The Readings
1

Reading #0
Select Your Means
(Name your ends)
3

Reading #1
What Do the Signs Say?
(Clue me in)
7

Reading #2
How Am I Headed?
(Point me)
26

Reading #3
How Did I Get Here?
(Go fast forward)
40

Reading #4
What's the Score?
(Hedge my bet)
63

Reading #5
What's It All About?
(Play ball!)
81

Reading #6
Tell It Like It Is
(Get real)
96

Reading #7
How's It Going Today?
(Update me)
102

Reading #8
How's It Look For Tomorrow?
(Tip me off)
112

Reading #9
What's on the Agenda?
(Block out my calendar)
120

Reading #10
Year-at-a-Glance
(Give it some time)
127

Reading #11
What Can I Envision?
(Show me the larger picture)
137

Reading #12
Fit Me In
(Book my time)
165

Contents

Reading #13
What's My Destiny?
(Give me my horoscope)
188

Quick Reference Guide
215

Intructions
217

Master Answer Section
223

The 20 Day Signs
223

The 13 Day Numbers
247

The 260 Combinations
265

Almanac 1909–2012
425

Part I—
The Sacred Calendar
438

Part II—
The Secular Calendar
473

Your Magic Lightning Cards
(Day Sign & Day Number Cutouts)
491

Index: All the Questions You Can Ask
507

Selected Bibliography
513

Acknowledgments
517

THE READINGS

I am making it my gifts to you again
for your welfare. . . .
May they not be affected by crumble,
may they not separate. . . .
May they not break, my gifts to you.
See me making my gifts to you,
oh father.

—LANCANDONE CHANT, CIRCA 1900
(AT THE CEREMONY FOR RENEWING THE INCENSE BURNERS)
ADAPTED FROM ALFRED TOZZER

Reading #0

Select Your Means
(Name your ends)

Some books are made to be read from cover to cover....
Some books are more like an experience.
This is one to touch and feel. In this Reading you will map
out your own path through the book. Everyone starts here.

TOOLS

You will map out your path first by choosing a means ... and then by choosing an end.

As for the means: You will have your choice of three methods for asking questions of, and getting answers from, this oracle. For example, you can simply close your eyes and point to one of the symbols on page 14—much as you would "point and click" your computer's cursor to select an icon. Or you can use the Magic Lightning Cards in the back of the book. Bean counting is the traditional way to consult this oracle—and if you like, you can do that too.

SELECT YOUR METHOD

Choose whichever method appeals to you. All work equally well.

Bean Counting. The most traditional method of consulting these oracles is bean counting. Using a bowl of dried soup beans, you draw a handful at random and count them off into bunches of four. The number of bunches points you to your sign, which you then look up in the Answer section. To take this route, follow the instructions for bean counting.

Point-n-Click. Get your answer by simply pointing your finger at one of the tables in the book to choose a sign. Then look up your sign in the Answer section. To take this route, follow the instructions for Point-n-Click.

Magic Lightning Cards. To use this method, photocopy and cut out the "Lightning Cards" in the back of the book. Swirl them around in front of you and choose one to answer your question. The Lightning Card you choose will direct you to the sign that will give you your answer. To take this route, follow the instructions for Lightning Cards.

STEP II—NAME YOUR ENDS

This book offers you a means of thinking about—and planning—your life. There are several paths laid out for you. Choose the one that meets your needs today:

FASTraCK Bring any current question—any specific issue—to this "table." Ask about your ambition, problem, desire, or concern from each of the angles provided by Readings #1 through #13. Your path is marked with the "FASTraCK" icon.

SoulSearcH To learn your Aztec and Mayan horoscope, discover your destiny, and plan your own fate, follow the "SoulSearcH" icon from Readings #1 through #13.

GamePlan The Maya and Aztecs were consummate ball players. To consider any issue that requires you to map out a strategy, follow the "GamePlan" icon, starting at Reading #1 and on through Reading #13.

Heart'sHunt To evaluate a love interest or to explore your passionate depths, follow the "Heart'sHunt" icon through the 13 Readings of this book.

Viz'nQuest For a deeply spiritual experience, seek your soul's purpose by following the "Viz'nQuest" icons in Readings #1 through #13.

STEP 3—NOTE YOUR CHOICES

Throughout the book, you'll find places to jot stuff down. At this point, jot down the means and ends you've chosen to follow for now.

Jot down your ends and means here.

HOW TO PROCEED

Regardless of which means and which ends you've chosen, the object of this book is for you to ask a series of questions about something that matters to you. The "oracle," in the form of this book's answer sets, will then give you a series of answers. The answers are written in the hope that they will make you think for yourself... for in the end, only you can answer your questions and resolve your issues. The book will give you guidance. But it's your life... and your choice.

To get your answers, you will be using authentic Mayan and Aztec signs and symbols. Using the method you have chosen (beans, Magic Lighting Cards, or Point-n-Click), you will ask a question and select one or more signs—each Reading will walk you through the process. Once you have your signs, all you have to do is look them up in the book's Answer sections.

BACKGROUND

The signs we will mostly be using are the 20 Day Signs of the Aztec or Mayan peoples, and the 13 Day Numbers. Depending on which Reading you are doing, you will be working with the Day Signs or Day Numbers—both individually and in combination. The instructions in each Reading will tell you which signs to choose from at the time.

THE ANSWERS

Each of the book's Readings will tell you where to look for the answer to the question you asked in that Reading. Sometimes the answers will be part of the Reading. Sometimes you will be directed to the Quick Reference Guide in the back of the book. Regardless, your answer will be selected based on the method—bean counting, Point-n-Click, or Lightning Cards—you have chosen. And you can't choose wrong.

EXTRA CREDIT

Opening Exercise. Each Reading's Extra Credit section will give you something additional to try. For openers, let's ask the oracle to reveal the nature of the matter that brings you here. To find the answer, turn to the Master Answer Section starting on page 223 in the back of the book, and flip through the pages until you feel like stopping. Point to an answer, and read the Strategy section on that page.

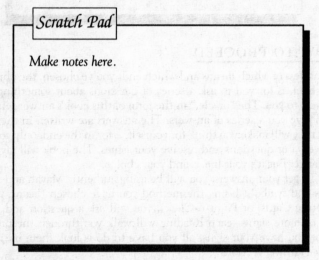

Scratch Pad

Make notes here.

EXTRA, EXTRA CREDIT!

For the ultimate experience . . . Live with the oracle for 260 days, the traditional time span for the vision quest of a Mayan priest. To take this thought-provoking route through the book, follow the instructions in the Extra, Extra Credit section of each Reading. These sections will show you how to find and interpret the naturally occurring signs in your own life.

Go on to Reading #1 whenever you are ready to continue.

Reading #1

WHAT DO THE SIGNS SAY?
(Clue me in)

In this Reading you will start working with the ancient symbols
of the original peoples of Mexico. Use the method you chose
in Reading #0 to pursue the ends you have established for yourself.

TOOLS

The 20 basic Day Signs you will be using in this Reading to think about
and plan your life in the new millennium were originally developed by
the Maya of Mexico as early as 600 B.C. As recently as 500 years ago,
when Europeans arrived in the Americas, the Aztecs of Mexico were
still using similar signs.

To their inventors, these signs were used to "indicate" the days of
the month. And in this context, they were read as horoscopic auspices—in other words, they were interpreted as omens for the day, much
as we consult our newspaper horoscopes. These Day Signs were also
employed as a means of divining what any future day might bring.

In this Reading you will start to think about any issue or question
in terms of the type of day it represents, for according to this tradition,
any event, circumstance, or unfolding situation is locked into its time
frame. Everything that happens in our lives is "like a day."

To arrive at your sign, you can do as Mayan diviners still do, by simply counting beans (corn kernels, pebbles, crystals, or other small
objects of your choice). Or you can Point-n-Click or use the Magic
Lightning Cards. Just look for your method in the How To section.

The results of your divination will point you toward a Day Sign.
Once you have found your sign, look it up in this Reading's Answer section. The text here will describe how your question is like a day... and
more specifically, which of the 20 days it is like.

7

THE 20 DAY SIGNS (A-J)

	MAYAN	AZTEC
SIGN A Bunch 1	Sea Creature	Alligator
SIGN B Bunch 2	Air	Wind
SIGN C Bunch 3	Night	House
SIGN D Bunch 4	Corn	Lizard
SIGN E Bunch 5	Serpent	Snake
SIGN F Bunch 6	Death	Death
SIGN G Bunch 7	Deer	Deer
SIGN H Bunch 8	Rabbit	Rabbit
SIGN I Bunch 9	Rain	Rain
SIGN J Bunch 10	Dog	Dog

THE 20 DAY SIGNS (K-T)

	MAYAN	AZTEC
SIGN K **Bunch 11**	Monkey	Monkey
SIGN L **Bunch 12**	Broom	Grass
SIGN M **Bunch 13**	Reed	Reed
SIGN N **Bunch 14**	Jaguar	Ocelot
SIGN O **Bunch 15**	Eagle	Eagle
SIGN P **Bunch 16**	Owl	Vulture
SIGN Q **Bunch 17**	Earthquake	Earthquake
SIGN R **Bunch 18**	Blade	Flint
SIGN S **Bunch 19**	Storm	Storm
SIGN T **Bunch 20**	Lord	Flower

BACKGROUND

The mystery and meaning of these ancient hieroglyphic symbols—"glyphs" for short—is still being unraveled, decoded, and deciphered by scientists and scholars today. The answers for this Reading are based on a very convincing theory, put forward in 1994 by leading Mayan experts, that all Mayan symbols are actually "maps of the sky." These symbols, the experts say, represent stars, planets, constellations, eclipses, and other cosmic events. It's a fact that the Maya—and their Aztec followers—were both astronomers and astrologers, blending science and art into one unified system of beliefs. In this Reading you will start to get a feeling for what the 20 Day Signs meant to their original creators, as well as an initial reading on the question you have brought with you today.

HOW TO

First, light some incense (copal is appropriate) or burn a candle of your choice and—if you like—say a blessing or repeat a favorite prayer.

Bean Counting. In order to read these signs like a Mayan Highland Priest, you will first need a bagful of beans. The modern Maya still use red beans in consulting their oracles. But any kind or color of dried soup beans will do—or even popcorn or pumpkin seeds would be appropriate. Or how about kernels of Indian corn (sold in groceries stores "in season")? These were the foods the ancient Maya grew. If you don't have any of these foodstuffs in the cupboard, how about some kind of roundish dry breakfast cereal? Whole coffee beans? Tiny beach pebbles? It doesn't really matter what small objects you use, as long as you have a bowlful of them. As soon as you have your "bowl of stuff" in front of you, you're ready to ask your question, so flip to that section of this Reading. Or use one of the other methods supported by this book. . . .

Magic Lightning Cards. Mayan Highland Priests also conduct divinations by handling and sorting their personal collections of "Magic Lightning Stones," gathered during their priestly initiation period. You'll be learning how to gather your own set of personal Lightning Stones in the Extra, Extra Credit sections. Until you've obtained your own set of stones, photocopy the paper cutouts in the back of the book. Mount them on card stock if you like. To get an answer, you'll just swish them around in front of you until you feel like selecting one. To use this method, go to the Ask Your Question section below. Or try this. . . .

Point-n-Click. If you don't have your beans or Magic Lightning Cards prepared yet—or if you'd just like to take a simpler approach—you can select a Day Sign by simply closing your eyes and pointing a finger at the Point-n-Click diagram below. The diagram has been modeled after the famous Aztec calendar unearthed in Mexico. It features the Day Signs arrayed around a central figure. Both the Mayan and Aztec symbols are included on the diagram in this book, with each sign keyed to one of the letters of our alphabet for easy lookup. Go on to the Ask Your Question section now.

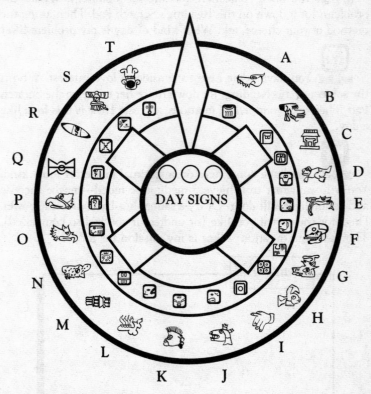

ASK YOUR QUESTION

Follow your icon for the ends you defined in Reading #0, or ask any question listed in **boldface** (below) that appeals to you at this moment.

FASTRACK You have brought an issue to the table today. In your own words, what is it? Jot it down on the Scratch Pad. Then, using the method you have selected, ask: **In a nutshell, what's the story here?**

SOUL SEARCH You have come to discover yourself or learn your destiny. Ask: **What's in the stars for today?** or **What's in my stars?**

GAME PLAN You have come here looking for a strategy. What's the problem? Jot it down on this Reading's Scratch Pad. Then, using the method of your choice, ask: **What kind of day is my problem like?**

HEART'S HUNT You have come here to consider a love interest. Who is the subject of this Reading? Jot down his or her name on the Scratch Pad. Then take your pick of methods, and ask: **How is this love like a day?**

VIZ'N QUEST You have come here on a spiritual matter of some kind. You will want first to achieve a meditative mood—maybe incense and candlelight will do it. Or try a sauna, hot bath, or cold shower. Dress for the part if you like (or undress if you feel so compelled). Then ask your question: **What is my mission for today?**

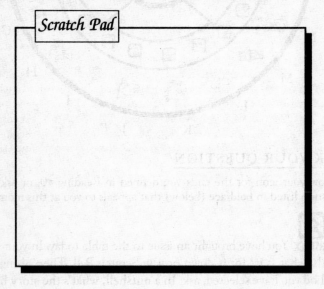

Scratch Pad

SELECT YOUR SIGN

With your question in mind...

Bean Counting. Grab a handful of beans, then count off your handful by bunches of four (or divide the total number of beans in your hand by 4). If the number of bunches exceeds 20, put 20 back and start counting again. Ignore any remaining beans (1, 2, 3) you have left over at the end. Look up your answer by the number of bunches.

Magic Lightning Cards. You will need the 20 Day Sign Lightning Cards from the back of the book. These signs are marked A through T. You do not need the other cards yet. Mix your 20 Lightning Cards together, or lay them out, facedown, in front of you. Choose one card.

Point-n-Click. Point-n-Click on one of the Mayan or Aztec Day Signs, using the special diagram in the preceding How To section.

LOOK UP YOUR ANSWER

Regardless of which method you have used and what question you have asked, find your Day Sign now in the following Answer section.

Each answer is introduced with a brief lesson in Mayan mythology, which helps to explain where the answers in the book "come from." If you'd just as soon focus on the book's interpretation of the sign, skip the portion of the answer set in *italics*.

For those who choose to consider the mythology portion too, you need to know one more thing. Each myth ends with an authentic and important date in Mayan and Aztec symbolism. The date—which is expressed in terms of the number of Baktuns (centuries), Katuns (decades), Tuns (years), Uinals (months), and Kins (days)—is a "long count" from the start of the current millennium, the first day of which was 0 Baktuns, 0 Katuns, 0 Tuns, 0 Uinals, and 0 Kins. This is a date that in our calendar is equivalent to August 12, 3114 B.C. According to the mythology, the current era ends and the next era begins on December 21, 2012—0 Baktuns, 0 Katuns, 0 Tuns, 0 Uinals, and 0 Kins once again.

THE ANSWERS

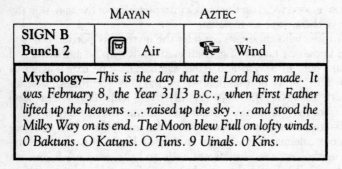

	MAYAN	AZTEC
SIGN A **Bunch 1**	🏛 Sea Creature	🐊 Alligator
Mythology—*This is the day that the Lord has made. It was August 12, the Year 3114* B.C.*, when First Father came in his Alligator canoe across the void to kindle First Fire in the Hearthstones of Heaven. The Moon was not yet formed. 0 Baktuns. 0 Katuns. 0 Tuns. 0 Uinals. 0 Kins.*		

The Day you have inquired after favors things rising up and taking shape out of nothing. Creative efforts are encouraged. The improbable is possible. Whole new beginnings, fresh starts, and clean slates are all on the agenda. This is the Day Sea Creature. This is the Day Alligator. Like a half-submerged beast peering up from still waters, keep your eyes open for the opportunity that lies before you.

	MAYAN	AZTEC
SIGN B **Bunch 2**	🏛 Air	🐦 Wind
Mythology—*This is the day that the Lord has made. It was February 8, the Year 3113* B.C.*, when First Father lifted up the heavens . . . raised up the sky . . . and stood the Milky Way on its end. The Moon blew Full on lofty winds. 0 Baktuns. 0 Katuns. 0 Tuns. 9 Uinals. 0 Kins.*		

The Day you have inquired after favors high, lofty, and elevated matters. It is a good day for pursuing dreams, stretching to reach goals, and shooting for the stars. The Way suddenly becomes clear as doors open, the road stretches out in front of you, and the breeze pushes you into motion. This is the Day Air. This is the Day Wind. Sail like the Moon cruising the heavens. Be part of the sky dream.

	MAYAN	AZTEC
SIGN C **Bunch 3**	⊞ Night	🏛 House

Mythology—*This is the day that the Lord has made. It was 542 Days after First Father struck First Fire in the Hearthstones in Orion, when he rose up to create his House of the North—great darkness at the center of the Universe. The Moon was Dark. 0 Baktuns. 0 Katuns. 1 Tun. 9 Uinals. 1 Kin.*

The Day you have inquired after favors things that are centered...directed...aligned...positioned...and perfectly balanced. The things that matter most will come past Twilight. It is a good day for going home. Even those who did not set the world on fire today can make their own sparks this night. Let the home fires burn bright. It is the Day Night. It is the Day House.

	MAYAN	AZTEC
SIGN D **Bunch 4**	⊡ Corn	🦎 Lizard

Mythology—*This is the day that the Lord has made. It was August 12, 3114 B.C., when First Fire was struck and the Great Nebula of Orion first glowed. From this ash and smoke issued the Corn God himself. Up he arose, from the cracked shell of a tortoise. Up he came, from the back of an amphibian. It was Itzamna, the Sky Lizard, who watched over his rebirth. The Moon was not yet born when it happened. 0 Baktuns. 0 Katuns. 0 Tuns. 0 Uinals. 0 Kins.*

The Day you have inquired after favors transformations of the most amazing sort. Out of nowhere, up from nothing, comes a new outlook. Startling events occur. And miracles do happen. Swift changes transform one thing into another. It is the Day Corn...time to crack out of that hard skin. It is the Day Lizard...time to stand up on your hind legs and walk like a human.

	MAYAN	AZTEC
SIGN E **Bunch 5**	Serpent	Snake

Mythology—*This is the day that the Lord has made. It was August 12, 3114 B.C., when the Corn God was born among the touchstones of Orion. The two Peccaries of Gemini immediately started copulating. It was 180 days later that the rest of the Zodiac appeared, suddenly stretched along the great back of the Two-Headed Serpent. The Moon was born Full. All was set in motion. 0 Baktuns. 0 Katuns. 0 Tuns. 9 Uinals. 0 Kins.*

The Day you have inquired after favors appearances, visions, and revelations. The pieces of a puzzle fall together before your very eyes. A seemingly random pattern takes on meaning in your life. It is the Day Serpent. It is the Day Snake. With its headdress of beautiful feathers the serpent of the sky reveals the hidden meaning in everything, and the Great Road has been opened.

	MAYAN	AZTEC
SIGN F **Bunch 6**	Death	Death

Mythology—*This is the day that the Lord has made. It was August 12, 3114 B.C., when First Father laid down the sky in the void at the Black Dreamplace. Over this vast emptiness his canoe rode the river we call White Bone Snake to the place of his rebirth. Thirteen Cycles had just been completed. Nothing else existed anymore. 0 Baktuns. 0 Katuns. 0 Tuns. 0 Uinals. 0 Kins.*

The Day you have inquired after favors the completion of things started long ago. An era ends. Another is about to start. All that's left now is to make the transition . . . and the transformation. It is the Day Death. It is Death's Day. Take heart. It is not an ending . . . merely a passage. A brand-new day awaits you the day after tomorrow.

	MAYAN	AZTEC
SIGN G **Bunch 7**	🦌 Deer	🦌 Deer

> **Mythology**—*This is the day that the Lord has made. It was February 8, 3113 B.C., when First Father set the Zodiac in motion as his last act of creation. At the time the stars started moving, the Horned Deer (the constellation Aquarius—or was it Pegasus?) rose first from the East to lead the way. The Moon came high and Full upon its heels. 0 Baktuns. 0 Katuns. 0 Tuns. 9 Uinals. 0 Kins.*

The Day you have inquired after favors quick starts and fast progress. It is as if a fire were lit under everyone at once today. There is great motion—maybe even a little chaos. It is the Day Deer. Deer is the name of the Day. Be ready to hit the ground running as you leap out of your silence.

	MAYAN	AZTEC
SIGN H **Bunch 8**	🐰 Rabbit	🐰 Rabbit

> **Mythology**—*This is the day that the Lord has made. It was 360 Days after the Corn God was reborn. It was 360 Days after his Fifth Creation began. It was August 7, 3113 B.C., when the Rabbit Stars (our constellation Leo) rose in the East at sunset to mark the completion of the first of the 5,200 "years." The Moon was nowhere to be seen. 0 Baktuns. 0 Katuns. 1 Tun. 0 Uinals. 0 Kins.*

The Day you have inquired after favors the marking of an anniversary, the turning of a calendar page, the completion of a cycle—great or small. We come to a turning point. We come to a crossing-over place. We come to a milestone. It is the Day Rabbit. Rabbit is the name of the day. At times like this, you can either sit and listen to the stillness that completion brings, or you can kick up your heels.

MAYAN   AZTEC

SIGN I Bunch 9	⬚ Rain	✍ Rain

Mythology—*This is the day that the Lord has made. It was July 25, 3113 B.C. It was the Feast Day of Saint Santiago, when the rains of creation let up for the first time, and the rain gods took their first rest. As the clouds cleared, the Zodiac stretched overhead at right angles with the Milky Way, forming a cross. This cross is the Wakah-Chan. This cross is the Tree of Life. It was a Quarter Moon. 0 Baktuns. O Katuns. 0 Tuns. 17 Uinals. 7 Kins.*

The Day you have inquired after favors matters of great significance, major importance, and utmost relevance. Though everything may not be a matter of life and death, this Day will surely bring a lesson in the facts of life. Details would be better left to slip into the background, as the larger picture comes into full view. Take the signs both for what they are and for what they are not. This is the Day Rain. Rain is the name of the Day. It is good to see a welcome relief come. It is good to see even a blessing reach its natural end.

MAYAN   AZTEC

SIGN J Bunch 10	⬚ Dog	✍ Dog

Mythology—*This is the day that the Lord has made. It was September 6, 3113 B.C., when the Dog Stars—the constellation Virgo—rose for the first time, and light rains returned after a period of clear skies. The Moon was Quartered again. And it was time to tend the second crops. 0 Baktuns. O Katuns. 1 Tun. 1 Uinal. 10 Kins.*

The Day you have inquired after favors the cultivating of ideas. As things cycle back around today, it is a good time to tend to long-term projects—especially for self-improvement or self-preservation. Think ahead. Take steps this day to assure the meeting of future needs and desires. It is the Day Dog. Dog is the name of this day. It is not enough to take the food from a hand that feeds you. Give something of yourself in return.

Reading #1

	MAYAN	AZTEC
SIGN K **Bunch 11**	🐵 Monkey	🐵 Monkey

Mythology—*This is the day that the Lord has made. It was long, long ago—during the second Creation Epoch—that the gods made a divination. It was long, long before August 12, 3114 B.C., when the gods divined to learn the secret of making creatures who could call them by name. The people they made of earth crumbled. The Wood People snapped. The gods sent a great flood to wash their mistakes away. But the Wood People floated and survived as Monkeys to the present day. It was so long ago when this happened that there were no Baktuns, Katuns, Tuns, Uinals, or Kins to count. There was not even a moon.*

The Day you have inquired after favors tests, trials, and experimental efforts. It is a good time to learn from past mistakes. Throw away the outworn and worthless. Go back to the drawing board if you have to. Wipe the slate clean if you must. In attempting to make a decision, don't forget to divine. It is the Day Monkey. Monkey is the name of the Day. Chattering voices have a way of saying nothing worth remembering or repeating. If you must speak out, let it be in the name of God.

	MAYAN	AZTEC
SIGN L **Bunch 12**	Broom	Grass

Mythology—*This is the day that the Lord has made. It was February 8, 3113 B.C., the day the Sky was Raised. It was the day when the first of the all-night vigils at San Antonio was held. The Sun, the Moon, and Venus were invoked—and all the Powers that Be—that the rain might, for the first time, return the parched grass to green. 0 Baktuns. 0 Katuns. 0 Tuns. 9 Uinals. 0 Kins.*

The Day you have inquired after favors solemn activities and profound, devoted, dedicated, and sincere acts. It is time to show your respect to the Powers that Be. (You might even consider pulling an all-nighter if you think that might be key.) Religion is favored. It is a good day for prayer and meditation. Come clean if you should. Ask what you would. Things green up for a purpose. Things brown for a purpose, too. It is the Day Broom. It is the Day Grass. Sweep up the old before planting new seeds.

	MAYAN	AZTEC
SIGN M **Bunch 13**	⬛ Reed	▦▦ Reed

Mythology—*This is the day that the Lord has made. It was August 12, 3114 B.C., when the Aztec gods made the Sun, Moon, and Stars. Reed was the name of the first year. It was 4,633 years later when the White Gods came from the place of the sunrise, as foretold. It was the Year Reed, just as the diviners had said, when the White Gods returned to the City of Reeds. It was November 8, A.D. 1519, when it happened. 11 Baktuns. 14 Katuns. 19 Tuns. 13 Uinals. 1 Kin.*

The Day you have inquired after favors discoveries and rediscoveries...births and rebirths. The signs you see this Day are especially important. Recognize a promise when you hear it. Recognize an omen when you see it. Recognize a threat when you smell it. Recognize a feeling when you sense it. Something long suspected happens. Something long anticipated comes to pass. This is the Day Reed. Reed is the name of the Day. A new King passes a sharpened reed through his penis to inspire his reading of the signs (but let's not get carried away).

MAYAN AZTEC

SIGN N Bunch 14	Jaguar	Ocelot

Mythology—*This is the day that the Lord has made. It was August 12, 3114 B.C., when the three took the Alligator Canoe across the dark heavens to set the Hearthstones of Orion. It was the first Day of Creation when the three crossed the sky. Itzamna, the first shaman, Stingray, and Jaguar: It was they who set the first three stones. 0 Baktuns. 0 Katuns. 0 Tuns. 0 Uinals. 0 Kins.*

The Day you have inquired after favors significant developments, phenomenal events—even magical moments. A journey, passage, or transition may be involved. Unified efforts, joint projects, and collective tasks are encouraged. Everything works in harmony. Things click. Pieces fall into place. The dots are connected. This is the Day Jaguar. This is the Day Ocelot. Pay attention to the animals you dream about tonight.

MAYAN AZTEC

SIGN O Bunch 15	Eagle	Eagle

Mythology—*This is the day that the Lord has made. It was August 12, 3114 B.C., when the Aztecs left Atzlan to begin their long journey in search of the sign their gods said they would give when the time and place were right. It was 4,439 years later that they saw it: The eagle sitting on a cactus devouring a snake. It was A.D.1325 when it happened in a marsh filled with reeds. And on this spot, Mexico City was built. 11 Baktuns. 5 Katuns. 2 Tuns. 11 Uinals. 16 Kins.*

The Day you have inquired after favors the resolution of long-standing matters, the completion of long-term projects, and the fulfillment of long-understood promises. Keep a sharp lookout for a message that eluded you in the past. When you see it, you shall know the truth at last. It is the Day Eagle. Eagle is the name of the Day. From a high vantage point, everything is seen. The whole depends on each of its parts.

MAYAN   AZTEC

SIGN P Bunch 16	🔲 Owl	🐦 Vulture

Mythology—*This is the day that the Lord has made. It was August 15, 3114* B.C., *when Speared Owl ruled. He was the third Lord of the Night. It was three days after the Creation that Owl ruled the night for the first time—and for the first time served as an omen. He said, "144,000 times 13." He said, "1,872,000 Days." "It will be the Year* A.D. *2012," he said. "This era ends. The Vulture comes." It was three days after Creation that Owl foretold Creation's end. 0 Baktuns. 0 Katuns. 0 Tuns. 0 Uinals. 3 Kins.*

The Day you have inquired after favors efforts that require insight, foresight, and intuition. The past is projected into the future. Add things up, tally the results, and compute the odds. But don't forget to read between the lines once the math is done. Avoid pooh-poohing an ominous feeling. Do not ignore a hunch. This is the Day Owl. This is the Day Vulture. When something sweeps down from out of the blue, best take it as a sign.

MAYAN   AZTEC

SIGN Q Bunch 17	🔲 Earthquake	🎗 Earthquake

Mythology—*This is the day that the Lord has made. It was December 21,* A.D. *2012, and the Earth was quaking. It was (144,000 x 13) Days after Creation. It was 1,872,000 Days since the Three-Stone Hearth was laid and the Fifth Era began. It was then that all the cycles cycled back upon themselves again. 0 Baktuns. 0 Katuns. 0 Tuns. 0 Uinals. 0 Kins.*

The Day you have inquired after favors things that need to be wound up, wrapped up, or tied up. Everything is done at this point. Something that was pending gets resolved. Some laugh. Some weep. Some wail. Some shriek. Some feel the earth move beneath their seats. It is the Day

Reading #1

Earthquake. Earthquake is the name of the Day. Take nothing for granted—especially the Will of God.

	MAYAN		AZTEC	
SIGN R **Bunch 18**	⊠	Blade	⬳	Flint

Mythology—*This is the day that the Lord has made. It was December 21, A.D. 2012, when the new millennium came to pass and the Earth started rumbling. On this day, the Incense Priest, with Black Glass Obsidian Point, went into the chamber to pierce his skin, see visions, and divine the nature of the new Creation—5,200 great cycles were complete and starting over again. 0 Baktuns. 0 Katuns. 0 Tuns. 0 Uinals. 0 Kins.*

The Day you have inquired after favors acts of deep devotion and divine love. A small personal sacrifice is called for. Carry out your duties with faith and diligence. Do something that benefits everyone involved. Act as if everything depends on you . . . but be careful not to overdo. It is the Day Blade. It is the Day Flint. It is by chipping away at things that flames are sparked. It is by chipping away at ourselves that we grow sharp.

	MAYAN		AZTEC	
SIGN S **Bunch 19**	▨	Storm	▥	Storm

Mythology—*This is the day that the Lord has made. It was December 22, A.D. 2012, when the Sixth Creation Epoch started to unwind. It was one day after 0 Baktuns. 0 Katuns. 0 Uinals. And 0 Kins. All night before, the Earth had rumbled and the volcanoes belched. Now, too, the sky began to swirl. The winds began to howl. And the rains began to pour. There was no moon. The clock had reset: 0 Baktuns. 0 Katuns. 0 Tuns. 0 Uinals. 1 Kin.*

The Day you have inquired after favors events that are out of your control. What can you do about the weather? How can you prepare for Acts of God? How can you control Mother Nature? Nothing comes of worrying but worry. Nothing comes of fear but fear. Take heed, but also take heart. Know strength. Feel courage. Prepare for the best, as well as the worst. The Day is Storm. Storm is the name of the Day. There will always be rumors of war.

	MAYAN	AZTEC
SIGN T **Bunch 20**	🁢 Lord	🝊 Flower

Mythology—*This is the day that the Lord has made. It was December 22, A.D. 2012, when the Sixth Creation Epoch started. It was the first day of a new era, when the Sky God laid the stars back down and raised the heavens back up again. Wak-Chan-Ahau was his name. And there was evening. And there was morning. And a new Day. 0 Baktuns. 0 Katuns. 0 Tuns. 0 Uinals. 1 Kin.*

The Day you have inquired after is like no other that ever was before...or that will ever be again. Each day is the same. Complete, entire, and unique. Each Day has its own destiny, its own identity. And this one can only be known once it has run its course. Every step of the way, you make the difference. Every hour, every minute, every second, you make your own choice. It is the Day Lord. It is the Day Flower. All we can ever do is plant seeds.

EXTRA CREDIT

To learn more about your sign . . . Consult the listing for your Day Sign in the Master Answer Section, starting on page 223. The text there contains specific answers expressed in terms of Work, Love, Money, and Strategy issues. At any point in your use of this book, you can consult the "back of the book" for more details or more specific guidance on any sign or number.

EXTRA, EXTRA CREDIT!

Day 1 through Day 20—Today begins your journey. Over the next 20 days (one Mayan month) keep a lookout for things you find lying on the ground . . . bits of glass, stones, scraps of wood, chips of concrete, coins, pebbles, shells. Gather up those that appeal to you and bring them home. Wash them, dry them, and add them to your beans. These objects are your *q'abawilob*—your magic Lightning Stones. In your Readings, just count them right along with your beans. Once you have collected enough of them—Mayan priests-in-training collect them for 260 days—you can substitute them entirely for your beans and use them exclusively for the rest of the Readings.[1]

Go on to the next Reading whenever you are ready to continue.

---

[1]Thanks to Linda Schele (University of Texas) for her valuable description of modern Mayan divination by use of Lightning Stones. Freidel, Schele, and Parker, *Maya Cosmos*, New York: William Morrow & Company, 1993, p. 226.

Reading #2

How Am I Headed?
(Point me)

In this Reading you will hear the ancient voice of this oracle speak to you of the four sacred directions, which—as you will soon learn—are waiting and willing to steer you in your quest today.

TOOLS

In this Reading you will be working with the same Day Signs you used in Reading #1. Both the Maya and the Aztecs associated each of these Day Signs with a compass point—East, North, West, and South, in that order.

Signs of the East	Signs of the North
Sea Creature/ Alligator	Air/Wind
Serpent/Snake	Death
Rain	Dog
Reed	Jaguar/Ocelot
Earthquake	Blade/Flint

Signs of the West			Signs of the South		
🔲	Night/House	🏛	🔲	Corn/Lizard	🐾
🔲	Deer	🦌	🔲	Rabbit	🐇
🔲	Monkey	🐵	🔲	Broom/Grass	🌾
🔲	Eagle	🦅	🔲	Owl/Vulture	🦅
🔲	Storm	🗿	🔲	Lord/Flower	🌼

In this Reading you will continue to use your bowl of dried beans or one of the other methods you have selected. Whatever question or issue is on your mind tonight, the oracle will answer this time in terms of the compass points.

BACKGROUND

The people who invented the symbols we are working with originally lived in the Yucatán Peninsula, in the southeast corner of present-day Mexico. To their East, lush jungles stretched to the Gulf of Mexico. To their South, the tropical rain forest extended into South America. To them, good things dwelled in these directions.

But to the far West lay the Pacific, into which the sun sank at night. And to their North were deserts. No wonder, then, that "North" to them meant "barrenness" and "dryness" . . . and "East," "abundance." Of all the compass points, West was most fearful; South, the very best.

Depending on where you live, the relative directions of East, North, West, and South probably conjure up different images than those of the Maya and Aztecs. But in this Reading we will be using their original imagery to interpret your answers.

Among the first of the Mayan hieroglyphs to be decrypted by scholars 125 years ago were the compass points. Later it was learned that each directional point was associated with a color, a bird, a god, and many other attributes. Each of the 20 Day Signs was assigned to a compass point, starting with Sea Creature/Alligator (to the East) and moving counterclockwise . . . North, West, and South . . . one Day Sign at a time. In order to deal with the issue or question you have brought, we will be selecting a Day Sign that will obtain some "direction" for you.

HOW TO

Light a candle or a stick of your favorite incense and choose your method: bean counting, Magic Lightning Cards, or Point-n-Click.

Bean Counting. Just use the beans, corn, crystals, or other small objects you gathered in Reading #1.

Magic Lightning Cards. Use the 20 cutouts from the back of the book to select a Day Sign.

Point-n-Click. Use the diagram in Reading #1 (page 11) to point to your answer.

But first, ask your question....

ASK YOUR QUESTION

Follow your icon for the ends you defined in Reading #0, or ask any question listed in **boldface** (below) that appeals to you at this moment.

FASTRACK You have come here looking for direction on a particular issue that concerns you. With the issue in mind, ask: **Where should I head with this?**

SOULSEARCH You have come looking for your destiny. Ask: **Where am I headed?**

GAMEPLAN You have come here looking for a plan. Give the command: **Point me in the right direction.**

HEARTSHUNT You have come here to consider your love life. Ask: **Where is this relationship heading?** Or give the command: **Show us some guidance.**

WIZNQUEST You have come here for spiritual guidance. Ask: **In what direction does my answer lie?**

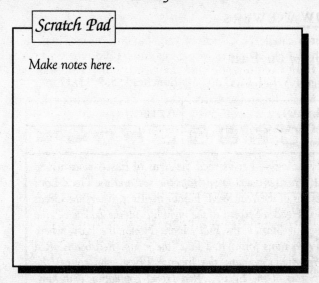

SELECT YOUR SIGN

With your question in mind...

Bean Counting. Grab a handful of beans and count them into bunches of four, then count the number of bunches. (If more than 20, put 20 back and count the rest.) This number corresponds to your Day Sign for this question.

Magic Lightning Cards. Mix up your Day Sign Lightning Cards, or turn all 20 of them facedown in front of you. Choose one to represent your Day Sign for this question.

Point-n-Click. Point-n-Click on one of the Mayan or Aztec Day Signs, using the special table on page 11 in Reading #1.

LOOK UP YOUR ANSWER

Find your Day Sign now in this Reading's Answers. The Day Signs are grouped according to the compass points they "belong" to (East, North, West, and South). For the full effect, read the *italic* text that describes the direction itself, then read the straightforward message that accompanies the particular sign you have drawn.

THE ANSWERS

Signs of the East

Signs: A, E, I, M, Q   Bunches 1, 5, 9, 13, 17

MAYAN	AZTEC

Mythology—*Let us read the signs of East—place where the sun rises each dawn from the sea and the Good Lord returns in the Year Reed. Honor the East, where the Great Two-Headed Serpent of the night lifts up the Zodiac . . . the Evening Star . . . the Full Moon. Honor the East, where the red rains form. Red flint, the stone. Red beans. Red corn. Red Shaman, the Incense Priest who counts the Crystals of the East . . . Red Ixchel copulating with him. Red Rain, the ruling deity. Let us read the signs of East. . . .*

	MAYAN	AZTEC
SIGN A **Bunch 1**	Sea Creature	Alligator

Something is arising in your life. Something is bubbling up from the depths where you have submerged your true feelings. This is a good time to bring things up to the surface. Go in the direction that the signs you see in your own life point. Let what will be, be. Or else, let well enough alone.

	MAYAN	AZTEC
SIGN E **Bunch 5**	Serpent	Snake

Something is rattling around here! Someone is making plans. Something is lying in wait. Someone is poised, coiled, and ready to strike. Go swiftly in the opposite direction when a timely warning tips you off. Be careful where you step. Watch out for the snake in the grass. Beware of the serpent in yourself.

MAYAN   AZTEC

SIGN I Bunch 9	Rain	Rain

Something is about to come gently into your life, soft as autumn rains kissing your face, gentle as fine mist. Something wells up and flows over in your heart. And you, my friend, will sleep well this night. It is not a time for going anywhere other than where you are right here...right now. Show kindness. Exhibit tenderness. Be a good friend.

MAYAN   AZTEC

SIGN M Bunch 13	Reed	Reed

Something you have waited long for comes to pass. A milestone is reached. A full cycle is complete. Congratulations! You have passed the test. The direction in which you should turn now is into yourself. What is it you really want to do? Set your sights. Pump yourself up. And go through with it.

MAYAN   AZTEC

SIGN Q Bunch 17	Earthquake	Earthquake

Something is about to happen. So don't be surprised when the Earth moves! Hold on to your hat. Hang on to your socks. It will all happen for you when you least expect it. (But when it does, just remember you read it here first.) The direction you should head in is this: Come out into the open, my friend. But don't forget to cover your...head.

Signs of the North

Signs: B, F, J, N, R   Bunches 2, 6, 10, 14, 18

MAYAN	AZTEC
🔳 🔲 🔳 🔳 🔳	🔳 🔳 🔳 🔳 🔳

Mythology—*Let us read the signs of North, where the Corn God makes his house and the Tree of Life soars . . . past the Dippers . . . into the darkness beyond the North Star . . . into the center of it all. Honor the North, where the gods in highest heaven are invisible . . . and all the Young Souls dwell. Honor the North, where everything is White. White flint, white beans, white corn . . . White Shaman's divining stones. White Itzamna—the Tobacco Priest—counting White Signs from the dish between his knees. White Ixchel consorting with him. White Rain coming forth. Let us read the Signs of North . . . .*

MAYAN   AZTEC

SIGN B **Bunch 2**	🔳 Air	🔳 Wind

Something blows into your life like a breath of fresh air. Something gently pushes, pumps, and gusts. It takes you in the direction you have pointed yourself. Keep doing what you're doing. Keep going where you're going. It's okay to let yourself be pushed this time. Let yourself be pulled. Let things take you along.

MAYAN   AZTEC

SIGN F **Bunch 6**	🔳 Death	🔳 Death

Something is about to change in your life. Something is about to alter, switch, or redirect. The past fades, dimmer and dimmer. The future glows brighter every day. And there is only one way to go. Ever onward, ever upward . . . without stopping to look back. Take no prisoners. Release the captives.

	MAYAN	AZTEC
SIGN J **Bunch 10**	🐶 Dog	🐕 Dog

There is a companion in your life. Someone accompanies you. Someone sits at your side. And when you need them, they are always there. Pick up on the signals for yourself. Follow the tug, when it pulls. And if it feels right, that is the direction you should head in. Be loyal. Be secret. Be true. Be a best friend.

	MAYAN	AZTEC
SIGN N **Bunch 14**	Jaguar	Ocelot

Something magical is happening in your life. Something mysterious is playing out. Something special is unfolding. It is a passage you are making. Listen to your spirit cat. The direction you should head in has already been revealed. And you know it. Perform a few spot checks if you must. Cast aside your own doubts. Let the magic flow into your life.

	MAYAN	AZTEC
SIGN R **Bunch 18**	Blade	Flint

Something is cutting away here . . . being cut free . . . cutting itself loose. And this severance is permanent. Once done, there is no turning back. Be sharp as steel, smooth as obsidian. The direction you should go in is an old one. Many have gone this way before you. Nevertheless, it is a path you must cut out for yourself. Go step by step.

Signs of the West

Signs: C, G, K, O, S   Bunches 3, 7, 11, 15, 19

MAYAN	AZTEC
📦 💀 👹 🗃 🗲	🏛 🐢 🦅 🐉 🗿

Mythology—Let us read the signs of West, leaving place of sun, place of sun's going down, point of rest for Venus, and the Crescent Moon's descent . . . deep, dark waters of the Underworld. Honor the West, where Corn Mother turns under the moldy mulch, and the Black Earth eats up the stalk. Black flint, black beans, black corn . . . Black Shaman's fingers counting Black Stones off by fours. Black Itzamna—Obsidian Priest—conjoined in darkness. Black Itzamna inside Black Ixchel. The two reflected in a smoking glass. Black God presiding over dust and ash. Black Rain forming into Black Glass. Let us read the Signs of West. . . .

MAYAN   AZTEC

SIGN C Bunch 3	📦 Night	🏛 House

When night falls, it is time to go to your house. When night comes, it is time for you to go to your home . . . wherever it is. Whatever you have been doing, your work on it is done for the day. The direction you should head in is into the arms of one you love . . . and one who loves you back. It should be spontaneous . . . but private. Let the night take its course.

MAYAN   AZTEC

SIGN G Bunch 7	💀 Deer	🐢 Deer

When dusk comes, the deer emerge timidly from the safety of the woods. Something is coming out in you, too. Something is coming out

34

about you. The direction you should take is open to interpretation. Watch your step. Look over your shoulder. Proceed with care. Handle with caution.

	MAYAN		AZTEC	
SIGN K **Bunch 11**	🐵	Monkey	🐵	Monkey

Something has been passing mouth to mouth and ear to ear on the grapevine. Someone has been up to old antics. Someone has been chattering a warning. The direction you should head in is up. . . to the top of the tree. There is no shame in running if it buys you a little time. Regroup. Rethink. Reconnoiter.

	MAYAN		AZTEC	
SIGN O **Bunch 15**	🦅	Eagle	🦅	Eagle

When night falls, it's time to roost. Someone who once flew the coop drops back into your life. Something is worked out at a distance, accomplished on the fly, or decided at the summits. The only way to go now is down, but from these heights, even down is up. Whatever suits your needs. Set up camp. Create a base. And operate from there.

	MAYAN		AZTEC	
SIGN S **Bunch 19**	⛈	Storm	⛈	Storm

As night falls, clouds gather—East, North, West, or South—and you should take it as a Sign. Something is brewing in the background, behind the backdrop. You will want to keep an eye on it . . . or not. The only way to go right now is with your gut. Sometimes you can smell it coming. Sometimes you can only smell it afterwards. Sniff out a situation before you jump into bed.

Signs of the South

Signs: D, H, L, P, T   Bunches: 4, 8, 12, 16, 20

MAYAN	AZTEC
🔲 🔲 🔲 🔲 🔲	🐊 🐇 🐟 🦅 👤

Mythology—*Let us read the signs of South, house to the right of Rising Sun . . . house to the left of Setting Moon . . . great expansiveness . . . abundant gathering. Right Side of Sun. Left Side of Moon. Yellow Heaven, where roots the Tree of Life in Sacrificial Dish. Yellow flint. Yellow bean. Yellow corn. Yellow squash. Yellow Shaman divining with his jaundiced eye. Gourds dried in the sun turn to rattles. Yellow Itzamna—Calendar Priest—color of the flesh from lack of sun . . . astride Pale Yellow Ixchel like a dog. Yellow Rain moving way down . . . far off. Yellow God kicking up Yellow Dust. Yellow Rain presiding in his Golden House. Let us read the signs of South . . . .*

	MAYAN	AZTEC
	MAYAN	AZTEC

SIGN D **Bunch 4**	🔲 Corn	🐊 Lizard

Something has come up. Something has crept out. Something is rustling like cornstalks in the dark. Though your skin seems thick, you are soft inside. Perhaps it's time to come out of your shell—or get a new one. The direction you should head in is up and out. Though your head be bent from the weight of your own success, keep aiming for the light.

	MAYAN	AZTEC

SIGN H **Bunch 8**	🔲 Rabbit	🐇 Rabbit

Something's been nibbling at something. Something's been eating at someone. These little things add up rapidly. Something's getting out of hand . . . again. The direction you should take is the one in which the tracks go. The Signs are as clear as the nose on your face . . . and the skin of your tail. Sit tight. Or else skedaddle.

	MAYAN		AZTEC	
SIGN L **Bunch 12**	🔲	Broom	🌿	Grass

Everything is winding down now. Everything is coming to its head. The passing of time has done its useful work. And all that's left to do now is pick up the pieces and find new uses for these leftovers. The direction you should go in is forward. Scrub the floor. Empty the ashtrays. Sweep the hearth. Light fresh incense. Renew the fire.

	MAYAN		AZTEC	
SIGN P **Bunch 16**	🦉	Owl	🦅	Vulture

Something is about to be revealed to, about, or for you. Some are exposed. Some are covered. Some are forewarned. There are signs aplenty in the world. A voice comes through loud and clear in your head. Take direction from your dreams. Keep an ear out for someone who calls. Reach out to a wise one when it's you who needs help.

	MAYAN		AZTEC	
SIGN T **Bunch 20**	🔲	Lord	🌸	Flower

Something meant to be is happening. Something meant to bloom is now burst forth. Things are unfolding according to plan. The picture is bigger than you think. And all the pieces are falling into place. When the road you are meant to take opens, go down it. Plant seeds.

Signs of the Center
(For Extra, Extra Credit Users)

> **Mythology**—*Let us read the signs at the Center, Zenith of the Sun . . . nadir of the Dark Moon . . . 13 heavens high . . . 9 hells low. All that is straight up. All that is below. Center of the hearth. Center of the room. Center of the soul. Blue Heaven, Green Earth. Blue-Green Scraper Flint. Green corn before it's formed. Blue diviner looking out of cat green eyes. Jade Itzamna—Sun-Counter Priest—counting days. Jade Ixchel—his counterpart at night. Green Rain pocking blue-green sea. Truth lies at the place where all things meet . . . the point of convergence.*

EXTRA CREDIT

Asking Yes/No Questions with Beans . . . Though we have been ignoring the "leftover" beans at the end of our counts, you can use them to answer simple yes/no questions. Here's how. Just ask any question that can be answered with a straightforward yes or no response. Take a handful of beans and count them off by fours. If, at the end, you have two beans left, or if you have no remainder, the answer is yes. If you have one or three beans left, the answer is no.

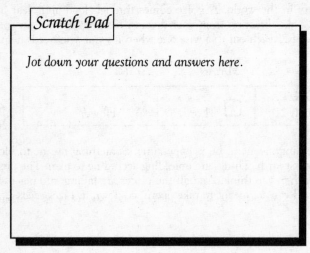

Scratch Pad

Jot down your questions and answers here.

NOTE: Some modern Mayan priests use these remainders to make a determination about whether or not the oracle wants to speak at all on any given question. The same rule applies: If one or three beans remain, the question itself is discarded, and no Reading takes place. If two beans are left, or if there is no remainder, the Reading proceeds. You are welcome to add this authentic touch to your Readings as well, if you like.

EXTRA, EXTRA CREDIT!

Day 21 through Day 40—The objects that you have been gathering for your q'abawilob not only add texture to your work with the beans, but also color. Colors, in turn, are traditionally associated with the compass points. So when you find that green pebble or red flint on the ground, you can also read it literally as a sign. To the Maya and Aztecs, the color red was associated with the East, white with the North, black with the West, yellow with the South, and green with the Center. The Mayan glyphs for these colors are shown in the center column of this table.

Mayan Color Key		
East	𒊹	Red
North	𒊹	White
West	𒊹	Black
South	𒊹	Yellow
Center	𒊹	Green/Blue

As you find each new item for your collection over the next 20 days, check its color against the chart above and note its "direction." Read the appropriate text in this Reading's Answer section for East, North, West, South, or Center.

Go on to the next Reading whenever you are ready to continue.

Reading #3

HOW DID I GET HERE?
(Go fast forward)

In this Reading you will learn to use the Day Signs to
conduct a past, present, and future analysis for the
question or issue that concerns you.

TOOLS

So far in this book, we have been using English names for the Day Signs.
For an authentic touch, you might like to try using the actual Mayan or
Aztec names for each. These names are shown in the tables on the next
two pages.

Tips for pronunciation: x = sh (Xochitl = sho-hitl)
                               z = s (Mazatl = mas-atl)
                               qu = k (kw before a)

THE 20 DAY SIGNS (A-J)

	MAYAN NAMES	AZTEC NAMES
SIGN A **Bunch 1**	Imix	Cipactli
SIGN B **Bunch 2**	Ik	Eecatl
SIGN C **Bunch 3**	Akbal	Calli
SIGN D **Bunch 4**	Kan	Cuetzpalin
SIGN E **Bunch 5**	Chicchan	Coatl
SIGN F **Bunch 6**	Cimi	Miquiztli
SIGN G **Bunch 7**	Manik	Mazatl
SIGN H **Bunch 8**	Lamat	Tochtli
SIGN I **Bunch 9**	Muluc	Atl
SIGN J **Bunch 10**	Oc	Itzcuintli

THE 20 DAY SIGNS (K-T)

	MAYAN NAMES	AZTEC NAMES
SIGN K **Bunch 11**	Chuen	Ozomatli
SIGN L **Bunch 12**	Eb	Malinalli
SIGN M **Bunch 13**	Ben	Acatl
SIGN N **Bunch 14**	Ix	Ocelotl
SIGN O **Bunch 15**	Men	Quauhtli
SIGN P **Bunch 16**	Cib	Cozcaquauhtli
SIGN Q **Bunch 17**	Caban	Ollin
SIGN R **Bunch 18**	Eznab	Tecpatl
SIGN S **Bunch 19**	Cauac	Quiauitl
SIGN T **Bunch 20**	Ahau	Xochitl

The names of the Mayan and Aztec Day Signs have been known to us for more than 100 years. But their entire meaning is still a mystery. Just as our Stars and Stripes, valentines, and four-leaf clovers mean something to us, each of these 20 signs meant something to the people who drew them. Each sign "conjured up"—if you will—emotions and feelings, as well as many layers of literal meanings. As we saw in Reading #2, each Day Sign was associated with a particular direction—and, therefore, everything that this direction stood for. As we will see here, each Day Sign also embodied Mayan myths, Aztec legends, and a plethora of gods.

BACKGROUND

Though the symbols here may be ancient, their lessons are immortal. In this Reading you will select three Day Signs for the particular question or matter you have brought to the oracle today. The first will describe the things of the past that are involved. The second will describe the present. And the third will talk about things to come.

The Mayan priests and their Aztec successors projected time deep into the past and far into the future. In their system of beliefs, everything is connected to everything else. Therefore, the first step in plotting the outcome of the matter before you now is to look to the past . . . then to the present...and on into the future. Here's how. . . .

HOW TO

Light your candle or a stick of your favorite incense, say a prayer, and choose your method: bean counting, Magic Lightning Cards, or Point-n-Click.

ASK YOUR QUESTION

Follow your icon for the ends you defined in Reading #0, or ask any question listed in **boldface** (below) that appeals to you at this moment.

FASTRACK You have come to consider a specific question, topic, or issue. With your subject in mind, ask: **What's the history?**

SOULSEARCH You have come to read your horoscope. Ask: **What powers are at play?**

GAME PLAN You have come to develop a strategy. Give the command: **Lay it out for me.**

HEARTS HUNT You have come here because of the one you love. Ask: **What's in store for her? him? us?**

VIZNQUEST You have come here for spiritual guidance. Give the command: **Lead me forward.**

SELECT YOUR SIGN

With your question in mind...

Bean Counting. Count your beans <u>three times,</u> to identify three Day Signs. (To get each Day sign, count a new handful of beans into bunches of four, then count the number of bunches. If more than 20, subtract 20.) Jot down your Day Signs, in the order in which you selected them, on this Reading's Scratch Pad.

Magic Lightning Cards. From the cutout Lightning Cards in the back of the book, use the 20 Day Signs (A through T). Swirl them around in front of you and pick <u>three</u>. Write down each of the signs, in the order in which you chose them, on the Scratch Pad.

Point-n-Click. Point-n-Click on <u>three</u> of the Mayan or Aztec Day Signs, using the special table on page 11 in Reading #1. Note each of your signs on the Scratch Pad in the order in which you picked them.

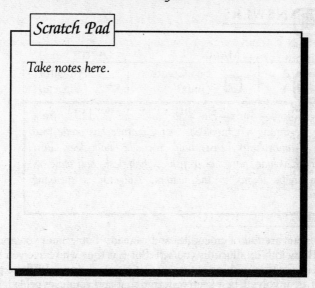

Scratch Pad

Take notes here.

LOOK UP YOUR ANSWER

Find your Day Signs now in this Reading's Answers. Each answer contains a bit of background on the sign and its meaning, then some specific prognostications, and finally a sentence or two that describes this sign as it might be read for the past, for the present, and for the future.

Read the whole answer for all three of your signs, and look for clues that trigger a spark of recognition in you. For the first sign you drew, focus on the part of the text that starts with **"In the past..."** For the second sign, focus on **"At present..."** And finally, for the third sign, focus on **"In the future..."**

THE ANSWERS

	MAYAN		AZTEC	
SIGN A **Bunch 1**		Sea Creature (*Imix*)		Alligator (*Cipactli*)

> **Mythology**—*Imix*—He Who Holds the World Up from
> the Beginning—is involved. Sea Creature has come into
> play—amorphous beast, half crocodile, half deer. Part
> smooth as hide, part slick as fish . . . half flesh, half scale. A
> dim shape looms in the waters. Alligator is speaking
> now. . . .

The rivers are full of crocodiles and caimans. Sometimes you are up to
your loincloth in alligators yourself. But is it they who have you by the
bowels? Or is something eating you up from the inside? Where primal
urges are involved, best keep your trap shut and your eyes peeled. *In the
past*—Your sights were lifted. And you tried to keep them up. *At present*—
Doubts and second thoughts have a mind to interfere. Maintain your firm
resolve in the face of opposition. *In the future*—What goes down must come
up. And everything up must come back down. In this case, people rise to the
occasion.

	MAYAN		AZTEC	
SIGN B **Bunch 2**		Air (*Ik*)		Wind (*Eecatl*)

> **Mythology**—*Ik*—Air—has come into play . . . breath of
> the gods . . . invisible power . . . transparent force. Wind is
> speaking: Wind is talking now. Save your breath! Let old
> Kukulchan do the speaking. Let Ik talk: There is no argu-
> ing with the Powers that Be. . . .

Might as well turn the other cheek (and cough!). Winds of change
sweep through the workplace. Government is reinvented. Hot air and
politics have always mixed. And love is constantly whispering, even if
it's in someone else's ear. Money flits and floats, as usual. Storms come
and go. The weather-worn endure. It is better to bend in the breeze than

be snapped in half. **In the past**—*It seemed like everything that was, would be—and would always stay the same.* **At present**—*It seems as if nothing is stable, constant, or for certain.* **In the future**—*Everything old is new again—including you—but different as Night and Day*

	MAYAN		AZTEC	
SIGN C **Bunch 3**	🔲	Night (Akbal)	🏠	House (Calli)

Mythology—*Akbal—Night—has come into play. . . dark ender of the long day, dark keeper of hushed sighs, maker of moans, and crier of both kinds of tears. Dark night is murmuring. Dark house is creaking . . . shadows dancing on the ceiling. Heavy breathing beneath the sheets. Dark night is whispering. Dark house is breathing. Akbal is speaking. . . .*

Things seen and unseen . . . things inside and things out . . . things above and things below—these things are involved. Work follows you home. So does the law of the land. Even in the privacy of your own four walls, someone watches what goes on. Someone counts. And someone knows you better than you know yourself. In dreams the spirit catches your fall. In dreams, your soul soars. **In the past**—*You remember it as if it all happened in black-and-white and slow motion. It was a little thing that made such a big impression—or was it a vivid dream?* **At present**—*It all seems like a blur. One day folds into the next. And it's difficult to remember what you did last week, let alone what you dreamt once.* **In the future**—*Suddenly it will dawn on you. An odd moment takes on new significance, as you see it all in context. All the pieces fit. A dream materializes.*

	MAYAN	AZTEC
SIGN D Bunch 4	🀫 Corn (Kan)	🦎 Lizard (Cuetzpalin)

Mythology—*Kan—The Corn God—has come into play . . . maker of sacred meal, the clay that molded male and female. It is Yum Kaax who is speaking, Lord of the Harvest, when the corn trees turn tan in the sun. It is Itzamna talking from his lizard lips about the time for planting when it comes. It is the Corn God himself, from his House of the North, who is talking. Kan himself is speaking. . . .*

Things go in one way . . . and come out another. Things go in one side . . . and come out the other end. Things cycle up until they cycle down again. Nothing winds up the way it started out—except when it starts all over again. What begins, ends. What ends, begins. **In the past**—*You chalked up a lesson to experience. It was a growth pang. It was a growth spurt.* **At present**—*You will mature a little bit more now before you are through. It is a natural course you are following. It is a natural cycle you are repeating. It is your own cycle unfolding again.* **In the future**—*Each time you learn "the same lesson," you will understand it more. The end that you are seeking comes, by and by. Each time, new. Each time, more.*

	MAYAN	AZTEC
SIGN E Bunch 5	🐍 Serpent (Chicchan)	🐍 Snake (Coatl)

Mythology—*Chicchan—the serpent-footed God "K," who smokes cigars before his dusty mirror—sees all . . . knows all . . . reveals nothing of the truth but its signs—it is he who is talking. Best read between the lines. Smoking Mirror is talking. Snake is coiled for striking. Heed these lines when they come. Chicchan is speaking. . . .*

At the moment when you least expect it...at the moment when you need it most...in the seconds when time slows to a standstill and you have to act fast...then—and only then—the sign you seek will come, and you will know. You'll have to play it by ear. Stand still. Or vamoose? Until then, things are not so clear. The truth speaks loudest from a full-length mirror...and visions come best in candlelight. *In the past—You came up against a smoke screen. Things were not as pretty as they seemed. Something lurked at your very feet.* **At present—***You must remain alert, lest smoke gets in your eyes. Do not be blinded to reality. Neither worry too much about an outside chance. Probability is only that. And the odds in this case are far and wide.* **In the future—***The smoke clears suddenly...and suddenly you see. A timely bit of news passes down. You are forewarned, and thereby forearmed.*

	MAYAN		AZTEC	
SIGN F Bunch 6	🪟	Death (Cimi)	🪦	Death (Miquiztli)

Mythology—*Cimi—Winking God of the Dead—has come into play...cavity in the side of the hill...pit underneath the deep lake...crevasse in the side of the mountain...great gateway into the mirror-world beneath. Toothless Cimi, his lips sewn shut, mumbles when he speaks. Cimi is talking from the Underworld. You will have to listen hard...listen well...and listen fast. Cimi's voice is always garbled at best....*

Something from a distance...someone from afar...a voice from out of the past...a wake-up call. Things are already not what they used to be. Suddenly...quickly...irreversibly, things change. Minute to minute. Day to day. Uinal to Uinal. Tun to Tun. Katun to Katun. The past adds up to this very day. And this is the moment you have waited for. *In the past—You died a little bit. You shed a little skin. You parted with a piece of innocence. You made a decision to grow.* **At present—***This is it. There is a sudden change of heart...a sudden flux in mood...a sudden reversal in attitude...and a sudden realization. Eureka! The past is done...over with...behind.* **In the future—***Things will be different, mark my words! The changes are coming fast and furious, even if you do not see them at first. And you, too, will change your mind.*

	MAYAN		AZTEC	
SIGN G **Bunch 7**		Deer (Manik)		Deer (Mazatl)

Mythology—Manik—*the Deer God*—has come into play, *still creature of the wood, timid invader of the corn-field, early riser of the dawn, latecomer at the dusk, swift evader of the human presence, darter into the underbrush, passer into the Underworld. Spirit deer is speaking. And all the Deer People are listening to their mascot tell the family secrets. Deer is speaking. Listen here. . . .*

Something is evading the detectors . . . eluding the trackers . . . deceiving the watchers . . . deluding the followers. Someone is going before you . . . behind you . . . right in front of you—and yet you cannot see. The signs are clear. But they all blend in with everything else going on. When the truth comes, you can only glimpse its fleeting form. Before the mind has seen, the white-tailed illusion disappears in a thicket. *In the past*—*There were a few fleeting moments that yet had their lasting effect. What you saw was yours alone to see. Who could you tell? Who would believe? How can you doubt your own good senses? At present*—*Something catches the attention, from the corner of an eye. But it is only when you look at a thing straight-on that you see. And this time you've gotten quite an eye-ful. In the future*—*An opportunity presents itself again. But how will you handle it this time? Take a lesson from the past. And get ready for a recurrence.*

	MAYAN		AZTEC	
SIGN H **Bunch 8**		Rabbit (Lamat)		Rabbit (Tochtli)

Mythology—Lamat—*the Rabbit Scribe of the Underworld, the Rabbit Face of the Moon*—has come into play . . . *scribbler of signs on bark pages covered with corn paste, drawer of pictures in the sky, imprinter of double-edged tracks on Earth . . . Rabbit is speaking. Rabbit is leaving a trail of pellet droppings as wide as a road. Rabbit People are hot on the scent. Rabbit is writing in the book. Rabbit is talking with puckered lips. . . .*

Some magic speaks loud as words. Some truths need not be uttered to be understood. Some signs are as clear as the nose on your face. You need no ears to hear. Your path is laid out clearly. Follow it. But hush...make no noise...utter not a sound. Some things are better left unsaid...especially at a time like this. **In the past—**You thought you knew what it was all about...where it was all going...and what it all meant. And there was something of the truth in the notes you made... though only half was said. **At present—**You are still looking...still seeking...still hunting...and still living to tell the tale. Where does it go next? How does this chapter end? You tell me! **In the future—**You catch up to something...or is it that something catches up to you? Take a deep breath. Say a silent prayer. And do what comes naturally...for you.

	MAYAN	AZTEC
SIGN I **Bunch 9**	Rain (Muluc)	Rain (Atl)

Mythology—Muluc—the Rain God, with his long nose...Chac, the god of the four directions and their rains, the piercer of ears...noses...tongues...and foreskins, opener of heaven's floodgates, he is the one talking to us here. Chac the Rain God is speaking, like a constant dripping in the Three-Stone Hearth at the center of the house all through the rainy season. Rain is speaking. Hear the beat....

Nothing that's as good as rain can come free. Everything has its price. And nothing comes without a little sacrifice—at least nothing that's good. Not much is assured. No rate is guaranteed. And there's no telling what the skies will look like tomorrow night. Everything that exists is dependent on everything else. Everything that is worth having is worth sweating, crying, even bleeding over. **In the past—**You believed in something, someone, somebody. You did what you thought was right by it, him, or her. And this is the way your kindness was repaid. **At present—**You believe in forces outside your control. And you still pray for rain sometimes, and sometimes for reprieve from storms. Believe what you will. Do all you can. And the Powers that Be will intervene. **In the future—**Your beliefs will be the deciding factor in the end. What you see is what you get...or don't get. If it's all in the eye of the beholder, behold!

51

	MAYAN	AZTEC
SIGN J **Bunch 10**	Dog (Oc)	Dog (Itzcuintli)

Mythology—*Oc—the Dog God—has come into play . . . Old Yellow, Dog of the Dead, leader of souls across the river of life, he who accompanied the Corn God on the day before Creation started all over again, it is Dog who is speaking. It is Oc speaking with his tongue and tail. It is Dog speaking with his bark and howl and growl. It is Dog speaking with upraised leg. Dog speaking. Hear Dog tell. . . .*

Some things don't seem to mind being tamed. Some get by with a pat on the head and a piece of fat to chew. Some live better than most humans can. Some have to fend for themselves, beginning to end. Sometimes you have to go with your instincts and senses. **In the past**—*You did things without questioning why. You more or less went along for the ride. And the flow took you to wherever the canoe went. What you learned along the way is what you learned.* **At present**—*You have no regrets . . . no second thoughts . . . no leftover baggage. Each day brings something new into focus. Nothing is wanting for any more than it needs.* **In the future**—*You find yourself arriving in a new place. And you can only conclude that you have been led.*

	MAYAN	AZTEC
SIGN K **Bunch 11**	Monkey (Chuen)	Monkey (Ozomatli)

Mythology—*Chuen—the Monkey-Faced God "C"—has come into play . . . he whose image adorns the Wacah Chan, the Tree of Heaven, the Milky Way, bridging Scorpio and the North Star—it is he, it is the North Star God who's speaking. It is the Monkey-Faced Chuen, chattering high up in the branches of the Wacah Chan, that is speaking. God "C" from the heights of the heavens is speaking. Better bow your head. Here is what he says. . . .*

Everything's small from this distance...even the trees, even the pyramids, even the volcanoes, even the mountains of the moon, even the stars. Everything...everything is rooted. Everything is connected. Everything hooks up to everything else. And it's all revolving around this turning point. **In the past**—*You came to a crossroads in your life, a juncture. Suddenly a road opened up to you. And suddenly you took your departure. How else could you go?* **At present**—*It's a pivotal moment. Who knows how, why, or wherefore? What? When? or Who? A portal opens. But will you step through?* **In the future**—*Everything becomes clearer...in hindsight...in looking back...once you have established some distance from it...in retrospect. And it could have been no other way, could it?*

	MAYAN	AZTEC
SIGN L **Bunch 12**	Broom (Eb)	Grass (Malinalli)

Mythology—*Eb—the God of the Underworld—has come into play...God "L," the old man of Xibalba, witness to Creation Day, is speaking. It is Old Eb puffing on his cigarette, dictating words of old-man wisdom to his Rabbit Scribe, it is he who is speaking. And every word he says is blown in tobacco smoke. His every word smokes like dry grass smoldering in the fields. His every word burns away what used to be. His every word sweeps clean. Here is what he has gleaned....*

Some things were made to be tasted...some touched...some felt. Some things were meant to be seen...and some things better left unseen. Some things were meant to be green as grass and dry as hemp. Some things were meant for smoke, some for ashes, and some for dust. Some things were meant to settle at the bottom. Some things were destined to float upward. Smoke the four corners of your house. Center yourself. And send your prayers all the way to the top. **In the past**—*Nothing that matters now even existed back then. Why dwell on ancient history...unless you think it might be happening all over again.* **At present**—*It's as if yesterday doesn't matter. It's as if tomorrow will never come. It's as if only this moment exists. Enjoy.* **In the future**—*Damned if I can see beyond this veil. What is, was, and will be must remain forever the same.*

	MAYAN	AZTEC
SIGN M **Bunch 13**	Reed (Ben)	Reed (Acatl)

Mythology—*Ben—The God of the Swamp—has come into play . . . Ben, the God of the Pond . . . God of Still Waters . . . Water Lily—living thing that rises out of nothing, beauty born of darkness—it is he who is speaking now. Hollow Reed is speaking. So much thin air is whistling through his hollow core. Reed, like a flute, is speaking. It is Reed that is piping now. Hear Reed sing. . . .*

Some things are exactly what they seem to be. Some things are exactly their opposite. Some things cross over into in-betweens. Some rise above. Some come out. Some go back in. Some transform themselves into other useful things. Some march to the sound of a different pipe. Some rise to the beat of a better drum. **In the past**—*You crawled at first, then lifted up your head and stood—at last—upon your own two feet. One small step, my friend . . . one helluva leap.* **At present**—*Shallowness is one thing. Hollowness its brother. Is it you who adapted to your environment? Or did your environment adapt to you?* **In the future**—*It's a symbiotic relationship you are enjoying. You change things. And things change you.*

	MAYAN	AZTEC
SIGN N **Bunch 14**	Jaguar (Ix)	Ocelot (Ocelotl)

Mythology—*Ix—the Jaguar God—has come into play . . . paddler of the great canoe that brought the Corn God across heaven, planter of the first of three hearthstones, it is Jaguar Paddler speaking. It is spotted cat talking with a low rumbling sound in his throat. It is Ocelot purring in the aftermath. God "G-III" is speaking, second-born of the first three. Transformed Shaman is talking with his cat eyes. Here is how he sees it. This is what he knows. . . .*

Everything is separate from everything else. But everything also connects. There is a way to get from one place to another . . . one point to the next. There is a way around every barrier . . . sometimes over, sometimes under. There is a way that the impossible gets done. Magic happens. Miracles occur. Transformations take place. **In the past**—*You believed in magic, fairy tales, and fantasy. You wished on a star. You split a wishbone. You picked a penny up for luck. You listened for reindeer on the roof. What did it do for you? What did it get you?* **At present**—*You are older, wiser, and more dubious than you once were. It takes as much to convince you as to trick you. Still, you keep the old ideas alive. Still, you are capable of suspending disbelief.* **In the future**—*A magical moment awaits you yet. Something just clicks. And you won't be able to believe your eyes, let alone what's come over you, and what is yet in store. Why question it? This is magic, after all—even if it's only done with mirrors.*

	MAYAN		AZTEC	
SIGN O Bunch 15	🔲	Eagle (Men)	🐾	Eagle (Quauhtli)

Mythology—*Men*—The Celestial Bird God—*has come into play . . . Eagle, the high-perched one on the Wacah Chan, the high-soaring bird of the heavens, one with the Sun, the Moon, and the Clouds. It is Eagle who is speaking now. Eagle is talking from way up high, majestic wings sprouting from the body of a snake. Plumed serpent of the sky. Eagle is speaking. Hear him shriek. . . .*

There are 13 layers to heaven. There are 9 layers to hell. And the earth floats between the two extremes. Everything that is—and is not—fits into the scheme. Some live in the rarefied air above . . . and some in the mirror-world below. It is a stratified and parallel existence. But now and then the realms collide. This is one of those times. **In the past**—*You were but a fledgling at your craft, a mere apprentice, an entry-level novice. Like a falcon tethered to the falconer's thread, your realm was defined. But the time came to journey on your own. And you have been traveling ever since.* **At present**—*Your position is admirable, honored, and respected. That which is beautiful is also envied. Though you may be endangered, you may yet be protected.* **In the future**—*One does what one does. One performs as one can. One steps out on a limb. Take a risk.*

	MAYAN	AZTEC
SIGN P **Bunch 16**	🦉 Owl (Cib)	🦅 Vulture (Cozcaquauhtli)

> **Mythology**—*Cib—the War God's Companion—has come into play . . . Owl, foreteller of outcomes in advance; Vulture, clearer-away of casual mistakes . . . it is these who are speaking now, War's Comrades. Owl, at the mouth of the cave, is nodding his head wisely and speaking of what will be. Vulture, at the top of the tree, looking out hungrily, is speaking of what will be no more. Both are speaking, but what does it mean? Look for the signs. Listen for the clues. . . .*

Time goes on and on and on without stopping, without faltering, without losing a beat. Powers rise and fall in one fell swoop. And hardly anything survives a whole millennium. The only thing that can be counted upon is change. **In the past**—*You saw a sign. You heard a timely warning. You were tipped off to something that was about to happen. And it was how you reacted that changed everything since.* **At present**—*There is new writing on the wall. The past has summed up into a new total. Divide by four and find your answer.* **In the future**—*You will know a thing when you see it. You will see a thing when you feel it. You will feel a thing when you open yourself to the signals all around you.*

	MAYAN	AZTEC
SIGN Q **Bunch 17**	🌍 Earthquake (Caban)	⋈ Earthquake (Ollin)

> **Mythology**—*Caban—The Earth God—has come into play . . . substantial ground beneath your feet, great firmness on the back of Crocodile, great floater between the heavens and the Underworld, it is Earth who speaks. And Earthquake who answers, frightening rumble underneath, upheaval and cave-in all around the place. Earth rumbles when she speaks. This is what Earth says. . . .*

Everything . . . Everything . . . Everything. Nothing that is firm remains firm. Nothing that is fluid remains fluid. Nothing that is invisible remains unseen forever. Nothing that is hidden remains forever unrevealed. Something from the past is heaved up. **In the past**—*You had quite a shock. You felt quite a jolt. You trembled all the way to the toes of your socks. Shivers went up and down your spine. (Wish I could have been there.)* **At present**—*Things seem a little rocky right now. You're standing on shaky ground. Something's making you weak in the knees. (Was it a kiss? or a near miss?)* **In the future**—*You feel the Earth move. And what a rush! What a grand finale! What a climax (hopefully for both of you).*

	MAYAN	AZTEC
SIGN R **Bunch 18**	⊠ Blade *(Eznab)*	◕ Flint *(Tecpatl)*

Mythology—*Eznab—the Four-Part God of Blades—has come into play . . . the one who cuts the world into East, North, West, and South . . . the one who is sharp as a stingray spine, sharper even than an obsidian knife . . . it is Blade who is speaking now. It is Blade tearing the hide from the meat. It is Flint Scraper, Spear Point, and Lancing Needle doing the speaking: And they are very sharp. See how they cut like a sharpened knife. . . .*

Some things chop like a hatchet. Some things shuck like a knife. Some things skin. And some things pierce. It takes all 10 fingers and all 10 toes to keep the Kins, Uinals, Tuns, and Katuns right. But it takes tools to build a house. And it takes utensils to cook in Three-Stone Hearth. **In the past**—*You were pretty sharp yourself . . . at least about certain things. You delved. You examined. You penetrated. You thought. And what did you conclude?* **At present**—*The truth cuts like a knife. And things fall to one side or the other. But is it cleft? Or is it cleavage?* **In the future**—*A keen wit comes in handy. Sometimes you need to laugh at things . . . maybe even yourself. The barb of humor cuts as finely as a razor's point.*

	MAYAN		AZTEC	
SIGN S **Bunch 19**	🁢	Storm (Cauac)	🁢	Storm (Quiauitl)

Mythology—*Cauac—The God of the Hurricane—has come into play . . . decorating the robe of Old Man "N," one storm a year and 20 to the decade. Storm Signs framing the cave where the Great Spirit of Mountain Dwells, Storm God is speaking now from the high hills. Hurricane and Tornado are speaking so loud, you can hardly make them out above their own roar. Best get inside to hear them go by . . . .*

Some things can be foreseen . . . expected . . . anticipated . . . and prepared for. Some things can even be avoided by making the right move at the right time. But some things turn suddenly, veer left or right, or blow off course. There is no way to foresee these things. They are simply unpredictable . . . random . . . and unavoidable. **In the past**—*There was some turbulence in your life . . . a sudden change in the pressure . . . a sudden rise in the humidity . . . a sudden drop in the temperature. It was a temporary disturbance.* **At present**—*Storm clouds may have gathered, but it is not yet certain whether it will just blow over . . . again. You'll have to watch, wait, and see how the Signs change.* **In the future**—*It will always be something. If it's not rain, it's no rain. If it's not breeze, there's no breeze. Learn to enjoy both the storms and the calms.*

	MAYAN		AZTEC	
SIGN T **Bunch 20**	🁢	Lord (Ahau)	🁢	Flower (Xochitl)

Mythology—*Ahau—It is Kinich Ahau, the Sun God— who has come into play . . . Ahau, Lord of the Year, marker of Tuns, Katuns, and Creation Epochs . . . good luck sign dangling from the sash between the legs of kings . . . Kinich Ahau, Face of the Sun, is speaking. Water Lily turns its head upward. Flower is talking now. The seasons are turning. Time is speaking. Hear time tell . . . .*

Some things rise and some things set. Some things go from East to West...some things, West to East. Some things move to the North, some to the South. Some things turn clockwise...some things go in reverse. Some things pass beneath your feet. Some things go right over the head. ***In the past**—The days passed so slowly that you thought the Big Day would never arrive, let alone the Big Night. **At present**—You mark off squares and book your dates. In choosing between conflicting commitments, anticipate where you want to be at this time next year. Choose accordingly. **In the future**—An anniversary is celebrated... a date is commemorated... an event is marked. As a full cycle draws to its close, look back and reflect. As a new cycle begins, step aggressively forward, onward, and upward.*

EXTRA CREDIT

Random thoughts...You do not necessarily need to have a burning issue or a life-altering question on your mind in order to gain insight from this oracle. For a quick Reading at any specific time, simply say, **Speak!** And using the method of your choice, select one Day Sign. Look it up in this Reading's Answer section and read the entire text. In this application, the oracle is likely to talk about things that matter to you but that haven't completely materialized yet or that have not quite bubbled up to the surface of your thoughts. On nights when you're not really sure what you want to ask about, it's a good way to start. This approach also gives the oracle the chance to tell you something you had no idea you should even be asking about. Give it a shot now and then, and note how things turn out.

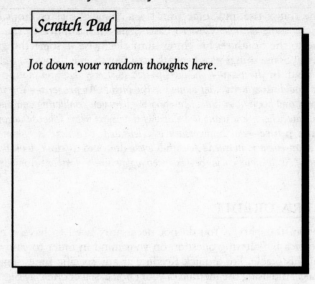

Scratch Pad

Jot down your random thoughts here.

EXTRA, EXTRA CREDIT!

Day 41 through Day 60—Keep looking for Lightning Stones this week (see Reading #1). Keep interpreting them on the basis of their color (see Reading #2). But also keep a lookout for the animals that you happen across or that happen across your path. They can also be interpreted as signs. And this goes doubly for animals that make an appearance in your dreams. To interpret animal signs, use this handy list that links the 20 Day Signs to animals you might actually encounter in the flesh, see on TV, or be attracted to in a work of art.

ANIMALS	DAY SIGNS	ANIMALS	DAY SIGNS
Alligators, Caimans, Crocodiles, Turtles, Any sea creature		Monkeys, Apes, Chimpanzees, Squirrels	
Birds, Flying insects		Cows, Sheep, Goats, All grazing animals	
House pets, House mice, House flies, Crickets, Bats		Frogs, Toads, Tadpoles, Beavers, Geese, Ducks	
Crows, Rodents, Lizards, Salamanders, Chameleons		Cats of all kinds	
Snakes		Eagles	
Flies		Owls, Vultures, Hawks	
Deer, Ticks		Prairie dogs, Moles, Ground hogs	

Animals	Day Signs		Animals	Day Signs	
Rabbits			Porcupines, Anything with sharp teeth		
Fish worms			Flocks of birds, Fireflies		
Dogs, Coyotes, Wolves			Bees, Butterflies, Peacocks		

Over the next 20 days, whenever you see an animal sign, look up the corresponding Day Sign in this Reading's Answer section to see what it might mean.

Go on to the next Reading whenever you are ready to continue.

Reading #4

WHAT'S THE SCORE?
(Hedge my bet)

In this Reading, you'll start working with the ancient Mesoamerican numerals, which—in addition to the 20 signs you already know—are the basic tools you'll use in the rest of your consultation with these oracles.

TOOLS

If you've ever counted things off by fives using tick marks (| | | |) and then drawing a line through the lot for the five count, you should have no trouble catching on to this counting system used by the Maya. Numbers one through four are comprised of dots: •, •• , ••• , and •••• . Number five is a bar: | . It all builds from there. Number six is a bar, with a dot beside it: •| . Ten is two bars: || . The Aztecs used dots only for all the numbers one through thirteen. Though simpler, their system is actually harder to count up. So we will be using the Mayan bar-and-dot system here. The thirteen numbers we will be working with are shown on the next page.

63

THE 13 DAY NUMBERS

• 1	⦙• 4	⦙• 7	‖ 10
•• 2	❙ 5	⦙❙ 8	•‖ 11
••• 3	•❙ 6	⦙❙ 9	⦙‖ 12
			⦙‖ 13

In this Reading we'll be using these Mayan numerals to size up the question or issue you have brought to the table.

BACKGROUND

Every culture has developed its own system of counting. We use a decimal system, based on the number 10. Where did we get this idea? As some experts have observed, 10 is the number of fingers we have, and since we probably first learned to count on our fingers... You get the idea. For the Maya and Aztecs, the basic unit of measure was not 10, but 20—the number of fingers <u>and</u> toes that we have. Thus there were 20 Day Signs, which you have been using in the previous three Readings.

Twenty was also a "prime" number in counting up larger time periods, such as the year, decade, century, and millennium. In their long counts, the priests expressed dates from the very starting point of their calendar, which to their reckoning was in 3114 B.C. Just as we might say this is the 260th day of the year, the Maya might say—and the Aztec would agree—the count is actually 12 centuries, 19 decades, 18 years, 13 months, and 0 days. In this ancient timekeeping system, every day has its own unique number.

HOW TO

Light your candle or favorite incense, say your prayers, and choose your method—bean counting, Magic Lightning Cards, or Point-n-Click. Once you have selected your method, ask your question.

ASK YOUR QUESTION

Follow your icon for the ends you defined in Reading #0, or ask any of the questions listed in **boldface** that appeals to you now.

FASTRACK You have come to get "the" answer to a specific question. It has many dimensions. With the subject in mind, ask: **What's the score?**

SOUL SEARCH You have come here to find out about yourself. There are many aspects. Ask: **How will things compute for me?**

![icon] **GAME PLAN** You have come here to form a plan. There are many things to consider. Ask the question: **What's it look like on the bottom line?**

![icon] **HEART'S HUNT** You have come to consider what love is. There are many facets. With your love interest in mind, command the oracle to rate the relationship: **On a scale from 1 to 13 . . .**

![icon] **VIZ'N QUEST** You have come in search of spiritual fulfillment. There are many dimensions to this quest. Ask: **What is my truth?**

SELECT YOUR SIGN

With your question in mind . . .
   Bean Counting. Draw a handful of beans and count them into bunches of four. Then count the number of bunches. (Or count all the beans in your hand and divide by four). If the number of bunches

exceeds 13, put those 13 bunches back and start counting again from one. Write your number on the Scratch Pad.

Magic Lightning Cards. Up until now, you've been using the 20 Day Sign Lightning Cards from the back of the book. Put these aside for now, and switch to the 13 Day Number cards included with this book. (If you haven't already photocopied and cut them out, go ahead and do that now.) While you think about your question, swirl the Day Number cards in front of you and choose one. Write your choice on the Scratch Pad.

Point-n-Click. As in other Readings, you can use the Point-n-Click method to find your answer. But for this Reading—and for others that will depend on numbers for their answers—Point-n-Click on the table below. Jot down your choice on the Scratch Pad.

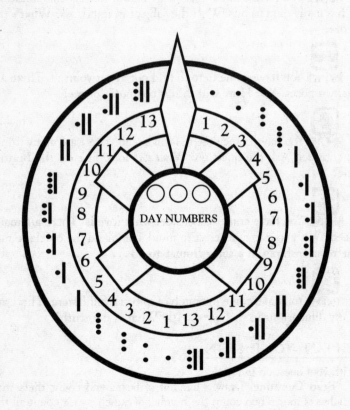

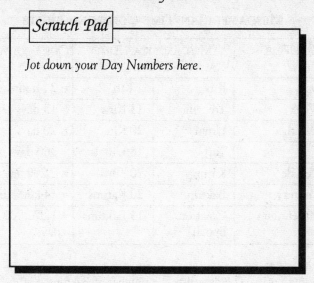

Scratch Pad

Jot down your Day Numbers here.

LOOK UP YOUR ANSWER

Find your numeral now in this Reading's Answers. Each answer includes a magical date, which you should consider, but your "real answer" follows immediately after the date.

NOTE ON LONG-COUNT DATES: As in the mythology answers for Reading #1, this Reading's answers include long-count dates. Though you will not need to do any math to read and understand your answer, you can decipher the dates if you like. All you need to know is the secret code...the magic formula, which is really just arithmetic.

Here's the trick: In Mayan terms a "year" is not 365 days, but rather 360. A "decade" is not 10 years, but the magical 20. A "century" is not 10 decades, but also 20. And a millennium is not 10 centuries, but 13— the other magical number in this system. The chart on the next page summarizes the values for each unit of time used most frequently....

MESOAMERICAN TIME-COUNTING UNITS

OUR TIME	MESOAMERICAN TIME UNITS		OUR EQUIVALENT
Day	Kin	1 Kin	= 24 hours
Week	Trecena	13 Kins	= 13 days
Month	Uinal	20 Kins	= 20 days
Year	Tun	18 Uinals	= 360 days
Decade	Katun	20 Tuns	= 7,200 days
Century	Baktun	20 Katuns	= 144,000 days
Millennium	Creation Epoch	13 Baktuns	= 1,872,000 days

A long-count date is a unique way of indicating every single day as a distinct entity. The date lists the number of Baktuns, Katuns, Tuns, Uinals, and Kins. You literally add them up to get the day count. Take the date "1 Baktun, 1 Katun, 1 Tun, 1 Uinal, and 1 Kin." By adding up the number of days in each unit, we can see that this date equals:

1 Baktun	144,000 days
1 Katun	+ 7,200 days
1 Tun	+ 360 days
1 Uinal	+ 20 days
1 Kin	+ 1 day
	151,581 days

The day "1 Baktun, 1 Katun, 1 Tun, 1 Uinal, and 1 Kin" represents the 151,581st day of the current millennium—which in our terms places it in the year 2699 B.C.

In this Reading we will be using some of the most magical dates that can occur in the ancient Mesoamerican calendars...those in which all the place values are equal. Look up your answer now.

THE ANSWERS

		MAYAN	AZTEC
DAY NUMBER 1 BUNCH 1	•	HUN	CE

Timeline—One. *1 Baktun, 1 Katun, 1 Tun, 1 Uinal, 1 Kin (2699 B.C., A.D. 2427). One of everything had cycled for the first time. Four hundred fifteen years, six days, had passed since Creation, when this number came up for the first time in this era. In a few hundred years, it will return again.*

One is the magic number that describes a thing that is happening for the first time . . . or a thing that is happening for the first time all over again. The distinction is academic. Each day is uniquely countable; each place, definable; each person, recognizable. But these are only the appearances. What you see in the mirror is not necessarily how you feel about yourself. But which is the real thing? and which, the illusion? You are who you are, my friend. And I will not reveal your secrets . . . even to you. Some things must be discovered by yourself, for yourself, through yourself. Your lucky number is 1. **Best bets:** 1, 11, and the hour 1:11.

		MAYAN	AZTEC
DAY NUMBER 2 BUNCH 2	• •	CA	OME

Timeline—Two. *2 Baktuns, 2 Katuns, 2 Tuns, 2 Uinals, 2 Kins (2284 B.C., A.D. 2843). Two of everything had now occurred. Eight hundred thirty years, eleven days, had passed since Creation. It will have been 830 years, eleven days, now since the start of the new era.*

Two is the magic number that describes a thing that has dual aspects, dual purposes, two identities. Opposites may attract, but likes hang out together. Night and day . . . black and white . . . male and female . . . left and right . . . up and down . . . in and out . . . and side to side—everything involves opposition and union. Equal forces are at work to keep things united . . . and split up. You feel both push and pull. You go both off and on. You pass both back and forth. And at any given moment, you are likely to be left or right of center. The important thing is to know your own range—to know when to push forward and when to pull back. **Best bets:** 2, 22, and the hour 2:22.

		MAYAN	AZTEC
DAY NUMBER 3 BUNCH 3	• • •	OX	YEI

Timeline—Three. *3 Baktuns, 3 Katuns, 3 Tuns, 3 Uinals, 3 Kins (1869 B.C., A.D. 3258). The cycles had all turned three times now. It was 1,245 years, seventeen days, since Creation. It will have been 1,245 years, seventeen days, since the start of the new era.*

Three is the magic number of stones it takes to build a Mayan fireplace. Three is the container of fire . . . and soul stuff. And it takes flesh, blood, and soul—all three—to make a person whole. It is the glimmer in your eye that we see. But it is the fire inside that puts it there. Some things burn faster than others. Some things produce more sparks than light. Some things put off mostly smoke. There is a wide range. And no three energy levels are alike. Learn to recognize your own pattern of behavior. Three is the magic number. The third time is the charm. **Best bets:** 3, 33, and the hour 3:33.

		MAYAN	AZTEC
DAY NUMBER 4 BUNCH 4	• • • •	CAN	NAHUI

Timeline—Four. *4 Baktuns, 4 Katuns, 4 Tuns, 4 Uinals, 4 Kins (1454 B.C., A.D. 3673). The cycles had run through four times over now. It was 1,660 years, twenty-two days, since Creation. It will have been 1,660 years, twenty-two days, since the start of the new era.*

Reading #4

Four is the magic number of corners in a house, the magic number of mythical pillars it took to hold the skies up and keep the earth afloat. Four is the number of directions (East, North, West, and South). Four is the number of sides it takes to make things square and evened out. Four sides to a temple, plaza, cornfield, and ball court. There are four views to be had of everything there is. But only you can see the view from your vantage point. Define your own space, boundaries, borders, and limits. Align your four sides. This is the space you have to operate within...this is your playing field (level or not)...this is your home turf. This is your power base. Here is where you gather your energy. Here is where you put your energy to work. This is your magical space, where it all takes place. Everyone is entitled to an opinion. Everyone has a unique point of view. What's yours? **Best bets: 4, 44, and the hour 4:44.**

		MAYAN	AZTEC
DAY NUMBER 5 BUNCH 5	—	HO	MACUILLI
Timeline—Five. *5 Baktuns, 5 Katuns, 5 Tuns, 5 Uinals, 5 Kins (1039 B.C., A.D. 4088). The cycles have all run themselves five times now. It was 2,075 years, twenty-eight days, since Creation. It will have been 2,075 years, twenty-eight days, since the start of the new era.*			

Five is the magic number that represents the center of a place, a sacred spot. It is the point equidistant from the four corners of the house. It is the place in the middle of the temple, the hole in the side of the mountain, the magical vortex, portal, and opening into both heaven and hell. The number five is about centering yourself, physically and spiritually. To make the external connection first requires turning inward. Define your four-cornered space—East, North, South, and West—and place yourself at its sacred center. If life is a ball game, go to center court or midfield to begin. If life is a play, place yourself at center stage and wait for the curtain to be raised. If your body is the temple, retreat into its central chamber. Matters of the heart, conscience, and gut are involved. In all cases, take a deep breath now. And let the spirits do the rest. You are about to have a religious experience. **Best bets: 5, 55, and the hour 5:55.**

	MAYAN	AZTEC
DAY NUMBER 6 BUNCH 6	**⨪** Uc	CHICUACE

Timeline—Six. *6 Baktuns, 6 Katuns, 6 Tuns, 6 Uinals, 6 Kins (624 B.C., A.D. 4503). Six cycles are completing. It was 2,490 years, thirty-three days, since Creation. It will have been 2,490 years, thirty-three days, since the start of the new era. Six is the magical number of all the directions. There is East, North, West, and South. But there is also "above," where lie the Heavens, and "below," which is the Underworld. Up is the zenith, down is the nadir. The perpendicular line cuts straight through center, and all six points converge, as if on an X.*

The number six is about the entire range of human experience. It's about the bad as well as the good, the agony as well as the ecstasy, the ugly as well as the beautiful, the profane as well as the holy. It's about life, death, and sex. It's about the convergence of natural forces. When you open yourself to all the powers of the Universe—all the possibilities, and all the options—you want to make sure you're grounded. Burn incense. Wear amulets. Touch sacred water to your forehead and lips. **Best bets:** 6, 66, and the hour—dare I say?—6:66.

	MAYAN	AZTEC
DAY NUMBER 7 BUNCH 7	**⨪⨪** Uac	CHICOME

Timeline—Seven. *7 Baktuns, 7 Katuns, 7 Tuns, 7 Uinals, 7 Kins (209 B.C., A.D. 4918). Seven cycles are done. It was 2,905 years, thirty-nine days, since Creation. It will have been 2,905 years, thirty-nine days, since the start of the new era. It was the bird known as 7 Macaw, whose death signaled the end of the previous Creation Epoch, the prior Mayan millennium. It is "7 Black Yellow Place" that the soul must cross to journey to its eternal resting place in the Underworld of Xibalba.*

Seven is the magical number of beginnings and endings. Seven is the magical number of things in the process of making a transition. A point is reached. A line is crossed. A river is forged. A sky is leaped. Destiny—with all its subtleties, nuances, and intricacies—is directly involved. Call it luck, if you will, or call it fate...the will of God, or the writing of the stars. Doors open. Doors close. Doors revolve in your head. But you determine which you will pass through, which you will fling wide, and which you will hide behind. **Best bets:** 7, 77, and the hour 7:07.

		MAYAN	AZTEC
DAY NUMBER 8 BUNCH 8	•••	UAXAC	CHICUEI

Timeline—Eight. *8 Baktuns, 8 Katuns, 8 Tuns, 8 Uinals, 8 Kins* (A.D. 207, A.D. 5333). *Eight cycles were done. It was 3,320 years, forty-four days, since Creation. It will have been 3,320 years, forty-four days, since the start of the new era. Eight, the number of rooms in the Corn God's House of the North . . . Eight, the number of the compass points (E, NE, N, NW, W, SW, S, and SE) . . . "8 Cumku," the date of the Fifth Creation.*

Eight is the magic number of things that are complete, done, and perfect in their completion. There is no way to improve this wheel. There is no better mousetrap. All's right with this world...at least your world...at least at this moment. Things move in sequence, harmony, rhythm, and frequency. Events unfold as they should. Time's infinite and majestic passage stops for no one—but opens ways for everyone. Here you are, my friend. This is here. Then is now. Nothing else counts. Nothing else matters. What is, is. **Best bets:** 8, 88, and the hour 8:08.

		MAYAN	AZTEC
DAY NUMBER 9 BUNCH 9	●●●●	BOLOM	CHICONAHUI

Timeline—Nine. *9 Baktuns, 9 Katuns, 9 Tuns, 9 Uinals, 9 Kins (A.D. 622, A.D. 5748). Nine cycles had come and gone. It was 3,735 years, fifty days, since Creation. It will have been 3,735 years, fifty days, since the start of the new era. Nine hours has the night, and to each hour one Lord of the Night is assigned. There are nine tests the soul must pass before it reaches eternal rest in Xibalba.*

Nine is the magic number of challenge. It can be a tad disturbing, a little disconcerting. Whether the light has suddenly shifted, lowered, dimmed, or gone out completely, your vision is more or less impaired. You will have to go more now on how a thing sounds and smells than how it looks. Be careful the eyes do not play tricks on you. Do not be taken in by optical illusions. A false alarm sounds. An instinctive fear turns into sudden relief. The night is not as long as you think. Keep quiet vigil in it. **Best bets:** 9, 99, and the hour 9:09.

		MAYAN	AZTEC
DAY NUMBER 10 BUNCH 10	═	LAHUN	MATLACTLI

Timeline—Ten. *10 Baktuns, 10 Katuns, 10 Tuns, 10 Uinals, 10 Kins (A.D.1037, A.D. 6163). Ten cycles have turned over. It was 4,150 years, fifty-five days, since Creation. It will have been 4,150 years, fifty-five days, since the start of the new era. Ten, the digits on two hands . . . ten fingers . . . the handprints of a human being. Ten, the toes on the feet . . . the footprints of a fellow traveler. But it takes 20 in all to make the "whole man."*

Ten is the magic number. . . half the magic 20. Things are going halfway. Things are half-completed. Things have met in the middle. Therefore, the auspices are good—especially for a rendezvous, a romantic liaison, or a return to the one you love. Matters of the heart, hand, and soul are involved. The 10th layer of Heaven is where the Sun Gods dwell.

"Yellow Heaven" is where prayers must reach, rising on the smoke of incense, to be heard. It never hurts to ask for the things your heart desires—even if it does mean you might later have second thoughts. **Best bets:** 10 and the hour 10:10.

		MAYAN	AZTEC
DAY NUMBER 11 BUNCH 11	≐	BULUC	MATLACTLI ONCE

> **Timeline—Eleven**. *11 Baktuns, 11 Katuns, 11 Tuns, 11 Uinals, 11 Kins* (A.D. *1452,* A.D. *6578). Eleven cycles are complete. It was 4,565 years, sixty-one days, since Creation. It will have been 4,565 years, sixty-one days, since the start of the new era. Eleven, the layer of Heaven where the Fire Gods live. As at the beginning, and again every 52 years, the sacred fire is rekindled, and everyone shares in the fresh new light. It is a time for cleaning up and throwing out what you can no longer use.*

Eleven is the magic number. It's about refreshing what is old and renewing what is worn. Eleven is also about making connections—with others, perhaps, but with spiritual forces, certainly. It is time to tap into the energies of those around you. It is time to share in the whole. Nothing lasts for long without renewal. It's time to charge up your creative, physical, and spiritual juices. Observe the customs, protocols, and rituals of your people. Keep in tune...in touch...networked...wired. **Best bets:** 11 and, especially, the hour 11:11.

		MAYAN	AZTEC
DAY NUMBER 12 BUNCH 12	••	LAH CA	MATLACTLI OMOME

> **Timeline—Twelve**. *12 Baktuns, 12 Katuns, 12 Tuns, 12 Uinals, 12 Kins (A.D. 1867, A.D. 6993). Twelve cycles are complete. It was 4,980 years, sixty-six days, since Creation. It will have been 4,980 years, sixty-six days, since the start of the new era. Twelve, the penultimate Heaven, where First Mother and First Father dwell, along with the souls of stillborn children. It is a beautiful and perfect place, but invisible to human eyes.*

Twelve is the magical number for things that are deep, dark, and mysterious. Things do not need to be obvious or apparent to influence you. Things unseen, unheard, unfelt, unnoticed, and unobserved are involved. Destinies collide. Someone is looking out for you. Someone is guiding your steps. There is a great and glorious plan for everything and everyone, including YOU. Go where your footsteps take you. Let yourself be guided, and you will find what is right for you and your soul's progress. **Best bets:** 12 and the hour 12:12.

		MAYAN	AZTEC
DAY NUMBER 13 BUNCH 13	•••	OX LA HUN	MATLACTLI OMEI

> **Timeline—Thirteen**. *12 Baktuns, 19 Katuns, 19 Tuns, 17 Uinals, 19 Kins[1] (3114 B.C., A.D. 2012 and 7138). Thirteen Baktuns will just be about to turn. Thirteen Baktuns, shy a day. But when that day ends, all the wheels will turn: 0 Baktuns, 0 Katuns, 0 Tuns, 0 Uinals, and 0 Kins. It will have been 5,125 years, 132 days, since Creation. It will be 5,125 years from now that this new era of ours will end.*

Thirteen is one of the most magical of numbers. Thirteen, the number of "months" in the holy year...thirteen, the number of hours of daylight in Mesoamerican terms. The number indicates continuity, regu-

---

[1]In Mayan date counting, this is the closest we can get to the number 13. After one more day is completed, the calendar will cycle back to its beginning.

76

larity, predictability...that thing that can be counted upon in your world...the firm earth beneath your feet...the sun in the morning...the moon at night—even death and taxes. There is a lovely rhythm to time's unfolding. Sing with the songs of the day. Dance with the beat of the night's noise—and its silence. Everything fits. Each belongs. All are involved. It is a good time for unlocking secrets, solving problems, and uncovering missing links. There is a factor or value that is the key to unlocking the puzzle. Keep working on your winning formula. Keep calculating. Keep computing. Keep at it until you figure it out. Mastery of a thing worth mastering may not always come overnight, but don't be surprised if one morning you awaken to the answer. **Best bets:** 13 and the hour 3:13.

EXTRA CREDIT

Who will it be? In addition to the bar-and-dot numbering system you have just used, the Maya sometimes used "face glyphs" to depict the various numbers 1 through 13. Each face or head glyph represented a specific Mayan god or goddess, but each could also be thought of as a type of person. For an interesting diversion, ask: **Who's coming into my life?** Select a number from 1 through 13, using your beans, Lighting Cards, or the Point-n-Click diagram in this Reading. Then consult the chart below.

THE NUMBERS & THEIR GODS

#1	Earth Goddess	She who wears her hair long and with flowers. She who wears flowers in her hair. There will be a young girl in your life—or else, a woman who, to you, will be forever young.
#2	God of the Sacrifice	He with an extended hand. He with his palm turned up. Whoever it is who is coming into your life...there will be a price to pay—for one or the other.
#3	The God of Wind	The one who blows in the wind. The one with wind-blown hair. The one who is coming may shout, but a whisper can also be heard loud and clear.

THE NUMBERS & THEIR GODS *(continued)*

#4	The Sun God	The one with the sharp nose. The one with the sharp eye. The one who is coming will dazzle you in broad daylight!
#5	God of the End of the Year	An older one. The one with older lines and wizened eyes. Whoever is coming will have advice to give. Follow it until New Year's.
#6	The Storm God	One whose eyes shoot daggers. One who sees red from time to time. Whoever is coming will come swiftly... and with little warning. Watch for the omens.
#7	God of the Ages Past	The one from out of the past. The one who still means something after all these years. Some things change, but not what was. Welcome a long-lost friend.
#8	The Corn God	One who grows on you in time. One who grows with you. A firm one—if not a tall one—is coming into your life. The two of you will sustain each other.
#9	The Summer God	The one with the pug nose. The one with the cat's eyes. The one with the five o'clock shadow. Though it might not be summer, your relationship will be a growing experience—at least for a season.
#10	The God of the Dead	The one who is too thin. The one who is more bone than flesh. The one whose mouth has forgotten its purpose. The one who is coming has little to say.

THE NUMBERS & THEIR GODS *(continued)*

#11	God of Earth & Quake	The one who is firm and yet soft. The one who can be depended upon ... at least most of the time. The one who is coming may arrive on the Full Moon.
#12	Lord of the Harvest	The one who has come full circle. The one who has been completed ... or fulfilled. The one who is coming is destined to come ... and has been here before.
#13	The Plumed Serpent	The one who appears as if in a vision. The one who comes as if in a dream. Whoever is coming will change you forever.

EXTRA, EXTRA CREDIT!

Day 61 through Day 80—Continue to look for the signs that come to you in the way of your magic Lightning Stones. Continue to look for the creatures who pass through your life and into your dreams. Also watch for the appearance of numbers. Check out the numbers that pop out at you during the next 20 days. When a number pops up, consult this Reading's Answer section. If the number is between 0 and 13, just look it up. For signs containing numbers of 14 and above, break the number into its individual parts (21 would break down into 2 and 1), then look up each of the integers. What sticks out? Take notes. . . .

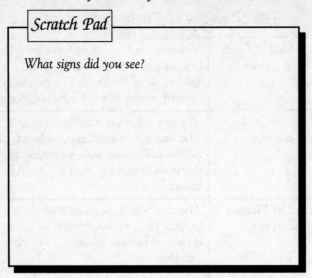

Scratch Pad

What signs did you see?

Go on to the next Reading whenever you are ready to continue.

Reading #5

WHAT'S IT ALL ABOUT?
(Play ball!)

In this Reading you'll be using the 13 Day Numbers as a looking glass—or a pair of binoculars—to ponder the big question on the tip of your tongue today.

TOOLS

In the last Reading, we saw that the counting system of the Maya and Aztecs was based on the number 13. Some experts have observed that the numerals 1 (.), 2 (. .), 3 (...), and 4 (....), look like fingerprints. The Mayan number 5 (—) looks like the upturned or outstretched thumb of the five-count.

In this Reading, we'll continue to work with these lucky-13 numerals....

THE 13 DAY NUMBERS

• 1	⋮ 4	•│ 7	‖ 10
• 2	│ 5	⋮ 8	•‖ 11
⋮ 3	•│ 6	⋮│ 9	⋮‖ 12
			⋮‖ 13

These Day Numbers are very versatile and function in a variety of ways for divination and timekeeping purposes. In this Reading we'll just be using them to get a feeling for what they mean in the context of your question or issue.

BACKGROUND

The Maya and Aztecs acknowledge two numbers as being practically sacred. One, as we have seen in the earlier Readings, is 20. The other sacred number is 13. Thirteen was the number of days in the Mayan and Aztec "week." And together with 20, it formed the basis for not only their famous calendars, but for their astrology as well.

In horoscopic terms, each of the thirteen days—numbered consecutively 1 through 13—had its own aura and influence. Just as our "Friday," "Sunday," and "Monday" conjure up images, feelings, and emotions for us, each numbered day in the Mayan week had a significance of its own. It was the diviner's job to interpret what the particular aspects or auspices of each day were and to thus help people determine what they should or should not do on any given day.

In this Reading you will get to use the ancient Day Numbers as indicators of what you can reasonably hope to accomplish with regard to the issue or question you are presenting to the oracle at this time.

HOW TO

Light your candle or favorite incense, say your prayers, and choose your method—bean counting, the 13 Day Number Cards from the back of the book, or Point-n-Click. Once you have selected your method, ask your question.

ASK YOUR QUESTION

Follow your icon for the ends you defined in Reading #0, or ask any question listed in **boldface** (below) that appeals to you now.

FASTRACK You have come here to get a straightforward answer. But every question itself needs delving into. With your most important subject in mind, ask: **What's it about?**

SOULSEARCH You have come to have your fortune told. This time ask: **What about my potential?**

GAMEPLAN You have come here for help in formulating a strategy. With your subject or plan in mind, ask: **What about it?**

HEARTSHUNT You have come here about love. Now is the time to ask: **What about this thing I have with _____ ? or for _____ ?**

VIZ'NQUEST You have come on a spiritual quest. It's time for you to ask: **What's it all about?**

SELECT YOUR SIGN

With your question in mind . . .

Bean Counting. Draw a handful of beans and count them into bunches of four. Then count the number of bunches. (Or count all the beans in your hand and divide by four.) If you have more than 13 bunches, put 13 back in the bowl and count out the remainder. For example, if you wind up with 18 bunches of beans, subtract 13, and look up the answer for the numeral 5. Jot the number down on this Reading's Scratch Pad.

Magic Lightning Cards. Use the 13 Day Number Cards from the back of the book. Just swirl them around in front of you, and choose one to represent the answer for the question you bring today. Write the number down on the Scratch Pad below.

Point-n-Click. Point-n-Click on one of the 13 Day Numbers, using the special table on page 66 in Reading #4. Jot down your choice on the Scratch Pad, then look up the Answers.

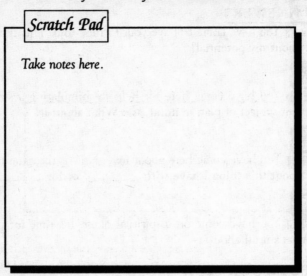

Scratch Pad

Take notes here.

LOOK UP YOUR ANSWER

Find your numeral now in this Reading's Answers. The Answers here call upon Mayan and Aztec mythology, images, and traditions in their interpretation of the Day Numbers. In particular, you will find many references to their national sport, the ball game.

Ball was played in a sacred court, itself cornered and centered, and usually constructed within the religious complex of temples and holy portals. Two teams played—seven to a squad—with one player (perhaps the King) in the position of captain. The object was to keep a large rubber ball in play.

Once the command *pitz* ("play ball") was given, the ball was put into play at center court. Once served, the ball was allowed to touch neither the ground nor any of the players' hands. Instead the ball would strike and bounce off the players' hips, sides, or—in a particularly sensitive maneuver—off a stone yoke attached to their loincloths. Talk about your contact sports!

The object was to maneuver the bouncing ball down the court and off benches at the other side—a goal that was eventually modified in some places to include "shooting" the ball through the middle of an elevated stone disk. As with Greek and Roman sporting events, these games occurred with much pomp and ceremony, often accompanied by sacrifices to the gods.

THE ANSWERS

		MAYAN	AZTEC
DAY NUMBER 1 BUNCH 1	•	HUN	CE

Mythology—One. *First principle. First cause. One, the number of reflections in a single mirror. One, the individual. One, the First Father. One, the number of the God of creation . . . and procreation. One, the point of the winning score in the ball game. One, the basic unit of counting, without which there would be nothing to count upon.*

This Day Number is about the basics. It's about primary power. It's about primal urges. It's about the energy that surges within you . . . and radiates out. The whole person emerges. The entire experience unfolds . . . albeit one step at a time. It's a Day Number that manifests the essence of the signs it couples with. Pure energy. Pure essence. You can hope to accomplish the things you are best at doing yourself. You can hope to achieve much with whatever you are good at. Apply your energies to the task that causes your soul to stir.

		MAYAN	AZTEC
DAY NUMBER 2 BUNCH 2	• •	CA	OME

Mythology—Two. *Second principle. Equal and opposite cause. Duality. Two, the number of the couple. Two, the number of images from conjoining mirrors. Two, the number of teams in the ball game. Two, the number of the Hero Twins who played the game for their lives.*

It's about equals, opposites, and things at the two extremes. Male and female. Black and white. It's about two differences that are somehow the same. It's about the inner and outer selves. A thing's opposite nature comes out. The mirror image comes to the fore. It's a Day Number that manifests the counteressence of the signs it is paired with. A thing is defined both by what it is and what it is not. You can hope to accomplish something by doing it in an opposite way. You can hope to achieve something counterintuitive or counterlogical, whichever is opposite your normal inclination. Apply your energies to tasks you would not normally handle yourself.

		MAYAN	AZTEC
DAY NUMBER 3 BUNCH 3	●●●	OX	YEI

> **Mythology—Three**. *Third principle. Third cause. Three, the number of angles in a three-way mirror. Three, the number of points in a triangle. Three, the number of stones in First Hearth. Three, the number of the bouncing ball in play, striking first the body, then the bench, and then the body again in a continuous series of events.*

It's about three things happening before a single thing is complete. Flesh, intellect, and soul must come together... body, mind, and spirit. In the end, it's about perfect balance of weight and counterweight on the pivot. A thing's divine nature reveals itself in the process. Neither the picture nor the mirror does a thing justice. It's a Day Number that manifests the spiritual significance of the signs it appears in conjunction with. Actions may speak louder than words, but in this case, it is a greater truth that shows its face. You can hope to accomplish something that involves a matter of faith or spiritual devotion. You can hope to achieve something by giving it not only your best effort, but your best prayer.

		MAYAN	AZTEC
DAY NUMBER 4 BUNCH 4	••••	CAN	NAHUI

Mythology—Four. *Fourth principle. Fourth cause. Four, the number of sides in a square. Four, the number of corners in the house. Four, the number of mirrored walls in a house of mirrors. Four, the number of pillars holding up the sky. Four, the number of sides it takes to center the ball court.*

It's about things that are "straight," "square," and "cornered." It's about things that are as neat and orderly as a grid. It's about things that are ruled . . . and defined by their rules, borders, or outer lines and limits. It's a number that reveals the range and limitations—the "parameters"—of its accompanying sign. Everything has a territory. Everything operates within a sphere of influence. You can hope to accomplish something that is already within your experience set. You can hope to achieve something by keeping it to your home turf. Set down some basic rules, before you start to play.

		MAYAN	AZTEC
DAY NUMBER 5 BUNCH 5	—	HO	MACUILLI

Mythology—Five. *Fifth principle. Fifth cause. Five, the spot that four-squared mirrors focus in on. Five, the focal point. Five, the center of a square . . . the center of a house . . . the center of the Universe . . . the center of the self. Five, the place where the ball is put in play.*

It's about proper placement. It's about proper alignment. Five is about the divine power that takes over when you become centered. Five is the silence in your own center. It's about being quietly aware. It's about understanding without needing to ask why or how. It's about being tapped into the right channels. It's about letting the Powers that Be operate through you. It's a Day Number that is perfectly in sync with the signs it is matched with. Things behave as they "should" here. Things behave in a way that is true . . . to them. Every being has a character...every power, a personality...and every force, a temperament. You can hope to accomplish things that are in keeping with the mood of the moment. You can hope to achieve something by opening yourself to your impulses. To learn what you should do, go to a place where you can hear yourself think...and your heart beat.

		MAYAN	AZTEC
DAY NUMBER 6 BUNCH 6	•	UC	CHICUACE

Mythology—Six. *Sixth principle. Sixth cause. Six, the last side of a cube. Six, the number of the floor in a sacred room. Six, the playing surface of the court. "Six-Stair-Place," the location for the sacrifices following the game. Six, the direction pointing down . . . into the Underworld. Six, the view from a mirror on the ceiling. To look up is to see down.*

It's about things that are completely and perfectly contained and defined by the "box" they are in. It stands for breadth, but also height and especially depth, for everything here is in 3-D. Things tend to extend into their confinements. Things take up the space they are allotted and allowed. It is a Day Number that emphasizes the natural definitions and, therefore, limitations of the sign it is accompanied by. You can hope to accomplish things that require you to stretch to your own limits. You can hope to achieve something either by reaching as far up as you can reach or—especially—by digging as far down as you can go. Only the sky knows the limits, and only the Earth knows the full extent. When hemmed in, stretch. Draw from your depths.

		MAYAN	AZTEC
DAY NUMBER 7 BUNCH 7	•• •	UAC	CHICOME

> **Mythology—Seven**. *Seventh principle. Seventh cause. Seven, the middle of the 13 days. Seven, the halfway point. Seven, the number of ball players on each of two teams. Seven, half the players on the court. Seven, the four primary directions, plus up, down, and "center" itself.*

It's about things that are equally matched and therefore balanced. It's about things that are paired and faced off. Everything is present. Everything is accounted for. And even though odd, everything is even. Seven takes everything in. Seven averages everything together. It's a number that combines all aspects of the sign it comes with. There is not too much or too little of anything. . . . It's a little of the best, and the best of the worst. You can hope to accomplish something that takes teamwork. You can hope to achieve something by taking the whole thing into account. If you want to go all the way, go halfway first. Level the playing field before attempting to serve the ball.

		MAYAN	AZTEC
DAY NUMBER 8 BUNCH 8	•••	UAXAC	CHICUEI

> **Mythology—Eight**. *Eighth principle. Eighth cause. Eight, the number of distinct reflections in two facing mirrors. Eight, the number of views within a view, within a view, within a view, within a view. Eight, the sum total of the compass points (E, NE, N, NW, W, SW, S, and SE). Eight ways to go. Eight ways to turn in saying your complete prayers.*

It's about various factors coming into simultaneous play. It's about facets, angles, and bevels. It's about the complete range of forces at work. It's about all the relationships that exist between all the stages and stations of life. Eight is also about multiplication (2x2x2) and duplication. As a Day Number, it doubles all the aspects of any sign it accompanies. You can hope to accomplish tasks that require you to outperform yourself—or at least rise to your ultimate potential. You can hope to achieve something by throwing yourself into it. Keep your eye on the ball, but let your reflexes do the rest.

		MAYAN	AZTEC
DAY NUMBER 9 BUNCH 9	●●●●	BOLOM	CHICONAHUI

Mythology—Nine. *Ninth principle. Ninth cause. Nine, the number of dark hours in a Mesoamerican night. Nine, the number of Lords of the Night, taking turns influencing the darkness: Flint Knife, Young Maize, Corn, Death, Jade Skirt, Earth, Mountain's Heart, and Rain. Nine, the number of the glyph often written on the ball. Nine, the images trailing off into the inner workings of facing mirrors. Nine, the resting place of the soul in Xibalba.*

It's about the tests of courage and strength that the Universe demands of us. It's about things that make it through the night. It's about things that run the gauntlet and withstand the test of time. It's about things that must somehow prove their ability to endure, withstand, or at least muddle through. It's a Day Number that brings out the challenge in the sign that appears along with it. You do not always know what you are getting into, until you are already into it. You can hope to accomplish that which requires a dedicated, devoted, or earnest effort on your own part. You can hope to achieve things by taking one step at a time. There are times when it is the last few minutes that count the most. But in retrospect, any play you make and any error you commit can mean the whole game. Give it your best at every point, but save some reserves for the end.

		MAYAN	AZTEC
DAY NUMBER 10 BUNCH 10	═	LAHUN	MATLACTLI

Mythology—Ten. *Tenth principle. Tenth cause. Ten, the number of fingers on both hands. Ten, the number of toes on both feet. (But it is illegal to use either fist or foot in the ball game.) Ten, the layer of heaven through which the Sun passes on its journey both above and below our field of play. Ten, the ball, as Sun itself . . . that which cannot touch the Earth, but without which there would be no purpose. Ten, the mirror of the cosmos.*

It's about things that are loosely connected. It's about things that are outside ourselves and yet make a connection with us. It is about the things that go right over our heads—sometimes without notice. It is about the things that may be right under our feet, and yet we do not see them. The Day Number puts a new spin on every sign it is matched up with. You see now how it all curves to fit the larger scheme of things. You can hope to accomplish things that do not depend entirely on the dexterity of your hands or the swiftness of your feet. Fly by the seat of your pants, instead. You can hope to achieve something by placing it into its proper context. If you want to win this game, you will have to play by its rules—not yours.

		MAYAN	AZTEC
DAY NUMBER 11 BUNCH 11	÷	BULUC	MATLACTLI ONCE

Mythology—Eleven. *Eleventh principle. Eleventh cause. Ten plus one. Eleven, the number of the first High Heaven. Eleven, the invisible. Eleven, the depth behind the mirror. Eleven, the marker of the portal to the Otherworld lying below the ball field's surface. Eleven, the cache of spirit stuff buried in the Earth.*

It's about connections that are made without being seen. It's about passages that suddenly open up and let us pass through. It is a Day Number that emphasizes the illusive aspects of the sign it is associated with... the truth within the truth. There is more here than meets the eye, but you may not be able to put your finger on it at first. You can hope to accomplish things that initially may seem outside your reach or grasp. You can hope to achieve something by making intuitive leaps of faith. Prepare yourself. Then let the inspiration wash over you. See into your magic mirror.

		MAYAN	AZTEC
DAY NUMBER 12 BUNCH 12	⠒	LAH CA	MATLACTLI OMOME

Mythology—Twelve. *Twelfth principle. Twelfth cause. Ten plus two. Twelve, the second of the high, invisible heavens. Twelve, the resting place of the Hero Twins, below the ball court. Twelve, the quicksilver on the back of the mirror, the veil that lets you see in only so far... and no farther.*

It's about depth difficult to penetrate. It's about all the things we cannot know for sure. It's about all the things we cannot comprehend, yet we try desperately to understand. Why? Wherefore? And how? It's about the unreachable, unseeing, indiscernible, that yet cannot be denied. It's a Day Number that reveals the unpredictability of the sign it accompanies. Anything can happen at any moment, especially the unexpected. You can hope to accomplish things that require you to keep an open mind. You can hope to achieve something by doing all you can do and then waiting for the next instruction. You do not have to be actively looking for a sign in order to receive one. In fact, signs generally come from out of left field, if not from out of the blue.

		MAYAN	AZTEC
DAY NUMBER 13 BUNCH 13	**⋮** ▬▬	OX LA HUN	MATLACTLI OMEI

> **Mythology—Thirteen**. *Thirteenth principle. Thirteenth cause. Ten plus three. Thirteen, the uppermost, high holiest realm of heaven. Thirteen, the number of days in the Mayan week. Thirteen, the number of daylight hours in the Mesoamerican day.[1] Thirteen, the number on the ball used at Bird-Jaguar's court in Yaxchilán. It was a woman who put it into play.*

Thirteen is about things that are perfect. It is about things that cannot be improved upon—at least not during this Creation. Everything fits together with everything else into a web that cannot be untangled for all our vain efforts to rise above—or put ourselves outside—what is real. The only thing residing outside is the gods, who made it all and set it all into motion. Everything else has no choice but to fit in and go along for the ride. It's a Day Number that emphasizes the true but underlying nature of the sign it is paired up with. You will have to draw your own conclusions about the truths you see. You can hope to accomplish things that depend on prayer and intercession. The Powers that Be will either support or stonewall you in your undertaking—hopefully at their will and not their whim. You can achieve something by making it fit in with the overall agenda. The emphasis is on the larger picture. The ball court has its limits, and the game cannot be extended beyond its four walls.

---

[1] The Maya and Aztec counted hours of a slightly longer length than ours. Consistent with their tropical location, a day was counted as 13 hours of daylight and nine hours of darkness.

EXTRA CREDIT

Triple Play. In Reading #3 you learned how to do a past, present, and future reading using the Day Signs. Let's update it now to this very moment in time, using Day Numbers. With the same subject you asked about back there (or a new one if your interests have changed), ask your question now:

 FASTRACK   What's the story?

 SOULSEARCH   What powers are at play?

 GAMEPLAN   Lay it out for me.

 HEARTSHUNT   What's in store for her? him? us?

 VIZNQUEST   Lead me forward.

Now, using the method of your choice from this Reading, select <u>three</u> Day Numbers. Look each one up in this Reading's Answers. The first number will talk to you about the past. The second number will talk to you about the present. And the third number will talk to you about the future. Focus on the last few lines of each text.

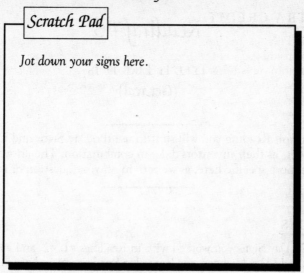

Scratch Pad

Jot down your signs here.

EXTRA, EXTRA CREDIT!

Day 81 through Day 100—To psych up for the "big game," Mayan and Aztec ballplayers performed very intense rituals, much like the ones that priests performed before attempting to divine. Preparation was a very personal and private act. The ballplayer retreated into an inner chamber to prepare himself. The priest went inside the temple to be alone with his own thoughts. During the next 20 days set aside a little time for yourself. Give yourself a little space. Set yourself a little mood. Take the phone off the hook, turn your beeper off, and let your thoughts fly. Sometimes the questions we ask are as important as the answers we receive. What thought presents itself? This, too, is a sign... that only you can read.

Go on to the next Reading whenever you are ready to continue.

Reading #6

TELL IT LIKE IT IS
(Get real)

In this Reading you will start to use the Day Signs and Day
Numbers as their inventors did—in combination. The answers will
get more specific here, as we zero in on your question or issue.

TOOLS

The 20 Day Signs you worked with in Readings #1, #2, and #3, along
with the 13 Day Numbers you learned in Readings #4 and #5, were read
in combination by the Mayan and Aztec priests to make their prognostications. By determining first one of the 20 Mayan or Aztec Day
Signs...

MAYAN DAY SIGNS

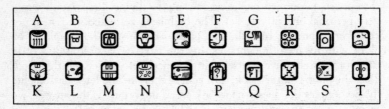

AZTEC DAY SIGNS

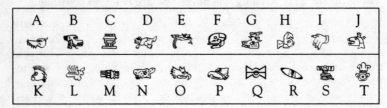

Reading #6

...and then one of the thirteen Day Numbers...

DAY NUMBERS

| 1 | 2 | 3 | 4 | 5 | 6 | 7 | 8 | 9 | 10 | 11 | 12 | 13 |

...any question asked of the oracle could have 260 possible answers, such as...

• 🔲	❙ 🔲	⦙ 🔲	⦙❙ 🔲
1 Corn	5 Deer	8 Monkey	13 Rain

In this Reading you will combine the Day Signs and Day Numbers just as the ancient priests did in order to get an in-depth Reading about any situation you face.

BACKGROUND

To the pre-Columbian peoples of Mexico, everything was explained with numbers—especially the numbers 13 and 20, which, when combined, seemed to be the secret combination...the magical formula...the mathematical equation for revealing universal truth. Just as our modern-day astronomers and mathematicians use our base-10 number system to calculate the movements of the heavenly bodies, 2,000 years ago Mayan astronomer priests used multiples of 13 and 20 to do the very same thing—with an accuracy that astounds present-day scientists.

It was the holy number 13 that, multiplied by the 20 Day Signs, measured the approximate length of a human pregnancy. It was 13 times 20 days that served as the basis for the holy year of 260 days, which determined when various festivals, feasts, and contests would be held. And it was 260 days that the priest needed for his vision quest. Thirteen and twenty, combined, seemed to determine everything there was to know about the Universe. So it is no surprise that these same combinations were put to use in forecasting what the outcome of various endeavors might be.

In this Reading you will begin to get your answers by combining the

Day Signs and Day Numbers—into any of 260 combinations—in order to focus in on your questions and answers.

HOW TO

Light your candle or favorite incense, say your prayers, and choose your method—bean counting, Magic Lightning Cards (both Day Sign and Day Number Cards), or Point-n-Click. Once you have selected your method, ask your question.

ASK YOUR QUESTION

Follow your icon for the ends you defined in Reading #0, or ask any question listed in **boldface** (below) that appeals to you now.

FASTRACK You have come here looking for the facts. It's time we got down to establishing them. With your question in mind, say to the oracle: **Zoom in!**

SOULSEARCH You have come to get your bearings. Pick an aspect: Work, Love, Money, or Strategy. Say: **Give me focus.**

GAMEPLAN You have come here to get your game plan. Let's see if we can get a close-up of it. Command the oracle: **Be specific.**

HEARTS HUNT You have come here for love. With your love interest in mind, say: **Spare no details on...** who? what? when? why? or how?

VIZ'N QUEST You have come for both spiritual counsel and personal advice. The two aims meet here in a pair of dual signs. Command the oracle: **Give me my mission.**

SELECT YOUR SIGN

With your question in mind...

Bean Counting. First, choose your Day Sign. Grab a handful of beans and count them into bunches of four, then count the number of bunches. If you have more than 20 bunches, put 20 back in the bowl and count the remaining bunches. Use that number to find your Day Sign...

BUNCH COUNTS KEYED TO DAY SIGNS

... and note its alphabet key on the Scratch Pad for lookup in a minute.

BUNCH COUNTS AND THEIR ALPHABET KEYS

1	2	3	4	5	6	7	8	9	10
A	B	C	D	E	F	G	H	I	J
K	L	M	N	O	P	Q	R	S	T
11	12	13	14	15	16	17	18	19	20

Then choose your Day Number. With your question in mind, draw a handful of beans and count them into bunches of four. Then count the number of bunches. (Or count all the beans in your hand and divide by four.) If you have more than 13 bunches, put 13 back in the bowl and count the remaining bunches. That number is your Day Number. Write your Day Number on the Scratch Pad below, then turn to the Answers.

Magic Lightning Cards. Get out your 20 Day Sign Cards, swirl them in front of you, and choose one. Write your Day Sign on the Scratch Pad.

Then swirl your 13 Day Number Cards in front of you, and choose one of those. Write your Day Number on the Scratch Pad, too. Then turn to the Answers.

Point-n-Click. Point-n-Click on one of the 20 Day Signs on page 11 in Reading #1. Then Point-n-Click on one of the 13 Day Numbers using the Day Number table on page 66 in Reading #4. Jot down your two choices on the Scratch Pad, then turn to the Answers.

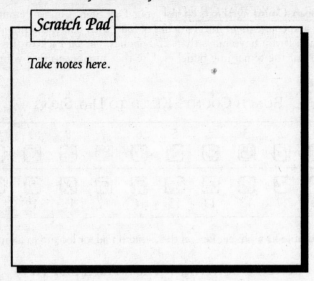

Scratch Pad

Take notes here.

LOOK UP YOUR ANSWER

The answers to this Reading are found "at the back of the book," in a section called the Quick Reference Guide, which starts on page 223.

First look up the Day Sign that you counted or cast, and read the section of the text—Horoscope, Work, Love, Money, or Strategy—that best suits your question. If you asked about a general subject, read the whole answer. For those who asked about their mission, you'll find it in the Strategy section.

Then look up the Day Number, and read your answer there as well.

EXTRA CREDIT

What's the clincher? To find out what your Day Sign and Day Number mean in combination, turn to the "260 Combinations" Section of the Quick Reference Guide. Look up your Day Sign first, then find your number underneath it. This brief passage of text—in 20 words or less—will give a sentiment that combines both the Day Sign and its number into a single "bottom line."

EXTRA, EXTRA CREDIT!

Day 101 through Day 120—You are now over two fifths of the way through your journey of 260 days. While continuing to be aware of the signs and symbols that appear to you in your world, it's time to create a little sacred space for yourself. "Sacred Space," in Mayan and Aztec terms, is simply space that has been "cornered." You "corner" a space by marking it off according to the compass points (East, North, West, and South). The Maya place four stones at these points outside their houses in order to corner the entire structure. But it's also possible (and perhaps more practical) to corner a room of the house—or at least your niche. You can do this by placing a small object of your choice (or a candle) in the direction of the sunrise (East) and sunset (West) and at right angles to these (North and South). The center of your space is in between the markers you have placed. Sometime during the next 20 days, mark off some space, seat yourself at the center, and do a little thinking from there. Jot down the thoughts that come to you. They will be visions.

Go on to the next Reading whenever you are ready to continue.

Reading #7

How's It Going Today?
(Update me)

In this Reading you will use the ancient number signs and symbols as their inventors did, to determine the auspices of any given day. So get ready... get set, let's synchronize our watches. In the 5,000 year-old calendar, what is today's date? And what does it mean for you and your question?

TOOLS

The signs you have been using in the first six Readings were not only used to answer everyday questions. Their original use (and principal purpose) was for telling time.

In this timekeeping system, each of the 20 Day Signs was assigned to a day. Much like our "Monday," "Tuesday," and "Wednesday," the Maya had "Sea Creature," "Air," "Night," "Corn," etc.... And the Aztecs, who adopted the calendar from the Maya, had "Alligator," "Wind," "House," "Lizard," etc. The 20 Day Signs cycled endlessly through time, just as our days cycle continuously through our months and years.

As an added touch, the ancient timekeepers also numbered each day, from 1 through 13.

They gave a sign and a number to each day, starting with "1 Sea Creature," and counting forward—"2 Air," "3 Night," "4 Corn". See the chart on page 103.

FIRST 24 DAY SIGNS AND NUMBERS

1 Sea Creature	2 Air	3 Night	4 Corn
5 Serpent	6 Death	7 Deer	8 Rabbit
9 Rain	10 Dog	11 Monkey	12 Broom
13 Reed	1 Jaguar	2 Eagle	3 Owl
4 Earthquake	5 Blade	6 Storm	7 Lord
8 Sea Creature	9 Air	10 Night	11 Corn

...and so on, through 260 days, never repeating the same sign-and-number combination.

In this Reading you'll be using this book's Almanac and some blank calendars to quickly determine which Day Sign and Day Number the Maya and Aztecs would have given to this very day—for their early calendars extended into our own times. This information will, in turn, lead us to a Reading for your specific question.

BACKGROUND

Even now there are Mayan priests in the hills of Mesoamerica who not only tell fortunes with their beans, stones, and crystals, but who track the holy days of the ancient calendar using the ancient ways. For many centuries these ways have included the use of holy timekeeping books.

Those few books that have survived from earlier times contain charts, tables, formulas, and calculations for keeping track not only of the days, but of the movements of the sun, moon, Venus, and all the other visible planets. In other words, these books are very much like our almanacs. By consulting the books, the priestly timekeepers were able to assign the proper numbers and symbols to each day, and thus were prepared to tell the people when to plant the corn, when to honor certain gods, and how to plan their daily lives.

As you complete this Reading, you'll get your first lesson in using this book's Almanac to compute past, present, and future dates, with the accuracy of a bona fide sun-counting priest. And once you know the signs and numbers for any given day, you will have the tools you need to look at your questions and issues in a whole new way.

HOW TO

Attention: Users of All Methods: Put your beans, cards, and pointing finger away for a second. The first part of this Reading is based on today's date. But in the Extra Credit section you'll need your tools again to find out how today's date affects your question or issue.

ASK YOUR QUESTION

Follow your icon for the ends you defined in Reading #0, or ask any question listed in **boldface** (below) that appeals to you now.

FASTRACK You have come here looking for the facts. The oracle can only answer based on how things are at the moment you ask the question. Ask: **How does today factor in?**

SOULSEARCH You have come to get your horoscope. It changes every moment! But each day has its overall effect. Ask: **What is today's outlook?**

GAMEPLAN You have come here to get your game plan. But conditions are constantly changing, and flexibility is key. Ask: **What are the environmental influences?**

HEARTS HUNT You have come here on a matter of love. Love is the sum total of a number of days. But each contributes to the whole impression. Ask: **What kind of love does the day favor?**

UIZ'N QUEST You have come to seek the higher spiritual meaning in your day-to-day affairs. You would be best advised to come every day for a while, for there are 260 days to experience, and this is but one of them. Ask: **What is the thought for this day?**

SELECT YOUR SIGN

All users follow the same method here . . . . Turn now to the back of the book, to the section called the "Almanac"—but keep a finger here. For this Reading you will be referring to Part I of the Almanac—The Sacred Calendar, starting on page 438.

For example, if this is 1998, find the column that says 1998 at the top. . . .

The table on page 106 lists every 20th date of our calendar. This is the date on which the Mayan "Sea Creature" Day Sign A (🔲) cycles up again, and a new 20-day period starts. Shown to the right of each date is a Day Sign (indicated by a letter of the alphabet) and a Day Number (1, 2, 3 . . . 13). Given these two pieces of information, you can quickly "count your way" to the Day Sign and Day Number for any date.

Find your date in the main table. The Day Sign and Day Number are listed to the right. Let's say the date you are looking for is December 26, 1996; the table lists Day Sign A, Day Number 2, for this date.

If your date isn't in the table, find the date right *before* yours. Counting this date as "1," count forward, up to and including your date. Jot down this count on the Scratch Pad. For example, if you were looking for December 28, 1996, the closest listed date is December 26. Counting December 26th as 1, you would count forward—December 27 = 2, December 28 = 3—three is the count. Jot down yours.

Put your finger on Day Sign A on page 107 (or at the top of most Almanac pages).

Sample Almanac Page

1996	Day #		1997	Day #		1998	Day #
JAN 1	A 6		JAN 15	A 9		JAN 10	A 5
JAN 21	A 13		FEB 4	A 3		JAN 30	A 12
FEB 10	A 7		FEB 24	A 10		FEB 19	A 6
MAR 1	*A 1*		MAR 16	A 4		MAR 11	A 13
MAR 21	A 8		APR 5	A 11		MAR 31	A 7
APR 10	A 2		APR 25	A 5		*APR 20*	*A 1*
APR 30	A 9		MAY 15	A 12		MAY 10	A 8
MAY 20	A 3		JUN 4	A 6		MAY 30	A 2
JUN 9	A 10		JUN 24	A 13		JUN 19	A 9
JUN 29	A 4		JUL 14	A 7		JUL 9	A 3
JUL 19	A 11		*AUG 3*	*A 1*		JUL 29	A 10
AUG 8	A 5		AUG 23	A 8		AUG 18	A 4
AUG 28	A 12		SEP 12	A 2		SEP 7	A 11
SEP 17	A 6		OCT 2	A 9		SEP 27	A 5
OCT 7	A 13		OCT 22	A 3		OCT 17	A 12
OCT 27	A 7		NOV 11	A 10		NOV 6	A 6
NOV 16	*A 1*		DEC 1	A 4		NOV 26	A 13
DEC 6	A 8		DEC 21	A 11		DEC 16	A 7
DEC 26	A 2						

TUN
3 AHAU   ⁞ 🔲
STARTS MAR 21ST

TUN
12 AHAU   ▌▌⁞ 🔲
STARTS MAR 16TH

TUN
8 AHAU   ⁞ 🔲
STARTS MAR 11TH

| 1 | 2 | 3 | 4 | 5 | 6 | 7 | 8 | 9 | 10 | 11 | 12 | 13 |

MAYAN DAY SIGNS

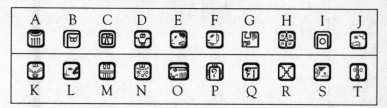

AZTEC DAY SIGNS

Count forward by your number. You have just fingered your Day Sign. Jot it down. In our example, December 28, 1996, is a count of three away from Day Sign A. Starting with A as 1, we count 2 = B, and 3 = C. C would be the Day Sign in this case. Note your Day Sign now.

Using the Day Number table here (or at the bottom of most Almanac pages), put your finger on the Day Number of the closest listed date to yours. Counting this Day as "1," count forward to yours.

DAY NUMBERS

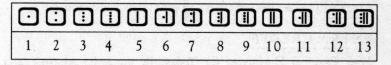

You have just fingered your Day Number. Jot it down beside your Day Sign. Turn to the Answers. In our example, the Day Number listed for December 26, 1996 (the closest calendar date), is 2. You are looking for the number that is a three-count, starting at 2. So, 2, 3, 4—four is the Day Number for December 28, 1996.

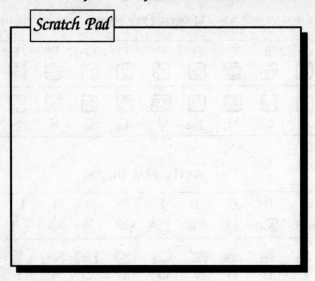

Scratch Pad

THE ANSWERS

Look up today's Day Sign in the Quick Reference Guide and read the section of text called Horoscope. Then look up today's Day Number (1 through 13) and read the Strategy section of that text. Together the two pieces of information will provide today's general horoscope, which applies to everyone and to everything that will happen today, including your specific question or issue.

And don't forget to consult the 260 Combinations section (starting on page 265) to see how today's unique sign/number combination will have an impact on the day's auspices. Look up your Day Sign first in the Combinations section and then find your Day Number beneath it.

EXTRA CREDIT

Your Personal Horoscope for Today. By using the Almanac and today's date, you just found the signs that apply to everyone today. But what does this general reading have to do with you personally and your specific question? To find out, let's factor in a divination on top of today's date. For this activity you will need to divine a number between 1 and 20. If you are counting beans, just count them as you would to select a Day Sign—take a handful, and count them off by bunches of four. If you reach 20 bunches, put those 20 back and keep counting. If you're using your Magic Lightning Cards, choose from among the Day Sign cards, and go by the bunch number at the top of the one you select. For Point-n-Click, use the diagram below to get your count between 1 and 20.

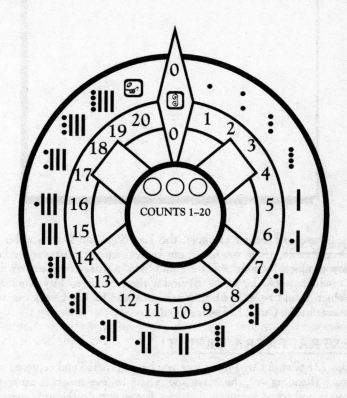

Now just "add" this count to today's Day Sign and Day Number. Turn to the Master Answer section and consult your resulting Day Sign, Day Number, and combination for your personal slant on this day.

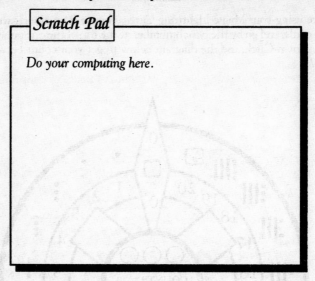

Scratch Pad

Do your computing here.

Using our earlier example, the Day Sign and Day Number for December 28, 1996, was C4. If our bean count (or whatever method) now produces a count of 3, we would "add" a three-count to Day Sign C (which would be C, D, **E**) and a three-count to Day Number 4 (which would be 4, 5, **6**). Our answer would be **E6**. Check out your answer in the Quick Reference Guide.

EXTRA, EXTRA CREDIT!

Day 121 through Day 140—Once you have cornered and centered your space (Reading #6), the Maya and Aztecs believe it acts as an energy vortex and portal for spiritual visions. For an extra authentic ceremonial touch, you might like to "smoke" the four corners of your space sometime over the next 20 days and then at intervals, as the spirit moves you. Incense of any kind—copal if you can get it—is traditional for this kind of smoking purpose. Just light a stick of your favorite blend at each compass point. Since a three-stone hearth is traditionally placed in the center of the house, you could burn a scented candle at the center of your space. While the incense burns down, say prayers for blessings, deliverance, mercy, guidance, or for whatever your spiritual need is at this time. At the end of this renewal ceremony, conduct a divination with your beans, your Lightning Cards, or your pointing finger. Select a Day Sign and Day Number and consult the Master Answer section for each.

Reading #7

Unless you ask otherwise, the oracle at this time will usually answer the issue you have presented in your prayer or will in some general way advise you for the coming period.

Go on to the next Reading whenever you are ready to continue.

Reading #8

HOW'S IT LOOK FOR TOMORROW?
(Tip me off)

Time—as they say—is relative. Today's signs are important in and of themselves, but so is their sequence in the larger scheme of things. In this Reading you will put your question or issue in the context of what tomorrow will bring.

TOOLS

Once you know the Day Sign and Day Number for any date in our calendar, it's easy to start counting time like a Mayan. As they cycle, the 20 Day Signs and 13 Day Numbers form a continuous, recurring, and repeating cycle of days. In the antique almanacs that survive, tables not dissimilar to the one shown on the next page were used to chart the sequence of days.

To read the table, start in the upper left-hand corner at Day A1. The next day is B2. And the day after that is C3. When you get to the bottom of the first column (Day T7), go to the top of the second column (Day A8). And so on, down one column and to the top of the next, until the last day—T13. Then start over at A1.

THE SEQUENCE OF DAYS
(REPEATS EVERY 260 DAYS)

▼ ▼ ▼ ▼ ▼ ▼ ▼ ▼ ▼ ▼ ▼ ▼ ▼

A	1	8	2	9	3	10	4	11	5	12	6	13	7
B	2	9	3	10	4	11	5	12	6	13	7	1	8
C	3	10	4	11	5	12	6	13	7	1	8	2	9
D	4	11	5	12	6	13	7	1	8	2	9	3	10
E	5	12	6	13	7	1	8	2	9	3	10	4	11
F	6	13	7	1	8	2	9	3	10	4	11	5	12
G	7	1	8	2	9	3	10	4	11	5	12	6	13
H	8	2	9	3	10	4	11	5	12	6	13	7	1
I	9	3	10	4	11	5	12	6	13	7	1	8	2
J	10	4	11	5	12	6	13	7	1	8	2	9	3
K	11	5	12	6	13	7	1	8	2	9	3	10	4
L	12	6	13	7	1	8	2	9	3	10	4	11	5
M	13	7	1	8	2	9	3	10	4	11	5	12	6
N	1	8	2	9	3	10	4	11	5	12	6	13	7
O	2	9	3	10	4	11	5	12	6	13	7	1	8
P	3	10	4	11	5	12	6	13	7	1	8	2	9
Q	4	11	5	12	6	13	7	1	8	2	9	3	10
R	5	12	6	13	7	1	8	2	9	3	10	4	11
S	6	13	7	1	8	2	9	3	10	4	11	5	12
T	7	1	8	2	9	3	10	4	11	5	12	6	13

BACKGROUND

The 260 holy-day sequence—called the *Tzolkin* by the Maya, the *Tonalpoualli* by the Aztecs, and the "Book of Fate" by English-speaking observers—was used to fix the religious festivals and other sacred events in a cycle of worship in which each day was regarded as special and holy.

Many of the tables that were hand-copied into Mayan and Aztec books were much more complicated than the table above. Some of these required mathematical computations to "fill in" the intentional gaps and blanks that were left to mystify those uninitiated in the priestly secrets. But you will be able to use your table just as the priests used theirs—and just as you use a wall calendar to check off days as they occur. This table gives you a practical way of following where you are in the Mayan holy year.

HOW TO

Attention: Users of All Methods: The first part of this Reading is based on an analysis of tomorrow's date. But in the Extra Credit section you'll get to use your beans, Magic Lightning Cards, or pointing finger to see how tomorrow will affect your question or issue.

ASK YOUR QUESTION

Follow your icon for the ends you defined in Reading #0, or ask any question listed in **boldface** (below) that appeals to you now.

FASTRACK You have come here looking for a quick answer to your question. But these things are always more complex than we initially think. Ask: **What's coming tomorrow?**

SOULSEARCH You have come here for your own well-being. We are getting down to the real thing. Ask: **What will I do tomorrow?**

GAMEPLAN You have come here to get your plan down in writing. Do not overlook the forces outside your control. Ask: **What will conditions be like tomorrow?**

HEARTSHUNT You have come here to ask about the matters of the heart. But love can be a fickle bedmate. Ask: **Will _____ still love me tomorrow?**

VIZ'nQUEST You have come seeking spiritual sustenance. You've come to the right place. Ask: **What is sacred?**

114

SELECT YOUR SIGN

All users follow the same method here.... If you just completed Reading #7, you're in luck. All you have to do is add one Day Sign and one Day Number to the date you computed, and turn to the answers. If today is 3 Jaguar (3N), tomorrow must be 4 Eagle (4O). You can verify this by circling the date you computed in Reading #7 on the table on page 113. Tomorrow's date will be the date right beneath it.

If it's been more than a day since you last read, count down the column, one date for every day that has passed. When you reach the bottom of one column, go to the top of the next. If you reach the end of the table, go back to the beginning.

Or you can always use the Almanac and the method you learned in Reading #7 to find tomorrow's date (or any date you choose). Here's a quick reminder of how to use the Almanac:

Find the current year in Part I of the Almanac, starting on page 438. Find the date you are looking for in that table. If it is listed, copy down its sign and number, and consult the answers. If your date isn't in the table, find the date right before yours. Counting this date as "1," count forward, up to and including your date. Jot down this count on the Scratch Pad.

Put your finger on Day Sign A in the tables here (or at the top of most Almanac pages).

MAYAN DAY SIGNS

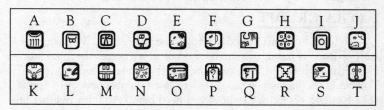

AZTEC DAY SIGNS

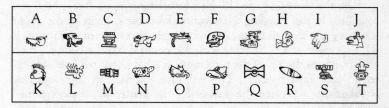

Count forward by your number. You have just fingered your Day Sign. Jot it down.

Using the Day Number table here (or at the bottom of most Almanac pages), put your finger on the Day Number of the closest listed date to yours. Counting this Day as "1," count forward to yours.

DAY NUMBERS

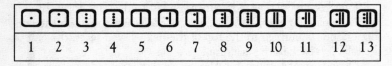

You have just fingered your Day Number. Jot it down beside your Day Sign. Turn to the Answers.

THE ANSWERS

You will find your answer at the back of the book, in the Quick Reference Guide's Master Answer Section, starting on page 223. First look up your Day Sign, then your Day Number. Read the Horoscope for each day as well as the section of text (Work, Love, Money, or Strategy) that relates best to your topic of interest.

Finally, turn to the Combinations section to get a little food for thought, related to tomorrow's sign/number combination.

EXTRA CREDIT

To learn how this holy day affects your question... With your question or issue in mind, use the method of your choice—bean counting, Day Sign Lightning Cards (use the bunch numbers), or Reading #7's Point-n-Click diagram on page 109—to cast a number between 1 and 20. (See Reading #7, Extra Credit, if you need help.) Add this number first to tomorrow's Day Sign, then to its Day Number, using the method you learned in Reading #7's Extra Credit section. Or—even easier...

Use the table on page 113. First locate tomorrow's date, which you computed in this Reading. Now count down the column by the count you just got with your beans, cards, or finger. (Let's say that tomorrow is R7, and you cast a 5. Starting with R7, count down the column, then continue from the top of the next, until you have counted five and gotten to your answer—B11.) This will give you the Day Sign and Day Number that represent the answer for the matter you are concerned with now.

Once you have found these signs, look each up in the Master Answer Section of the Quick Reference Guide, and read the portion of the text (Work, Love, Money, Strategy) that most relates to your question, as well as the text called Horoscope. Complete your reading by consulting the Combinations section for your Day Sign and Day Number combination.

Scratch Pad

Do your math here.

EXTRA, EXTRA CREDIT!

Day 141 through Day 160—Calibrate your vision quest! The 260-day journey you have embarked upon is a long-standing holy tradition. Using your understanding of the 260-Day Tzolkin (Tonalpoualli) calendar from this Reading, you can now discover how your own quest meshes with the actual 260-day holy period taking place. You will find the beginning of each new 260-day Tzolkin in the Almanac, printed in script, like this: *JAN 5*.

To find where you stand in the current holy cycle, turn to the Almanac page for this year. Find the date closest to today's in the table on page 118, then locate the date in *script* that immediately precedes this date.

1999	Day #		2000	Day #		2001	Day #
JAN 5	A 1		JAN 20	A 4		JAN 14	A 13
JAN 25	A 8		FEB 9	A 11		FEB 3	A 7
FEB 14	A 2		FEB 29	A 5		FEB 23	A 1
MAR 6	A 9		MAR 20	A 12		MAR 15	A 8
MAR 26	A 3		APR 9	A 6		APR 4	A 2
APR 15	A 10		APR 29	A 13		APR 24	A 9
MAY 5	A 4		MAY 19	A 7		MAY 14	A 3
MAY 25	A 11		JUN 8	A 1		JUN 3	A 10
JUN 14	A 5		JUN 28	A 8		JUN 23	A 4
JUL 4	A 12		JUL 18	A 2		JUL 13	A 11
JUL 24	A 6		AUG 7	A 9		AUG 2	A 5
AUG 13	A 13		AUG 27	A 3		AUG 22	A 12
SEP 2	A 7		SEP 16	A 10		SEP 11	A 6
SEP 22	A 1		OCT 6	A 4		OCT 1	A 13
OCT 12	A 8		OCT 26	A 11		OCT 21	A 7
NOV 1	A 2		NOV 15	A 5		NOV 10	A 1
NOV 21	A 9		DEC 5	A 12		NOV 30	A 8
DEC 11	A 3		DEC 25	A 6		DEC 20	A 2
DEC 31	A 10						

TUN 4 AHAU	TUN 13 AHAU	TUN 9 AHAU
STARTS MAR 6TH	STARTS FEB 29TH	STARTS FEB 23RD

For example, these three columns from the Almanac for 1999 to 2001 show five new holy periods starting—one on January 5, 1999; one on September 22, 1999; one on June 8, 2000; one on February 23, 2001; and one on November 10, 2001. (Holy periods always start on a day A1.)

Reading #8

Now turn to the table on page 113 and find your sign and number combination. Circle the start date you found for the current holy year in the tables in this Reading's Tools section. Voilà! You can immediately see where you are in the cycle. And you now have a handy means of computing the signs for each of the dates remaining in your quest. Just x them out as they occur over the next 20 days of vision questing. Consult the Combinations section for each new day.

Go on to the next Reading whenever you are ready to continue.

Reading #9

WHAT'S ON THE AGENDA?
(Block out my calendar)

In this Reading your forecast for today and tomorrow will be extended
to include the outlook for as many days as you want to look ahead.
Use it to project your question or issue out a Mayan Uinal—
or 20-day month.

TOOLS

In Readings #7 and #8 you learned how to figure out the Mayan or
Aztec symbols and numbers that go with any one of our dates. Once you
know any given Mayan date, it's relatively simple to count forward to
any date in the future or count backward to any date in the past. Since
the dates cycle in a recurring way, you can also just use a calendar, like
the one provided here:

THE HOLY YEAR
A PERPETUAL CALENDAR
(HOLY YEAR REPEATS EVERY 13 UINALS)

UINAL #1—20 DAYS, STARTING ON 1A

A	B	C	D	E	F	G	H	I	J
1	2	3	4	5	6	7	8	9	10
K	L	M	N	O	P	Q	R	S	T
11	12	13	1	2	3	4	5	6	7

Reading #9

UINAL #2—20 DAYS, STARTING ON 8A

A	B	C	D	E	F	G	H	I	J
8	9	10	11	12	13	1	2	3	4

K	L	M	N	O	P	Q	R	S	T
5	6	7	8	9	10	11	12	13	1

UINAL #3—20 DAYS, STARTING ON 2A

A	B	C	D	E	F	G	H	I	J
2	3	4	5	6	7	8	9	10	11

K	L	M	N	O	P	Q	R	S	T
12	13	1	2	3	4	5	6	7	8

UINAL #4—20 DAYS, STARTING ON 9A

A	B	C	D	E	F	G	H	I	J
9	10	11	12	13	1	2	3	4	5

K	L	M	N	O	P	Q	R	S	T
6	7	8	9	10	11	12	13	1	2

UINAL #5—20 DAYS, STARTING ON 3A

A	B	C	D	E	F	G	H	I	J
3	4	5	6	7	8	9	10	11	12

K	L	M	N	O	P	Q	R	S	T
13	1	2	3	4	5	6	7	8	9

UINAL #6—20 DAYS, STARTING ON 10A

A	B	C	D	E	F	G	H	I	J
10	11	12	13	1	2	3	4	5	6

K	L	M	N	O	P	Q	R	S	T
7	8	9	10	11	12	13	1	2	3

UINAL #7—20 DAYS, STARTING ON 4A

A	B	C	D	E	F	G	H	I	J
4	5	6	7	8	9	10	11	12	13

K	L	M	N	O	P	Q	R	S	T
1	2	3	4	5	6	7	8	9	10

UINAL #8—20 DAYS, STARTING ON 11A

A	B	C	D	E	F	G	H	I	J
11	12	13	1	2	3	4	5	6	7

K	L	M	N	O	P	Q	R	S	T
8	9	10	11	12	13	1	2	3	4

UINAL #9—20 DAYS, STARTING ON 5A

A	B	C	D	E	F	G	H	I	J
5	6	7	8	9	10	11	12	13	1

K	L	M	N	O	P	Q	R	S	T
2	3	4	5	6	7	8	9	10	11

UINAL #10—20 DAYS, STARTING ON 12A

A	B	C	D	E	F	G	H	I	J
12	13	1	2	3	4	5	6	7	8

K	L	M	N	O	P	Q	R	S	T
9	10	11	12	13	1	2	3	4	5

UINAL #11—20 DAYS, STARTING ON 6A

A	B	C	D	E	F	G	H	I	J
6	7	8	9	10	11	12	13	1	2

K	L	M	N	O	P	Q	R	S	T
3	4	5	6	7	8	9	10	11	12

UINAL #12—20 DAYS, STARTING ON 13A

A	B	C	D	E	F	G	H	I	J
13	1	2	3	4	5	6	7	8	9

K	L	M	N	O	P	Q	R	S	T
10	11	12	13	1	2	3	4	5	6

UINAL #13—20 DAYS, STARTING ON 7A

A	B	C	D	E	F	G	H	I	J
7	8	9	10	11	12	13	1	2	3

K	L	M	N	O	P	Q	R	S	T
4	5	6	7	8	9	10	11	12	13

Starting with any date listed in this book's Almanac—always an "A" date—you can quickly find the appropriate table starting with that A date. The table will tell you what the next 19 signs and numbers will be, without your having to do any additional math. And you can even see forward from that point by just going on to the next Uinal.

In this Reading we'll take a quick look at the next couple of weeks. You can then work the Extra Credit section to see what it all means to your question or issue.

BACKGROUND

Though the thirteen 20-day Uinals—pronounced "Ve-nal" and roughly equivalent to our concept of a month—did not have official names, the Maya and Aztecs recognized them by their starting date—always a Day Sign "A" and a number 1 through 13. The 13 Uinals cycle continuously in a set pattern: Uinal A1 is always followed by A8, which is always followed by A2, A9, A3, A10, A4, A11, A5, A12, A6, A13, and A7. Each Uinal was thought to take on the characteristic of the particular combination of signs that it opened with. By just looking at the first day of the Uinal in which you find yourself now, you can get an indication of the influences that will affect the entire 20-day period.

HOW TO

Attention: Users of All Methods: The first part of this Reading is based on an analysis of an upcoming time period. Once you have computed these dates, the Extra Credit section will give you the opportunity to use the method of your choice to consider your own question or ongoing issue.

ASK YOUR QUESTION

Follow your icon for the ends you defined in Reading #0, or ask any question listed in **boldface** (below) that appeals to you now.

FASTRACK You have come here for immediate gratification... and nothing's wrong with that. But any question worth asking is rarely resolved in a single day. To find out what this 20-day Uinal holds, say: **What's in store these 20 days?**

SOULSEARCH You have come here for guidance on your journey. Let's consider the aspects of this 20-day Uinal. Ask: **Where will I be when this Uinal ends?**

GAMEPLAN You have come here to plan your contingencies. It is easiest to foresee something that follows a predictable pattern. Let's see what's cycling up in the calendar. Ask: **Plot it out for 20 days.**

HEARTS HUNT You have come here to ask about love and life. Better plan ahead. Say: **Cast for us these 20 nights.**

VIZ'N'QUEST You have come seeking spiritual enlightenment. This itself is cyclical. Say: **Put me in the context of this Uinal.**

SELECT YOUR SIGN

All users follow the same method here.... If you do not know what Mayan Uinal you're in, turn to the Almanac, starting on page 438, and find the date listed that is closest to today's. Jot down this A-date on the Scratch Pad. This date will influence the entire 20-day period ahead of it. If today's date is near the end of a 20-day Uinal, you may wish to identify the next Uinal in the Almanac as well.

Armed with this information, turn to the Answers.

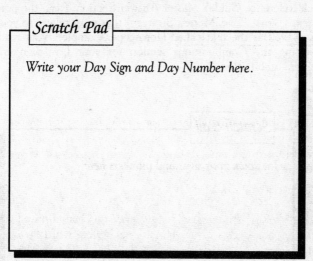

Scratch Pad

Write your Day Sign and Day Number here.

THE ANSWERS

You will find your answer at the back of the book, in the Quick Reference Guide's Section, starting on page 265. First look up your Day Sign, then read the Combinations horoscope to get a feel for the influences dominating this Uinal. Then look up your day number.

You also can use the answer sets in earlier Readings to divine your answer. Look up your Day Sign in Reading #3's Answers. Look up your Day Number in Reading #5's Answers.

EXTRA CREDIT

To learn how this Uinal affects your question... With your question or issue in mind, use the method of your choice—bean counting, Day Sign Lightning Cards (use the bunch numbers), or Reading #7's Point-n-Click diagram—to cast a number between 1 and 20. (See Reading #7, Extra Credit, if you need help.) Add this number first to this Uinal's Day Sign, then to its Day Number, using the method you learned in Reading #7 or #8's Extra Credit section. Or—even easier...

Use the tables in this Reading's Tools section. First locate this Uinal's table, according to its start date (A1 through A13). Now, starting with the A-date, count ahead by the count you just got with your beans, cards, or finger. The sign and number that your finger ends up on is your answer. Look up both the Day Sign and Day Number in the Quick Reference Guide's Master Answer Section. Read the portion of the text (Work, Love, Money, Strategy) that most relates to your question, as well as the text called Horoscope. Complete your reading by consulting the Combinations section for your Day Sign and Day Number combination.

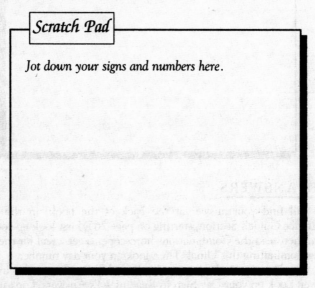

| Scratch Pad |

Jot down your signs and numbers here.

EXTRA, EXTRA CREDIT!

Day 161 through Day 180—When a Mayan priest (or king, who served as the ultimate priest) wanted to stimulate a vision, he retired to the dark inner chamber of the temple, which itself was oriented to the compass points and therefore cornered and centered. You can achieve a similar effect by taking a candlelit herbal bath. In the hushed light, let your thoughts go . . . and see where they lead. As part of your meditation, periodically shift direction so that you are facing, in turn, East, North, West, and South. Listen for the messages that come from each direction. . . . These are your visions.

Go on to the next Reading whenever you are ready to continue.

Reading #10

In this Reading, you will continue to build your forecast as you
learn to interpret the overriding signs for any given year.
What will the Mayan New Year bring for your
question or issue? Let's find out here.

TOOLS

As you are starting to appreciate, the Mayan timekeeper priests had to
take many things into consideration before they could completely
determine the auspices for the day. First there were the 20 Day Signs
and Day Numbers to be read. What day was it? And which signs
applied? Furthermore, where did this day fall in the sacred calendar?
And, last but not least, which sign was ruling the year itself?

In the previous Readings you've been working with the 260-day
divinatory calendar, or Tzolkin, of 13 Uinals. But for this Reading we'll
be learning about another one of the Maya's time-counting units—the
Tun, which is a 360-day year made up of 18 Uinals. Using the Almanac
at the back of the book, it's easy to determine what Tun year it is.

Let's say you want to know what year it is on July 23, 2003. Turn to
the table for 2003 (page 469). The start date for each Tun year is listed
at the bottom of the column. In 2003 a new Tun starts on February 13th
and runs for 360 days to February 7, 2004, concluding on a day "1
Ahau," for which it is named. Since July 23, 2003 is after February 13th
and before February 8th of the folling year, July 23rd is in the year 1
Ahau.

127

2002	Day #	2003	Day #	2004	Day #
JAN 9	A 9	JAN 4	A 5	JAN 19	A 8
JAN 29	A 3	JAN 24	A 12	FEB 8	A 2
FEB 18	A 10	FEB 13	A 6	FEB 28	A 9
MAR 10	A 4	MAR 5	A 13	MAR 19	A 3
MAR 30	A 11	MAR 25	A 7	APR 8	A 10
APR 19	A 5	*APR 14*	*A 1*	APR 28	A 4
MAY 9	A 12	MAY 4	A 8	MAY 18	A 11
MAY 29	A 6	MAY 24	A 2	JUN 7	A 5
JUN 18	A 13	JUN 13	A 9	JUN 27	A 12
JUL 8	A 7	JUL 3	A 3	JUL 17	A 6
JUL 28	*A 1*	JUL 23	A 10	AUG 6	A 13
AUG 17	A 8	AUG 12	A 4	AUG 26	A 7
SEP 6	A 2	SEP 1	A 11	*SEP 15*	*A 1*
SEP 26	A 9	SEP 21	A 5	OCT 5	A 8
OCT 16	A 3	OCT 11	A 12	OCT 25	A 2
NOV 5	A 10	OCT 31	A 6	NOV 14	A 9
NOV 25	A 4	NOV 20	A 13	NOV 4	A 3
DEC 15	A 11	DEC 10	A 7	DEC 24	A 10
		DEC 30	*A 1*		

TUN 5 AHAU	TUN 1 AHAU	TUN 10 AHAU
STARTS FEB 18TH	STARTS FEB 13TH	STARTS FEB 8TH

The start date for each Tun is listed at the bottom of the columns.

BACKGROUND

The Maya were aware that their 260-day holy calendar did not reflect the solar year, whose measurement—with its anticipation of the seasons—meant greater success in agriculture. As a result, using the same signs and numbers, they also counted 360-day periods to keep track of a "year" they called a Tun. A Tun, which is eighteen 20-day Uinals, is about the length of our own calendar year, but is actually short by about five and one quarter days. The term *Tun* stands for "stone," since at the end of each 360-day period, the ancients erected a stone monument to commemorate the passing of a complete cycle of seasons.

The Tuns were each named for their <u>last</u> day, which is always a day marked by the Day Sign T. The Maya called this day *Ahau,* or Lord. The thing that made each Tun unique was the number (1 through 13) that accompanied Ahau in the calendar. Depending on what this number was, the year itself would take on an attitude, and all events that year would be affected by this sign.

Due to the cyclical nature of the calendar, these year numbers cycle in a recurring sequence of Ahau numbers in this order: 5, 1, 10, 6, 2, 11, 7, 3, 12, 8, 4, 13, 9, and then back to 5 again. Here is a useful chart for looking at the sequence as it appears in the Almanac. Reading left to right in Mayan symbols:

THE TUN YEARS

5 Ahau	1 Ahau	10 Ahau	6 Ahau
2 Ahau	11 Ahau	7 Ahau	3 Ahau
12 Ahau	8 Ahau	4 Ahau	13 Ahau
9 Ahau			

In this Reading you will be determining what Ahau year it is, and then, in the Extra Credit, what this sign means to you and your specific question.

HOW TO

Attention: Users of All Methods: You do not need your beans, Lightning Cards, or pointing finger to do the first part of this Reading. Put them on standby. Your initial answer only requires a simple lookup in the Almanac.

ASK YOUR QUESTION

Follow your icon for the ends you defined in Reading #0, or ask any question listed in **boldface** (below) that appeals to you now.

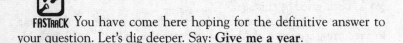

FASTTRACK You have come here hoping for the definitive answer to your question. Let's dig deeper. Say: **Give me a year**.

SOULSEARCH You have come here for your horoscope. So let's consider the influence of the coming year. Say: **Cycle the seasons.**

GAMEPLAN You have come here to plan ahead. Might as well take it out a year. Say: **Plot it out for 360 days.**

HEARTSHUNT You have come here to ask about love and life. Better plan ahead. Ask: **Where will we be in a year?**

VIZNQUEST You have come seeking spiritual pursuits. These things always take at least a full cycle to run their current course. What a difference a year makes. Ask: **How will this year change me?**

SELECT YOUR SIGN

All users follow the same method here.... You will not need your beans, Lightning Cards, or pointing finger to figure out what Ahau year this is. All you have to do is flip to the Almanac, which starts on page 438.

As is traditional, the <u>end</u> date of each Tun is the sign that designates the year. But for easier lookup, the Almanac lists each Ahau's start date. For example, using the table in the Tools section of this Reading, we can see that Tun 5 Ahau, which begins February 18, 2002, ends with the date 5 Ahau on February 12, 2003. A new year starts February 13, 2003, named for its end date—1 Ahau (February 7, 2004).

Turn to the Almanac and find today's date. Look at the bottom of that column to see when the Ahau starts this year. If today's date is before the start day of this Ahau, you will find your sign listed at the bottom of the previous column. If today's date is after the Ahau start date listed, you are living in that Ahau year.

Scratch Pad

Jot down your Ahau year here.

THE ANSWERS

Look up the Day Number for your Ahau in the Quick Reference Guide at the back of the book. Read the Key Dates and Horoscope sections of the text. These answers will give you a feeling for the types of events that may occur this year. Then consult the Combinations section of the

Quick Reference Guide. The text here will give you a feeling for the nature of the entire year you're living through right now.

The answers in earlier Readings also can add dimension to your answer. Look up this year's Day Number in the Answer sections to Readings #4 and #5.

EXTRA CREDIT

What sayeth the Ahau? To determine how the current Tun year will affect your question or issue: With your question or issue in mind, use the method of your choice—bean counting, Day Sign Lightning Cards (use the bunch numbers), or Reading #7's Point-n-Click diagram—to cast a number between 1 and 20. (See Reading #7's Extra Credit section if you need help.) Using the following tables, count forward from your present Ahau sign by that count. When you are done counting, your finger will be on your new Day Sign and Day Number.

TABLES FOR COUNTING FORWARD
FROM AHAU DATES

5 AHAU

T 5	A 6	B 7	C 8	D 9	E 10	F 11	G 12	H 13	I 1
J 2	K 3	L 4	M 5	N 6	O 7	P 8	Q 9	R 10	S 11

1 AHAU

T 1	A 2	B 3	C 4	D 5	E 6	F 7	G 8	H 9	I 10
J 11	K 12	L 13	M 1	N 2	O 3	P 4	Q 5	R 6	S 7

10 Ahau

T	A	B	C	D	E	F	G	H	I
10	11	12	13	1	2	3	4	5	6
J	K	L	M	N	O	P	Q	R	S
7	8	9	10	11	12	13	1	2	3

6 Ahau

T	A	B	C	D	E	F	G	H	I
6	7	8	9	10	11	12	13	1	2
J	K	L	M	N	O	P	Q	R	S
3	4	5	6	7	8	9	10	11	12

2 Ahau

T	A	B	C	D	E	F	G	H	I
2	3	4	5	6	7	8	9	10	11
J	K	L	M	N	O	P	Q	R	S
12	13	1	2	3	4	5	6	7	8

11 Ahau

T	A	B	C	D	E	F	G	H	I
11	12	13	1	2	3	4	5	6	7
J	K	L	M	N	O	P	Q	R	S
8	9	10	11	12	13	1	2	3	4

7 Ahau

T	A	B	C	D	E	F	G	H	I
7	8	9	10	11	12	13	1	2	3
J	K	L	M	N	O	P	Q	R	S
4	5	6	7	8	9	10	11	12	13

3 AHAU

T	A	B	C	D	E	F	G	H	I
3	4	5	6	7	8	9	10	11	12

J	K	L	M	N	O	P	Q	R	S
13	1	2	3	4	5	6	7	8	9

12 AHAU

T	A	B	C	D	E	F	G	H	I
12	13	1	2	3	4	5	6	7	8

J	K	L	M	N	O	P	Q	R	S
9	10	11	12	13	1	2	3	4	5

8 AHAU

T	A	B	C	D	E	F	G	H	I
8	9	10	11	12	13	1	2	3	4

J	K	L	M	N	O	P	Q	R	S
5	6	7	8	9	10	11	12	13	1

4 AHAU

T	A	B	C	D	E	F	G	H	I
4	5	6	7	8	9	10	11	12	13

J	K	L	M	N	O	P	Q	R	S
1	2	3	4	5	6	7	8	9	10

13 AHAU

T	A	B	C	D	E	F	G	H	I
13	1	2	3	4	5	6	7	8	9

J	K	L	M	N	O	P	Q	R	S
10	11	12	13	1	2	3	4	5	6

9 AHAU

T	A	B	C	D	E	F	G	H	I
9	10	11	12	13	1	2	3	4	5
J	K	L	M	N	O	P	Q	R	S
6	7	8	9	10	11	12	13	1	2

Look up your resulting Day Sign and Day Number in the Quick Reference Guide's Master Answer section. Read the portion of the text (Work, Love, Money, Strategy) that most relates to your question, as well as the text called Horoscope. Complete your Reading by consulting the Combinations section for your Day Sign and Day Number combination.

Scratch Pad

Jot down your signs and numbers here.

EXTRA, EXTRA CREDIT!

Day 181 through Day 200—By now you should have quite a collection of Magic Lightning Stones in your possession. You may have so many, in fact, that it's difficult to count them by the handful. Mayan priests who still practice this ancient art often simply shift the objects around on a table or other flat surface. They shift them until the objects have "sorted themselves" into a pile. There is no right or wrong way to do this. You simply have to go with how the stones feel to you. As you shift them, they will arrange themselves. You will sense when they are done. When this happens, you can either count them, like beans, to get a Day Sign... and then repeat the procedure to get a Day Number; or you can start to interpret them on their own merits... based on your understanding of colors, compass points, and the Mayan and Aztec symbols in general. Each one of your Magic Lightning Stones also has the capability of taking on the meanings you have associated with it. As such, each can be interpreted using your own personal definition. Over the next 20 days, try out this method of shifting your Lightning Stones around. Which objects gather themselves into your pile? And what does this say to you?

Go on to the next Reading whenever you are ready to continue.

Reading #11

WHAT CAN I ENVISION?
(Show me the larger picture)

In this Reading you will expand your ability to interpret
your signs with the aid of some pictures drawn from an
ancient Mayan book. Each is worth a thousand words, of course.
But their interpretation is all in the eye of the beholder,
which—right here, right now—is you.

TOOLS

The Day Signs and Day Numbers that you became acquainted with in
the previous Readings were the core symbols that the Mayan and Aztec
priests used to read the auspices of the day and answer specific questions. But the holy books they used in their consultations contained
many additional drawings and illustrations . . . of gods, kings, astronomical symbols, and other figures that helped to explain the meaning of
the Day Numbers and Day Signs they accompanied.

This Reading features 20 drawings based on the many hundreds of
illustrations found in the *Dresden Codex*, one of only three or four
Mayan books that survived the European conquest—and subsequent
book-burning—of 16th-century Mexico.

BACKGROUND

Scholars are still attempting to unravel the mysteries contained in the
100-page *Dresden Codex* (named for the place where the manuscript
now resides). Certain sections of the book are understood to contain
detailed information on predicting eclipses. Other drawings clearly
show particular gods, including many renderings of Chac, the long-
nosed Rain God. In addition, many series of related illustrations appear
to tell stories.

Some of the *Codex* drawings bear a striking resemblance to Tarot
cards. In fact, the 20 drawings that have been selected to illustrate this
Reading's Answers were chosen based on their similarity to the images

137

found in modern-day Tarot decks.[1] For those already familiar with the Tarot, this presentation will help you understand how the Mayan symbols can be related to the symbols you already know and love. But no prior knowledge of the Tarot is needed for you to use these drawings for personal edification and enlightenment.

Just like any drawing, photograph, or picture, there are many dimensions to these illustrations, and different people will see different things. It's like looking at one of the ink blots used by psychologists. What strikes you about each drawing is its significance for you . . . tonight.

Let's get the feel for it, all right?

HOW TO

Light your candle or favorite incense, say your prayers, and choose your method—bean counting, Magic Lightning Cards, or Point-n-Click. Once you have selected your method, ask your question.

ASK YOUR QUESTION

Follow your icon for the ends you defined in Reading #0, or ask any question listed in **boldface** (below) that appeals to you now.

FASTRACK You have come here to find out something specific. But even a single answer can have many points of view. Let's see if we can find the one that's right for you. Say: **Sharpen my view.** (It's also interesting to ask about how other individuals, in turn, view it too. Ask: **Sharpen the view of so-and-so.**)

SOUL SEARCH You have come for your horoscope. It changes moment to moment. Let's see if we can get a snapshot of "right now." Say: **Capture the moment.**

---

[1] My deep thanks to Pittsburgh artist and musician Wild Bill Cox for his inspired interpretation and rendering of this "Mayan Tarot."

GAME PLAN You have come here to plan a method for achieving your goal. But before we can hope to know how, we must appreciate why. To crystallize your objective, say: **Picture it in my head.** (It's also interesting to ask how others might view the same goal by saying, **Picture it for them.** Or **Picture it for so-and-so.**)

HEARTS HUNT You have come here with love in your heart—or is it all in your head? Let's see it from your inner point of view. Say: **Tell how I feel.** (You can also ask about others, from their point of view. **Tell how ____ feels.**)

VIZ'N QUEST You have come on a spiritual quest. As with any journey, half the experience is the getting there. Take time to view the scenery and you will never be wanting for signs to read. Say: **Magic mirror, let me see.**

SELECT YOUR SIGN

With your question in mind, use your favorite method—bean counting, Lightning Cards, Point-n-Click—to choose a Day Sign.

Bean Counting. Count your beans and use the number of bunches (1 through 20) to find your Day Sign for this question. Jot down the name of your sign on this Reading's Scratch Pad.

Magic Lightning Cards. Swirl your Day Sign Lightning Cards in front of you. Choose one, and write its name on the Scratch Pad on the next page.

Point-n-Click. Point-n-Click on one of the Mayan or Aztec Day Signs, using the table on page 11 in Reading #1. Note your sign on the Scratch Pad.

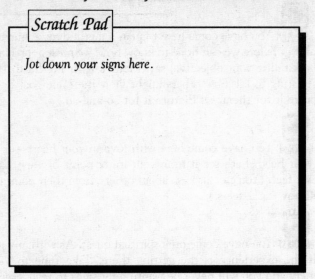

Scratch Pad

Jot down your signs here.

LOOK UP YOUR ANSWER

Find your Day Sign now in this Reading's Answers. Your answer consists of both the picture for your Day Sign and the text that accompanies the picture. To interpret the response, first look at the picture as if it were a piece of art and you were trying to figure out what the artist meant. Then read the text for clues, and look back to the picture again. The object here is to determine for yourself what it means to you.

THE ANSWERS

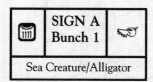

	SIGN A Bunch 1	
Sea Creature/Alligator		

The Old Man—or is it Youth?—with walking stick going off to vision quest . . . cornmeal in his backpack, some fish, and the clothes on his back. It is a journey of 260 days . . . at the end of which the Old Man feels young again, and the Lad, old. As once the legendary Corn God came rowing in his Alligator canoe to the place where Creation renewed, so you approach the point of your rebirth.

Keywords—Up Side: New beginnings. Fresh Starts. To be. To go. Journey. Great Adventure. Spontaneity. A Vision Quest. A Learning Experience. Go for it. **Flip Side:** Opposition. False Starts. Has Been. Return. A Close Call. Inertia. Scant Progress. Nothing New. An Old Refrain. Come back.

Tarot Correlation: Card 0—The Fool
Illustration Notes: Based on a rendering of a "Father Time" figure, who guards the difficult last five days of the year. In his knapsack are the signs for Sea Creature and Corn. (See: p. 16, *Dresden Codex*, where it introduces a complete set of 20 Day Signs.) This is the sign for Sea Creature: 🏺; and this is the sign for Corn: 🎴.

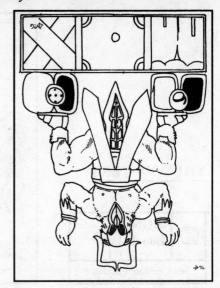

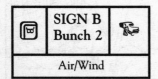

	SIGN B Bunch 2	
	Air/Wind	

*Venus—the bright, wandering "star"... companion of Sun... going back
and forth, horizon to horizon... Morning Star... Evening Star... a light
suspended in midair and blown on constant winds. It takes 37,960 days for
Venus and the 260-day holy calendar to realign. Some prophecies take longer
than others to be fulfilled. But it's always possible to spot a past behavior pattern resurfacing.*

Keywords—Up Side: Recurring Cycles. A Day. A Week. A Month. A
Year. Time frames. To Repeat. To Circle Around. Synchronization. To
Cycle Up. An Occurrence. Progression. A Sequence of Events: Past,
Present, and Future. **Flip Side:** Randomization. Serendipity. Chance
Meeting. Coincidences. Cycles too Long to Appreciate. Retrogression.
Backwards Motion. Mirror Image.

Tarot Correlation: Card 17—The Star
Illustration Notes: Based on a "constellation glyph." A god descends,
suspended from the sign for Venus, with feet resting on the signs for sun
and moon. (See: p. 58, *Dresden Codex*, following a series of dates on
planetary movements.) This is a constellation glyph: ⊠.

142

	SIGN C Bunch 3	
	Night/House	

Dusk & Dawn—The sun has set, and another Day of the Sun can be counted as done. Venus sparkles in the West, darkening clouds descending from its rays. Or is it morning, with Venus sparkling in the East? Sooner or later a thing reverses itself into its mirror image. For there are two sides to everything—but three aspects. Without force and opposition, there would be no direction.

Keywords—Up Side: Opposites Attract. The Length of a Day. A Matter of Hours. Things Done in the Daytime. The Out-of-Doors. Extroversion. Energy from Being Out and About. Work. Efficiency. Effectiveness. Productivity. **Flip Side:** Likes Repel. Night. The Length of a Day . . . and a Night. Family. Hearth. Home. Activities in Twilight. Moonlight Serenades. The Witching Hour. The Dead of Night. Sleep. Rest. Dreams. Motivations.

Tarot Correlation: Card 19—The Sun
Illustration Notes: Based on a rendering of a "Kin" (or sun) sign. "Kin" is also the word for "day." Chac, the Rain God, is suspended from star glyphs. (See: p. 56, *Dresden Codex*.) This is a Kin Sign: ⊕.

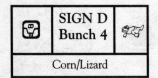

SIGN D Bunch 4	
Corn/Lizard	

Cornmeal—*She grinds the corn into sacred meal, with the intensity of one striking New Fire. Energy is energy. And it all cycles round and round. It was the Sun that grew the seeds, stalks, and ears. It was the Sun that ripened and browned the fields. And now all that is left is the grinding. Take what you need, but take nothing for granted. Scatter cornmeal to the four directions. Return a token.*

Keywords—**Upside:** Fertility. Creativity. Procreativity. Fecundity. Time Between Spring and Autumn. Planting. Growth. Harvest. Reaping What You Plant. A Matter of Timing. To Be. To Become. Potential. Firm Predictions. **Flip Side:** Infertility. Impotence. Inability to Act. Failure to Act at the Right Time. Weather Permitting. Period between Fall and Spring. Counting on Eggs to Hatch. Wishful Predictions. False Hopes.

Tarot Correlation: Card 3—The Empress
Illustration Notes: Fourth of the four fire gods, having transformed into a woman just as the fire ignites. (See: p. 6, *Dresden Codex*, within a series dedicated to the lighting of New Fire.)

	**SIGN E** **Bunch 5**	🐾
	Serpent/Snake	

Vision Serpent—A storm is brewing. The face of Chac is written in the clouds. All you have to do is look. All you have to do is see. The Rain God rears his ugly head. The serpent coils . . . rattles . . . and is about to strike. Rumble. Crash. And boom! Everything goes through periods of instability—especially when two fronts collide, when two opposites knock heads. By observing a thing, you will know it when you see it again. Apply your experience. Use your wits. Think fast.

Keywords—Up Side: Disturbance. Disruption. Turbulence. A Dark Cloud. A Test to Pass. Obstacle Course. Diversionary Tactic. Standoff. Staring Match. A Timely Warning. Near Miss. Close Call. A Brush with the Inevitable. **Flip Side:** Violence. Victimization. Sacrificial Cow. Dirty Politics. Wrong Place. Wrong Time. Bad Move. Indiscretion. Poor Tactics. Tragic Flaw. False Pretense. Mental Cruelty. Ambush. Captivity. Subservience.

Tarot Correlation: Card 16—The Devil
Illustration Notes: Based on a drawing of Chac, the Rain God, forming in the clouds of a Sky Snake or Vision Serpent. (See: p. 36, *Dresden Codex*.)

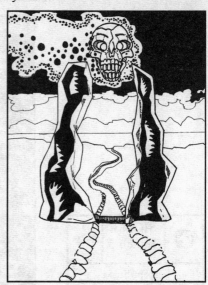

	SIGN F Bunch 6	
Death/Death		

Death—It's just a bundle of bones dressed in its grave goods. The spine that once held up a proud human head is crumbled to dust, and the skull is emptied of thought. The soul has flown on the last breath. Everything that comes around goes back . . . down the path that leads through clashing mountains into the Underworld. Everything changes. Nothing lasts—not even a good thing. Tend to your body, and it will betray you yet. Take care rather of the soul that goes with you.

Keywords—Up Side: Sudden Change. Change of State. Change of Condition. Life Alteration. Change of Outlook. Attitudinal Adjustment. Natural Progression. Physical Change. New Stage. Next Phase. Giant Leap. **Flip Side:** Slow Evolution. Day-to-Day Differences. Little Things Add Up. A Mountain Out of a Molehill. Shift in Point of View. First Appearances Deceive. Little by Little. Bit by Bit. Step by Step. Inch by Inch.

Tarot Correlation: Card 13—Death
Illustration Notes: Based on a picture of the Death God exhaling the last breath and giving up the ghost. (See: p. 11, *Dresden Codex*, where it denotes dark dates subject to violence.)

146

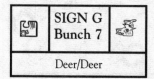

SIGN G Bunch 7	
Deer/Deer	

The Deer Carcass—He is dead. The eyes are closed. The antlers are being turned into amulets somewhere else. And the skinned, split carcass hangs suspended by its hooves. The meat is curing. The sinew has been turned to thread. The herd has been thinned. And a feast is planned. We will make soft loincloths from the skin—or are we above these things? Everything in the Universe feeds from itself. Everything is constantly being recycled and reclaimed. Take all you need. Use all you take.

Keywords—Up Side: Process. Thin Skin. Thick Hide. Use. Reuse. Forward Advancement. Transition. New Purpose. Stiffness Becoming Softness. The Point in Between. Juncture. Crossroads. Turning Point. Decision Spot. **Flip Side:** Progress. Passage Made. Things Firming Up. New Conditions. Reapplications. New Uses. Purpose Fulfilled. Meaning Realized. Contribution Made. The Payoff. A Worthwhile Effort. Profitable Sacrifice.

Tarot Correlation: Card 12—The Hanged Man
Illustration Notes: Based on a pair of drawings showing the Rain God and a woman (or perhaps the Maize God) falling to Earth head over heels. The rain nurtures, but drought destroys. (See: p. 15, *Dresden Codex*, where it denotes a section of difficult dates.)

	SIGN H Bunch 8	
	Rabbit/Rabbit	

The Moon—There are four quarters to the Moon, half of them light, half of them dark. Full Moon. New Moon. And the 27 stages in between. It all unfolds predictably, from Crescent to Quarter. Rabbit Scribe among the lunar craters jotting down the figures of the 20 days. Everything that's born can be numbered by its age. Everything can be discussed in terms of its phase. Life is a cycle.

Keywords—Up Side: Upswing. From New Moon to Full Moon. About a Fortnight. Fourteen or Fifteen Days. Waxing. Increasing. Formation. Energy Buildup. Growth. Suspense. Creative Tension. Climax. Well-Being. Planting. **Flip Side:** Downturn. From Full Moon to New Moon. Two Weeks. Waning. Decreasing. Disintegration. Anticlimactic Experience. A Downer. A Bummer. A Poignant Feeling. Melancholy. Drawing from Reserves.

Tarot Correlation: Card 18—The Moon
Illustration Notes: Based on a depiction of the phasing moon, along with signs indicating planets and stars. (See: p. 56, *Dresden Codex*, where it illustrates a series of 405 lunations—11,958 days.) We have combined it with Itzamna Making First Fire from p. 5 of the *Codex*.

The Rainy Season—For weeks and weeks on end, the gift of the gods has kept coming and coming. Rain, like a blessing, is falling from the endless depths of the Sky Wells. No sun has shown in days. No moon at night . . . and not a single star. The gray sky swirls. The gray day absorbs. And the rain beats down like a drum. Thank God for small miracles. We've all lucked out again. And now, let's dance.

Keywords—Up Side: Gathering. Collecting. Assembling. Pieces Falling into Place. Fortuitous Event. Welcome News. Sudden Reprieve. Good Sign. Catching What Falls. Saving Up. Storing. Restoring Reserves. Gaining Strength. **Flip Side:** Releasing. Welcome Relief. Picking Up the Pieces. Spillage. Spoilage. Waste. Disassociation. Separation. Parting Waves. Expending Energy. Using Reserves. Dribs and Drabs. Penny Here . . . Penny There.

Tarot Correlation: Card 14—Temperance
Illustration Notes: Based on a picture of the Rain God Chac catching water in a vase. The rain falls from a Moon sign as well as from the signs for Mercury and Jupiter. (See: p. 37, *Dresden Codex*.)

	SIGN J	
	Bunch 10	
Dog/Dog		

Kindred Spirits—Face-to-face they sit, a woman staring into the eyes of her Dog Man. She has become like putty in his hands. Is it true love? Or is it only hypnotism? There is an edge. There is a line. A wild and hungry look creeps into otherwise sane pupils. Everyone is part human and part beast, but we do not always reveal our claws. We talk without speaking. We act without thinking. The only sound here is of two souls engaging. It is a primal noise.

Keywords—Up Side: Interchange. Mental Telepathy. Electronic Mail. Like Minds. Shared Views. Mutual Desires. Commonalties. Two Peas in a Pod. Two Kernels on a Cob. Common Destiny. Instinctive Feelings. Acting on Impulse. **Flip Side:** Blockage. Failure to Communicate. Abortive Attempt. Wrong Chemistry. Disagreement. Lack of Control. A Dropped Ball. The Magic Gone. The Spell Broken. The Animal Unmasked.

Tarot Correlation: Card 11—Strength
Illustration Notes: Based on the image of a woman facing off a dog or man in the skin of an animal. (See: p. 21, *Dresden Codex*, where it appears in a series of lovemaking figures.)

	SIGN K Bunch 11	
Monkey/Monkey		

The Courtship Ritual—He has bathed, shaved, and dressed for the occasion. She has perfumed her hair. And now they wait to see if small talk and body language will spark a fire. It was all so much simpler—maybe even more honest—when we were naked in the trees. The end is the same. It is the children who finish what the father and mother start. We are all sprung from the same desire.

Keywords—Up Side: Intercourse. Union. Interactive Exchange. Heated Conversation. Single-mindedness. Mutual Desire. Common Ground. Recurring Attraction. Joint Participation. To Come and Go Together. Arrive at a Meeting of the Minds. **Flip Side:** Masturbation. Self-Gratification. Self-Centering. Self-Grounding. Talking to Yourself. Seeing Yourself. Self-Reflection. Self-Inspection. Personal Handling. Mull It Over. To Go and Come Alone. Reach Your Own Conclusions.

Tarot Correlation: Card 6—The Lovers
Illustration Notes: Based on a series of erotic drawings, this one showing the Shaman Itzamna in an embrace with his consort, Ixchel. (See: p. 23, *Dresden Codex*.)

SIGN L Bunch 12	
Broom/Grass	

The Tree of Life—It is from a sacrificial dish the Tree of Life rises. One year to the next, it re-arises. What sprouts in the spring, in the fall becomes dry grass—or else the makings of a corn-husk broom . . . provided the rains come. Nothing is for certain when it comes to recurrences. Anything worth achieving is worth a little sacrifice. The seasons are dancing, and things hang in the balance. Each year is different from the one just past. It's time to start all over from scratch.

Keywords—Up Side: Birth. Rebirth. Offspring. Offshoot. Sprout. A Chip off the Old Block. A Spittin' Image. Small Fry. To Be. To Develop. To Rise Up. Emergence. Reintroduction. Resurrection. Incarnation. Substance. Form. **Flip Side:** Renewal. Reinvigoration. Restoration. Second Childhood. Something Arising. Up from Smoke and Ashes. Making a Comeback. Everything Old Is New Again. Reincarnation. New Identity. New Name.

Tarot Correlation: Card 21—The World
Illustration Notes: Based on a drawing of the Tree of Life emerging from the Corn Goddess. (See: p. 3, *Dresden Codex*.)

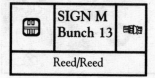

| | SIGN M Bunch 13 | |
| Reed/Reed | | |

Leadership—The king kneels on his reed mat, spine of the stingray in hand, to say his prayers and to prepare himself for the challenge stretched before him. The fate of the empire depends on these hands and this moment. Will they be subject to waver? Will he be subject to crumble? In a while he will step from these chambers with the proof in his hand. What choice is there between the lesser of evils?

Keywords—Up Side: Firmness. Strong Exterior. Stiff Upper Lip. Steady Hand. Feel No Pain. See No Evil. Remain Brave. Act like a Man. Go Through with It. Do What You Gotta Do. Ready. Steady. Aim. Fire. Follow Through. **Flip Side:** Hollowness. Weak Interior. Shaky Knees. Momentary Doubt. On Second Thought. Vacillation. Lack of Resolve. A Bitten Bullet. A Cry for Help.

Tarot Correlation: Card 4—The Emperor
Illustration Notes: Based on a drawing of the Storm God sitting on a reed mat in the attitude of a King about to pierce his penis as a sacrifice. (See: p. 20, *Dresden Codex*.)

SIGN N
Bunch 14

Jaguar/Ocelot

The Spirit Guide—He comes as if in a dream . . . to teach, warn, and advise. He comes as if in a trance, from out of clouds of wafting incense, to speak in a human voice. What can he possibly tell us, smartest of all beasts? As if from the clouding of a mirror, he comes. Is it man? Or is it Creature? And which is which? Everything has the power to change shape—if not its form, then its substance. If not change from without, then change from within.

Keywords—Up Side: Transformation. Reconfiguration. Realignment. Put on a New Face. Get behind a Mask. Subliminal Message. Interesting Dream. The Power of Suggestion. Imagination. Interpretation. Similes. Metaphors. **Flip Side:** Retransformation. Changing Back. Coming to Your Senses. Waking Up. Vague Memories. Random Bits and Pieces. Flashbacks. Mirror Images. Dim Reflections. Sudden Realizations. Understanding a Sign.

Tarot Correlation: Card 1—The Magician
Illustration Notes: Based on a picture of a Jaguar, or shaman transformed into a Jaguar. (See p. 8, *Dresden Codex*.) We have combined it with an image of the male Jaguar spirit "Waterlily Jaguar" from a codex-style vase. This spirit represents a person's animal counterpart, a *wayhel*.

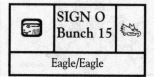

Eagle/Eagle

The Shaman—The Incense Priest burning copal in a dish and seeing visions in the rising smoke. There is a time and place for every offering. There is a ritual for each and every day. And only he can keep the calendar straight and say for sure when the seasons change. Seated cross-legged on the earth, he guards the secrets of the stars. Divine wisdom is a curious thing. And knowledge has always been power.

Keywords—Up Side: Common Prayer. The Power of Prayer. Wherever Two or More are Gathered. Set Ritual. Well-worn Words. Devotions. Litanies. The Holy Year. Feasts. Festivals. Done by the Book. By the Holidays. **Flip Side:** Silent Prayer. Personal Intercession. Direct Connection. Outreach. From the Bottom of the Heart. In Your Own Words. Fasts. Vigils. Private Rituals. Personal Sacrifices. Acts of Silent Heroism. At the Full Moon.

Tarot Correlation: Card 5—The Hierophant
Illustration Notes: Based on a drawing of Itzamna seated on a platform of star, moon, and sun glyphs. (See: p. 46, *Dresden Codex.*)

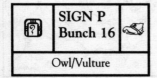

SIGN P Bunch 16	
Owl/Vulture	

Justice?—He was probably just minding his own business out in the hills when the ambush came. Not that it was fair, mind you, but here the captive throws himself upon the mercy of the court. The wounded elk cannot negotiate with the vulture. The mouse cannot strike a deal with the owl. But one does not have to be captured to be captivated. A human trophy is claimed. A notch is added to the belt. A number is written into the book. Chalk one up.

Keywords—Up Side: Offense. Swift Maneuver. Surprise Attack. Running Circles Around. Outdistancing. One-upping. Outmaneuvering. Dropping by Unexpectedly. Forcing a Move. Begging a Response. Actions Speak Louder. **Flip Side:** Defense. Quick Thinking. Fast Response Time. Standing Off an Attack. Avoiding Victimization. Holding the Line. Standing up for Yourself. Putting Up a Good Fight. Turning the Tide.

Tarot Correlation: Card 8—Justice
Illustration Notes: Based on a drawing showing the Rain God Chac as a warrior about to decapitate the Grain God, indicating the harvest season. (See: p. 42, *Dresden Codex*, in a section discussing how every 65 days a "cardinal point" is "discarded" and a new one takes its turn influencing things. In this case the South is being discarded for the East.)

156

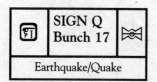

Earthquake/Quake

Acts of God—The Rain God turns back the Dragon of the West. . . the rattles rattling, and the giant feet causing the earth to quake. The sun, moon, and stars all rotate through the heavens. It is time now for the boundaries of Earth to change. It is time for the powers to shift. It is time for a new balance to be achieved. Even the firmest thing around cannot manage to escape alteration. And a tottering stone does not like to remain in balance for long.

Keywords—Up Side: Earth Force. Magnetism. Gravity. Geothermal Energy. Strength of the Soil. Minerals. Rocks. Magic Lightning Stones. Cornering. Centering. Get Your Bearings. Measurements. Properties. Possessions. **Flip Side:** Earthquake. Freak Event. Sudden Shift. Upheaval. Tremors. Shaky Footholds. False Assumptions. Poor Foundations. Thin Walls. The Tables Are Turned. Cracks. Fissures. Portals Opening. Nothing Is Certain.

Tarot Correlation: Card 20—Judgement
Illustration Notes: Based on an image of the Rain God displacing the serpent of the West and thus turning back to the South. (See: p. 45, *Dresden Codex*, in the context of how the various compass points influence certain days.)

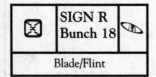

☒	SIGN R Bunch 18	⬭
	Blade/Flint	

The Obsidian Blade—The warrior clad for battle kneels waiting, his spear points sharp as steel—offered up. Has he surrendered? Will he turn and thrust them into the ground? Or is he about to breathe upon them, to give them battle life? The razor cuts both ways, and both ways are equally sharp. Flints and points will be no match for the muskets that are coming. The hero of the moment plays his part. But no record stands forever. There is always someone bigger and faster and better.

Keywords—Up Side: New Technology. New Means. New Tools. New Capabilities. On the Cutting Edge. At the Forefront. Innovation. Pioneering. Forging. Inventing New Rules. New Relationships. Edging. Cutting. Incising. Leaving your Mark. **Flip Side:** Old Technology. Tradition. The Way It's Done. Entrenchment. Vested Interest. Hard Habit to Break. The Old Grind. A Regular Routine. Standard Mode of Operation. It's Always Worked Before.

Tarot Correlation: Card 7—The Chariot
Illustration Notes: Based on the drawing of a kneeling warrior. (See: p. 49, *Dresden Codex*, in a series on the movements of the planet Venus. The planets were perceived to be involved in a race or contest.)

SIGN S
Bunch 19

Storm/Storm

The Hurricane—Chac the Rain God gears up to go to fight with Sky. Already you can see his spiral clouds moving in from the East. Already there is the silence that precedes all hell breaking loose. Winds. Rains. And tides . . . with the worst around the edges of the eye. Things go in a circular, cyclonic motion here. But that which comes on so swiftly is sure to blow away as fast. Lord have mercy.

Keywords—Up Side: The Prelude. Things Leading Up to Other Things. Escalation. Intensification. Foreshadowings. Omens. Rumblings. Ominous Signs. Threatening Danger. Stillness. Quietness. Anticipation. Excitement. **Flip Side:** The Aftermath. Reemergence. Clean up. Put away. Inspection. Reflection. Taking It All In. Wondering. What if . . . Rejoicing at a Timely Deliverance. Withstanding. Perseverance. Resolve to Rebuild.

Tarot Correlation: Card 15—The Devil
Illustration Notes: Based on a drawing of the Rain God armed to go to battle in the form of a storm. (See: pp. 38–39, *Dresden Codex*, where it refers to the length of the rainy season—104 days.)

SIGN T Bunch 20
Lord/Flower

The Calendar Wheel—It is a cycle within a cycle within a cycle within a cycle. . . . It is a reflection within a reflection in the looking glass. A wheel within a wheel. Each day has its signs. And each year, its Lord. All things can be broken down into their parts. Each thing that exists can be assigned a number, if not also a name. What does it prove in the end? To know is to understand. To understand is to appreciate. To appreciate is to respect. To respect is to honor. To honor is to obey. Whatever rules you establish, live by them yourself.

Keywords—Up Side: This Year. By the End of the Year. Within the Year. In 12 months. In 18 Uinals. In 360 days. Let It Ride. Give It Some Time. Give It a Chance. Give It a Break. Things Unfold as They Should. Day by Day. Don't Fight It. **Flip Side:** Next Year. By this Time Next Year. In Another Year. Extended Forecast. Ultimately. Eventually. As Time Permits. As Time Allows. As Time Passes. As Time Favors. Watch and Wait. Look for the Signs.

Tarot Correlation: Card 10—The Wheel of Fortune
Illustration Notes: Based on the famous calendar wheel of the Aztecs. There are four suns at the center, with the Day Signs circling them.

160

BONUS ANSWERS FOR EXTRA CREDIT USERS

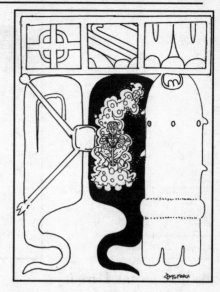

Answer for the High Priestess

First Fire—It happened first in the sky. First Father grinding out First Fire with First Fire Stick in the basin of a turtle shell. As in the skies, so on the Earth. It takes energy to make energy. It takes friction to set off a spark. It takes timing—and even patience—to get a thing done right. Everything is conditional. Everything has a rhythm, a cycle, and an interval. Everything is connected. Everything is tied to everything else.

Keywords—Up Side: Universal Truth. Basic Principles. Common Sense. Secrets of Survival. To Be. To Know. To Exist. To Experience. Participate. Become Involved. Countdown, Ignition, and Liftoff. Go with the Flow. Spark and Sparkle. **Flip Side:** Universal Truth. Tragic Flaws. Human Nature. Hidden Knowledge. Self-Denial. Timing Error. Miscue. Caught in the Act. Waning Light. A Fire Gone Out.

Tarot Correlation: Card 2—The High Priestess
Illustration Notes: Based on a series of drawings showing the four fire gods making new fire. The figure shown here becomes a woman as the series progresses. (See: p. 5, *Dresden Codex*, within a series of 52-day periods. By tradition New Fire is lit every 52 years.) We have shown her against a moon sign—possibly an eclipse.

Answer for the Hermit

The Rain Dancer—Wearing the mask of an eagle, the Rain Priest rejoices in the downpour he has delivered for his people once again . . . and just in the nick of time. We are all dependent on something. We are all beholden to someone. We are affected by forces outside our control. A semblance of order calms the nerves. We call to the Powers that Be to save us from the chaos of their own creation. Bowing our heads before us, we wait for a sign. Eagle is circling in gathering clouds.

Keywords—Up Side: Public Display. Public Welfare. Public Works. Common Understanding. Common Knowledge. Right Action. Right Timing. Popular Belief. Cause-and-Effect Relationship. Kicking Up Dust. Gestures. Motions. **Flip Side:** Private Ritual. Personal Oblation. Personal Preference. Secrets. Hidden Knowledge. Personal Understanding. Individual Truth. Inner Wisdom. Inner Voices. Private Belief. The Beat of a Different Drum.

Tarot Correlation: Card 9—The Hermit
Illustration Notes: Based on a picture of a shaman wearing the mask of a bird and doing a rain dance. (See: p. 38, *Dresden Codex*, in the context of the 104-day period denoting the rainy season.)

EXTRA CREDIT

Attention Tarot Users: You can use any deck of Tarot cards to get your answer for this Reading. Just shuffle your 22 Major Arcana Tarot cards, (0–XXI) and deal up a single card. Then consult the table below to see which Mayan Day Sign you have selected. Consult this Reading's Answer section for your message. Since there are two more Tarot cards than there are Mayan Day Signs, you will find the answers for Tarot Card II (The High Priestess) and Tarot Card IX (The Hermit) at the end of the Answer section.

TAROT READER'S LOOK-UP TABLE

Tarot Card #	Day Signs	Tarot Card #	Day Signs
0	A	11	J
1	N	12	G
2	—	13	F
3	D	14	I
4	M	15	S
5	O	16	E
6	K	17	B
7	R	18	H
8	P	19	C
9	—	20	Q
10	T	21	L

EXTRA, EXTRA CREDIT!

Day 201 through Day 220—It is not always necessary to wait for a sign to come to you, for you always have the power to ask. To ask for a sign, first say a prayer. Your prayer can be as simple as "Give me guidance," "Give me strength," or "Give me direction." Or it can be as specific as you like. Pray, in turn, to each compass point, starting with the East and moving North, West, and South. You can extend your prayer by also acknowledging the "half" directions as you turn (E, NE, N, NW, W, SW, S, and SE). If you would like to address these prayers to the God of your native religion, that's fine. Or, more in keeping with this tradition, you can also say, "Oh, Great Spirit of the East (North, West, or South), give me direction." Upon completing your prayers, let your thoughts go. An idea will come to you. If nothing comes right away, sleep on it, and note your first conscious thoughts the next day.

Go on to the next Reading whenever you are ready to continue.

Reading #12

Fit Me In
(Book my time)

In this Reading you will expand your priestly time-keeping skills, by adding 19 additional Mayan symbols to your collection of glyphs. These 19 "seasonal" signs are great tools for planning activities and fitting your life into the larger scheme of things.

TOOLS

The 19 new signs you will be using here each designate a "month" in another calendar developed in Mesoamerica. This calendar is entirely separate from the holy Tzolkin and Tun you have been working with in the previous Readings. The Maya called this secular calendar the *Haab*. The Aztecs knew it as their *Xihuitl*. Like our calendar, the Haab counted months and days in a set order, for a complete 365-day year. This calendar consisted of eighteen 20-day months...plus a special "leap" month at the end (a *Uayeb* or *Nemontemi*), which counted only five "dark" days.

BACKGROUND

The Haab has one small flaw. Though we add a "leap year" every four to make up for the extra quarter day of the solar year, the Maya made no such adjustment. What this means is, every four years the Haab "loses" a whole day. Given the passage of several centuries, "July" would be coming in "January." In the period covered by the current Creation Epoch, the Haab has, in fact, slipped back two full turns through the seasons, plus about another half turn. What was once fall is now spring.

But, interestingly enough, as the Haab cycles up to the end of the Creation Epoch, it falls neatly back in line with the seasons as they existed when the Maya recorded most of their dates...presuming, of course, that we are living in an equatorial zone. The area experiences two rainy seasons a year (including hurricane season), a moderate period of drought, and a short, dry period when the harvest is brought in.

MONTHS OF THE HAAB YEAR

Month 1		Pop		Month 11		Zac
Month 2		Uo		Month 12		Ceh
Month 3		Zip		Month 13		Macl
Month 4		Zotz		Month 14		Kankin
Month 5		Tzec		Month 15		Muan
Month 6		Xul		Month 16		Pax
Month 7		Yaxkin		Month 17		Kayab
Month 8		Mol		Month 18		Cumku
Month 9		Chen		Month 19		Uayeb
Month 10		Yax				

HAAB DATES AND WEATHER CONDITIONS
A.D. 488 & A.D. 2000

M O N T H	Maya Name		A.D. 2000 (Also A.D. 488)	Weather (2000–2012)	To Do
1		Pop	Apr 6–Apr 25	Hot & Dry	Burn Trees
2		Uo	Apr 26–May 15	Hot & Dry	Make Fences
3		Zip	May 16–Jun 4	Hot & Dry	Till Soil
4		Zotz	Jun 5–Jun 24	Heavy Rains	Plant
5		Tzec	Jun 25–Jul 14	Heavy Rains	Plant & Weed
6		Xul	Jul 15–Aug 3	Heavy Rains	Weed
7		Yaxkin	Aug 4–Aug 23	Heavy Rains	Watch & Wait
8		Mol	Aug 24–Sep 12	Heavy Rains	Watch & Wait
9		Chen	Sep 13–Oct 2	Hurricanes	Watch & Wait
10		Yax	Oct 3–Oct 22	Hurricanes	Watch & Wait
11		Zac	Oct 23–Nov 11	Hurricanes	Bend Corn
12		Ceh	Nov 12–Dec 1	Dry	Harvest
13		Mac	Dec 2–Dec 21	Dry	Harvest
14		Kankin	Dec 22–Jan 11	Dry	Harvest
15		Muan	Jan 12–Jan 31	Light Rains	Fell Trees
16		Pax	Feb 1–Feb 20	Light Rains	Fell Trees
17		Kayab	Feb 21–Mar 11	Light Rains	Fell Trees
18		Cumku	Mar 12–Mar 31	Hot & Dry	Burn Trees
19		Uayeb	Apr 1–Apr 5	Hot & Dry	Attempt Nothing

Corn and rain were the two basic ingredients of Mayan sustenance. And as you will see, the Haab is largely about the "cob."

The Aztecs had their own names for each month and their own festivals.

AZTEC DATES AND WEATHER CONDITIONS
A.D. 488 & A.D. 2000

M O N T H	Aztec Name	A.D. 2000 (Also A.D. 488)	Weather (2000–2012)	Aztec Meanings
1	Atlcahualo	Apr 6– Apr 25	Dry	Stopping of Water, Want of Water
2	Tlacaxi- pehualiztli	Apr 26– May 15	Dry	Human Flaying, Boning of Men
3	Tozoztontli	May 16– Jun 4	Dry	The Lesser Vigil, Fasting for Rain
4	Hueytozoztli	Jun 5– Jun 24	Heavy Rains	The Great Vigil, Worship of New Corn
5	Toxcatl	Jun 25– Jul 14	Heavy Rains	The Drought, Impersonation Ceremonies
6	Etzalcualiztli	Jul 15– Aug 3	Heavy Rains	Time of Eating Succotash
7	Tecuil- huitontli	Aug 4– Aug 23	Heavy Rains	Lesser Feast of the Lords, Adoration of the Corn

AZTEC DATES AND WEATHER CONDITIONS

A.D. 488 & A.D. 2000 *(continued)*

MONTH	Aztec Name	A.D. 2000 (Also A.D. 488)	Weather (2000–2012)	Aztec Meanings
8	Huey-tecuilhuitl	Aug 24–Sep 12	Heavy Rains	Great Feast of the Lords
9	Tlaxoc-himaco	Sep 13–Oct 2	Hurricane Season	Offering of Flowers
10	Xocotl-huetzi	Oct 3–Oct 22	Hurricane Season	Falling of Fruit
11	Ochpaniztli	Oct 23–Nov 11	Hurricane Season	Month of Brooms
12	Teotleco	Nov 12–Dec 1	Dry	Return of the Gods
13	Tepeilhuitl	Dec 2–Dec 21	Dry	Feast of Mountains
14	Quecholli	Dec 22–Jan 11	Dry	Hunting of Birds
15	Penquet-zaliztli	Jan 12–Jan 31	Light Rains	Raising of Banners, Feast of Flags
16	Atemoztli	Feb 1–Feb 20	Light Rains	Coming Down of the Water, Fall of Waters
17	Tititl	Feb 21–Mar 11	Light Rains	White Woman Month, Flagellations

AZTEC DATES AND WEATHER CONDITIONS
A.D. 488 & A.D. 2000 *(continued)*

MONTH	Aztec Name	A.D. 2000 (Also A.D. 488)	Weather (2000–2012)	Aztec Meanings
18	Itzcalli	Mar 12–Mar 31	Dry	Growth by Fire, Immolation of Women
19	Nemontemi	Apr 1–Apr 5	Dry	Five Empty Days

In this Reading, we'll be using the Mayan and Aztec agricultural months to obtain some seasonal advice, first for today's date, then for your current question.

HOW TO

Attention: Users of All Methods: You do not need your beans, Lightning Cards, or pointing finger to do the first part of this Reading. Your answer only requires a simple lookup in the Almanac. The Extra Credit section contains instructions for using beans, Magic Lightning Cards, or Point-n-Click to get ask a specific question.

ASK YOUR QUESTION

Follow your icon for the ends you defined in Reading #0, or ask any question listed in **boldface** (below) that appeals to you now.

FASTTRACK You have come here with a question in mind. Ask it again, one more time. Say: **What should I do now?**

SOULSEARCH You have come for your horoscope. In the next Reading you'll compute your own chart! But first let's find out about today. Say: **Give me the time.**

GAME PLAN You have come here to finalize your plans. Here's where you consider the logistics: Say: **Is this the right time?**

HEARTS HUNT You have come here on a matter of love. Love has its season and cycle, too. Ask, **What season are we in?**

VIZ'N QUEST You have come for spiritual counseling. Counsel this.... Ask, **How do I fit into these times?**

SELECT YOUR SIGN

For this Reading you will be using Part II of the Almanac, starting on page 473, at the back of the book. This part of the Almanac lists the first day of every Haab month. Each day in a 20-day Haab month was numbered continuously. The count started each month with a Day 0, known as the *seating* of the new month. The days of the month were then counted 1 through 19, with the final day being counted as 0 again—the seating of the next month. For every year in our calendar from 1909 to 2012, this Almanac lists the date on which each Haab month is seated—the 0 day.

2004 Leap Year					
JAN 1-9	See 2003	APR 4	*Pop*	AUG 22	*Mol*
JAN 10	*Muan*	APR 24	*Uo*	SEP 11	*Chen*
JAN 30	*Pax*	MAY 14	*Zip*	OCT 1	*Yax*
FEB 19	*Kayab*	JUN 3	*Zotz*	OCT 21	*Zac*
MAR 10	*Cumku*	JUN 23	*Tzec*	NOV 10	*Ceh*
MAR 30	*Uayeb*	JUL 13	*Xul*	NOV 30	*Mac*
		AUG 2	*Yaxkin*	DEC 20	*Kankin*

The Year 7 Flint starts Apr. 4, 2004

Turn to the listing for the current year and find the date just preceding today's. For example, if today is April 20, 2004, the closest preceding date in the table is April 4, which is the seating of the month Pop. The next 19 days will also be known as Pop days. So your month is Pop, which is all you need to know to find your answer for this Reading.

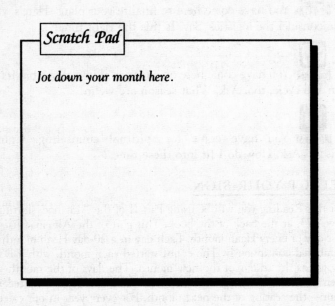

LOOK UP YOUR ANSWER

Find your Month Signs now in this Reading's Answers.

Your answer is preceded by a table listing a date or two from Mayan history. The dates referenced here are taken from Mayan monuments and other artifacts.

THE ANSWERS

Month 1			
🔲	MAYAN: **Pop** AZTEC: **Atlcahualo**		
Apr 6– Apr 25	Hot & Dry	Stopping of Water, Want of Water	Burn Trees
THIS MONTH IN HISTORY: Earliest dated Mayan object—an inscribed blade (8 Pop, A.D. 120).			

Beginnings and endings are noted.... It is the time of renewal and of wearing new clothes. It is the time when the rains stop and the skies clear. This is like spring. And in spring you will fit in by helping to prepare the fields for planting soon. You will fit in by preparing yourself as well. Get ready to launch new projects and explore fresh ideas. The right time is between the 6th and 25th of this month. We will not feel this motivated again until hurricane season. Either time is fine for making plans—especially contingency plans. What should you do next? A "what if" analysis wouldn't hurt.

Month 2			
🔲	MAYAN: **Uo** AZTEC: **Tlacaxipehualiztli**		
Apr 26– May 15	Hot & Dry	Flaying, Wearing of Skins	Make Fences
THIS MONTH IN HISTORY: King Ah-Cacaw honors 9 Baktuns, 13 Katuns, with twin pyramids. (8 Uo, A.D. 692).			

Time's passage is indicated.... It will be sooner than you think when the rains fall. It is a good time to do honor to your profession. It is also a good time to make love. It is like the time when the sun shines warm and bright. The days are hot, and the nights are even hotter. This is like spring, my friend. And in spring you will fit in best by blossoming yourself. You will fit in by feeling the springtime in your own veins. Get creative. Allow yourself to be spontaneous. The right time is between the 26th of this month and the 15th of next month. What should you do next? Try to put yourself into the other guy's skin ... or at least into her shoes. (You know what I mean.) Try to see it from the other person's point of view.

Month 3			
	MAYAN: **Zip** AZTEC: **Tozoztontli**		
May 16– Jun 4	Hot & Dry	The Lesser Vigil, Fasting for Rain	Till Soil
THIS MONTH IN HISTORY: First dated stone erected to the passage of a Tun year (13 Zip, A.D. 199).			

The erection of monuments is discussed.... In these final days before the rainy season, it's a good time to wrap up outstanding projects. It's a good time to memorialize and remember. Keep vigils. Make an offering in someone's name. It is the time when we don't know whether to adore or fear the face of the sun. Will we remember fondly these warm days? Or will we have to humble ourselves to get rain? This is like the end of spring, my friend, when everything depends on everything else. You will fit in by not indulging yourself. Fast instead of feast. The right time is between the 16th of this month and the 4th of next month. It will be entirely different a half year from now when we bring the feast in. Now and later, take none of this for granted. What should you do next? Pay your respects to the dead. Lay something of your own heart to rest. Cleanse your own thoughts.

Month 4			
🗿	MAYAN: **Zotz** AZTEC: **Hueytozoztli**		
Jun 5– Jun 24	Heavy Rains	Great Vigil, Worship of New Corn	Plant
THIS MONTH IN HISTORY: Last recorded date at several Mayan cities, despite sacrifices (Jun 22 A.D. 810).			

Devout worship is required.... In these critcal days (which at any moment could be final) the essential rains will either come or they will resist coming. Something needed desperately, desperately needs to happen right now. So pray, even if the signs are promising at first. We never know for sure how these things will go. This is like the beginning of summer. And with any luck it will be a growing season. You will fit in by dedicating yourself to the task of doing what you need to do now to assure something will happen later. You will fit in by adjusting your thoughts to the prevailing circumstances. Take on the role of a leader. The right time is between the 5th and the 24th of this month. Half a year from now, the same advice will apply. It is a time to appeal to your God for sustenance, deliverance, mercy, and strength. What should you do next? Burn some incense.

Month 5			
🗿	MAYAN: **Tzec** AZTEC: **Toxcatl**		
Jun 25– Jul 14	Heavy Rains	The Drought, Impersonation Ceremonies	Plant & Weed
THIS MONTH IN HISTORY: King "Bird-Jaguar," Lady "Evening-Star," and others dance for rain (Jun 25, A.D. 741).			

The weather must cooperate.... If the rains haven't come by now, it's getting serious. And there could even be a devastating drought. Drastic measures could (but hopefully won't) be called for. Things are just as likely to suddenly change for the better. This is like the beginning of summer; and this is how summer starts . . . or doesn't start at all. You will fit in by doing a little dance in keeping with the thing you need the most. Pretend to be the animal that would know how to handle a situation like this. The right time is between the 25th of this month and the 14th of next month. In another half year you will feel like dancing again. It's a good time to ask for rain or whatever other blessings you require. What should you do next? Turn up the volume on the CD player. And at least tap your feet, my friend. This is the dance of life we're dancing.

Month 6			
MAYAN: **Xul** AZTEC: **Etzalcualiztli**			
Jul 15– Aug 3	Heavy Rains	Time of Eating Succotash	Weed
THIS MONTH IN HISTORY: Lady Xoc dedicates the sculpture of Temple 23 (July 30, A.D. 723).			

The mood picks up.... The first of the beans are in, fresh from the fields—as long as all has gone according to plan and the rains held. Everyone is feeling festive. Things are going our way. It's time for a party. It's time for a carnival. This is like the middle of summer . . . and things are improving. We are gaining confidence that the gods have shined upon us again. You will fit in by wearing a costume that suits you. Dress the part that you desire to play—but never The Fool. The right time is between the 15th of this month and the 3rd of next. It will not be this lively again until another half year is through, and again, come January. What should you do next? Eat some succotash. Let your hair down. And let the mood of the moment command you.

Month 7			
🎴	MAYAN: **Yaxkin** AZTEC: **Tecuilhuitontli**		
Aug 4– Aug 23	Heavy Rains	Lesser Feast of the Lords, Adoration of the Corn	Watch & Wait
THIS MONTH IN HISTORY: Ball game at La Amelia (Aug 10, A.D. 807).			

The tension builds.... By this time the corn is standing at least knee-high. The rains have come. The crop is healthy. And everything looks all right with the world. But when is it safe to say the worst is over? Best to keep the gods enthused and enthralled. Suit up. Let's play a little ball. This is like the middle of summer. The middle of summer is the time for games. Groups are forming. Players are taking sides. And every day it's a new contest. Every day there's a fresh strategy. You will fit in on the sidelines by wearing the colors of the winning team. You will fit into the game's play by not letting the ball drop when it bounces your way. The right time is between the 4th and the 23rd of this month. We will not feel this invigorated again until the rains have gone and returned. What should you do next? Play to win. Or else eat the dust at your opponent's feet. Remain loyal to a good cause.

Month 8			
🎴	MAYAN: **Mol** AZTEC: **Hueytecuilhuitl**		
Aug 24– Sep 12	Heavy Rains	Great Feast of the Lords	Watch & Wait
THIS MONTH IN HISTORY: First ceremony at Chichén Itzá, a bloodletting (Sep 9, A.D. 869). Chichén Itzá abandoned forever (Sep 9, A.D. 1204).			

Things are building to a fevered pitch.... It is still raining, but soon the worst will subside. The first sweet corn is in. But only the sweet corn is assured. Everything's fine for now. But the fight is only half over. Let's roast a few ears of this first crop and celebrate another year of potential being fulfilled. It is like midsummer. And in midsummer, everything is improving. You will fit in by admiring your collective handiwork. You will fit in by smacking your lips. Nothing has ever tasted quite as fresh as this. Partake of God's early blessings. Count your early returns. The right time is between the 24th of this month and the 12th of next. It will be an entirely different story in another half year. What should you do next? Pass the pepper, if not also the salt. And how about a little Tabasco sauce? Appreciate what you've got right now.

Month 9			
🐖	MAYAN: **Chen** AZTEC: **Tlaxochimaco**		
Sep 13– Oct 2	Hurricane Season	Offering of Flowers	Watch & Wait
THIS MONTH IN HISTORY: Copán is established as a kingdom on the occasion of the 6th Katun's passing (3 Chen, A.D. 150).			

Late blooming is happening now.... The rains have let up their glorious gift just when they should, and the late, dark flowers have opened to the face of the sun. The thistles are turning to seed. And the signs are clear. In a final burst of activity, things are actually starting to wind down here. You will fit in by gathering in as much as you can consume, process for later, or give away. Assemble your assets and store your energies. Bring nuts and flowers to the ones you love. The right time is between the 13th of this month and the 2nd of next month. A half year from now, it will be time to burn what is now green. What should you do next? Hunt. Gather. Pit. Clean. Cook. Prepare. Gather up what you will need for later. Hold some strength in reserve.

Month 10			
🗿 MAYAN: **Yax** AZTEC: **Xocotlhuetzi**			
Oct 3– Oct 22	Hurricane Season	Falling of Fruit	Watch & Wait
THIS MONTH IN HISTORY: "Smoking Imix" celebrates the 11th Katun's end (Oct 9 A.D. 652).			

This is a time for appreciating smells on the air.... It is still raining off and on, and every once in a while a hurricane blows through. But the fruits have ripened and are ready to fall anyway—the wind only helps convince them. It is like late summer. And in late summer we eat fresh fruits from the vine. It is a time for honoring <u>all</u> the things that sustain and keep us throughout the year: plants, animals, vegetables, vitamins, fats, and minerals. You will fit in by making full use of everything. You will fit in by exchanging compliments and bartering surplus. So far, so good. The right time is between the 3rd and the 22nd of this month. In another half year there will be five empty days and then a fresh start. What should you do next? Attune. Atone. Get on. There is much work to do, but this will be the last of it for a while. With any energy you have left at the end of the day, don't forget to celebrate your good fortune.

Month 11			
🗿 MAYAN: **Zac** AZTEC: **Ochpaniztli**			
Oct 23– Nov 11	Hurricane Season	Month of Brooms	Bend Corn
THIS MONTH IN HISTORY: "Kinichil-Cab" performs a ritual at Ucanal (15 Zac, A.D. 698).			

Everything is business here.... The corn is done, except for the cutting and shucking. So, too, the pumpkins have finished getting larger, and the gourds are done forming into their peculiar shapes. It is a time for doing the last of the work—for this season at least—and for getting

179

ready for the next job. It is still a time for gathering. But it is also a good time to close up shop. You will fit in by doing your share of the sweeping out. You will fit in by bending at the knees, especially when you lift. There is no work quite as hard as this. But there is also no greater reward. The right time is between the 23rd of this month and the 11th of next. In just a half year you will feel like shedding your winter skin again. But that is far from now. What should you do next? Forget about the distant possibilities. You have done enough for now... provided you have done your very best.

Month 12			
📖	MAYAN: **Ceh** AZTEC: **Teotleco**		
Nov 12– Dec 1	Dry	Return of the Gods	Harvest
THIS MONTH IN HISTORY: Construction begins on the Temple of Inscriptions (19 Ceh, A.D. 675).			

A celebration is called for.... The harvest is in the basket. The fruit is in the cellar. The corn is in the crib. There is something that can be counted up now, sorted, measured, and weighed. How tips the scale? In sum, what do the accountants say? Did the gods shine on us this year, or what? It's time to thank them anyway. It's time to count blessings. You will fit in by bowing your head when the prayer of thanks is said. You will fit in even better by feeling the thanks in your heart and soul. We will stay up all night now, to watch one full turning of the stars. As above, so below. The right time is between the 12th of this month and the 1st of next. In one more half year you will be keeping watch again. What should you do next? Eat your fill, my friend. Take in all your stomach can hold. It doesn't get much better than this. This is, at any rate, as good as it can get right now.

Month 13

	MAYAN:	**Mac**	
	AZTEC:	**Tepeilhuitl**	
Dec 2– Dec 21	Dry	Feast of Mountains	Harvest

THIS MONTH IN HISTORY: Caracol Victory
Stair dedicated in honor of conquests (Dec 2,
A.D. 642).

It is time to give thanks again...this time to the mountains...and the
stairs. Hurdles and barriers serve their purpose, too. It is one thing to
climb over. It is another to go around. And it is quite another to tunnel
through. The portals are opening. And anything is possible. It is a time
for recognizing no obstacle too large...no challenge too great...no
task too daunting. You will fit in by getting into the spirit of the season.
You will fit in by becoming part of the pageantry...even if it's mostly
glitz. The right time is between the 2nd and the 21st of this month. In
one more half year you will be celebrating again. What should you do
next? Light candles. Sing songs. Honor those who bring you your sustenance. Say thanks for yet another Year in the Sun.

Month 14

	MAYAN:	**Kankin**	
	AZTEC:	**Quecholli**	
Dec 22– Jan 11	Dry	Hunting of Birds	Harvest

THIS MONTH IN HISTORY: Last date at
Caracol (3 Kankin, A.D. 859). Last independent
Mayan kingdom falls (17 Kankin, A.D. 1697).

Turning outward is required now....The work in the fields is all done
and over. We are still feasting to our heart's content. (We never even
get finished cleaning up from the feasting.) Yet more? The geese have
come down now from the North. The partridge is in the pear tree. And
seven swans are swimming. In any kind of hunt, you will fit in by imi-

tating the call of the game you seek. You will fit in even better if you paint your face to match the landscape. And it wouldn't hurt to learn a few lessons from the well-traveled and experienced. It is like winter now, for sure. But instead of snow, we get the blazing sun, sweeping back North from the tropics. The right time is between the 22nd of this month and the 11th of next month. In another half year it will be much the same. And we will be doing the Bird Dance again. What should you do next? Bring surprises back from the commercial forest. Book reservations. Exchange gifts. Make resolutions. Life is great. And God is good to us.

Month 15

	MAYAN: **Muan** AZTEC: **Penquetzaliztli**		
Jan 12– Jan 31	Light Rains	Raising of Banners, Feast of Flags, Military Procession	Fell Trees

THIS MONTH IN HISTORY: Caracol wages "Star War" against Naranjo (16 Muan, A.D. 631). Columbus met by canoe in Bay of Honduras (8 Muan, A.D. 1502).

Demonstrations and contests occur here.... There is not much else to do at this time. It's mostly miserable out-of-doors—foggy and rainy down here. And what we really need is something to keep our hands busy and our minds occupied. How about a ball game? How about a super ball game? You will fit in by mustering to the call of your team leader. You will fit in by rallying to a common battle cry. You will fit in by waving your flag and by repeating the cheer of your people. It's like winter. What else are we going to do? The right time for the play-offs is between the 12th and the 31st of this month. In another half year you will be eating beans. But for now, it's stadium tacos. What should you do next? Hang out with your buddies, comrades-in-arms, or best friends. Drop the tailgate. And let the games begin. Winner take all, pal.

Month 16			
🔲	MAYAN: **Pax** AZTEC: **Atemoztli**		
Feb 1– Feb 20	Light Rains	Coming Down of the Water, Fall of Waters	Fell Trees
THIS MONTH IN HISTORY: Founding of Mayapán (Feb 2, A.D. 1254). Fall of Mayapán (Feb 17, 1451).			

This is the time for paper-shredding.... The rains are back. And we must fast before we feast again so that the rains will not forget to come when we need them later. At this time we cut out the shapes of spirit animals from paper mats and hang them in the woods. We pledge ourselves. We make our vows of the heart. And we invite others to be one with us. You will fit in by sending greeting cards to those you would like to keep active in your day-to-day life. You will fit in by sending your heart out to touch someone else. The right time for doing this is between the 1st and the 20th of this month. In another half year you will be watching how the relationships you form now have developed. What should you do next? Invite into your life the things you must have. Foster attachments that are not only convenient but necessary. Create conditions that are both necessary and sufficient. Sustain a competitive edge.

Month 17			
🔲	MAYAN: **Kayab** AZTEC: **Tititl**		
Feb 21– Mar 11	Light Rains	White Woman Sacrifice, Self-Flagellation	Fell Trees
THIS MONTH IN HISTORY: Second "Star War" against Naranjo by Caracol (Feb 28, A.D. 636). Last date recorded on the Altar of Sacrifices (3 Kayab, A.D. 849).			

This is a time of conflict.... It is raining again, and we have been cooped up too long in the house, with nothing to do but pace. We are antsy, tense, and nervous. You will fit in by exposing a raw nerve. You will fit in by revealing your true feelings. (We have encountered worse.) But you will also fit in by holding back on negative impulses. It is like a late winter. And in late winter it gets a little kinky. We get tied up in our own knots. We become victims of what we have kept pent up. We split hairs with one another now. We cut and snip. The most likely time is between the 21st of this month and the 11th of next month. You'll want to bite your tongue then, or else rue the day. In another half year it will all be behind you, except for just a taste of bittersweetness. What should you do next? Put a lid on it. Take it outside. Think twice before you speak. Count to 20 before you act. And never, ever throw the first punch.

Month 18			
💀	MAYAN: **Cumku** AZTEC: **Itzcalli**		
Mar 12– Mar 31	Hot & Dry	Growth by Fire, Immolation of Women	Burn Trees
THIS MONTH IN HISTORY: Yax Pac dedicates a temple (Mar 13, A.D. 783).			

This is the time of inner sanctum. . . . It is time to burn the fields. It is time to burn what we have cut down. You will fit in by burning bridges now. You will fit in by burning up that which has served you well, but now has no further purpose. It is like late winter. And in late winter, already we must prepare for the next winter's coming. There is never enough to last forever. We must constantly be preparing for whatever must happen next. We must always be preparing ourselves for whatever may come. And may it always be for the best . . . or at worst, for the better. The best time to start preparing yourself again is between the 12th and 31st of this month. In another half year, that which you prepare for now will all be turning to seed. What should you do next? Are you ready? Are you on your mark? Are you all set? Then go.

Month 19			
🔢	MAYAN: **Uayeb** AZTEC: **Nemontemi**		
Apr 1– Apr 5	Hot & Dry	Five Empty Days	Attempt Nothing
THIS MONTH IN HISTORY: Nothing happened.			

And so we come to five blank days. What is there to say about it that you don't already know? Things are just as inclined to fizzle out as to explode. Things are just as likely to cave in as upheave. And anything can always change with the weather. If you want to fit in, try shutting yourself off. Crawl into your cave. Curl up under your favorite book. And hang in there for the duration. Do this between the 1st and 5th of this month. Your own mind may play tricks on you. But a retreat works wonders, even if it's not fully appreciated at the time. You will not need to do this again for a whole other year. What should you do next? Take a breather.

EXTRA CREDIT

Ask a question of the months. The Haab was used by the priests more for agricultural and religious purposes than for casting horoscopes. But you can also use the Haab months in your fortune-telling work. Ask,

How is my concern like a season? With your question in mind, use your favorite method to choose a Day Sign....

   Bean Counting. Count your beans into bunches of four, then count the bunches. (If you get to 19 bunches, put those bunches back and count the remainder of your handful into bunches.) That number represents your Month Sign for this question. Jot down the name of your Month Sign on this Reading's Scratch Pad. Consult this Reading's Answers.

   Magic Lightning Cards. For this Reading, use the first 19 Day Sign Lightning Cards to represent the 19 months. (Go by the bean counts printed on the cards.) Swirl the Cards and choose one. Look up the name of the corresponding Month Sign on the table in this Reading's Tools section, and write it down on the Scratch Pad. Then consult this Reading's Answers.

   Point-n-Click. Point-n-Click on one of the Month Signs, using the diagram below. Note your Month Sign on the Scratch Pad. Consult this Reading's Answers.

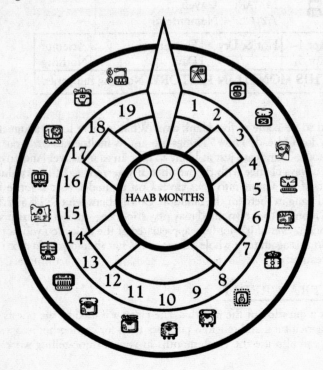

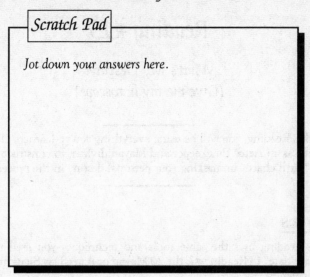

Scratch Pad

Jot down your answers here.

EXTRA, EXTRA CREDIT!

Day 221 through Day 240—If you haven't been out stargazing in a while, this is the time to do it. Over the next 20 days, catch a sunrise, get a glimpse of the moon, and pick out a star. Enjoy and note your experiences. What thoughts do these wonders inspire in you? What impressions do you walk away thinking about? What have these most ancient of signs and symbols told you? Note especially where the sun rises and sets and what phase the moon is in. It is good to note and acknowledge these things every day. These are the signs and symbols that can tip you off not only to the time of year and changing weather, but to your own cycles, rhythms, and mood swings. Since time immemorial, we have seen stories in the sky. As above, so below. This month, go in search of your sky tale.

Go on to the next Reading whenever you are ready to continue.

Reading #13

What's My Destiny?
(Give me my horoscope)

In this Reading, you will be using everything you've learned, all your skills as an Aztec timekeeper and Mayan diviner, to construct your "birth chart," unmasking your personal destiny in the process.

TOOLS

This Reading uses the same tools and techniques you used to find "today's date" in Reading #7: the 20 Mayan or Aztec Day Signs from the holy calendar.

Once you have computed these signs for your very own birth date (or for the birth date of a friend), you will be able to "run your horoscope" back through the rest of the book, getting a complete analysis in the process.

BACKGROUND

To the founders of these systems, there was nothing more important in determining an individual's destiny than the specific date on which he or she was born. Based on the signs that were present in the calendar on that date, each person's fate was sealed—except, of course, for the things that could be done to accentuate the positive and minimize the negative.

By interpreting all the signs from the calendar, the priest would forecast your occupation, marital possibilities, social status, and even your most likely cause of demise. In this Reading you will start to construct your personal astrological profile by interpreting your Day Sign and Day Number—the key indicators of your sacred destiny.

HOW TO

Attention: Users of All Methods: Put your beans, Lightning Cards, or pointing-finger away. This Reading is based on your date of birth.

ASK YOUR QUESTION

Follow your icon for the ends you defined in Reading #0, or ask any question listed in **boldface** (below) that appeals to you now.

FASTRACK You have come in search of a specific answer. But no question can be fully answered without considering the individual destinies of the people involved. Ask: **What do I have to do with it?** What does each of us?

SOULSEARCH You have come to find out about yourself. And so we come here to the bottom line. Ask: **What's my sign?**

GAMEPLAN You have come here to get your game plan. But a game is only as good as its players and their coaches. Ask: **What's my field position?**

HEARTSHUNT You have come here on a matter involving love. It usually takes two to do the Lambada. But, starting with yourself, ask: **What kind of love will hunt me out?**

VIZ'NQUEST You have come to seek the spiritual dimension of yourself. It is a search without beginning or ending that only continued on the day of your birth. Ask: **What am I supposed to learn, this time around?**

SELECT YOUR SIGN

All users follow the same method here.... Turn now to the back of the book, to the Almanac, starting on page 438. Look up the year of your birth. The Almanac covers all birthdays from 1909 to 2012. For example, for a baby born on April 22, 2007, find the column that says 2007 at the top....

2005	Day #	2006	Day #	2007	Day #
JAN 13	A 4	JAN 8	A 13	JAN 3	A 9
FEB 2	A 11	JAN 28	A 7	JAN 23	A 3
FEB 22	A 5	*FEB 17*	*A 1*	FEB 12	A 10
MAR 14	A 12	MAR 9	A 8	MAR 4	A 4
APR 3	A 6	MAR 29	A 2	MAR 24	A 11
APR 23	A 13	APR 18	A 9	APR 13	A 5
MAY 13	A 7	MAY 8	A 3	MAY 3	A 12
JUN 2	*A 1*	MAY 28	A 10	MAY 23	A 6
JUN 22	A 8	JUN 17	A 4	JUN 12	A 13
JUL 12	A 2	JUL 7	A 11	JUL 2	A 7
AUG 1	A 9	JUL 27	A 5	*JUL 22*	*A 1*
AUG 21	A 3	AUG 16	A 12	AUG 11	A 8
SEP 10	A 10	SEP 5	A 6	AUG 31	A 2
SEP 30	A 4	SEP 25	A 13	SEP 20	A 9
OCT 20	A 11	OCT 15	A 7	OCT 10	A 3
NOV 9	A 5	*NOV 4*	*A 1*	OCT 30	A 10
NOV 29	A 12	NOV 24	A 8	NOV 19	A 4
DEC 19	A 6	DEC 14	A 2	DEC 9	A 11
				DEC 29	A 5

TUN 6 AHAU	TUN 2 AHAU	TUN 11 AHAU
STARTS FEB 2ND	STARTS JAN 28TH	STARTS JAN 23RD

The Almanac lists every 20th day of our calendar. This is the date on which the Mayan "Sea Creature" (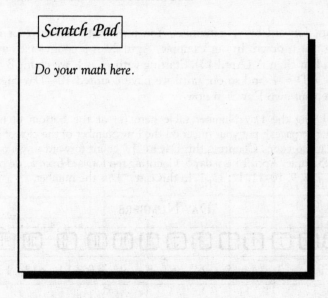) Sign A or the Aztec "Alligator" Sign A (🐊) cycles up again, and a new 20-day period begins. Shown to the right of the sign for each date is its Day Number (1–13). If your date is listed in the table, just copy down your Day Sign and Day Number and consult the Answers in this Reading.

If your date isn't in the table, find the date right before yours. Counting this date as "1," count forward, up to and including your date. Jot down this count on the Scratch Pad.

Scratch Pad

Do your math here.

Put your finger on Day Sign A in one of the tables here (or at the top of most Almanac pages).

MAYAN DAY SIGNS

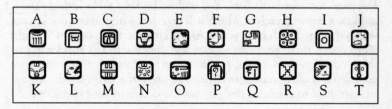

A	B	C	D	E	F	G	H	I	J
K	L	M	N	O	P	Q	R	S	T

AZTEC DAY SIGNS

Count forward by your number. You have just fingered your Day Sign. Jot it down. In our example, April 22 is a count of 10 away from Day Sign A (April 13). Starting with A as 1, we count B = 2, C = 3, D = 4, and so on, until we have counted 10—Day Sign J. Note your own Day Sign now.

Using the Day Number table here (or at the bottom of most Almanac pages), put your finger on the Day Number of the closest listed date to yours. Counting this Day as "1," count forward to yours. In our example, April 13 is a day 5. Counting ten forward from 5, we have 5, 6, 7, 8, 9, 10, 11, 12, 13, 1. In this case, "1" is the number.

DAY NUMBERS

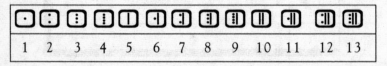

Jot down your Day Number beside your Day Sign. Turn to the Answers.

LOOK UP YOUR ANSWERS

Your answer begins in this Reading's Answer section. Just look up the Day Sign for your birth date. You will find a brief table listing various aspects of destiny, each of which will give you a hint about the sorts of things that are involved in yours. As with interpreting our own Western Horoscopes, there are many aspects and dimensions to consider in giving a complete astrological profile for any individual. Once you have completed reading your answer here, go on to the Extra Credit section to learn how to continue fleshing out the details of your horoscope.

THE ANSWERS

	MAYAN	AZTEC
SIGN A **Bunch 1**	🏺 Sea Creature Person	〰️ Alligator Person
Play	Play on, in, or under water.	
Work	Do something in keeping with your environment.	
Place	Live near the sea, on a river, out at the lake, or in a marsh.	
Mate	Repel slippery critters; attract the strongest and the fittest.	
Point	Face East, toward the rising sun and the Full Moon, both of which charge you up.	
Lineage	Hand down your "whale song," legend of the road, ghost stories, and other tall tales.	
Wealth	Live off life's bounty, nature's reserve, and your own energy.	
Sexual Preference	You prefer doing it on the fly and in motion.	
Hobbies	You like to fish around for your collection of things.	
Politics	Vote for the lesser of evils.	
Religion	Pray for the greater good.	
Ethics	Help out the strays and the stranded.	
Spirit	Sing the song you know by heart. Follow the song in your soul.	

See also your mirror image: Monkey.
Go on to Extra Credit.

SIGN B Bunch 2	🔲 Air Person	🐾 Wind Person
Play	Participate in sports wherein the wind can be a factor.	
Work	Do something that requires hot air, is a breath of fresh air, or requires a breezy attitude.	
Place	On a hill. Up in a building. At the top of the stairs.	
Mate	Repel those who would try to slow you. Attract those who go along for the ride.	
Point	Face North, toward the place where winds are born.	
Lineage	Hand down your free-spirited, entrepreneurial temperament.	
Wealth	Live off the energy you yourself create. Work for yourself.	
Sexual Preference	You prefer those who blow in your ear.	
Hobbies	You like something that will keep you busy in between moods.	
Politics	Vote for the one who is not just a windbag.	
Religion	Hear out the long-winded.	
Ethics	Pitch in during a crisis.	
Spirit	Let yourself be pushed along by the breeze at your back, and you will never be misled.	

See also your mirror image: Broom/Grass.
Go on to Extra Credit.

	MAYAN	AZTEC
SIGN C Bunch 3	🀅 Night Person	🏛 House Person
Play	Choose an indoor sport, or one played under lights.	
Work	Do something with everyone else's "odd" hours.	
Place	Work at home, out of the home, or from home.	
Mate	Repel early-to-bed-and-early-to-risers; attract night owls.	
Point	Face West, toward the setting sun and New Moon.	
Lineage	Hand down your alternative lifestyle.	
Wealth	Live off the services you deliver and the value you add.	
Sexual Preference	You prefer the privacy of your own bedroom (no doubt with the lights out).	
Hobbies	You like home-improvement projects.	
Politics	Vote for the one who supports your values.	
Religion	Tune in to a voice late at night.	
Ethics	Watch out for your neighbors.	
Spirit	Be guided by the stillness of the nighttime and your inner silence.	

See also your mirror image: Reed.
Go on to Extra Credit.

	MAYAN	AZTEC
SIGN D **Bunch 4**	🔲 Corn Person	🦎 Lizard Person
Play	You enjoy all sports played on a field.	
Work	Do something that involves a tough skin or thick hide.	
Place	Work out-of-doors, in the sun, or with the earth.	
Mate	Repel crows, attract butterflies.	
Point	Face South, toward the sun at all times.	
Lineage	Hand down your strongest, biggest, hardiest genes.	
Wealth	Live off the elements and your will to endure.	
Sexual Preference	You prefer something in a hybrid stock.	
Hobbies	You like to do something connected with your roots.	
Politics	Vote for the one who favors subsidies.	
Religion	Hear the one who pitches a tent.	
Ethics	Neither borrow nor steal.	
Spirit	Look to the earth itself for your own answer.	

See also your mirror image: Jaguar/Ocelot.
Go on to Extra Credit.

SIGN E Bunch 5	🔲 Serpent Person	🐍 Snake Person
	MAYAN	AZTEC
Play	Play a sport that requires crouching or sliding.	
Work	Do something that kicks up dust, takes a winding route, or leaves a trail.	
Place	The desert suits you, but also grasslands. A borough is good.	
Mate	Repel hawks, attract bunnies and mice.	
Point	Face East, with your face to the sun.	
Lineage	Hand down your colors, stripes, and distinctive markings.	
Wealth	Live off the fat of the land.	
Sexual Preference	You prefer to be entwined and entangled.	
Hobbies	You like rocks, ledges, caves, and sleeping bags.	
Politics	Vote for the one whose body is still warm.	
Religion	Worship whenever tempted.	
Ethics	Sound a warning before you strike.	
Spirit	To keep growing, keep shedding your used-up skins. You have many identities.	

See also your mirror image: Eagle.
Go on to Extra Credit.

	MAYAN	AZTEC
SIGN F **Bunch 6**	🎴 Death Person	💀 Death Person
Play	Play a sport that involves the wearing of protective gear.	
Work	Do something with minimal risk and few occupational hazards.	
Place	Stand well back from the edge, line, or brink. Obey all lighted signs and placards.	
Mate	Repel the reckless, attract the cautious, careful, and conservative.	
Point	Face North, away from the sun (and always wear sunblock).	
Lineage	Hand down your healthy lifestyles, provided they, too, don't kill you in the end.	
Wealth	Live off your retirement accounts and pension for as long as you can.	
Sexual Preference	You prefer to wash your hands before and after....	
Hobbies	You like to do things that have a therapeutic value.	
Politics	Vote for the one who's outlived the most rivals.	
Religion	Follow a faith that prescribes what to eat.	
Ethics	Honor your elders, and remember the ancestors.	
Spirit	Cram for the final. The only question is: What have you learned?	

See also your mirror image: Owl/Vulture.
Go on to Extra Credit.

Reading #13

SIGN G Bunch 7	MAYAN — Deer Person	AZTEC — Deer Person
Play	Play a sport that involves the wearing of camouflage or the jumping of hurdles.	
Work	Do something that allows you to stay more or less still, but also requires quick reflexes.	
Place	Go to a familiar neck of the woods, across a highway, or over some walls and fences.	
Mate	Repel those who smell sinister. Attract those with the same taste.	
Point	Face West, and the twilight that is your best time.	
Lineage	Hand down your ability to blend in.	
Wealth	Live off the things that grow on and under other things.	
Sexual Preference	You prefer the sound of nature in the background.	
Hobbies	You like to do things that can be put away fast.	
Politics	Vote for the one with the shortest, cleanest tail.	
Religion	Always worship out-of-doors.	
Ethics	Take a thing only when it's in season.	
Spirit	Listen to your spirit guide. Seek the animal that would lead you.	

See also your mirror image: Earthquake.
Go on to Extra Credit.

199

SIGN H Bunch 8	MAYAN 🎲 Rabbit Person	AZTEC 🐇 Rabbit Person
Play	Participate in a sport that is played on grass.	
Work	Do something that requires you to keep creating, producing, or reproducing.	
Place	Keep out in the open, and yet stay hidden from full view.	
Mate	Repel those who would sniff you out. Attract those who respect you for more than your clothes.	
Point	Face South, between the rising and setting moons, your fertility signs.	
Lineage	Hand down your ability to be prolific, creative, and nonviolent.	
Wealth	Avoid your tendency to freeze your assets all in one place.	
Sexual Preference	You like it fast and spontaneous ... maybe even often.	
Hobbies	You like to snuggle up with a good pastime.	
Politics	Vote for the one with the most impressive off-spring.	
Religion	Choose a faith that requires you to sit still.	
Ethics	Treat all things with respect.	
Spirit	Follow the trail left for you. Look for the tracks and the traces. See the signs.	

See also your mirror image: Blade/Flint.
Go on to Extra Credit.

	MAYAN	AZTEC
SIGN I Bunch 9	🔲 Rain Person	👆 Rain Person
Play	Participate in water sports.	
Work	Do something that requires exposure to the elements.	
Place	Anywhere suits you, as long as it has a dry bed and a roof overhead when you need it.	
Mate	Repel those who are a wet blanket. Attract the ones who fit your ever-changing mood.	
Point	Face East, the home of the rainbow.	
Lineage	Hand down your affinity for shaking things up.	
Wealth	Depend on your liquid assets. Freeze no more than you can manage without.	
Sexual Preference	You prefer stormy and impetuous encounters.	
Hobbies	You like things that involve puttering, dabbling, and dribbling, as the spirit moves you.	
Politics	Vote for the one who comes on the strongest.	
Religion	Practice a faith founded in the Agricultural Age.	
Ethics	Never rain on a parade.	
Spirit	Be sensitive to and aware of changing weather conditions. These are your primal cues.	

See also your mirror image: Storm.
Go on to Extra Credit.

	MAYAN	AZTEC
SIGN J **Bunch 10**	😐 Dog Person	🐕 Dog Person
Play	Participate in sports that require catching a ball or throwing a disc.	
Work	Do something that requires loyalty above all else.	
Place	Position yourself at the foot of your master, your mistress, or the one you belong with.	
Mate	Repel those who come around on the prowl. Gravitate to those with good traits, if not also the best credentials.	
Point	Face North, the path that the Baying Moon takes.	
Lineage	Hand down your most desired and admired characteristics.	
Wealth	Depend on your sponsor, benefactor, contributor, or patron.	
Sexual Preference	You like to linger for a while afterwards.	
Hobbies	You like pastimes that involve chewing at the same time.	
Politics	Vote for the one who shakes your hand.	
Religion	Take to the faith that keeps your belly full, your head patted, and your back scratched.	
Ethics	Never lift your leg on a guest.	
Spirit	Be open to the messages that pass unspoken between kindred spirits.	

See also your mirror image: Lord/Flower.
Go on to Extra Credit.

	MAYAN	AZTEC
SIGN K **Bunch 11**	🐵 Monkey Person	🐒 Monkey Person
Play	Participate in sports that require gymnastic equipment.	
Work	Do something that involves climbing up the ladder or into the ranks.	
Place	Position yourself at a good vantage point. A nest, cave, or even cage would suit you.	
Mate	Repel those who would crawl up after you. Attract those who lift you higher.	
Point	Face West, the path of least resistance for you.	
Lineage	Hand down your knowledge of tools, your vocabulary, and other survival skills.	
Wealth	Live as high as you can, for as long as you can keep it up.	
Sexual Preference	For you, nothing is indecent, improper, or private. You prefer anything involving your own parts.	
Hobbies	Practically anything will keep you amused and interested, for at least a little while.	
Politics	Vote for the one who chooses discreet partners.	
Religion	Practice a faith that doesn't require abstinence.	
Ethics	Do not feed the other animals at the zoo.	
Spirit	Be open to your primal impulses. Behave instinctively, sensuously. And you will see.	

See also your mirror image: Sea Creature/Alligator.
Go on to Extra Credit.

	MAYAN	AZTEC
SIGN L **Bunch 12**	📛 Broom Person	🌿 Grass Person
Play	Participate in games played on a lawn or in a park.	
Work	Do something that involves seasonal patterns of activity, cycles, or processes.	
Place	Position yourself in a place where the drainage is good and you are naturally exposed to the things that nourish you.	
Mate	Repel those who try to cut you down. Attract the ones who will give you some space.	
Point	Face South, for maximum exposure to the light.	
Lineage	Hand down your resilience, resistance, and tolerance.	
Wealth	Live off the things in your general vicinity. Go after what is in reach.	
Sexual Preference	You prefer them tall, lean, and turgid, but at arm's length.	
Hobbies	You enjoy things that touch or have touched the earth.	
Politics	Vote for the one with the best manicure.	
Religion	Worship in the suburbs.	
Ethics	Do not start your mower before 9 A.M. on Saturday.	
Spirit	Feel your roots. Draw up from the wells beneath you. Take in what you need.	

See also your mirror image: Wind/Air.
Go on to Extra Credit.

	MAYAN	AZTEC
SIGN M Bunch 13	🔲 Reed Person	▦ Reed Person
Play	You would enjoy playing a musical instrument.	
Work	Do something that requires you to perfect a talent, skill, craft, or trade.	
Place	Position yourself in a low-lying place, along a river, near a seaport, or on the water itself.	
Mate	Repel those who are hollow. Attract those who are tender in their core.	
Point	Face East, for the morning light.	
Lineage	Hand down your ability to stand proud and tall.	
Wealth	Live off the things that others may regard as worthless these days.	
Sexual Preference	You prefer something with a hollow center.	
Hobbies	You enjoy dabbling in a number of things at once.	
Politics	Vote for the one who stands up and out.	
Religion	Pray to the accompaniment of an organ.	
Ethics	Do not make slurping noises with your straw.	
Spirit	Look for signs everywhere you go, but especially where there are marshes.	

See also your mirror image: Night/House.
Go on to Extra Credit.

	MAYAN	AZTEC
SIGN N **Bunch 14**	🎲 Jaguar Person	🐾 Ocelot Person
Play	You enjoy games involving pips, points, and spots.	
Work	Do something that keeps you out of the hot afternoon sun.	
Place	Position yourself in a place that offers shade, a good view, and a stiff breeze.	
Mate	Repel those who admire you for your coat. Attract those who make you purr in the throat.	
Point	Face North, and out of the constant glare.	
Lineage	Hand down your ability to go after a moving target.	
Wealth	Live off the things that fall or come within your territory.	
Sexual Preference	You prefer to do it again and again and again . . . and again.	
Hobbies	You enjoy things that require strategy, finesse, and preferably can be done lying down.	
Politics	Vote for the one who puts up the best fight.	
Religion	Pray within your own sanctuary.	
Ethics	Do not harm an endangered species.	
Spirit	Pay attention to the animals who appear in your life and in your dreams.	

See also your mirror image: Corn/Lizard.
Go on to Extra Credit.

	MAYAN	AZTEC
SIGN O Bunch 15	🔲 Eagle Person	🔥 Eagle Person
Play	You enjoy sports played at high points.	
Work	Do something that keeps you flying high, far, and wide.	
Place	Position yourself at a good height, overlooking the surrounding sights.	
Mate	Repel those who enter your space without permission. Attract those who will remain with you for longer than a year.	
Point	Face West, so you will know when dusk comes and it is time to go home.	
Lineage	Hand down your insights, foresights, and hindsights.	
Wealth	Live off the things that capture your attention from afar.	
Sexual Preference	You prefer to take a single mate for life.	
Hobbies	You enjoy working on the roost.	
Politics	Vote for the one with the best beak.	
Religion	Pray in a place with a steeple.	
Ethics	Do not drop by without an invitation.	
Spirit	Allow your free spirit the space that it needs to soar, glide, and swoop.	

See also your mirror image: Serpent/Snake.
Go on to Extra Credit.

SIGN P Bunch 16	🦉 Owl Person	🪶 Vulture Person
	MAYAN	AZTEC

Play	You would enjoy any spectator sport, especially if you own binoculars.
Work	Do something that involves watching over things.
Place	Position yourself where you can see everything.
Mate	Repel competitors, especially birds of a feather. Attract those who leave you alone.
Point	Face South, so you can watch the sky turn bloodred at dusk and read the omens in the shapes of clouds.
Lineage	Hand down your skills of observation. Hand down your symbols.
Wealth	Live off the things you can see coming in advance.
Sexual Preference	You prefer places where others have slept before.
Hobbies	You enjoy activities that require your head to move from side to side.
Politics	Vote for the one who will watch out for your interests.
Religion	Practice a faith founded on prophecy, truth, and vision.
Ethics	Wait till the body is cold before claiming an inheritance.
Spirit	Appreciate an omen when you see one, and you will not need to be warned a second time.

See also your mirror image: Death.
Go on to Extra Credit.

SIGN Q Bunch 17	🝰 Earthquake Person (MAYAN)	⋈ Earthquake Person (AZTEC)
Play	Participate in a sport that is played on a pulsing screen.	
Work	Do something that requires basically steady hands, but also firm or sudden actions.	
Place	Position yourself on or near a fault line . . . and take your risk.	
Mate	Repel those who would set you off. Attract those who support and steady you.	
Point	Face East, where you can appreciate the pull of a Full Moon. . . . Stay steady now.	
Lineage	Hand down both your stability and instability, but especially your sense of balance.	
Wealth	Live off the securities you have built up and placed around yourself.	
Sexual Preference	You prefer the earth to move at the end.	
Hobbies	You enjoy things that involve a calculated risk, as long as the odds are in your favor.	
Politics	Vote for the one who seems the most stable.	
Religion	Practice a faith built on a firm foundation.	
Ethics	Always use materials that measure up to code.	
Spirit	Put your ear to the ground if you want to hear something. Keep an eye out for Lightning Stones.	

See also your mirror image: Deer.
Go on to Extra Credit.

	MAYAN	AZTEC
SIGN R **Bunch 18**	⊠ Blade Person	🜂 Flint Person
Play	Participate in a sport that requires you to hit a target.	
Work	Do something that demands you be sharp, quick, and keen-witted. Do something you are cut out for.	
Place	Position yourself at a strategic location, base, or compound.	
Mate	Repel those who chill you to the bone. Attract those that make your blood run warm.	
Point	Face North, where the compass point is pulled.	
Lineage	Hand down your ability to cut clean, smooth, and swift.	
Wealth	Live from the things you are able to cut off for yourself.	
Sexual Preference	You prefer a partner with a short haircut . . . or is it uncut?	
Hobbies	You enjoy cutting things out, or cutting things up. But do you also piece them back together?	
Politics	Vote for the one who cuts the most impressive figure.	
Religion	Worship at a place where the priest cuts to the chase.	
Ethics	Always hand off a knife with the blade toward you.	
Spirit	Draw from yourself the energy and strength to endure, survive, achieve.	

See also your mirror image: Rabbit.
Go on to Extra Credit.

SIGN S Bunch 19	MAYAN 🔲 Storm Person	AZTEC 🔲 Storm Person
Play	Participate in a sport that requires you to perform in fits, peaks, and bursts.	
Work	Do something that forces you to channel your energy into a constructive outlet.	
Place	Position yourself to one side or the other of an imaginary line... then go forward.	
Mate	Repel those who pressure you. Attract those who let you develop in your own way.	
Point	Face West, which is to say, come from the East.	
Lineage	Hand down your passionate side, but not your temper.	
Wealth	Live off the momentum you built up in youth.	
Sexual Preference	You prefer lusty encounters, which crash, bang, and boom.	
Hobbies	You enjoy doing things that are suited for a rainy day.	
Politics	Vote for the one who charges you up, without charging you more.	
Religion	Worship in a way that ends with crescendo, or at least a high note.	
Ethics	Do not loiter in a danger zone.	
Spirit	Take your cues from the things you know and feel in your own bones.	

See also your mirror image: Rain.
Go on to Extra Credit.

	MAYAN	AZTEC
SIGN T **Bunch 20**	🔲 Lord Person	🔱 Flower Person
Play	You would enjoy a sport that includes pomp and pageantry among its circumstances.	
Work	Do something that might win you honors—or at least a bouquet of flowers.	
Place	Position yourself to be at a certain place, by a certain time... especially the right place at the right time.	
Mate	Repel those who would rob you of your bloom. Attract those who appeal to your highly refined senses.	
Point	Face South, to get all the exposure you need.	
Lineage	Hand down your beauty secrets and other charms.	
Wealth	Live off the compliments that people pay you and the favors you exchange.	
Sexual Preference	You prefer the ones who smell like a bed of roses.	
Hobbies	You enjoy doing things that require attention to detail.	
Politics	Vote for the one with the best teeth.	
Religion	Practice a faith that encourages you to bloom.	
Ethics	When in doubt, send roses.	
Spirit	Take time to appreciate all the Good Lord gives you. Say thanks. Give grace.	

See also your mirror image: Dog.
Go on to Extra Credit.

EXTRA CREDIT

How to Complete Your Horoscope...

Flesh out your signs. For more detail, look up the Day Sign you computed in this Reading in the Master Answer section and read the entire text. Then look up your Day Number and read this text too. Together, these two answer sets will provide many additional details on your love life, home life, work life, and other aspects of your destiny.

Find your picture. Look up your Day Sign in Reading #11's Answers, look at your picture, read your story, and consider the keywords that describe the meaning of your sign.

Consider your mirror image. Every Day Sign is linked to and influenced by an opposite or complimentary sign in the set. Your opposite sign is listed at the end of your profile in Reading #13's Answers. To learn more about your mirror image, look up your opposite sign in the Master Answer section and read the entire text.

Learn your mythology. Look up your Day Sign in the Answer sections to Readings #1, #2, and #3. Read the boxed text (and the rest of the answer if you like). You can consult for your mirror image as well. Also, look up your Day Number in Readings #4 and #5.

Find your holy day. There are 260 combinations of the 20 Day Signs and 13 Day Numbers—260 kinds of birth dates, and 260 kinds of basic personalities. Each combination is represented by a specific day in the Mayan and Aztec holy calendar's "Book of Days." Since each day in this calendar has specific spiritual meaning, your birth date also bears spiritual significance. Whenever your holy day cycles up—whether it is your birth date or not—you should have pause for thought. For something to think about right now, turn to the Combinations section of the Quick Reference Guide and find your unique Day Sign/Day Number combination.

Compute your Month Sign. You can also find and interpret your Month Signs from the Haab, or seasonal calendar. These signs reveal environmental influences and the conditions at the time of your birth that have had a lasting impact on you. To find your Month Sign, follow the instructions in Reading #12's How To section for computing these signs. Once you have computed yours, look up your Month Sign in the Answers for Reading #12.

Find the Year Bearer. Use Almanac II to find the Year Bearer that rules your year of birth. Year Bearers are listed at the bottom of the tables. Find the one that was ruling at the time you were born, and consult the Master Answer section for the Day Sign and Day Number associated with your Year Bearer. (There are only four Year Bearer signs, which cycle every fourth Haab year. At times your birth sign will be complemented, and at times contradicted.)

Consider your Ahau influence. In addition to considering the specific day at a specific point in a certain month when you were born—and on which holy day—your natal horoscope needs to take into consideration the particular year (or Tun) in progress at the time of birth. These Tun years are named for their last day—always a Day Lord (*Ahau* in native Mayan) or a Day Flower (*Xochitl* in Aztec terms). There are 13 such years, numbered 1 through 13, but not in sequential order. You will find the Ahau date listed at the bottom of the Almanac column for your birth year. Or see Reading #10 if you need some help.

Get your personal horoscope for today. You can update your personal horoscope every day of the year by simply computing today's Day Sign (using the method described in this Reading). Then "add" your Day Number to today's Day Number and Day Sign. For example, if today is 4 Lord (4T) and your birthday is 5 Sea Creature (5A), count 5 forward from today's Number 4, for a Day 8. Now start at today's Lord date (Sign T) and move five signs forward, to Sign D—Corn. In our example you would look up 8 Corn (8D) for your personal slant on the day. Compute your sign now.

To find out how compatible you are. For evaluating any love interest, business partner, or friend, simply add your two Day Signs and Day Numbers together, to see how you two compute. Add your personal Day Number to the Day Sign and Day Number of the potential partner. Then Consult the Quick Reference Guide's Day Signs and Day Numbers for a reading of how you will get along with this person. To find out how they will get along with you, add their personal Day Number to your Day Sign and Day Number. Look up the resulting sign/number combination in the Master Answer Section.

EXTRA, EXTRA CREDIT!

Day 241 through Day 260—This is the most important Uinal in your journey of 260 days. Remain open to everything that your senses take in... but also stay calm and centered. Devote extra time to cleansing and purification. Take plenty of baths or showers. Burn lots of incense. Wear your good luck charms and amulets. A sign might come from anywhere at any time. But don't look too hard. There is no way to seek it out in advance. Relax. When the time is right, you will make contact... and then you will reemerge. At the end of these final days, honor the experience. The time is coming when you must return to your everyday life. Take your own lessons with you. And always treat your Magic Lightning Stones with the deepest respect. They have become one with you. Make them a part of your life. And remember, as above, so below. May you have the strength of New Fire.

QUICK
REFERENCE
GUIDE

I am restoring it, my offering of copal to you . . .
my offering of posol to you again
for your welfare
for you to restore it to the father.
I will pay it to you my offering of posol—
to you for yourself.

—LANCANDONE CHANT
("WHEN COPAL AND POSOLE ARE
DISTRIBUTED IN THE CEREMONY OF
RENEWING THE INCENSE BURNERS")
ADAPTED FROM ALFRED TOZZER

Instructions

HOW TO FIND YOUR ANSWERS

There are three ways to ask questions and get answers of this oracle.

Bean counting. This way is a traditional method. Just take a handful of dried soup beans and count them out into bunches of four, and then count the number of bunches. The number of bunches you wind up with will point you to a Day Sign or Day Number, which is all you need to access the Master Answer section. The method for counting beans to get a Day Sign is described in Reading #1. The method for counting beans to get a Day Number is described in Reading #4.

Magic Lightning Cards. This method is based on practices of modern Mayan priests, who often shuffle crystals around on a table before reading them as signs. A set of cards is included at the back of the book. Just photocopy the pages, cut them out, mount them on card stock if you like, and shuffle them in front of you to select a Day Sign and Day Number. Then look up your answers in this Quick Reference Guide.

Point-n-Click. For those who prefer absolute simplicity, let your fingers do the walking! Special Point-n-Click diagrams are included in Readings #1, #4, #7, and #12. Point at the diagram in Reading #1 to get a Day Sign. Point at the diagram in Reading #4 to get a Day Number. Then look up your answers here. The Point-n-Click diagrams have been modeled after the famous Aztec calendar wheel.

Another way to consult this oracle is to use today's (or any day's) date along with the Alamanac at the back of the book to find the Mayan Day Sign and Day Number. Full instructions are in Reading #7. Once you have computed a date, a general horoscope can be found by looking up the Day Sign, Day Number, and Sign/Number Combination in the Master Answer Section. This will give you the "auspices of the day." To find your personal horoscope, see Reading #13.

How to find your answer. All you have to do is look up your signs in the Master Answer section. First, look up the Day Sign. These 20 signs are arranged in the Master Answers in their traditional order:

THE 20 DAY SIGNS (A-J)

	MAYAN	AZTEC
SIGN A Bunch 1	Sea Creature	Alligator
SIGN B Bunch 2	Air	Wind
SIGN C Bunch 3	Night	House
SIGN D Bunch 4	Corn	Lizard
SIGN E Bunch 5	Serpent	Snake
SIGN F Bunch 6	Death	Death
SIGN G Bunch 7	Deer	Deer
SIGN H Bunch 8	Rabbit	Rabbit
SIGN I Bunch 9	Rain	Rain
SIGN J Bunch 10	Dog	Dog

	MAYAN	AZTEC
SIGN K Bunch 11	Monkey	Monkey
SIGN L Bunch 12	Broom	Grass
SIGN M Bunch 13	Reed	Reed
SIGN N Bunch 14	Jaguar	Ocelot
SIGN O Bunch 15	Eagle	Eagle
SIGN P Bunch 16	Owl	Vulture
SIGN Q Bunch 17	Earthquake	Earthquake
SIGN R Bunch 18	Blade	Flint
SIGN S Bunch 19	Storm	Storm
SIGN T Bunch 20	Lord	Flower

Your answer consists of whatever portion of the text you feel like reading today....

The Answer is divided into various parts. First, you'll find a chart at the top. Here's the chart for the ninth Day Sign, Rain....

	MAYAN		AZTEC	
SIGN I **Bunch 9**	🔲	Rain Muluc	☞	Rain Atl
Direction: East		Color: Red		
Key Date: 6 Muluc, 7 Ceh—Prohibition ends. Everything dry is wet again (Dec. 5, 1933).				

The top of this table will confirm that this is the Day Sign you have drawn, based on whichever method you are using from Reading #0 (bean counting, Magic Lightning Cards, or Point-n-Click). The middle boxes tell you the direction and color that are traditionally associated with this sign. Those listed in the table are of the Highland Maya tradition. Various Mesoamerican groups use slightly different systems.

And finally, you'll find a "key date" from recent times that is associated with this Day Sign. The dates used throughout the Master Answer section have been selected based on a sampling of key events from the 20th century, as recognized by American historians. The real date, and actual event, listed with your Day Sign, is—in the author's estimation—a good representation of the types of events that have recently tended to be associated with this sign, based on his review of several thousand selected dates.

The Maya used both their Tzolkin/Tun calendar and their Haab calendar at the same time. So a complete Mayan date is expressed both as a Day Sign/Day Number combination and a Haab count. The two most famous of these dates are:

- **4 Ahau** (the Tzolkin date), **8 Cumku** (the Haab date), the day when the Fifth Creation Epoch began (August 12, 3114 B.C.); and

- **4 Ahau** (the Tzolkin date), **3 Kankin** (the Haab date), which is December 21, A.D. 2012, the day on which the current millennium will end.

The key dates in this Master Answer section are expressed in the classic Mayan tradition of citing both the Tzolkin (the Sacred Calendar) and the Haab (the Secular Calendar) dates.

You can skip over the information in the table if it doesn't interest you. But for some, it will aid in the use and interpretation of the oracle.

The text below the chart for your Day Sign is divided into sections: **Work, Love, Money, Strategy,** and **Horoscope.** Depending on the type of question you have asked or the issue that faces you today, you might choose to zero in on the particular part of the text that is most logical. If nothing else fits, try the Strategy section. You can, naturally, read the whole text that goes with your sign, if you like . . . in which case, you may find that an answer simply pops out at you as being right today.

In general, the text here is just one impression that a Day Sign might leave. As you become more and more familiar with the signs, you will probably start to develop your own feelings about what they mean. If it ever comes down to a choice between "what the book says" and what your own intuition tells you, go with your gut.

Once you have looked up your Day Sign, go on to find the Day Number in these Master Answers, starting on page 247. In reading the text that goes with your number, the same general rules apply. Look at the chart, if you like, and read the passage of text under it that would seem to most relate to your question (Work, Love, Money, Strategy, and Horoscope) . . . or read all the sections if you feel like it. Try it various ways to see what works best for you.

Then—for the clincher!—find out what your unique combination of Day Sign and Day Number means by consulting the Combinations section of these Master Answers, starting on page 265. All 260 possible combinations are listed, along with a selected date and brief narrative text. Read the whole thing.

For convenient lookup, these combinations are listed in Day-Sign order, with each Day Sign immediately followed by its thirteen combinations (1 through 13).[1] First, find your Day Sign in the Combinations section, then find your Day Number under it. Space has been left in the tables here for you to enter your own "key dates" as personal reference points, cues, and clues to the meaning of the signs. If, as you use this book, you jot down a little something about each combination you look up, you'll soon have a very personalized oracle at work in your life.

Once you've gotten your first answer, start the process over again by asking another question or computing another date. To compute today's date, use the Almanac at the end of the Quick Reference Guide. Full instructions are in Reading #7.

---

[1]The actual sequence that the Day Signs take is much less logical. Consult the Tzolkin and Tonalpoualli charts in Reading #8 for their actual day-to-day sequence.

Friendly words of advice. In general, you will have the best results if you bring real questions, problems, and issues to the table. For a self-guided tour of the oracle on any question or issue, follow one of the paths outlined in Reading #0 . . . and carried out in Readings #1 through #13. It's possible to "run a question" through the entire book in a very short period of time. But important issues are often best considered over a number of days, weeks, or even years. So don't feel as if you have to rush.

However you choose to proceed, and whatever you choose to ask, I wish you the best. My thoughts and incense prayers are with you throughout your vision quest.

Master Answer Section

THE 20 DAY SIGNS

	MAYAN		AZTEC
SIGN A **Bunch 1**	🏛	Sea Creature Imix	🐊 Alligator Cipactli

Direction: East	Color: Red	

Key Date: 2 Imix, 14 Mac—Scientists announce theory that Universe was formed by Big Bang (Dec. 27, 1954).

HOROSCOPE

The truth may be stark once it's laid out bare-naked in black and white before you. But the outlook in general is no more grim than it's ever been. At least the weather will be dry. The day favors brotherly love, as well as its opposite. The thought is: For every story, there's a moral.

For WORK questions. Public Relations, for sure. But PR is half of just about everything. Take your pick of careers or offers. Don the appropriate outfit, then get out there and wait for the right opportunity to fall into your lap. Catch hold of the golden ring, snatch, clean and jerk. It's a swamp out there. And the game is played dirty. But just the same, keep your own nose clean and dry.

For LOVE questions. You may seem like a tough cookie, but just let me scratch your belly for a while. It may be the raw and sultry power that's the come-on. But it's the softer side that really gets us going. Crocodile Woman—the ultimate challenge, but the Genuine Article, down to her shoes. Crocodile Man—the Real Thing, but an Endangered Species. Be careful that at a particularly vulnerable moment, you do not lose the advantage.

For MONEY questions. Though at times you may feel like you're worth more dead than alive, you will always have enough to eat. Self-sufficiency is your motto, and self-sufficient you will be. Survival of the fittest and wittiest is involved. Take advantage of your species' claim to fame. Do as your parents taught you about money, not as they did.

For STRATEGY issues. Lie low until the time is right. Cunning and plotting are involved, but the most important element is that of surprise. Though a tried-and-true formula may work most of the time, a sudden movement catches everyone off-guard. Do not just watch, but also observe. And pay attention to your gut instincts. When the moment is right, act—or react—just as fast as you can.

MAYAN			AZTEC	
SIGN B **Bunch 2**	🔲	Air Ik	🔳	Wind Eecatl
Direction: North			Color: White	
Key Date: 9 Ik, 0 Uo—Shepard is first American in space (May 5, 1961).				

HOROSCOPE

An occasional miracle occurs this day . . . but do not overlook the possibility for disaster. Charismatic people may be involved in both good <u>and</u> ill purposes. Some curses may be blessings in disguise. Atmospheric conditions beg you to appeal. The day favors a love of conviction. The thought is: Take a deep breath.

For WORK questions. The winds of change sweep through the workplace. But is it a breath of fresh air? Or an old bag of breeze? The speed is picking up. Everything gets done in a flurry, if not a fury. You are buffeted. You are blustered. Your hair may even be tousled at the end of the day. But your voice carries, even against the wind. And what's that I smell nuking in the corporate microwave?

For LOVE questions. Where air is involved, it's difficult to tell which way the wind blows . . . let alone what direction it might be coming from tomorrow. Whatever it is, it's probably just a temporary thing. A fickle tendency gains strength from time to time. Momentum builds. And tempers collide. But on other days, it will be like a sweet breath brushing your lips . . . the kind that draws an inadvertent gasp. Calm or gusty? Whichever suits you best at the moment. This is what the wind brings.

For MONEY questions. In this period things will pick up quickly . . . or as suddenly slow down. Keep one eye on your barometer at all times. Take readings of the indicators and the signs. Monitor market fluctuations, interest rates, stocks, and bonds. Watch for small blips that might signal a trend. And whatever you do, hold on to your checkbook . . . as well as your hat.

For STRATEGY issues. Your mission is the same as the air's. You must permit yourself to be flexible. In that way you will be able to get around many things that others view as obstacles. You must be like the breeze. You must be like the wind. There is a time to float. There is a time to sail. There is even a time to howl . . . and wail. Be wary of your temper. But respect your temperament. Trust in the things you feel. Follow the mood.

	MAYAN		AZTEC	
SIGN C **Bunch 3**	🔳	Night Akbal	🏛	House Calli
	Direction: West		Color: Black	
Key Date: 1 Akbal, 6 Zotz—Five burglars are caught in The Watergate (Jun. 17, 1972).				

HOROSCOPE

Some dirty, dark, and dastardly deeds happen from time to time, but this day tends to nip them in the bud. Records set in the past are overturned. A silence is broken. A secret is out. The skies will be but partly overcast tonight. The day favors the love of truth. The thought is: Come out of your secret room.

For WORK questions. Around you are four walls. Above you is a ceiling. And below you is the floor. An office may be central. But home is where the real work gets down. Something after hours has your attention. Something at the end of the day. Something into the dead of night. Someone remains silent on a subject. But is it sinister? Or just suspense building up?

For LOVE questions. It's hard to describe it really.... It's that dark, calm feeling you feel inside when you hold each other close. It's about feeling centered, it's about being rooted. Things grow best in a blackened soil. Life comes out of a narrow hole. It is both darkness and light that make a thing grow. May you strike an even balance, between the two of you. Your ideal lover is a deep, dark, mysterious, strong-but-silent type. If it works for the two of you, it's right.

For MONEY questions. In this period things will be in the black, which should make you feel pretty good. It's a fine time for putting it all down in black and white and signing on the bottom line. A change in property (particularly real estate, especially the development of a part-time business) could be indicated. Money from, in, or around the house is involved. Don't keep it all in one place. Don't spend it all at one time.

For STRATEGY issues. Your mission is to delve into the dark. The silence at the center, as still as a house at night, is where the answer lies. You will have to dig deeper for this one. It's something about your motivations and the things that make you tick. If I were you, I'd sleep on it, with all the lights out. It will all be clearer in the morning. Trust me on this one.

	MAYAN		AZTEC	
SIGN D **Bunch 4**	🀫	Corn Kan	🦎	Lizard Cuetzpalin
	Direction: South		Color: Yellow	
Key Date: 3 Kan, 17 Zac—Rev. Moon mass-marries 4,000 prearranged couples in Madison Square Garden ceremonies (Jul. 16, 1982).				

HOROSCOPE

Things that might capture our attention, captivate us, or draw us in this day, do. All eyes are focused on the screen. There are spectacles and public displays. "We are coming to you live from the scene." The day favors a love that is simple, but subject to the test. With any luck, the weather will be fair. The thought is: Measure up—not down—to expectation.

For WORK questions. It may not always be a laugh a minute, but one thing's for sure: It's always entertaining. Seasonal work is involved.

Certain things happen at certain times. And you have to be there at the critical moment. What you do at the start determines how you will wind up at the end of each day. There are only so many hours you're paid for. So when the sun sets, go home and get some sleep. Tomorrow is another day, and the night is for growing, and restoring.

For LOVE questions. Oh, I know it's corny. But it's just like a growing season: a springtime in the rain; a summer in the sun. And then that poignant fall. May cold winter bypass us who are each other's lovers. (And may we at least always remain friends.) The two of you grow together. You share the same space. You eat in the same place. You weather the same conditions. You share the same foundation and roof over your head.... You succeed or fail together. For it takes two, baby.

For MONEY questions. In this period commodities are the big thing. You'll want to watch the grain prices out in Chicago. And don't forget the pork bellies. You're betting that the current good conditions are going to hold up, until the time when your investment matures. Or else you're hoping that things may turn sour, but the prices will soar. How can you lose? It has something to do with brokers and financial advisors. Select both carefully.

For STRATEGY issues. Your mission is an ancient one. First you hold your head up. Then you sit. Then you crawl. Then you walk. And suddenly you find yourself driving 65 miles an hour past cornfields on the Pennsylvania Turnpike. You're here to live out your cycle . . . to witness your times. . . to experience from your unique vantage point what only you can ever know, if not completely understand yourself. Give things the time they need to work themselves out. Most things worth the energy take a year to complete. At least give it a season. Or how about 260 days?

MAYAN			AZTEC	
SIGN E **Bunch 5**	🔲	Serpent Chicchan	🐍	Snake Coatl
Direction: East			Color: Red	
Key Date: 3 Chicchan, 18 Xul—President Nixon announces he will resign rather than face impeachment (Aug. 8, 1974).				

HOROSCOPE

It's a day that carries a sting—or packs a wallop—with it. Things that are sinister or suspect come out into the light. Things rattle in the overhead compartment or the seat pocket in front of you. The weather may turn suddenly. The day favors love, both in and out of control. The thought is: Watch out for broken glass . . . especially if it's silvered on the back.

For WORK questions. If this isn't a cage of vipers . . . or a pit of rattlesnakes . . . then I don't know what is. Oh, how sharper than a serpent's tooth . . . and get a load of that tongue! It seems like everyone is slithering around and going behind each other's backs . . . again. And there's all this hissing and posturing and rattling. If I were you, I'd let them eat my dust.

For LOVE questions. Are you peeling again? Well scratch my back, and I'll scratch yours. Together forever, right? Friends to the end, for sure. And at this moment you're feeling really tight. But if I were you, I wouldn't close my eyes for a second. And I'd be cautious about making any sudden moves. Though the dance you two are doing may be erotic, it can also hypnotize and intoxicate. It could be harmless for a time. But it may yet bite you in the bitter behind.

For MONEY questions. In this period things are not as tranquil and peaceful as they might appear on the surface. The grain sways gently in the breeze. But if I were you, I wouldn't go in there, not even with a ten-foot stick in my hand. There are snakes in the grass, my friend. (Don't be one of them.) Someone is talking about striking. Someone is about to make a killing. Someone has insider information. Don't get caught with the wrong kind of friends.

For STRATEGY issues. Your mission is of a clandestine, secret, or mysterious nature. It all happens underfoot and in full view, yet it would be dangerous for you if you got caught. Both right and wrong come to play in everything. Opposing forces clash. The "bad guys" take on the "good guys." And, sorry to observe, the ones in the White Hats don't always win. If you must strike out, do it for truth, justice, and light. Do it on account of the principle.

MAYAN   AZTEC

SIGN F Bunch 6	🁢 Death Cimi	🁢 Death Miquiztli
Direction: North		Color: White

Key Date: 13 Cimi, 14 Mac—General Motors restructures, 70,000 jobs cut (Dec. 18, 1991).

HOROSCOPE

Issues of life and death are involved. Some things will be decided. Some things will resolve. Some, dissolve. And some will disappear for good. Not all terminations are fatal. The weather is nothing to speak of. The day favors a love that goes beyond the grave. The thought is: Leave behind what you cannot take along.

For WORK questions. It could mean "heads will roll" around here soon. But more than likely, it will be a small death. A boss leaves. A key player quits. The company gets bought out. The store changes hands, and then its name. It's an identity crisis of some kind. The old way of doing things is out, but the new way is not necessarily fully defined yet. Say good riddance to all that was bad about the past. And say a fond farewell to all that was good for as long as it lasted.

For LOVE questions. This one is history. Perhaps you feel a loss in your heart. Perhaps you feel a catch in your throat. And maybe a tear or two rolls down your cheek. A period of separation is implied. Every relationship brings its share of grief, as well as joy. And this is a sad moment—for both of you, you know. May it not yet turn to bitterness.

For MONEY questions. In this period, things are pretty dead. Not much activity is in progress. Assets are frozen for a time. The offices are closed. And you'll have to wait to find out how you stand. The will is read. The bottom line tells all. It is as clear as black ink on newsprint. It's a done deal now.

For STRATEGY issues. Your mission is to put an end to something that has occupied your time. An old habit, tie, or bond perhaps . . . something you have put off reckoning (or coming to terms) with, for lo, these many years. Some fear the inevitable, while others court it. Each day is a new chance to alter the human destiny. Sinners, repent. Saints, perfect. Poor souls, nourish. Disbelievers, find comfort in the odds. All forms of resistance fail in the end. For what will be, will be. If not one fate, then another.

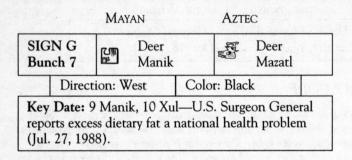

	MAYAN		AZTEC	
SIGN G **Bunch 7**		Deer Manik		Deer Mazatl
Direction: West			Color: Black	

Key Date: 9 Manik, 10 Xul—U.S. Surgeon General reports excess dietary fat a national health problem (Jul. 27, 1988).

HOROSCOPE

The day occurs against an ideological backdrop. Facts of life are incontestable, but truth changes, age to age. Do you believe everything you hear? . . . and everything they say? The weather will be mostly clear, with an occasional flurry of activity. The day favors a love on the run. The thought is: Best to keep your own tail down . . . but your head high.

For **WORK** *questions.* Somebody's hightailing it. Watch out for falling rocks, for debris, and especially for roadkill. Somebody's been running around without any supervision. Someone's gone out of control, maybe even shooting off at the mouth or from the hip. Some think they have the license. But all things serve a purpose in the larger scheme. And those who stick their necks out take their own risks. It could mean the workforce needs to be thinned out again. To be a fighting machine, one can never be too lean . . . or too mean.

For **LOVE** *questions.* Oh, dear. But, darling. Sweetheart! The two of you bump into each other at dawn and dusk . . . providing the moon is right. Well, better to be fleet than fleeting. And better to go quietly about your own business than become a constant intrusion on each other's space. Don't let the distance fool you. It is not aversion but introversion. And don't let the silence trouble you. It is good to feel peaceful in each other's company. Keep an ear out for intruders.

For **MONEY** *questions.* In this period things become dear. Every little bit counts. Every little piece needs to be used. And it wouldn't hurt to utter a silent prayer for the blessings that you have. In times like this, the things that really count and actually matter tend to come to the fore. Reduce the excess fat. Tighten your belt. Cut back. Slender down. There are times of plenty, and there are times when less works just as well. This is one of them, and you know which.

For **STRATEGY** *issues.* Your mission is to blend in as much as you can with your surroundings. Go about your own business. Try not to get yourself noticed by the wrong kind of people. And don't ever place yourself in front of the spotlight. We can all stand to be a little shy, at least about some things. And we can all identify with Disney's deer. It's something subliminal. Or maybe it's just what the mind reads into things. The sign is Deer. Are you going to shoot it? or pet it?

	MAYAN		AZTEC	
SIGN H **Bunch 8**		Rabbit Lamat		Rabbit Tochtli
Direction: South			Color: Yellow	
Key Date: 5 Lamat, 6 Pop—47 nations meet to organize the UN (Apr. 25, 1945).				

HOROSCOPE

Things get together, come together, or even ride off into the sunset together by the time this day is done. New periods are started. New eras are born. Old chapters come to a timely close. The day favors acquisitions and mergers. A love is repositioned. The weather changes with the moon. The thought is: Everything old renews again.

———————

For **WORK** *questions.* Oh, I know some days it seems like everyone has gone down the rabbit hatch. Some days it even seems like everyone is hopping just to hop. And someone's always getting caught in the supply closet with someone else. The grass is always greener.... Such is life. In such a diverse environment, it takes diversity to fit in. Don't be afraid to show your colors. Go ahead and shine.

For LOVE questions. It's just like in the movies. But don't be surprised if this affair is over before it's even intermission. Rabbits like to proliferate as fast as they can, then part and go their separate ways. The events here occur in a predictable, time-honored sequence. From innuendo to expectation to shared experience, the sequence of events is repeated and repeated. Keep one eye on the clock and the other on the moon, and you'll have all the clues you need. All the rest is written in the eyes.

For MONEY questions. In this period the financial situation is bullish. It calls for bold, decisive, aggressive moves. If you think you're being premature, it's too late to speculate. Investments you started recently are likely to come to early fruition, paying off manyfold for the relatively small effort you put in. If not now, then give it one more moon. Bear in mind that the market is cyclical. Chart performance from the past, and project your earnings forward. Then close your eyes, and Point-n-Click.

For STRATEGY issues. Your mission is of the most central and critical kind. Yet the task is not very complex. And you don't need a rule book to master it. In fact, you can pretty much play this one by ear... eyes, nose, throat, and other vital parts. The drama of your life unfolds, scene to scene, in a spontaneous and instantaneous way. But you better take precautions in the Age of AIDS, air raids, and other sneak attacks. I know it's tempting to freeze in your tracks, but sooner or later you'll have to react.

	MAYAN		AZTEC	
SIGN I **Bunch 9**	🔲	Rain Muluc	☞	Rain Atl
Direction: East		Color: Red		

Key Date: 6 Muluc, 7 Ceh—Prohibition ends.
Everything dry is wet again (Dec. 5, 1933).

HOROSCOPE

The world is a powder keg. And there is always thunder somewhere. Is there nothing we can agree upon besides gold medalists? If the weather is dreary, read poetry, listen to sad songs, and mix tears with the rain. The day favors a love based on matters of principle. The thought is: Ain't a fit night out for man nor beast.

For WORK questions. When it's not raining, it's pouring. And if it's not pouring, well, then it's a dry spell. Any change in conditions spells a relief of some kind . . . for a while. Too much of a good thing is not necessarily better than too little. To grow in any job is to experience it from all sides. If the work climate cooperates, you should have a good year. But even if this one's a dud, there's always next year. Nothing stays up forever, and nothing bottoms out for long. At least, let's pray not.

For LOVE questions. Love likes a good rain. Love likes the little patter on the windowpane. And, well, if the electricity goes out, who necessarily would complain? When the tube has been silenced, and the computers have shut themselves down, it's best to take it as a sign. Light candles. Tell ghost stories. Toast marshmallows. And share the same blankey. The best candle lasts longer than a single night; so does the true love of your life. If I were you two, we'd turn in early tonight so that we could . . . listen to the rain on the roof.

For MONEY questions. In this period things will trickle down to you—maybe even a tax cut! In fact, there is the possibility of being showered—maybe even deluged—with, in this case, financial blessings. If you see twenty-dollar bills raining from the sky, stop and pick them up—they're for you. Rain is a good sign, in general. It is a thing to say thanks over . . . and for.

For STRATEGY issues. Your mission is to constantly change and adjust to prevailing conditions. There are gentle rains. There are drizzles. There are cloudbursts. And there are piddles. It is amazing, the range and variation that's required to get the job done. No two situations are ever exactly the same. And most plans take some twists and turns before they finish their natural—but unique—course. Monitor the sonar, radar, or whatever instrument you use to chart the path of a work in progress. Also, keep your eye on the horizon.

	MAYAN		AZTEC	
SIGN J **Bunch 10**	🂠	Dog Oc	🐕	Dog Itzcuintli
	Direction: North		Color: White	
Key Date: 8 Oc, 18 Pax—Evangelist Swaggart confesses he has sinned (Feb. 21, 1988).				

HOROSCOPE

There are good dogs, bad dogs, and mad dogs. There are top dogs, under-dogs, dirty dogs, lapdogs, show dogs. And each one will have its day. You, too, will exhibit your tendencies. The weather will seem hot, even if it is not unseasonably warm. The day favors a love that's on the prowl. The thought is: If you hear the call of the wild, tilt up your head and bay back.

For WORK questions. You're either in the doghouse or you're running with a pack of wolves. Perhaps the product is a dog? Or, dawgone it, maybe you just can't teach an old one new tricks. If someone throws you a bone, retrieve it. But don't snarl if they start demanding more of you in return. A pat on the back had better go a long way, because more lucrative rewards are harder to get. Conditions require dedication and devotion to the job, but they don't require you to slaver all over the boss. Keep a civil tongue.

For LOVE questions. Puppy love is not just for puppies, you know. And no matter how old you get, or how many times you've gone through the same paces, it can still excite you like the first time. When will you learn? Hopefully never, since no two encounters are ever alike. And no two situations turn out quite the same. You can walk the same block every night, and still there's something new and different to see. Dogs do not mate for life. But then again, they can be taught to shake hands, instead of sniff crotches. Be as loyal and trustworthy as you can.

For MONEY questions. Don't be so quick to call it a dog . . . at least not until you have watched it behave for a few days. Orders you give to buy, sell, or pay will be obeyed. Make sure your instructions are clear. There could be a little bonus or an extra treat of some kind thrown your way. Receive it graciously, no matter how small the scrap.

For STRATEGY issues. Your mission is to find a place for yourself in the heart of another—and once you grab hold of it, to never willingly let go. Not every animal takes an immediate liking to everyone. And there is no forcing an affection that is not felt. A boy and his dog know what they know. The chemistry has to be there, and you'll simply know when it's right. But will you ever acknowledge? Or will you choose to fight?

234

	MAYAN		AZTEC	
SIGN K Bunch 11	🐵	Monkey Chuen	🐵	Monkey Ozomatli

Direction: West	Color: Black

Key Date: 5 Chuen, 14 Uo—Cheetah's pal Tarzan (Johnny Weismuller) born (Jun. 2, 1904).

HOROSCOPE

Chimps will be chimps. Chumps will be chumps. The primate in each of us comes out this day, sometimes as comic relief or irony. Watch out for tragic flaws, Achilles' heels, and fatal errors. Bombshells drop. Plans backfire. The weather will turn by the end of the day. If you see a funnel cloud, get out of the way. The day favors a love that is superficial. The thought is: The soul is willing and the flesh is weak.

For WORK questions. Sometimes it seems as if you're just hanging around, one-armed from a limb. Sometimes a warning call comes down the grapevine, and everybody chatters . . . and scatters. Whoever pounds his chest the hardest makes the decisions for today. It's an environment where everyone eats banana bread instead of meat. (And nobody had better light a cigarette.) Some invent solutions. Some make rules. Some even come up with new tools. But most just play with their computers. You can always handle it yourself.

For LOVE questions. It looks like monkey business to me. But which kind? Monkeys have no rules in this department, and anything goes this time. Haven't we come a long way, baby? And aren't we better off, pal? No, ma'am. Yes, sir. Take an about-turn . . . right about now. What I have to say here is not politically correct. And neither are your true thoughts on the subject.

For MONEY questions. In this period, watch for shenanigans. Shocking revelations of former mistresses, wives, and houseboys cause ratings to fluctuate for a time . . . at least until the shock value wears off or until the next crisis takes center stage. Follow politics as well as other sports. Keep your eye on the latest medical reports. And watch the marketplace respond . . . according to plan? The Fed may control the flow of money, but it has no corner on monkey business.

For STRATEGY issues. Your mission is to help your species evolve. So be the strongest and fittest you can be. Or else use more of that bigger brain of yours. Monkeys are social creatures, but they are also prone to "antisocial" behavior. We can't seem to get along with or without each other. Even where there could be harmony in our own houses, we create stress. Some even thrive on it. It would be easier if we could convince everybody to think the same way about everything and behave just exactly right at all moments. But wouldn't that kind of take the sport—and the adventure—out of it?

MAYAN			AZTEC		
SIGN L **Bunch 12**	🔲	Broom Eb	🌿	Grass Malinalli	
	Direction: South		Color: Yellow		
Key Date: 4 Eb, 15 Mac—Apollo astronauts, broadcasting from the moon, read from the book of Genesis (Dec. 24, 1968).					

HOROSCOPE

Great feats occur this day. Legends that are later made are born now. We achieve a harvest of some kind. You will be thrilled, amazed, enthralled, and saddened—all at the same time. The weather will be cooler than average . . . and drier than normal. The day favors a love that lasts long enough to tell its story. The thought is: Every moment has the potential for glory.

———————

For WORK questions. Here today, gone tomorrow. The world is full of ephemera, like headlines in the newspaper that tomorrow will line the bottom of the birdcage. Today's crises become the folders filling up tomorrow's files. And when the corporate history is written, what will it say about your times? What you do here is like dry grass blowing in the wind. It is time to mow things down and start all over again.

For LOVE questions. Memories. The petals in the scrapbook are dried and pressed now. And the best photos of the times you want to remember are in plastic sleeves. No one but the two of you will ever know what the particular instant meant—or what it still means. Memories are like old jeans and a favorite shirt. Both have been lived in . . . and through. Carry a picture in your wallet. Or a lock of hair. It is dry grass now. Remember.

For MONEY questions. In this period things are inclined to dry. A source of funding goes away. A revenue stream dries up. In general, things come of age now. A fine wine matures. A cheese ages gracefully. Investments that have matured fully should be cashed in. The crop should be harvested, neither too late nor too soon. As always, timing is everything. Let the thing itself tell you when the moment is right. Listen to the dry grass when it whispers in your ear.

For STRATEGY issues. Your mission is to come full circle. It may seem as if the seeds you plant are so small that they have no chance of becoming anything but bird food. Plant many, and the odds will shift in your favor. Some sprouts will actually take root and turn into slender shoots. Some of these will escape the rabbits. And, to make a long story short, eventually some will live long enough to tan in the low light of fall. We'll make them into brooms. For the time has come, my friend, to clean house. Sweep out the cobwebs. And empty the ashes. In a little while there will be no traces left. It will all be behind you. It will all be dry grass—except for the memory.

	MAYAN		AZTEC	
SIGN M Bunch 13	🔲	Reed Ben	▦	Reed Acatl
	Direction: East		Color: Red	
Key Date: 4 Ben, 1 Ceh—John F. Kennedy assassinated in Dallas motorcade (Nov. 22, 1963).				

HOROSCOPE

Dire, dread, and painful events may turn as easily to triumph as to tragedy. The best and worst in us comes out this day. Some will dare to be brave. Some will only be bold. The weather will be darker than it first appears. The day favors a love that endures beyond the present moment. The thought is: What is the price of your beliefs?

For WORK questions. The environment is like quicksand. You're never exactly sure of your foothold. Yet many things can and do flourish in this place. And there can be an eco-balance. Reeds do their best work in shallow places. (They are a bit hollow themselves.) But in the right hands and between the right lips, they can make deep, beautiful music. The important thing is to all get tuned to the same pitch. At a critical moment, try not to squeak.

For LOVE questions. You may feel a song in your heart. Or was that a wolf whistle from behind you? This relationship might yet prove light and hollow, but for the moment it is firm of resolve. A critical test will be telling. Love must measure up and prove itself on a regular basis to survive long. Try not to bite your tongue too hard. And be careful not to injure anything else while you are at it. (Blow in my ear, and I'll follow you everywhere.)

For MONEY questions. In this period things are inclined to go down the tube. Something drains your accounts. A leak occurs somewhere. Or something is siphoned off when nobody is looking. A catheter is inserted (ouch!). Or you at least feel victim to a punch below the belt. Reeds present you with a difficult challenge. It's time once again to prove that you can make it on your own. I leave you to your own devices.

For STRATEGY issues. Your mission is critical. The reed is passed to you. And you must take things into your own hands now. A rite of passage may be involved. An initiation may need to be gotten through. Or an entrance exam may require your full attention for a few nights. Reeds are powerful signs in and of themselves. They indicate that where there is will, there can also be wherewithal. Remain brave. Keep a stiff upper lip. I know you can do what you need to do.

MAYAN   AZTEC

SIGN N Bunch 14		Jaguar Ix		Ocelot Ocelotl	
Direction: North			Color: White		
Key Date: 7 Ix, 2 Muan—Supreme Court rules that citizens may use VCR's at home to record TV programs without infringing on copyright laws (Jan. 17, 1984).					

HOROSCOPE

The day is surprising. Anything can happen, but especially a random occurrence. Things drop out of the trees. There will always be the occasional coincidence. But does it always alter destiny or change fate? The day favors a love that takes you down as well as up. The weather is partly sunny. The thought is: An error is not necessarily an accident. An incident is not necessarily a statement.

For WORK questions. Sometimes it is hard to tell the tigers from the pussycats around here, especially if someone has gone without a timely lunch. The terrain is rocky. But Jaguars and Ocelots both like to climb. From the powerful heights of these rocky cliffs, everything below looks so small and vulnerable. Someone is climbing the ladder again. Someone else is lying in wait. Watch out for low-hanging branches. Try not to get spotted.

For LOVE questions. I can see that there is magic between you. But when cats like you go at it, it's hard to tell whether you are courting and sparking or sparring and fighting. A bucket of cold water on both of you! Don't you know the walls are thin as romance novels? And your neighbors don't want to hear you going at it all night <u>and</u> all day.

For MONEY questions. Some fat cats are born, while others are made. In this period stocks may climb, returns could mount, or things might even drop into your lap. If so, purr all the way to the bank. It's also possible, however, that someone you need to see about a money matter is playing cat and mouse with you. Keep leaving voice mail until you get an answer.

For STRATEGY issues. Your mission is to keep others guessing. In general, take the position that gives you a sustainable competitive advantage. When the opportunity you have been waiting for comes along, pounce. There is the possibility that several efforts will pay off at once. If it's too much for you to handle by yourself, call for backup.

	MAYAN		AZTEC	
SIGN O Bunch 15	🔲	Eagle Men	🦅	Eagle Quauhtli
	Direction: West		Color: Black	
Key Date: 7 Men, 3 Uayeb—Civil Rights Act becomes law. No discrimination in housing allowed (Apr. 11, 1968).				

HOROSCOPE

You soar with the eagles. But in this world, the sky is home to both hawks and doves, and you are free to choose sides. For some they come . . . for some they call. Lofty attitudes are respected—the sky is the limit and provides quite a range. The weather will be subject to updrafts and tailwinds. The day favors a love that can be both uplifting and frightening. The thought is: Seek to achieve your highest level of integrity.

For WORK questions. Everything ought to be clear sailing around here—at least for a while. But better buckle up just in case we encounter some unexpected turbulence. If someone in a high place unfurls a protective wing, crawl under. (But never take your eyes off the talons.) There are some people who have just been gliding along. Make sure you flap your wings fast when the conditions suddenly, surely, change. Watch out for the headwinds and the downdraft.

For LOVE questions. This is a marriage made in the heavens. Make your choice. Take your pick. But then stick with it. Stand with your woman. Be beside your man. Provide for each other. Maintain the night watch together. Divide the chores of the day. Share the same couch, the same dinner, and the same mattress ticking. And God willing, grow old together. Hand your best characteristics down to those who look up to you, follow after you, or take your lead. What's the secret? We're all dying to know.

For MONEY questions. In this period the sky's the only limit you need to fear or worry over. And right now the ceiling looks endless. All's well and good as long as you have the funds to cover yourself...or at least the credit lines to keep you afloat. Try not to hock the family estate over dinner and cocktails at eight. Interest rates, too, have been known to soar...and airplanes are not the only things that ever crash. Boom follows bust. And bust follow boom. Eat, drink, and be merry till then.

For STRATEGY issues. Your mission is to catch hold of a sky dream. But be cautious about latching on to someone else's dream catcher. (Who knows where those feathers have been! or what department of your interior might get bent out of whack.) Dreams are one of those things that each must experience by and for oneself. For no one but you can get inside your own head (and let's keep it that way). Soar as you must, and as your free spirit takes you. It is your right, honor, duty, and privilege. Looking up with mouths agape, we marvel at the graceful way you cut a curl.

MAYAN   AZTEC

SIGN P Bunch 16	Owl Cib	Vulture Cozcaquauhtli
Direction: South		Color: Yellow
Key Date: 3 Cib, 4 Uo—H-bomb predecessor exploded in the Pacific (May 12, 1951).		

HOROSCOPE

Diplomacy rules this day. Everything that appears to be conspiracy is not. Ignorance and absurdity also contribute. When a warning of impending doom passes around, some smack their lips. The weather will not matter much in comparison to this, but it may contribute to the mood. The day favors a love that is wide at the eyes and pointed at the chin. The thought is: Desire feeds on itself, rather than go hungry.

For WORK questions. Shadows fall across the office landscape. They are the shadows of hawks, crows, and vultures . . . and these are not the friendliest of beasts. There is a wise one who seems to have eyes in the back of the head, as well as in the front. Listen carefully when the Wise Old Owl speaks. The waiting and wondering is like a dark cloud that hovers. The writing may not be clearly on the wall yet, but you can already read the effects in the eyes of the beholders.

For LOVE questions. All you can do now is watch and wait . . . hope and pray. We never know for sure, do we? And just because the signs point one way or the other at the moment does not mean that things are chiseled in stone yet. Seek the advice of someone who is well connected. Perhaps a few strings can be pulled. And if all else fails, there is always the hope of a miracle.

For MONEY questions. There is the possibility of an inheritance, but you may wish to forgo the conditions of receiving it. At the very least, you stand to gain from something that someone else has done in your name. There could be an investigation, an audit, or an inquiry before you are off the hook. If the thought of making a certain investment gives you a bad taste in your mouth or an ill feeling in your gut, better pass it up. Stand watch, keep vigil, and wait.

For STRATEGY issues. Your mission is to prepare for the inevitable. Someone is looking over your shoulder now. Someone is just waiting and watching to see how you will do. Someone may have the idea that it's just a matter of time. Review papers, policies, and records. Get your books in order. Ambulance chasers—and other diabolical critters—may be involved. Trust only a revered counsel . . . and even then, only so far.

	MAYAN		AZTEC	
SIGN Q **Bunch 17**	🜂	Earthquake Caban	⋈	Earthquake Ollin
	Direction: East		Color: Red	
Key Date: 12 Caban, 10 Uo—U.S. Supreme Court orders school integration (May 17, 1954).				

HOROSCOPE

> *Things are shaken up this day. Knees tremble. Hips wobble. Minds are made to bend. Not only storms can be doozies. And if you feel a sudden shiver . . . rate it on a scale from 1 to 13. Movers and shakers rattle our mirrors from time to time. And in between, the weather relieves the monotony. The day favors a love that is natural but hard to size up. The thought is: How can you ever be sure? So ya might as well trust.*

For WORK questions. The environment around here is relatively predictable. There are times and seasons for everything. And in general, things roll along more or less evenly and predictably. Though a sporadic rumble is heard from the ranks from time to time, most would-be revolutions peter out after the initial uprising. It is the rare one that shakes everything to the foundations and brings the tower personnel to their knees. Wait long enough, and there will be a big one.

For LOVE questions. It is like a house overlooking the Pacific. The balcony continues to dangle over the creeping tides for another night and a day. (But . . . danger! No climbing up the shaky cliffs underneath.) Still, red sky at night, sailor's delight. In the gathering mist, the light from the glass walls travels wider than far. Best to hold your breath at a critical moment. Careful not to shake the bedrock too hard. And never utter a note that would shatter the wineglass on the nightstand.

For MONEY questions. In this period you may feel a few tremors as the market responds to the latest political bombshell dropped inside the Capital Beltway or out at the bunkers in Crystal City. Some will scurry now. A few will panic. But most will continue to hustle. The market could rise or fall with the word. Either place your bets or remove your ante from the kitty—but do it calmly. There will always be threats and rumors, but most of them amount to nothing more than a momentary tremble. And it is mostly political fortunes that are made and lost here.

For STRATEGY issues. Your mission is to come between opposing forces...to strike a balance between opposites. A lot of stress and tension are involved. The law of gravity also plays a part. In the event of an emergency, proceed calmly but quickly to the nearest exit sign. You do not want to be trapped inside a box you have built for yourself. Do not ignore an advance warning. Something stable starts to shake. Something brittle starts to break. When a gap tries to close itself, step out of the middle.

MAYAN		AZTEC	
SIGN R Bunch 18	☒ Blade Eznab	◀	Flint Tecpatl
Direction: North		Color: White	
Key Date: 9 Eznab, 16 Kayab—Doctors at Harvard announce that participation by women in athletics endangers their health (Mar. 31, 1906).			

HOROSCOPE

Things divide, split, and sever us this day. Things cut clean to the soul, even if the tool we are using is not a knife, arrow, or spearpoint. Words may sound mightier than they actually are. But nothing beats a truth when it's wielding a scalpel. The weather may or may not be a tactical consideration. Which way do the winds blow? And where does sentiment lie? The day favors a love on the cutting edge. The thought is: Every tool is a weapon in disguise.

For WORK questions. This is a manufacturing environment. (How quaint in the Information Age.) It takes a certain stroke to flake a rock into a blade. And it takes firm, fluid hands to throw a pot on the wheel. Long-lost arts are known for their comebacks. Keep your nose to the grindstone, as it were. Punch the clock. Skip your break. And put quality above quota. There's offshore price competition, you know. But a cottage industry is favored. You get out what you put in.

For LOVE questions. It is like a dart, an arrow, or a knife—all three kinds of love go as quick to the heart and as sharp to the bone. Love rips and rends the fabric from the fasteners. Love first crawls all over, then gets under, the skin. But love can also strip clean and tan the hide hung up to dry. Love should not, but wants to, change the object of its desire. Pleasure, pain, and ecstasy mix. A love turns sharp before it starts to cut.

For MONEY questions. In this period you will have to be sharp as a Swiss army knife, as direct as an arrow, and as effective as a razor. Contractual matters are involved. A legal argument requires its own set of weapons and wits. Try not to be obvious in going for the jugular. (Is that a pair of brass knuckles in your pocket?... or have you just gotten into *Oracles*?)

For STRATEGY issues. Your mission is to cut into things, cut off things, or cut through things. There is not much difference between a tool and a weapon. A new invention may be involved...or a novel technology. Everything can be employed for both good and ill. What's the latest rage in the streets? But if you are on the cutting edge, be careful you do not also bleed. (You know how I hate the sight....)

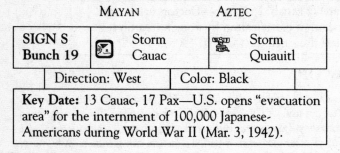

	MAYAN		AZTEC
SIGN S **Bunch 19**		Storm Cauac	Storm Quiauitl

Direction: West	Color: Black

Key Date: 13 Cauac, 17 Pax—U.S. opens "evacuation area" for the internment of 100,000 Japanese-Americans during World War II (Mar. 3, 1942).

HOROSCOPE

You'll be talking about this day for a while to come. Events are unforgettable... unbelievable... sometimes even inconceivable. Controversy brews in every crockpot, pressure cooker, and microwave. No wonder the lid blows off something somewhere every so many days. Don't even ask about the weather! The day favors a love that is stormy. The thought is: As it is above us, so it is below.

For WORK questions. It looks like a hurricane's blown through here. Is everybody okay? Do you need anything? And can I lend a helping hand? Perhaps it's not a total disaster, but it's still quite a mess. Independent contractors, temporary help, outside labor, or troops in reserve could be called in to bail you out. The gods may have been angry once, but they, too, are silent for now. With heads bowed and backs bent, we salvage what is left and go on with our lives.

For LOVE questions. It was wild while it lasted, wasn't it? (And believe me, I really had a blast. In fact, at one point, I even heard the shutters flap.) Some loves swirl through your life, some even run on unabated for a while, and some, from time to time, come round again. A whirlwind romance may be indicated. Watch out you are not devastated in its wake. Or it could be a whirlwind courtship, in which case we'll have to see how long the fair-weather friendship holds up. All others, beware of touching the wrong nerve.

For MONEY questions. In this period there will be cause for tracking conditions elsewhere than in your immediate neighborhood. A tropical depression may or may not turn into something that affects you directly. You'll just have to keep an eye on it. Watch. And wait. And see. Keep an ear out for sirens in your mind. Only then must you seriously consider getting out while you're still ahead.

For STRATEGY issues. Your mission is to withstand, overcome, and override the obstacles and temporary setbacks of life. You will walk out of a difficult situation by using your wits and exercising common sense. But if you want to fly, it will have to be by the seat of your pants. Try to control your own rage, temper, and foul moods. Though you may be tempted to look into the eye of the storm, once you get that close, it will be impossible to outrun.

	MAYAN		AZTEC	
SIGN T Bunch 20		Lord Ahau		Flower Xochitl
Direction: South		Color: Yellow		

Key Date: 6 Ahau, 3 Yaxkin—American women can vote, over 70 years after the birth of the suffrage movement (Aug. 26, 1920).

HOROSCOPE

*Wow! What a finish! Stunning and stupendous things happen this day.
Destinies are achieved. Benchmarks are passed. Landmarks are reached.
Rites of passage are survived, and their tale told. Not only the weather
should be taken for better or worse. The day favors a love that alters everything from here on in. The thought is: Do what it takes to prove your point.*

For WORK questions. We never promised you a bed of roses, but this
is getting awfully close. The right people get together at the right time
and the right place. As if by magic, they all cooperate long enough to
get an idea off the ground. What happens here changes things in a profound and lasting way. But it is a special situation that would be difficult
to duplicate again. It's a time for pulling together to reach a lofty goal.

For LOVE questions. What can I say? It's perfect for you. It fits you like
a glove. It suits you. You wear each other well. You match. You go
together. This is the sort of love that could prove legendary. But watch
out. Others are jealous.

For MONEY questions. In this period some will rise and some will fall.
Though you might be surprised which stocks, bonds, and brokers go
which way, yours <u>will</u> go your way. The ticker tape blows through the
streets. Light candles at your place of worship. Bring flowers to the altar.
Tithe 10% (but tip 15). And render to Caesar, Caesar's.

For STRATEGY issues. Your mission is to do something special,
unique, novel, and successful. Everything seems to hinge on a few key
dates, an important innovation, a significant observation, or a critical
statement. Many aspire to greatness, but those who least expect it are
the ones who often achieve it with the biggest bang.

The 13 Day Numbers

		MAYAN	AZTEC
Day Number 1 **Bunch 1**	•	Hun	Ce
Key Date: 1 Akbal, 1 Pax—Pentagon unveils first digital computer (Feb. 14, 1946).			

HOROSCOPE

Amazing things happen on number "one" days. Heroes rise. Political power shifts. Legends are made. . . . Weissmuller sets three world records in a single day. The Mets win the series! and New York is back in the ball game. Shah flees Iran. Five burglars arrested at the Watergate break-in. Plane crashes into Potomac . . . and a hero jumps in to the rescue. Chuck Berry and Dolly Parton are born. Rock 'n' roll lives . . . and so does Country.[1]
The beat goes on. . . .

For WORK questions. Smokin' now. Your Day Sign is smoking like the leaves under kindling, just before the fire ignites. Things here are going to be very hot. There is going to be a moment of glory coming up. The conditions are present here and now. But you must bring it together. Both history and destiny are in the making. And you are in the right place at the right time to witness and be a part of these exciting times.

---

[1]Johnny Weissmuller sets three swimming records: Apr. 5, 1927 ("1 Reed"). After years of waiting for a comeback, New York again takes the pennant: Oct. 16, 1969 ("1 Rabbit"). Shah flees Iran, following riots and strikes: Jan. 30, 1979 ("1 Alligator"). Watergate burglary: Jun. 17, 1972 ("1 Night"). Plane crashes into the Potomac; unknown rescuer becomes popular hero: Jan. 13, 1982 ("1 Lord"). Early rocker Chuck Berry is born: Oct. 18, 1926 ("1 Corn"). Country singer Dolly Parton is born: Jan. 19, 1946 ("1 Earthquake").

For LOVE questions. No smokin' after. Your Day Sign is modified by haze, mist, and the smoke of rising incense. Your prayers may be answered. (It is all in the eye of the beholder.) But the sign may be masked, obscured, or veiled. Myth and mystery are intertwined. Your sign is best observed through gauze, gossamer, or bedroom eyes. Why spoil the moment . . . or the illusion? You may have to stretch a point to reach your own conclusion.

For MONEY questions. Lightin' up. Whatever your Day Sign is today, it wants to be a winner . . . of one kind or another. There's a number "1" in front of it—and how many "0's" behind? The Day Sign this number accompanies will indicate the type of success you can expect . . . and the sort of investment you ought to make. Hope springs, forever and a day, eternal. Dream on. Dream big. And go for the goal.

For STRATEGY issues. Smokin' mirrors. The advice from your Day Sign is "right on" this time. But you may think it's just a trick being played on your eyes or on your mind. A mere coincidence. An uncanny fluke. A sign reveals itself for what it is. But each views it from a different angle. And not everyone is ready to see it for what it is. You be the judge. You make the call.

	MAYAN	AZTEC
Day Number 2 **Bunch 2**	• • • Ca	Ome
Key Date: 2 Ahau, 3 Cumku—European Common Market treaty signed in Rome (Mar. 25, 1957).		

HOROSCOPE

Partnerships are favored on number "two" days. Julie marries David at the White House. Chuck takes Di to be his lawful wife. Geraldine Ferraro runs on the Democratic ticket in the number-two slot. The Boy Scouts are incorporated. Blacks can now join the American Bowling Congress. Reagan is reelected. Mussolini arrested. And Elvis is in the army now.[2] Not all alliances are holy, and this day favors partnerships of all kinds.

---

[2]Nixon marries Eisenhower at the White House: Dec. 22, 1968 ("2 Dog"). Prince Charles makes Di his princess: July 29, 1981 ("2 Broom"). First woman nominated to run as vice president: July 12, 1984 ("2 Monkey"). Boy Scouts of

For **WORK** *questions.* Double vision. Your Day Sign is modified today by its opposing angle. Even the welcome news is somewhat tinged. Good guys and bad guys both duke it out, and the victor is not always an enlightened despot. Be a little sensitive when you choose sides. There are both undercurrents and riptides. Form a partnership with care.

For **LOVE** *questions.* Identical twins. Your Day Sign is influenced today by its mirror image. True opposites can and do attract. And stranger bedfellows have been known to match up (though not necessarily for more than a couple of nights). Best friends are born, not made. And only identical twins can ever truly relate. Friendships, courtships, and even marriages may be involved. The day was made for couples.

For **MONEY** *questions.* Two-dollar bills. The Day Sign you have received is multiplied by a compounding effect. An investment may eventually double on you. Or you may double-down your bet. The market is as odd this day as a two-dollar bill. Keep one in your wallet as a counter...and a reminder.

For **STRATEGY** *issues.* Double play. The advice from your Day Sign is double-sided, double-edged, and double-tongue-and-grooved. You may have to straddle the fence on this one. You may have to choose between the simple truth and its slick illusion. Point and counterpoint are at work. Someone who tries to steal second base risks being tagged...in a double play.

	MAYAN		AZTEC
Day Number 3 Bunch 3	**⋮**	Ox	Yei
Key Date: 3 Muluc, 17 Mac. The Soviet Union is dissolved (Dec. 21, 1991).			

America incorporated: Feb. 8, 1910 ("2 Rabbit"). Bowling Congress accepts blacks: May 12, 1950 ("2 Monkey"). Reagan elected for second term: Nov. 6, 1984 ("2 Rabbit"). Fascist dictator Mussolini deposed: July 25, 1943 (also "2 Rabbit"). Elvis reports for active duty: Mar. 24, 1958 ("2 Corn").

HOROSCOPE

The most amazing things happen on a "three" day. The very first car is made in Detroit. The moving pictures now speak . . . and the flicks have sync. The Mona Lisa is lifted out of its frame. Janis Joplin found dead . . . John Lennon is silenced. Hitler is elected President. Artificial insemination with frozen sperm is reported. And the war in the Gulf makes headlines.[3] Everything that goes on around us affects us. Only if we respond do we effect back.

For WORK questions. Three on a match. The Day Sign you have received today could just as soon stand for its counterpart. Where equal and opposite forces are concerned, there could be retaliation. Aggressive action begets its consequence. And violent reaction is not always possible to contain. But gratefully, it is also difficult to sustain. Things will even out in the end. They always have. They always will. We just need to live long enough to see it.

For LOVE questions. Three strikes, you're out. Your Day Sign is accompanied by three chances, three wishes, and three regrets. There is the possibility that whatever is indicated will backfire. Things go full circle here before they are done. One you admire greatly runs the risk of being victimized somehow. Controversy surrounds all solid affairs.

For MONEY questions. The odds are three to one. Your Day Sign is modified by a three-count. A champion will eventually be proclaimed. But it could take a knock-down, drag-out fight to achieve total victory. Three of a kind may be a winning hand, but it can be beaten easily by a flush. Try to keep a poker face.

For STRATEGY issues. Triple header . . . triple play. The advice of your Day Sign has three angles, three implications, and three views. It can be taken in all three ways. The clash of three opposing or competing views usually results in a compromise, created from the fallout of their collision. Consider both your sign and its opposite, but then combine the two and read between the lines.

---

[3]First Ford Model T comes off the line in Detroit: Aug. 12, 1908 ("3 Night"). Jolson premiers in *The Jazz Singer*—the screen also talks: Oct. 6, 1927 ("3 Earthquake"). Mona Lisa stolen (by a starving artist) from the Louvre in Paris: Aug. 22, 1911 ("3 Rabbit"). Janis Joplin dies of an overdose at 27: Oct. 4, 1970 ("3 Sea Creature"). John Lennon shot and killed outside his New York apartment building: Dec. 8, 1980 ("3 Storm"). Hitler is President of Germany: Aug. 19, 1934 ("3 Death"). Frozen sperm used successfully: Dec. 3, 1953 ("3 Broom"). First full day of the Persian Gulf War: Jan. 17, 1991 ("3 Monkey").

MAYAN   AZTEC

Day Number 4 Bunch 4	⋮	Can	Nahui
Key Date: 4 Imix, 4 Zip—U.S. Surgeon General reports second-hand smoke, a health risk (May 23, 1984).			

HOROSCOPE

Shocking things happen on the "four" days. Jews must wear the gold Star of David, as the Nazis command. Cuban Missile Crisis ends. JFK is shot. And would-be Reagan assassin gets off "by reason of insanity." Michael Jackson is born. Oliver North is found guilty. And 50,000 poor rally at the Lincoln Memorial.[4] What does it take to get our attention . . . let alone our sympathy?

For WORK questions. Cornered. The Day Sign you have drawn is modified by the four things that define its outer limits. Things this day are boxed in. The lines are drawn on the playing field. The limits are set. The rules are known (though not necessarily followed at all times). It's hard to beat four of a kind . . . especially if they're aces.

For LOVE questions. Centered. The Day Sign strikes dead center . . . the nail is hit on the head . . . it's a bull's-eye. Once a target is identified, it still takes a plan to pull it off . . . not to mention skill of execution and that oh-so-critical split-second timing. Four steps are involved in fulfilling your complete desire. Take the first step now.

For MONEY questions. Squared. The Day Sign you have received is modified by each of four separate components. Treat it as an equation to be worked out. What is the missing value? Hint: It's all in the numbers, both the evens and the odds. But are you willing to do the math?

---

[4]Jews ordered to wear yellow stars on their clothes when in public: Sept. 19, 1941 ("4 Jaguar"). Cuban Missile Crisis ends: Oct. 28, 1962 ("4 Night"). JFK assassinated in Dallas: Nov. 22, 1963 ("4 Reed"). John Hinckley found not guilty: June 21, 1982 ("4 Storm"). Michael Jackson born: Aug. 29, 1958 ("4 Air"). Oliver North found guilty (but later pardoned): May 4, 1989 ("4 Rabbit"). Poor People's March on Washington started: June, 25 1968 ("4 Dog").

For STRATEGY issues. Cubed. The advice that your Day Sign attempts to give may not always be welcome ... for sometimes it is "square" when it ought to be smooth on the edges. And sometimes, for all its definition, it's still rather vague. Well, what do ya know! As neatly as it can be defined in general, the world is full of unexpected events and random occurrences. Watch for the things that come at you from outside the box. Try not to be blindsided.

		MAYAN	AZTEC
Day Number 5 Bunch 5	**I**	Ho	Macuilli
Key Date: 5 Ik, 5 Pax—French doctors announce drug for treatment of AIDS (Feb. 8, 1985).			

HOROSCOPE

Fame and infamy mark the "five" days. Japanese attack Pearl Harbor. Nazis burn banned books and take away politically incorrect parents betrayed by their children. Bush declares victory over Iraq. Ben Vereen, Peggy Lee, and Randy Travis are born. Rockefeller Center opens in New York. Marilyn Monroe stars in Gentlemen Prefer Blondes.[5] *We each have our cross to bear.*

For WORK questions. Three of one kind, two of another. The Day Sign is a mixed one. Some grieve. And some cheer. But though it may all seem like a fight between good and evil, there may be other motivations as well. And even good deeds can have negative consequences. Take control of your own destiny by opening yourself to the possibilities.

For LOVE questions. Five-o'clock shadow. The Day Sign you have received carries with it a haunting, brooding feeling. Perhaps you will say later, "I should have known from the start." Each destiny is differ-

---

[5]Japanese attack Pearl Harbor: Dec. 7, 1941 ("5 Reed"). Nazis build bonfires of books at Berlin University: May 10, 1933 ("5 Lord"). Nazis begin to arrest "unfit" parents for failure to teach correct ideology: Nov. 29, 1937 ("5 Corn"). Bush declares blitz over: Feb. 27, 1991 ("5 Broom"). Dancer Ben Vereen born: Oct. 10, 1946 ("5 Sea Creature"). Torch singer Peggy Lee born: May 26, 1920 ("5 Rabbit"). Country singer Randy Travis born: May 4, 1959 ("5 Dog"). Rockefeller Center opens: Nov. 1, 1939. *Gentlemen Prefer Blondes* opens: July 15, 1953 ("5 Monkey").

ent. But always in looking back, you can see that it could have been no other way. All the pieces have always been there. All that is left is to put two and three together for yourself.

For MONEY questions. Give me five. The Day Sign you have received is unqualified, if not incontestable. One side is due to score a victory. But every champion's reign is only temporary. You may place your bets on a sure thing only to discover later that the game was fixed from the start. But there's always the hope you'll find yourself in the winningest part.

For STRATEGY issues. Best three out of five. The advice that your Day Sign attempts to give is that the majority of the message fits this time. One tends to confirm what is already believed. Another tends to seek out the comforting solution. But in general, it is the opinion held by the simple majority that wins out . . . sometimes with bare fists, sometimes with kid gloves.

		MAYAN	AZTEC
Day Number 6 **Bunch 6**	•|	Uc	Chicuace
Key Date: 6 Lamat, 6 Yaxkin—Woodstock Rock Festival in full swing (Aug. 17, 1969).			

HOROSCOPE

After "six" days, things will never be quite the same. Babe Ruth gets sold to the Yankees . . . the Yankees shut out the Series in four games . . . and the players all strike for more pay. Six is the history of baseball: "6 Death," "6 Lord." And "6 Jaguar" beast. It's never been the same since: Kent State. Robert Frost. And what about James Dean? Reagan testifies before Congress: "The Screen Actors Guild is not full of communists."[6] Things have never been the same since. . . . Things never happen the same way twice.

---

[6]Babe Ruth sold to Yankees for $125,000: Jan. 5, 1920 ("6 Death"). Yankees shut out the World Series in four games: Oct. 2, 1932 ("6 Lord"). Baseball players strike—no World Series this year: Aug. 12, 1994 ("6 Jaguar"). Four students killed by National Guardsmen at Kent State while protesting the U.S. invasion of Cambodia: May 4, 1970 ("6 Rabbit"). Yankee Poet Robert Frost is dead: Jan. 29, 1963 ("6 Owl"). Rebel actor James Dean is dead: Sept. 30, 1955 ("6 Blade"). Reagan testifies at Senate Hearings on communist activities: Oct. 23, 1947 ("6 Storm").

For WORK questions. !! Touchdown !! (6 points). Your Day Sign is amplified this time. The best that can be done is attempted...but depending upon the sign, it may be the best of good that is done here, or the worst of bad. And not to complicate things further, but it depends on which side you are on, as to how you'll have to read things this time around. Stand up and be counted—or else stand on the sidelines.

For LOVE questions. And a sixpence...Your choice of Day Sign, along with the number six, tends to be associated with partnerships, but not necessarily those that last. Some associations break up or are split apart; some are bombs, some are duds; some take a walk, and others take a hike. Love doesn't just exist in the fairy tales, but it is the rare story that gets written up. This is a variation on a remembered theme. There is an old record playing in your heart.

For MONEY questions. Six of one, half dozen of another. The Day Sign you have selected this time is qualified by the fact that there are always two ways of looking at everything. List three pros...and three cons for each venture and you will see what I mean. You may feel damned-if-you-do. But, in truth, damned-if-you-don't...You can't even get in the game if you don't choose sides and suit up.

For STRATEGY issues. Deep-six it. The advice your Day Sign attempts to give cannot always be fully understood until after the fact (darn it!). But would you always want to know the ending in advance? And if I were to tell you, could you hurry it?...or delay it? Could you reverse it? Einstein said we might go forward...but never back. The only way to find out where it all ends is to get on with it—your life, that is. Things are a certain way right now. But it is no guarantee of what will be valued tomorrow.

		MAYAN	AZTEC
Day Number 7 **Bunch 7**	**:|**	Uac	Chicome
Key Date: 7 Ix, 2 Pax—The Beatles play their first American concert for a general audience in Washington, D.C., as a warm-up for their appearance the next day on the *Ed Sullivan Show* (Feb. 11, 1964).			

HOROSCOPE

The "seven" days are action-packed. . . . Libya is bombed for the second day, troops land at Normandy, and—numbering 50,000—head for Vietnam . . . North Korea invades South . . . the siege on Waco ends. Occupied Berlin is divided into four zones. . . but in the end no wall can keep the city asunder. The first test-tube baby is born. The bioengineered mouse is perfected. And the Supreme Court rules, yes, you can tape TV programs with your VCR.[7] What would life be without a noble cause . . . or a good fight to the finish?

For WORK questions. Stay until seven o'clock. A sign's got to do what a sign's got to do. Dry Grass burns today. Snake stings. Dog performs. Knife cuts. Reed plays. The vultures gather not a moment too soon. But here and there a miracle occurs. (Lord knows, it does not need to be a big one.) A Day Sign will give you the gist, but the details are sure to amaze and mystify you yet. If life is like a hockey match, then this must be the power play.

For LOVE questions. Seven-year itch. The Day Sign you have received is neither lucky nor unlucky, but the outcome depends on a little of each. For every winner, there's a loser. And for every trick, there's a trap. It is the more untenable situation that will ultimately have to go. But which one is it? If it weren't for the good guys, nobody would fight back.

For MONEY questions. Lucky sevens. The Day Sign you have drawn is influenced by the luck of the draw. (And I assume you're playing with a full deck.) No sign has any greater shot at coming up than any other— all odds being equal. Sometimes I'm hot. Sometimes I'm not. And sometimes I just get lucky. But I have a feeling this one hits the nail on the head.

---

[7]Bombing of Libya continues: Apr. 15, 1986 ("7 Reed"). Allies land at Normandy: June 6, 1944 ("7 Serpent"). The first of 50,000 new troops promised by LBJ start toward Nam: July 28, 1965 ("7 Deer"). South Korea invaded by North: June 25, 1950 ("7 Eagle"). Siege on Branch Davidian cult at Waco ends: Apr. 19, 1993 ("7 Jaguar"). Berlin divided: June 5, 1945 ("7 Rain"). East and West Germany spend first day under new treaty: May 19, 1990 ("7 Rabbit"). First test-tube baby: July 25, 1978 ("7 Broom"). First patent for a bioengineered animal (a perfected lab mouse) awarded by U.S. Patent & Trademark Office: Apr. 12, 1988 ("7 Sea Creature"). Court rules home videotaping is not a copyright violation: Jan. 17, 1984 ("7 Jaguar").

For STRATEGY issues. Seventh-inning stretch? There's not much time for time-outs today, as events will move quickly, decisively, and without much opposition. What your Day Sign is trying to say with this number in front of it is, it's time to get the lead out and start maneuvering. Each sign will behave today in keeping with its nature—but very aggressively. If this were the Belmont Stakes, I'd say, "They're off and running . . . and jockeying for position."

		MAYAN	AZTEC
Day Number 8 Bunch 8	⁞	Uaxac	Chicuei
Key Date: 8 Ahau, 8 Kankin—Katie Mulchaey arrested in New York for smoking a cigarette in public (Jan. 22, 1908).			

HOROSCOPE

The "eight" days are quirky: Nazis double seats in Reichstag . . . announce
plans to breed a super race. Race riots rock L.A. And in New York,
800,000 protest. Jackie Kennedy gives televised tour of the East Room, Red
Room, Green Room, Blue Room. . . . White-House employs Astrologer—
special coverage following the local news.[8] Stay tuned for further details as
they become known.

For WORK questions. Eight ball in the corner pocket. The Day Signs are fairly true to themselves in this instance, but it's as if it's all shot from a different angle. The human side of the boss comes out . . . or else her fangs are revealed for the first time. Though everything is presented in color these days, the world still seems to prefer a black-and-white view of reality. You will have to decide for yourself what is good and bad about more than your Day Sign.

---

[8]Nazis double their representation in German legislature: July 31, 1932 ("8 Earthquake"). Nazis reverse moral restriction, encourage unmarried girls to breed (provided, of course, they are Aryan): Jan. 29, 1944 ("8 Owl"). Race riots start in Watts: Aug. 11, 1965 ("8 Sea Creature"). Eight hundred thousand protest nuclear arms in N.Y.C.: June 12, 1982 ("8 Dog"). Jackie gives tour of White House: Feb. 14, 1962 ("8 Deer"). Word leaks, the Reagans frequently consult an astrologer on matters of state: May 9, 1988 ("8 Rabbit").

For LOVE questions. Magic Eight Ball. The number eight adds a new angle to a relationship. Whatever Day Sign it accompanies, the larger nature of that sign is about to be revealed. And let it be a sign to you! Dogs and monkeys can both be trained to perform. But neither cares where the bathroom is... let alone the boudoir. Is it in the tea leaves? My sources say yes... Yes... YES!

For MONEY questions. Figure eight. The Day Sign this number accompanies simply adds up... calculates... computes. And all of a sudden you see the sum is but the total of its individual parts. You can read the bottom line for yourself... in black and white (no red this time). This is the moment you've been waiting for. It all comes down to what the raw numbers say. But beware of statistics, which can be manipulated.

For STRATEGY issues. Eighty miles an hour. The Day Sign you have drawn is trying to show you that you should call them as you see them. (Heck, I always do!) And besides, only you can see what it looks like from your angle. The ball is either outside or over the plate this time. It's either a strike or a ball... a hit or a miss. And only you can make this judgment call.

		Mayan	Aztec
Day Number 9 **Bunch 9**	⁞	Bolom	Chiconahui
Key Date: 9 Chicchan, 8 Yaxkin. Paris is liberated from the Nazis (Aug. 25, 1944).			

HOROSCOPE

Darkness and light compete on "nine" days. A buried Mayan city is unearthed. Martin Luther King, Jr., says, "I have a dream." A flag is raised at Iwo Jima. . . . Japanese Emperor Hirohito says he is no longer a god. The Pope declares—following scientific inspection—the Shroud of Turin is but a symbol of the Resurrection. The High Court bans prayer in school. Knute Rockne's undefeated Fighting Irish win the Rose Bowl. Republicans score major election victories in Congress.[9] It's a fact everybody around here still believes in Angels. And what about oracles?

---

[9]Six pyramids uncovered in the Yucatán: Feb. 8, 1926 ("9 Broom"). MLK's famous Washington, D.C. speech: Aug. 28, 1963 ("9 Deer"). U.S. Flag over Iwo Jima: Feb. 23, 1945 (also "9 Deer"). Hirohito denounces his divinity: Jan. 1,

For WORK questions. Nine to five. Your Day Sign is smoking again—but this time in the aftermath of an event, rather than at the start. What do you have at the end of the day? What have you earned? What do you know? And what do you owe? Some celebrate today. Some protest. But the many make the majority of the excuses. A myth is debunked as a new version of the truth makes the rounds. Well, I'll be damned. And what do ya know!

For LOVE questions. Sixty-nine?? Ninety-six?? (Are we alone? Can we speak frankly?) Heads are tails and tails are heads today. And all bets are off. The Day Sign you have received may be as clear as the nose on your face. But you may have to turn it upside down to read it. Bad guys tend to fall on their badness this day, while good guys tend to rise on their greatness. There are upsets. And overthrows. And by the time this dust clears, there will be no secrets left to tell.

For MONEY questions. Nine to one. The Day Sign you have drawn is under the influence of number nine's tendency to favor the long shot. The unlikely, improbable, and disconcerting tends to happen on this day—especially if it's an upset. So look for the "weakness" in your Day Sign. Underdogs are favored . . . while top dogs tend to fall. I'd bet my money on the outside chance. (But only you can decide.)

For STRATEGY issues. At sixes and nines. The number nine would seem to imply that you shouldn't take your Day Sign at its face value. There is a weakening here in general. But things that are already weak tend to strengthen in a sudden counterattack. Something is involved that could come back to haunt you . . . or to inspire you. If you feel nervous, all the better. A little stress will come in handy in times like this.

		MAYAN	AZTEC
Day Number 10 **Bunch 10**	**II**	Lahun	Matlactli
Key Date: 10 Imix, 4 Zac—U.S. celebrates 200th anniversary of the American Revolution (Jul 4, 1976).			

1946 ("9 Storm"). Vatican announces Shroud is not the burial robe of Christ: Oct. 13, 1988 ("9 Serpent"). Prayer banned in public schools: Jun. 25, 1962 ("9 Blade"). Notre Dame over Stanford: Jan. 1, 1925 ("9 Rain"). Republicans sweep Congress: Nov. 2, 1993 ("9 Monkey").

HOROSCOPE

On a "ten" day, lines will be drawn . . . or redrawn. Astronauts first orbit the moon, then return. Hawaii becomes the 50th state. Gone with the Wind premieres in theaters (and replays again and again). Picasso has his first show. The first Indy 500 is run. The first Nobel Prizes are awarded. Alexander Fleming discovers the cure for VD. The Pope denounces all forms of birth control. And Roger Maris breaks the Babe's seasonal home-run record, with 61.[10] The targets just keep moving further and further out the farther along you go.

For WORK questions. A 10K race. The Day Sign indicates a clean sweep. Records are made to be broken. But for the moment, you've got an entry in the books. The Day Sign that you have drawn comes on strong but also holds enough in reserve to finish well. Win, place, or show? Mark down your time. And we'll study the photos.

For LOVE questions. Ten minutes a day. When accompanied by a 10, a Day Sign will measure up consistently against its true character. Heroes are born, made, and die every day. But on this day, practice and patience tend to pay off. It may seem as if out of nowhere, a star rises or blinks out, but actually a lot has come before . . . and a lot will come after.

For MONEY questions. Ten percent rate. Your Day Sign is modified by a decimal point. A certain percentage of it will ring true immediately. But some of it will prove itself only over a number of days—or even months, or years. (We compound daily around here, but to three hundredths of a point.) Ten favors the climactic moment when everything comes together at last. The spoils go to the victor of the moment. But accolades are reserved for the heroes of the past.

For STRATEGY issues. *Tarot in 10 Minutes.* The advice from your Day Sign is to take your clues from the title. Your sign has a name. And you

---

[10]Apollo 8 astronauts, broadcasting from the moon, read from the book of Genesis: Dec. 24, 1968 ("10 Broom"). Apollo astronauts are again on the moon: Nov. 20, 1969 ("10 Night"). Hawaii admitted: Aug. 21, 1959 ("10 Storm"). *GWTW* premieres: Dec. 15, 1939 ("10 Dog"). Picasso opens in Paris: June 24, 1901 ("10 Earthquake"). First Indianapolis 500 auto race, with speeds averaging 74.5 mph, is run: May 30, 1911 ("10 Corn"). First Nobel awards given: Dec. 10, 1901 ("10 Death"). Fleming announces discovery of miracle drug penicillin: Sept. 15, 1928 ("10 Air"). Vatican denounces birth control: Jan. 8, 1931 ("10 Deer"). Roger Maris breaks the record: Oct. 9, 1961 ("10 Storm").

can take the name literally, figuratively, or critically. I give you a few ideas and hints. Let your own free associations do the rest. Everyone sees something different in both the picture on the wall and the face in the mirror. The Day Sign you have selected means exactly what you think it means . . . at least to you . . . at least this day.

		MAYAN	AZTEC
Day Number 11 **Bunch 11**	**·II**	Buluc	Matlactli Once
Key Date: 11 Chuen, 14 Zip—Robert F. Kennedy is assassinated in Los Angeles (Jun. 6, 1968).			

HOROSCOPE

On "eleven" days, you will be floored. An earthquake rocks Europe. Sandy Koufax pitches his fourth no-hitter in as many years. Tornadoes touch down in the Midwest. Hank Aaron hits his 715th homer. Worst flooding on record. California quakes. President takes a __third__ term.[11] Does it only seem in retrospect to have been destined from the start? Do the signs only seem to predict in hindsight?

For WORK questions. Eleven on a squad. Your Day Sign is being modified here by a very powerful combination of factors. Everyone will be touched by it in some way. Something that happens now will be passed down for years to come . . . as part of the collective consciousness and shared experience of the organization and its team. A corporate myth is in the making. This is a watershed period. You are living in special times.

For LOVE questions. In bed by 11 o'clock. Your Day Sign is under the influence of a ticking biological clock. And certain times will stand out as highlights. The sign you have drawn will go into effect at a specific moment. And at that very instant, you will know what it means to be singled out as special. Some may say it is only a coincidence that the

---

[11]Quake in Italy kills 100,000: Dec. 28, 1908 ("11 Sea Creature"). Koufax's fourth year of pitching a no-hitter game: Sept. 9, 1965 ("11 Dog"). Tornadoes hit Kansas: April 26, 1991 ("10 Dog"). Aaron breaks Babe Ruth's career record: Apr. 8, 1974 ("11 Night"). Flooding now the worst on record in central states: July 10, 1993 ("11 Owl"). Quakes in CA: June 28, 1992 ("11 Storm"). FDR reelected for third of four times: Nov. 5, 1940 ("11 Owl").

two of you have been drawn together like this, but no one can deny the importance of timing. Be open to suggestion.

For MONEY questions. Bet on the come (7 or 11 wins). They don't call 'em lucky numbers for nothin'. Your Day Sign today is under the influence of what we regard to be a lucky 11. In Mayan and Aztec terms, 11 is lucky too—but especially if the cause is good. Put your money into things that not only give you the return you're looking for but also serve a useful purpose. There will be hard times to weather. And it will not always come easy. That's why you need to believe.

For STRATEGY issues. 11:11. The advice your Day Sign is trying to give you today is to achieve your highest, finest, noblest purpose. Heroes are made on days with an 11 in front of them—and so are martyrs to a cause. Take your cues from the sign itself. The day favors the very best this sign is capable of presaging. Violent signs will be especially violent. Gentle signs will be particularly peaceful. It could happen at any time today. But pay particular attention when the digital clock reads 11:11.

		MAYAN	AZTEC
Day Number 12 **Bunch 12**	**∙‖**	Lah ca	Matlactli Omome
Key Date: 12 Cimi, 19 Zotz—Abortions are legal in New York (Jul. 1, 1970).			

HOROSCOPE

Rules are made—and made to be broken—on "twelve" days. Children under 14 may no longer work in factories at night. Tennessee bans teaching of evolution. FBI conducts "loyalty checks" on employees. Earhart becomes first of her gender to fly across Atlantic. Women rally in New York. Koop sends pamphlet to every U.S. household urging abstinence but promoting condom use.[12] Stranger things have happened, I guess . . . and stranger things than this will yet take place.

---

[12]International conference forbids nighttime child labor: Sept. 29, 1908 ("12 Monkey"). TN bans teaching of Darwin's controversial theory of evolution: Mar. 23, 1925 ("12 Dog"). FBI authorized to conduct checks of all federal employees: Mar. 22, 1947 ("12 Corn"). Earhart flies the Atlantic, with two male pilots: June 18, 1928 ("12 Reed"). Women's suffrage movement holds a rally in

For WORK questions. A dirty dozen. Your Day Sign develops an unconventional appearance when accompanied by a 12. Every now and again the hairstyles change . . . before changing back again. Every once in a while long-standing rules undergo a necessary, but surprising, shift— but only perhaps before reversing back. Though things done this day tend to get undone later, they have their moment in the spotlight now.

For LOVE questions. A dozen long-stemmed. Your Day Sign consists of both a rose and a thorn. So watch out. The message may be that a thing is about to take on its more difficult aspects. That is, of course, unless things are difficult already—in which case you're in luck. Change is inevitable for everything that exists, including love. When in doubt, evolve.

For MONEY questions. A dozen to one. Whatever your Day Sign is today, don't take too much stock in it or invest much long-term store. For it is about to be attacked. The respected way of doing things will soon apply no more to today's changing global conditions. The impossible is no longer highly unlikely. Things go back and forth as usual.

For STRATEGY issues. A dozen things to do. With a 12 in front of it, your Day Sign advises you to hold on to your hat, socks, and anything else that might fly off. Things are spinning here. The signs are blurring by like bells and cherries in Atlantic City slots. There is no stopping the world to get off . . . even if the rules do change in the middle of the game.

	MAYAN	AZTEC
Day Number 13 **Bunch 13** ᠅║	Ox la hun	Matlactli Omei
Key Date: 13 Lamat, 11 Zac—Supreme Court rules: No one must sit at the back of the bus (Nov. 13, 1956).		

HOROSCOPE

The stakes are large on "thirteen" days . . . the numbers are high. One hundred million dollars in aid goes to the Contras. The 15 millionth Model T rolls off the assembly line . . . and the first Volkswagen is made. Three hun-

---

N.Y.C.: Dec. 31, 1907 ("12 Blade"). Surgeon general's pamphlet on AIDS mailed: May 26, 1988 ("12 Serpent").

*dred fifty thousand phone workers remain on strike, and GM announces
plans to lay off 70,000. The 49ers win the Super Bowl . . . again. Grand
Central Station opens in New York. Sputnik launched.
Viking lands on Mars.[13] What will they think of next?*

———————

For WORK questions. Lucky 13. Accompanied by the number 13, your
Day Sign becomes capable of achieving its most obvious manifestations.
Unlucky, perhaps . . . for some. Fortunate for a few. A 13 brings things to
their logical head and natural conclusion.

For LOVE questions. Once in a blue moon. Your Day Sign is under a
rare influence. And it's a rare occasion you are about to witness.
Depending on its nature, the sign may shine on you or take a shameless
dump. But one thing is for sure, it will be something you do not soon
forget. May you remember with fondness this good old day.

For MONEY questions. Friday the 13th. A 13 indicates your Day Sign
is about to pay off. But will you personally see it as a Black Friday? or a
Red Monday? It might not get much better than this. (And let's hope it
never gets worse!) Everything that money does has a price.

For STRATEGY issues. Get off on the 13th floor. When your Day
Sign is accompanied by a number 13, it's clear your sign has reached its
highest strength and maximum intensity. A cause produces its natural
effect. A truth reveals its consequence. And everyone's true colors are
shown. Always keep your best side facing the cameras, but look square
into the eyes in the mirror.

———————

[13]Congress approves aid to Contra rebels: June 25, 1986 ("13 Corn"). Ford
Model T milestone reached: May 26, 1927 (also "13 Corn"). German plant
builds world's first VW: Feb. 26, 1936 ("13 Air"). Phone workers still on strike
for higher pay: Apr. 5, 1947 ("13 Blade"). GM announces layoffs and closings:
Dec. 18, 1991 ("13 Death"). San Francisco 49ers, featuring Joe Montana, win
the Super Bowl: Jan. 28, 1990 ("13 Earthquake"). Grand Central Station opens:
Feb. 2, 1913 ("13 Blade"). Soviets launch first satellite, vow to paint the moon
red: Oct. 4, 1957 ("13 Reed"). U.S. lands spaceship on the red planet: July 20,
1976 ("13 Earthquake").

	MAYAN	AZTEC
Day Number 0 **Bunch 0**	⟨ 𝒢 ⟩ Tulakal ("All")	Cintli
Key Date: 13 Caban, 0 Xul—*Viking* spacecraft lands on Mars (July 20, 1976).		

HOROSCOPE

There is no answer at this point in time that you do not already know.

———————

For WORK questions. Nothing to do. You've done everything you can do. It's all over now.

For LOVE questions. Nothing to wear. And nothing left to hide.

For MONEY questions. Nothing to spend. And nothing needed or wanted to spend it on. Plenty is good enough.

For STRATEGY issues. Nowhere to go . . . but back to the start again. Ask another question. Or come at it from a different angle.

> **<u>NOTE:</u>** Mesoamerican people discovered the concept of "zero" over 2,000 years ago. It was so important to their knowledge of mathematics, astronomy, and time-counting that there are at least 25 different glyphs designating the zero concept. The "squirly-gig" sign (𝒢) used in this book means "zero time." Though it does not play a role in the holy calendar we are using for divination purposes, zero was used to number the last (or 20th) day of each month in the Haab—the agricultural calendar (365-day year)—in which case the following month was said to be "seated" on what was actually the final day of the preceding month. Zero thus indicated completion, which, come to think of it, is not all that different from our concept of zero meaning emptiness at the start.
>
> Day Signs are numbered only 1 through 13. However, depending on what method you are using to select signs, it's possible that you could draw a "0." In these cases, we interpret it as a "no answer." Such a response is consistent with the authentic bean-counting method, wherein an answer is either provided to the consultant or not, depending on how many beans are left over at the end of counting them off by fours. (See Reading #2's Extra Credit section.)

The 260 Combinations

DAY SIGN A

SEA CREATURE/ALLIGATOR DAYS

DAY SIGN A HOROSCOPE:

"The truth may be stark once it's laid out bare-naked in black and white before you. But the outlook in general is no more grim than it's ever been. At least the weather will be dry. The day favors brotherly love, as well as its opposite. The thought is: For every story, there's a moral."

RECORD YOUR OWN "A" DATES:

EXPRESS YOUR OWN THOUGHTS:

NOW LOOK UP YOUR DAY NUMBER

MAYAN	AZTEC	
1 📿	**1** 🦅	DAY OF THE HOLY YEAR #1
1 Sea Creature (1 Imix)	1 Alligator (1 Cipactli)	

Key Dates: There's a quake in Iran (June 21, 1990). Shah Flees (Jan. 30, 1979).

Your Dates:

Horoscope. As at the very beginning, things are shaken up this time around. New ideas take the place of old lots.

MAYAN	AZTEC	
2 📿	**2** 🦅	DAY OF THE HOLY YEAR #41
2 Sea Creature (2 Imix)	2 Alligator (2 Cipactli)	

Key Dates: Dick Tracy artist is born (Nov. 20, 1900, Chester Gould). Schools remove apples from menu following a report on TV's *60 Minutes* (Feb. 26, 1989).

Your Dates:

Horoscope. Either the sky is raised up, or it's fallin'. Even far-fetched notions have their day in the sun.

MAYAN   AZTEC

3 ▥	3 🐊	DAY OF THE HOLY YEAR #81
3 Sea Creature (3 Imix)	3 Alligator (3 Cipactli)	
Key Dates: Blue whale named endangered species (May 15, 1959). House cancels covert aid to anti-Sandinistas (July 28, 1983). **Your Dates:**		

Horoscope. This, that, and the other thing. There are causes to support and causes to ignore. The truth is a secret.

MAYAN   AZTEC

4 ▥	4 🐊	DAY OF THE HOLY YEAR #121
4 Sea Creature (4 Imix)	4 Alligator (4 Cipactli)	
Key Dates: Truman orders Congress to establish Civil Rights Commission (Feb. 2, 1948). Surgeon General recommends no smoking in public (May 23, 1984). **Your Dates:**		

Horoscope. The truth, the whole truth, nothing but the truth. A half truth does not sit well for long with anyone.

MAYAN	AZTEC	
5 🗑	5 🐊	DAY OF THE HOLY YEAR #161
5 Sea Creature (5 Imix)	5 Alligator (5 Cipactli)	

Key Dates: Dancer, singer, Broadway actor Ben Vereen is born (Oct. 10, 1946).

Your Dates:

Horoscope. If the world's a stage—with life the plot—then each of us must be an actor... and a scriptwriter.

MAYAN	AZTEC	
6 🗑	6 🐊	DAY OF THE HOLY YEAR #201
6 Sea Creature (6 Imix)	6 Alligator (6 Cipactli)	

Key Dates: Federal study reports one third of students have smoked pot (Feb. 1, 1971).

Your Dates:

Horoscope. Before this, it was chaos. And after this, it will be chaos again. Does order come from stability... or imbalance?

MAYAN   AZTEC

7 [glyph]	7 [glyph]	DAY OF THE HOLY YEAR #241
7 Sea Creature (7 Imix)	7 Alligator (7 Cipactli)	
Key Dates: Death toll in concentration camps reaches one quarter million (Sept. 21, 1942). A mouse better suited for laboratory tests is patented (Apr. 12, 1988). **Your Dates:**		

Horoscope. That which furthers the good of the many tends to outweigh the few. Orders tend to be received...and fulfilled.

MAYAN   AZTEC

8 [glyph]	8 [glyph]	DAY OF THE HOLY YEAR #21
8 Sea Creature (8 Imix)	8 Alligator (8 Cipactli)	
Key Dates: Los Angeles in flames (Aug. 11, 1965). **Your Dates:**		

Horoscope. The truth, if it be fully revealed, is double-sided, double-edged and double-tongued. A smoking symbol is easier lit than interpreted.

MAYAN   AZTEC

9 🗳	9 🐚	DAY OF THE HOLY YEAR #61
9 Sea Creature (9 Imix)	9 Alligator (9 Cipactli)	
Key Dates: Israel and Egypt sign armistice (Mar. 31, 1979). Kennedy and Nixon in televised debate (Sep. 26, 1960). **Your Dates:**		

Horoscope. It is not so much what you say as what you do. A sense of false security is only that.

MAYAN   AZTEC

10 🗳	10 🐚	DAY OF THE HOLY YEAR #101
10 Sea Creature (10 Imix)	10 Alligator (10 Cipactli)	
Key Dates: America recalls its stirring past (Jul. 4, 1976). **Your Dates:**		

Horoscope. Today may be all that counts now, but without yesterday, there would be nothing to build upon tomorrow. Carry on.

MAYAN   AZTEC

11 📿	11 🐊	DAY OF THE HOLY YEAR #141
11 Sea Creature (11 Imix)	11 Alligator (11 Cipactli)	
Key Dates: Thousands die in Europe's worst earthquake (Dec. 28, 1908). **Your Dates:**		

Horoscope. The truth may shock us at first...both into and out of our senses. What moral, this dilemma? You tell.

MAYAN   AZTEC

12 📿	12 🐊	DAY OF THE HOLY YEAR #181
12 Sea Creature (12 Imix)	12 Alligator (12 Cipactli)	
Key Dates: People's Republic detonates most powerful nuclear bomb it has tested to date (May 21, 1992). Family and Medical Leave Act signed into law (Feb. 5, 1993). **Your Dates:**		

Horoscope. Powerful forces—constructive and destructive—are at work this day. Energy may be applied directly or leveraged, with similar effect.

MAYAN	AZTEC	
13 13 Sea Creature (13 Imix)	13 13 Alligator (13 Cipactli)	DAY OF THE HOLY YEAR #221
Key Dates: First atomic submarine launched: the *Nautilus* (Jan. 21, 1954). **Your Dates:**		

Horoscope. Creative energy eventually becomes spent, whether it is used or unused. May there always be more where that came from.

272

DAY SIGN B

AIR/WIND DAYS

DAY SIGN B HOROSCOPE:

"An occasional miracle occurs this day... but do not overlook the possibility for disaster. Charismatic people may be involved in both good <u>and</u> ill purpose. Some curses may be blessings in disguise. Atmospheric conditions beg you to appeal. The day favors a love of conviction. The thought is: Lay down your guns."

RECORD YOUR OWN "B" DATES:

EXPRESS YOUR OWN THOUGHTS:

NOW LOOK UP YOUR DAY NUMBER

MAYAN   AZTEC

1 📅	1 🐕	DAY OF THE HOLY YEAR #222
1 Air (1 Ik)	1 Wind (1 Eecatl)	

Key Dates: Pavlov wins Nobel Prize (Dec. 10, 1904). Carter is elected President (Nov. 2, 1976).

Your Dates:

Horoscope. Some make it look like a breeze. But you know it's all sweat of the brow. The proportions are cosmic. Don't be taken in.

MAYAN   AZTEC

2 📅	2 🐕	DAY OF THE HOLY YEAR #2
2 Air (2 Ik)	2 Wind (2 Eecatl)	

Key Dates: Resumption of diplomatic relations between China and the U.S. ends three decades of estrangement (Jan. 31, 1979).

Your Dates:

Horoscope. The breeze is a frequent flier. Here today and somewhere else tomorrow. Scatter seeds on the way. Anticipate the rains.

MAYAN   AZTEC

3 🔲	3 🐚	DAY OF THE HOLY YEAR #42
3 Air (3 Ik)	3 Wind (3 Eecatl)	
Key Dates: America declares "War to end all wars" (Apr. 6, 1917). The Grand Old Party makes a comeback after 40 years (Nov. 8, 1994). **Your Dates:**		

Horoscope. The wind is always whispering in circles. An argument turns back upon itself. A loop is closed. A cycle completes.

MAYAN   AZTEC

4 🔲	4 🐚	DAY OF THE HOLY YEAR #82
4 Air (4 Ik)	4 Wind (4 Eecatl)	
Key Dates: Pop Idol is born (Aug. 29, 1958, Michael Jackson). Living legend dies (Sep. 29, 1975, Casey Stengel). **Your Dates:**		

Horoscope. The winds "of" change are also "by" and "for" change. And from day to day you never know what's coming.

MAYAN   AZTEC

5 🔲	5 🐾	DAY OF THE HOLY YEAR #122
5 Air (5 Ik)	5 Wind (5 Eecatl)	

Key Dates: Supreme Court justice born (Feb. 27, 1886, Hugo Black).

Your Dates:

Horoscope. While you have the breath to speak, by all means...speak up and out. Let us hear your voice carry.

MAYAN   AZTEC

6 🔲	6 🐾	DAY OF THE HOLY YEAR #162
6 Air (6 Ik)	6 Wind (6 Eecatl)	

Key Dates: United Nations advocates the use of force in Iraq (Nov. 29, 1990).

Your Dates:

Horoscope. Try though we may to avoid them, a cyclone is always stirring somewhere. Don't kick dust in anyone's face today.

MAYAN	AZTEC	
7 🔲	7 🐚	DAY OF THE HOLY YEAR #202
7 Air (7 Ik)	7 Wind (7 Eecatl)	

Key Dates: Pan Am files for bankruptcy (Jan. 8, 1991). World Trade Center bombed (Feb. 26, 1993).

Your Dates:

Horoscope. Some things go with the wind that they blew in on. Some things stand firm, even in a stiff breeze.

MAYAN	AZTEC	
8 🔲	8 🐚	DAY OF THE HOLY YEAR #242
8 Air (8 Ik)	8 Wind (8 Eecatl)	

Key Dates: Hurricane Hugo is about to devastate the Caribbean and the southeast states (Sept. 15, 1989).

Your Dates:

Horoscope. Even a swirling mass dissipates at last. Something you thought would devour you did not. The weather turns in time.

MAYAN   AZTEC

9 🔲	9 🐌	DAY OF THE HOLY YEAR #22
9 Air (9 Ik)	9 Wind (9 Eecatl)	

Key Dates: Despite the fabled curse on the door, King Tut's tomb is opened (Nov. 26, 1922).

Your Dates:

Horoscope. No good comes of ill will. It is like a wind that sits still. Nothing moves. Nothing sails. Nothing flies.

MAYAN   AZTEC

10 🔲	10 🐌	DAY OF THE HOLY YEAR #62
10 Air (10 Ik)	10 Wind (10 Eecatl)	

Key Dates: Out of an old fungus comes a modern cure (Sep. 15, 1928, penicillin created, from airborne mold).

Your Dates:

Horoscope. A whirlwind kicks up a little dust. But later, it becomes difficult to recall... like a dream or a miracle.

MAYAN   AZTEC

11 🔲	11 🐾	DAY OF THE HOLY YEAR #102
11 Air (11 Ik)	11 Wind (11 Eecatl)	

Key Dates: Supreme Court Justice Thurgood Marshall is born (July 2, 1908; as a lawyer, Marshall presented winning arguments in many civil rights cases.)

Your Dates:

Horoscope. Things that go up do not remain there long. Use your position to change the way things will be remembered.

MAYAN   AZTEC

12 🔲	12 🐾	DAY OF THE HOLY YEAR #142
12 Air (12 Ik)	12 Wind (12 Eecatl)	

Key Dates: Poland and Soviet Union sign 15-year trade pact (May 4, 1984).

Your Dates:

Horoscope. All things are possible, from time to time. We never know what the winds will bring tomorrow, let alone today.

MAYAN	AZTEC	
13 ▣	13 🐌	DAY OF THE HOLY YEAR #182
13 Air (13 Ik)	13 Wind (13 Eecatl)	

Key Dates: British navy ship the *Courageous* sunk by U-boat; 500 lost (Sep. 18, 1939). Hostilities end in Grenada (Nov. 6, 1983).

Your Dates:

Horoscope. Some winds are remembered long after the air blows out of them. But it all blurs together in the end.

DAY SIGN C

NIGHT/HOUSE DAYS

DAY SIGN C HOROSCOPE:

"Some dirty, dark, and dastardly deeds happen from time to time, but this day tends to nip them in the bud. Records set in the past are overturned. A silence is broken. A secret is out. The skies will be but partly overcast tonight. The day favors the love of truth. The thought is: Come out of your room."

RECORD YOUR OWN "C" DATES:

EXPRESS YOUR OWN THOUGHTS:

NOW LOOK UP YOUR DAY NUMBER

MAYAN   AZTEC

1 ▦	1 ⛩	DAY OF THE HOLY YEAR #183
1 Night (1 Akbal)	1 House (1 Calli)	
Key Dates: Nineteen smaller countries join allies in endorsing League of Nations (Jan. 27, 1919). **Your Dates:**		

Horoscope. Home is the place for doing the right thing by each other. If not here and now, then where? When?

MAYAN   AZTEC

2 ▦	2 ⛩	DAY OF THE HOLY YEAR #223
2 Night (2 Akbal)	2 House (2 Calli)	
Key Dates: Supreme Court justice announces retirement in June (Mar. 19, 1993, Byron White). **Your Dates:**		

Horoscope. Every hour, whether dark or light, passes as time counts. Each Lord of the Night comes, and each departs again.

MAYAN   AZTEC

3 🔲	3 🏛	DAY OF THE HOLY YEAR #3
3 Night (3 Akbal)	3 House (3 Calli)	
Key Dates: Lt. Col. North takes the Fifth during Senate hearings on Iran-Contra investigation (Dec. 1, 1986). **Your Dates:**		

Horoscope. That which is quiet most of the time may yet alarm. To be forewarned is not necessarily to be forearmed.

MAYAN   AZTEC

4 🔲	4 🏛	DAY OF THE HOLY YEAR #43
4 Night (4 Akbal)	4 House (4 Calli)	
Key Dates: Cuban Missile Crisis ends (Oct. 28, 1962). **Your Dates:**		

Horoscope. This day is overshadowed by those who carry the weight of the world. A threatened doomsday passes. Till tomorrow, friend....

MAYAN	AZTEC	
5 🉐	5 🏠	DAY OF THE HOLY YEAR #83
5 Night (5 Akbal)	5 House (5 Calli)	

Key Dates: Family values advocate Jerry Falwell is born (Aug. 11, 1933).

Your Dates:

Horoscope. In every light is darkness. In every darkness is light. And in every just cause is a measure of hatred.

MAYAN	AZTEC	
6 🉐	6 🏠	DAY OF THE HOLY YEAR #123
6 Night (6 Akbal)	6 House (6 Calli)	

Key Dates: Wright Brothers fly (Dec. 17, 1903). The Chicago Seven are out on bail appealing their convictions (Feb. 28, 1970).

Your Dates:

Horoscope. We reach through thin air and dark matter for the truth. The questions you ask determine the answers you get.

MAYAN   AZTEC

7 🔲	7 🏛	DAY OF THE HOLY YEAR #163
7 Night (7 Akbal)	7 House (7 Calli)	
Key Dates: Red-hunting senator brands Truman administration "a communist haven" (Nov. 24, 1953, Joseph McCarthy in a televised broadcast). Shoe-pounding Kremlin chief dies in obscurity (Sep. 11, 1971, Nikita Khrushchev). **Your Dates:**		

Horoscope. Every darkness is neither revealed nor remembered. For it is by committee that history is written to conform to "truth."

MAYAN   AZTEC

8 🔲	8 🏛	DAY OF THE HOLY YEAR #203
8 Night (8 Akbal)	8 House (8 Calli)	
Key Dates: The eve of an era: Tomorrow a new recording medium is born! It will spin along at 45 rpm's (Jan. 9, 1949). **Your Dates:**		

Horoscope. The night spins ideas like discs on a jukebox. Certain tracks are worth replaying... until they become a familiar refrain.

MAYAN   AZTEC

9 ▣	9 ▤	DAY OF THE HOLY YEAR #243
9 Night (9 Akbal)	9 House (9 Calli)	
Key Dates: First gay and lesbian rally (Jun. 28, 1970, in New York). Khrushchev is out... Brezhnev is in (Oct. 17, 1964). **Your Dates:**		

Horoscope. The night was made both for concealing and hooking up. Easily applied labels are often the hardest to get off.

MAYAN   AZTEC

10 ▣	10 ▤	DAY OF THE HOLY YEAR #23
10 Night (10 Akbal)	10 House (10 Calli)	
Key Dates: We walk on the moon... again! (Nov. 20, 1969) **Your Dates:**		

Horoscope. The place you spend your nights is the house you now call home. May it serve and suit you well.

MAYAN   AZTEC

11 ▣	11 ▨	DAY OF THE HOLY YEAR #63
11 Night (11 Akbal)	11 House (11 Calli)	
Key Dates: AIDS quilt is unfolded in D.C.... for the first time (Oct. 10, 1992). **Your Dates:**		

Horoscope. Home is the place where the heart returns to remember. Things change. Feelings diminish, fade.... But not on this day.

MAYAN   AZTEC

12 ▣	12 ▨	DAY OF THE HOLY YEAR #103
12 Night (12 Akbal)	12 House (12 Calli)	
Key Dates: First heart transplant patient dead after 18 days (Dec. 21, 1967, Louis Washkansky, Cape Town, South Africa). **Your Dates:**		

Horoscope. Love is accepted or rejected this night. To give is not automatically to receive. Every offer is not immediately considered.

MAYAN	AZTEC	
13 ⏏	13 ⛩	DAY OF THE HOLY YEAR #143
13 Night (13 Akbal)	13 House (13 Calli)	

Key Dates: Convicted spies (the Rosenbergs) denied appeal (Feb. 17, 1953, later exonerated— after their execution).

Your Dates:

Horoscope. Things might seem bleak to you. But only time's passage will tell whether it isn't just justice in the making.

DAY SIGN D

CORN/LIZARD DAYS

DAY SIGN D HOROSCOPE:

"Things that capture our attention, captivate us, or draw us in this day, do. All eyes are focused on the screen. There are spectacles and public displays. 'We are coming to you live from the scene.' The day favors a love that is simple, but subject to the test. With any luck, the weather will be fair. The thought is: Measure up to expectation, not down."

RECORD YOUR OWN "D" DATES:

EXPRESS YOUR OWN THOUGHTS:

NOW LOOK UP YOUR DAY NUMBER

MAYAN	AZTEC	
1 ⬚	1 🦎	DAY OF THE HOLY YEAR #144
1 Corn (1 Kan)	1 Lizard (1 Cuetzpalin)	

Key Dates: Chuck Berry is born (Oct. 18, 1926).... You might say so is rock 'n' roll.

Your Dates:

Horoscope. Breakthroughs do occur. Every species mutates. A missing link is found. Mistakes are quickly balanced out. Only the best endures.

MAYAN	AZTEC	
2 ⬚	2 🦎	DAY OF THE HOLY YEAR #184
2 Corn (2 Kan)	2 Lizard (2 Cuetzpalin)	

Key Dates: Hitler opens the winter Olympics (Feb. 28, 1936). Elvis gets a haircut, trades tight jeans for khaki pants (Mar. 24, 1958).

Your Dates:

Horoscope. Though a cause be common, it may not be just...or nobly intended. A little publicity goes a long way.

MAYAN   AZTEC

3 🗿	3 🦎	DAY OF THE HOLY YEAR #224
3 Corn (3 Kan)	3 Lizard (3 Cuetzpalin)	
Key Dates: St. Louis Cardinal Pop Haines, of fastball and knuckleball fame, is born (Jul. 22, 1893, in Clayton, Ohio). President Ford grants amnesty to Vietnam draft evaders (Sep. 16, 1974). **Your Dates:**		

Horoscope. The story takes an ironic twist at this point, but no one seems to care or notice. Until later, then...

MAYAN   AZTEC

4 🗿	4 🦎	DAY OF THE HOLY YEAR #4
4 Corn (4 Kan)	4 Lizard (4 Cuetzpalin)	
Key Dates: Parisians attempt second French revolution (May 30, 1968). Arabs massacre 11 Israeli athletes at the Munich Olympic games (Jul. 8, 1972). Hijacked hostages freed in Beirut (June 30, 1985). **Your Dates:**		

Horoscope. Life can get really tough. It's been rough getting to the end of this day—but you did it. Viva!

MAYAN	AZTEC	
5 🔲	5 🐊	DAY OF THE HOLY YEAR #44
5 Corn (5 Kan)	5 Lizard (5 Cuetzpalin)	

Key Dates: Nazis remove "misfit" parents for failure to indoctrinate their young (Nov. 29, 1937).

Your Dates:

Horoscope. Some things need to be seen to be believed. Do not ignore signs.

MAYAN	AZTEC	
6 🔲	6 🐊	DAY OF THE HOLY YEAR #84
6 Corn (6 Kan)	6 Lizard (6 Cuetzpalin)	

Key Dates: Atomic bombs tested by U.S. in the Pacific (July 25, 1946, near Bikini Islands).

Your Dates:

Horoscope. Popcorn!?...or something blows the lid off the pressure cooker today. Rat-a-tat-tat. When one goes, they all follow. Do you?

MAYAN   AZTEC

7 🔲	7 🐊	DAY OF THE HOLY YEAR #124
7 Corn (7 Kan)	7 Lizard (7 Cuetzpalin)	

Key Dates: Feds raid Wyoming ranch...
biggest bust of bald eagle bones yet (Aug. 3, 1971).

Your Dates:

Horoscope. Tough hide. Thick skin. Protection is nice. But you do not want to be in a position to deserve it.

MAYAN   AZTEC

8 🔲	8 🐊	DAY OF THE HOLY YEAR #164
8 Corn (8 Kan)	8 Lizard (8 Cuetzpalin)	

Key Dates: Newspapers announce Nixon/Agnew ticket win (Nov. 6, 1968). The Beatles split up (Apr. 10, 1970).

Your Dates:

Horoscope. Are there accidents of nature? Or is it all one big, divine plan? What-if's don't matter as much as truths.

MAYAN	AZTEC	
9 🔲	9 🐊	DAY OF THE HOLY YEAR #204
9 Corn (9 Kan)	9 Lizard (9 Cuetzpalin)	

Key Dates: NFL calls cocaine biggest threat to the sport (June 26, 1982).

Your Dates:

Horoscope. A private life interferes with a public persona. You are a material witness to the truth as it is revealed.

MAYAN	AZTEC	
10 🔲	10 🐊	DAY OF THE HOLY YEAR #244
10 Corn (10 Kan)	10 Lizard (10 Cuetzpalin)	

Key Dates: They laughed when Goddard said we might go to the moon (Mar. 29, 1919). Late bloomer Grandma Moses leaves us her life's work (Dec. 13, 1961).

Your Dates:

Horoscope. Just because something is highly unlikely, extremely improbable, or difficult to imagine doesn't mean it can't and won't ever happen.

MAYAN   AZTEC

11 🐢	11 🦎	DAY OF THE HOLY YEAR #24
11 Corn (11 Kan)	11 Lizard (11 Cuetzpalin)	

Key Dates: Korea divided into North and South (Sep. 8, 1945). Kennedy speaks at wall dividing Berlin into East and West (June 26, 1963).

Your Dates:

Horoscope. Has everybody got their bearings? Are we all synchronized and coordinated yet? All right, then, everyone back in your niches.

MAYAN   AZTEC

12 🐢	12 🦎	DAY OF THE HOLY YEAR #64
12 Corn (12 Kan)	12 Lizard (12 Cuetzpalin)	

Key Dates: Retail merchandiser Sears is born (Dec. 7, 1863).

Your Dates:

Horoscope. There is a compartment for every field, a furrow for every seed, and a hoe for every weed. Plant ideas.

MAYAN	AZTEC	
13 ⬛	13 🦎	DAY OF THE HOLY YEAR #104
13 Corn (13 Kan)	13 Lizard (13 Cuetzpalin)	

Key Dates: Queen Victoria is dead. Long live the King (Jan. 22, 1901). Performing artist sometimes known as "Prince" is born (June 7, 1959, in Minneapolis).

Your Dates:

Horoscope. Is it life that imitates art? Or does art only mirror what we are willing to line up to witness?

DAY SIGN E

SERPENT/SNAKE DAYS

DAY SIGN E HOROSCOPE:

"It's a day that carries a sting with it or packs a wallop. Things that are sinister or suspect come out into the light. Things rattle in the overhead compartment or the seat pocket in front of you. The weather may turn suddenly. The day favors love both in and out of control. The thought is: Watch out for broken glass... especially if it's silvered on the back."

RECORD YOUR OWN "E" DATES:

EXPRESS YOUR OWN THOUGHTS:

NOW LOOK UP YOUR DAY NUMBER

MAYAN   AZTEC

1	1	DAY OF THE HOLY YEAR #105
1 Serpent (1 Chicchan)	1 Snake (1 Coatl)	

Key Dates: The world awakens to news that Kennedy has defeated Nixon (Nov. 9, 1960).

Your Dates:

Horoscope. It is not always the pattern on the back of the serpent that reveals its nature... but rather its underside.

MAYAN   AZTEC

2	2	DAY OF THE HOLY YEAR #145
2 Serpent (2 Chicchan)	2 Snake (2 Coatl)	

Key Dates: Memphis police slay seven cultists in shootout (Jan. 13, 1983). Smoking banned on all flights under six hours (Feb. 25, 1990).

Your Dates:

Horoscope. Some varieties are more deadly serious than others. It is not only a snake that can bite its own tail.

MAYAN   AZTEC

3 🔲	3 🐍	DAY OF THE HOLY YEAR #185
3 Serpent (3 Chicchan)	3 Snake (3 Coatl)	
Key Dates: The Constitution is amended to permit moral legislation (Jan. 29, 1919, Prohibition allowed). Nixon resigns (Aug. 8, 1974). Computer virus threatens U.S. infrastructure (Nov. 2, 1988). **Your Dates:**		

Horoscope. Some snakes blend in so well with their surroundings, they cannot be seen until the damage they do is done.

MAYAN   AZTEC

4 🔲	4 🐍	DAY OF THE HOLY YEAR #225
4 Serpent (4 Chicchan)	4 Snake (4 Coatl)	
Key Dates: American fairy-tale princess is born (Nov. 12, 1929, Grace Kelly). **Your Dates:**		

Horoscope. An old skin is left drying. The one who crawled out from under it has already assumed a new identity.

MAYAN	AZTEC	
5 🐍	5 🐍	DAY OF THE HOLY YEAR #5
5 Serpent (5 Chicchan)	5 Snake (5 Coatl)	

Key Dates: Rosenbergs wrongly executed for espionage (June 19, 1953). Fifty thousand troops ordered to Nam (July 26, 1965).

Your Dates:

Horoscope. It is later we correct our views. A wrong is more recognizable by its old pattern than its current color.

MAYAN	AZTEC	
6 🐍	6 🐍	DAY OF THE HOLY YEAR #45
6 Serpent (6 Chicchan)	6 Snake (6 Coatl)	

Key Dates: Congress overrides President's veto of "Anti-American Act." Communists shall be "routed out" (Sep. 23, 1950). Iceberg sinks Titanic (Apr. 15, 1912).

Your Dates:

Horoscope. It is the Great Water Serpent that curls around its victims, cutting off their breathing space. Watch out from below.

MAYAN	AZTEC	
7 😊	7 🐍	DAY OF THE HOLY YEAR #85
7 Serpent (7 Chicchan)	7 Snake (7 Coatl)	

Key Dates: Feds crack rum ring worth millions (Dec. 3, 1925). Twenty Speakeasies raided in New York (Oct. 8, 1928). Allies land at Normandy (June 6, 1944).

Your Dates:

Horoscope. Snakes get caught where they live this day...in the act...and by surprise attack. No time for flushing stash.

MAYAN	AZTEC	
8 😊	8 🐍	DAY OF THE HOLY YEAR #125
8 Serpent (8 Chicchan)	8 Snake (8 Coatl)	

Key Dates: U.S. airports begin screening all passengers (Jan. 5, 1973). Ronald Reagan is President (Nov. 4, 1980). Legendary pitcher Cy Young passes on (Dec. 6, 1955).

Your Dates:

Horoscope. Two offspring of earlier times. Two chips off a similar block. Two enraptured serpents. Two snakes mesmerizing us. Two legends.

MAYAN	AZTEC	
9 🐍	9 🐍	DAY OF THE HOLY YEAR #165
9 Serpent (9 Chicchan)	9 Snake (9 Coatl)	

Key Dates: Paris is liberated from the Nazis (Aug. 25, 1944). Eight hundred thousand U.S. Steel workers face their second week of a months-long strike (Jan. 27, 1946).

Your Dates:

Horoscope. Reality has a way of rearing its oft ugly face. For every force, there is an equivalent and opposite response.

MAYAN	AZTEC	
10 🐍	10 🐍	DAY OF THE HOLY YEAR #205
10 Serpent (10 Chicchan)	10 Snake (10 Coatl)	

Key Dates: King Tut's mummy is removed from its tomb (Feb. 12, 1924). Crowds protest the arrest of 115 in Montgomery bus boycott (Feb. 24, 1956, Alabama).

Your Dates:

Horoscope. Events this day may only appear to be significantly related. Every sequence has its cause . . . and every effect, its purpose.

MAYAN AZTEC

11 🌀	11 🐍	DAY OF THE HOLY YEAR #245
11 Serpent (11 Chicchan)	11 Snake (11 Coatl)	

Key Dates: Magic Johnson, Lakers star, announces he is infected with AIDS (Nov. 7, 1991).

Your Dates:

Horoscope. It is insidious, the snake that rules this day. And you will not see it coming... till it already arrives.

MAYAN AZTEC

12 🌀	12 🐍	DAY OF THE HOLY YEAR #25
12 Serpent (12 Chicchan)	12 Snake (12 Coatl)	

Key Dates: Oakland A's ace the Series in four games (Oct. 28, 1989).

Your Dates:

Horoscope. Each plays the same game, but some better than the others. Skill, practice, timing, and luck—each play a part.

MAYAN AZTEC

13 🐍	13 🐍	DAY OF THE HOLY YEAR #65
13 Serpent (13 Chicchan)	13 Snake (13 Coatl)	

Key Dates: It's the Washington Redskins over the Buffalo Bills in Super Bowl XXVI (Jan. 26, 1992). Earthquake rocks Cairo (Oct. 12, 1992).

Your Dates:

Horoscope. It is a clear decision this time. There are winners and losers, spoilers and victors, champions and might-have-beens. Cheers, guys.

DAY SIGN F

DEATH DAYS

DAY SIGN F HOROSCOPE:

"Issues of life and death are involved. Some things will be decided. Some things will resolve. Some, dissolve. And some will disappear for good. Not all terminations are fatal. The weather is nothing to speak of. The day favors a love that goes beyond the grave. The thought is: Leave behind what you cannot take along."

RECORD YOUR OWN "F" DATES:

EXPRESS YOUR OWN THOUGHTS:

NOW LOOK UP YOUR DAY NUMBER

MAYAN	AZTEC	
1 🂠	1 🂠	DAY OF THE HOLY YEAR #66
1 Death (1 Cimi)	1 Death (1 Maquiztli)	
Key Dates: General Colin Powell is born (Apr. 5, 1937). **Your Dates:**		

Horoscope. Are we warriors by nature? or just by trade? Everybody's got to do something. Might as well be the best....

MAYAN	AZTEC	
2 🂠	2 🂠	DAY OF THE HOLY YEAR #106
2 Death (2 Cimi)	2 Death (2 Maquiztli)	
Key Dates: Cease-fire in effect at 11:01 on 11/11 (Nov. 11, 1918, World War I is over). **Your Dates:**		

Horoscope. The worst is over. Though everything might not yet be completely resolved, at least it's decided...once and for all.

MAYAN   AZTEC

3 🝮	3 🝮	DAY OF THE HOLY YEAR #146
3 Death (3 Cimi)	3 Death (3 Maquiztli)	
Key Dates: Hitler is führer (Aug. 19, 1934). What else can we say? **Your Dates:**		

Horoscope. We get whomever we vote for. We get what we go along with. Sometimes it's for better, and sometimes worse.

MAYAN   AZTEC

4 🝮	4 🝮	DAY OF THE HOLY YEAR #186
4 Death (4 Cimi)	4 Death (4 Maquiztli)	
Key Dates: King Camp Gillette, of safety-razor fame, is born. As an inventor, he set out to create something disposable that would be in constant demand (Jan. 5, 1855, Fond du Lac, Wisconsin). **Your Dates:**		

Horoscope. Nothing lasts forever—not even a better mousetrap. Some things wear out from use, and others by design. Try software.

307

MAYAN   AZTEC

5 🝙	5 🝝	DAY OF THE HOLY YEAR #226
5 Death (5 Cimi)	5 Death (5 Maquiztli)	

Key Dates: League of Nations recommends the partitioning of Palestine to create a Jewish state (Aug. 31, 1937). Ford pardons Nixon (Sep. 16, 1974).

Your Dates:

Horoscope. A line is drawn, whether in the sand of the desert or at the bottom of letterhead. Initial here: _____.

MAYAN   AZTEC

6 🝙	6 🝝	DAY OF THE HOLY YEAR #6
6 Death (6 Cimi)	6 Death (6 Maquiztli)	

Key Dates: Babe Ruth's salary is doubled. "It's the death of baseball" (Jan. 5, 1920). Speed skater-to-be, Eric Heiden, is born (June 14, 1958, in Madison, Wisconsin).

Your Dates:

Horoscope. Nothing lasts forever—not even America's favorite sport. But not to fear: Something new is about to make it big-time.

MAYAN   AZTEC

7 🌀	7 💀	DAY OF THE HOLY YEAR #46
7 Death (7 Cimi)	7 Death (7 Maquiztli)	

Key Dates: Bootleg kingpin Al Capone is busted in Philly, after being sought since Valentine's Day (May 17, 1929).

Your Dates:

Horoscope. You can run, of course, but no one can hide forever. Look back over your shoulder. Keep on marking time.

MAYAN   AZTEC

8 🌀	8 💀	DAY OF THE HOLY YEAR #86
8 Death (8 Cimi)	8 Death (8 Maquiztli)	

Key Dates: New FBI chief nominated (July 20, 1993, Louis J. Freeh). Presidents of Rwanda and Burundi assassinated, after signing peace treaty (Apr. 6, 1994, the jet carrying Juvénal Habyarimana and Cyprien Ntaryamira is hit by rocket fire).

Your Dates:

Horoscope. Things can get pretty twisted around here. (And I'm not talking about pretzels.) Keep your eye on the bouncing ball.

MAYAN   AZTEC

9 🔲	9 🐚	DAY OF THE HOLY YEAR #126
9 Death (9 Cimi)	9 Death (9 Maquiztli)	

Key Dates: Second day of Nor'easter that is battering coast with snow, rain, wind, and surf. It's called "worst storm in decades" (Dec. 12, 1992).

Your Dates:

Horoscope. We've made quite a mess of things this time. Get out the shovels. Salvage what you can. Smoke the corners.

MAYAN   AZTEC

10 🔲	10 🐚	DAY OF THE HOLY YEAR #166
10 Death (10 Cimi)	10 Death (10 Maquiztli)	

Key Dates: First Nobel Prizes awarded (Dec. 10, 1901). Blues matron Ella Fitzgerald born (Apr. 25, 1918).

Your Dates:

Horoscope. Well, if this doesn't take the cake, we don't know what does! A pinnacle of success is a precarious point.

MAYAN   AZTEC

11 ⊙	11 ☻	DAY OF THE HOLY YEAR #206
11 Death (11 Cimi)	11 Death (11 Maquiztli)	

Key Dates: Black Thursday (Oct. 24, 1929, stock market crashes in New York).

Your Dates:

Horoscope. Is that a dark cloud we see hanging over a head? Has the sun not shown enough for one season?

MAYAN   AZTEC

12 ⊙	12 ☻	DAY OF THE HOLY YEAR #246
12 Death (12 Cimi)	12 Death (12 Maquiztli)	

Key Dates: Soviets are first to photo dark side of the moon (Oct. 27, 1959). Social Security enacted (Aug. 14, 1935).

Your Dates:

Horoscope. We are inclined to only see half...the side that points toward us in the looking glass...not the back.

MAYAN	AZTEC	
13 🔲	13 🐚	DAY OF THE HOLY YEAR #26
13 Death (13 Cimi)	13 Death (13 Maquiztli)	

Key Dates: Major corporate reorganization and downsizing takes place at GM . . . and throughout the land (Dec. 18, 1991).

Your Dates:

Horoscope. The killer is not so much the ends but the means. The best deaths are really fresh starts in disguise.

DAY SIGN G

DEER DAYS

DAY SIGN G HOROSCOPE:

"The day occurs against an ideological backdrop. Facts
of life are incontestable. But truth changes, age to age.
Do you believe everything you hear?... and everything
they say? The weather will be mostly clear, with an
occasional flurry of activity. The day favors a love on
the run. The thought is: Best to keep your own tail
down... but head high."

RECORD YOUR OWN "G" DATES:

EXPRESS YOUR OWN THOUGHTS:

NOW LOOK UP YOUR DAY NUMBER

MAYAN   AZTEC

1 🦌	1 🦌	DAY OF THE HOLY YEAR #27
1 Deer (1 Manik)	1 Deer (1 Mazatl)	

Key Dates: President McKinley reelected. But his running mate will succeed (Nov. 6, 1900, McKinley assassinated 10 months later).

Your Dates:

Horoscope. Go in pairs, instead of single file. And please hold hands, so no one gets left out or lags behind.

MAYAN   AZTEC

2 🦌	2 🦌	DAY OF THE HOLY YEAR #67
2 Deer (2 Manik)	2 Deer (2 Mazatl)	

Key Dates: Mae West fined $500 for "lewd improvisations." Courts judge her stage act "indecent" (Apr. 19, 1927).

Your Dates:

Horoscope. So are you getting off on this or what? It works for us. It can and will work for you.

MAYAN   AZTEC

3 🐾	3 🦌	DAY OF THE HOLY YEAR #107
3 Deer (3 Manik)	3 Deer (3 Mazatl)	

Key Dates: Two more tied to the stake in Georgia... (Aug. 17, 1904, two African-Americans lynched by white mob).

Your Dates:

Horoscope. Wow! What a pair of antlers...or are those horns? That's quite a performance you put on under the sheets.

MAYAN   AZTEC

4 🐾	4 🦌	DAY OF THE HOLY YEAR #147
4 Deer (4 Manik)	4 Deer (4 Mazatl)	

Key Dates: U.S. agrees to cease-fire in Vietnam at seven o'clock (Jan. 27, 1973). Researchers report eating may be hazardous to your health (Dec. 3, 1975).

Your Dates:

Horoscope. Bang. Bang. Double-banger. If there's not an enemy outside, then the enemy is within. Everybody seems to need a target.

MAYAN   AZTEC

5 [glyph]	5 [glyph]	DAY OF THE HOLY YEAR #187
5 Deer (5 Manik)	5 Deer (5 Mazatl)	
Key Dates: Congress says U.S. "internment" of Japanese-Americans during World War II was "unjust" (Feb. 24, 1983) . . . just 10 days after GM signs joint venture with Toyota. **Your Dates:**		

Horoscope. How can we be so transparent? Are we invisible within our own shadows? Face is saved for yet another day.

MAYAN   AZTEC

6 [glyph]	6 [glyph]	DAY OF THE HOLY YEAR #227
6 Deer (6 Manik)	6 Deer (6 Mazatl)	
Key Dates: U.S. Census Bureau reports poverty level at 14 percent—highest rate in 15 years (July 19, 1982). **Your Dates:**		

Horoscope. Whatever makes you feel better . . . a spoonful of sugar . . . a hot-water bottle . . . a bag of ice . . . a compress. Seek relief.

MAYAN   AZTEC

7 [glyph]	7 [glyph]	DAY OF THE HOLY YEAR #7
7 Deer (7 Manik)	7 Deer (7 Mazatl)	

Key Dates: For the second time this year, the Russian government has been overthrown—this time by the Bolsheviks (Nov. 7, 1917). Muhammad Ali regains heavyweight title (Oct. 29, 1974).

Your Dates:

Horoscope. Hunters are out in force...en masse...all over the place. (It must be open season...hopefully not for us.)

MAYAN   AZTEC

8 [glyph]	8 [glyph]	DAY OF THE HOLY YEAR #47
8 Deer (8 Manik)	8 Deer (8 Mazatl)	

Key Dates: First woman in U.S. to get her pilot's license (Aug. 1, 1911, Harriet Quimby). First American woman in space returns (June 24, 1983, Sally Ride).

Your Dates:

Horoscope. Careful where you point that finger, mister. Some classes are protected now...while others remain fair game. Abandon old metaphors.

317

MAYAN   AZTEC

9 [glyph]	9 [glyph]	DAY OF THE HOLY YEAR #87
9 Deer (9 Manik)	9 Deer (9 Mazatl)	

Key Dates: Color TV demoed at Bell Labs (Jun. 27, 1929). Surgeon General Koop says excess dietary fat is a no-no (July 27, 1988).

Your Dates:

Horoscope. It is 99.99% pure, FDA-inspected, lean. Don't worry... it's all "for your own good." (Life looked better in black and white.)

MAYAN   AZTEC

10 [glyph]	10 [glyph]	DAY OF THE HOLY YEAR #127
10 Deer (10 Manik)	10 Deer (10 Mazatl)	

Key Dates: Pope "just says no" to birth control, divorce, and trial marriage (Jan. 8, 1931, Pius XI). Communists surrender monopoly of power (Feb. 7, 1990).

Your Dates:

Horoscope. Never seen a rack like this one on a buck! How can one so strong and determined succumb so easily?

MAYAN   AZTEC

11 [glyph]	11 [glyph]	DAY OF THE HOLY YEAR #167
11 Deer (11 Manik)	11 Deer (11 Mazatl)	
Key Dates: Nine Nazis are punished, in Nuremburg (Oct. 16, 1946). **Your Dates:**		

Horoscope. Hang it up for another day. It was not necessarily a very pretty business we conducted, but someone had to.

MAYAN   AZTEC

12 [glyph]	12 [glyph]	DAY OF THE HOLY YEAR #207
12 Deer (12 Manik)	12 Deer (12 Mazatl)	
Key Dates: Hitler publishes *My Struggle* (Jul. 18, 1925). Mouthy Congresswoman from New York is born (July 24, 1920, Bella Abzug). **Your Dates:**		

Horoscope. You'll have to speak up if you ever want to be heard around these parts. Say something short and quotable.

MAYAN   AZTEC

13 🔯	13 🦌	DAY OF THE HOLY YEAR #247
13 Deer (13 Manik)	13 Deer (13 Mazatl)	

Key Dates: General MacArthur begins his "drive for the Pacific" (Feb. 29, 1944).

Your Dates:

Horoscope. We go two by two. They come in waves. There is the possibility that, despite conviction, you will be outnumbered.

DAY SIGN H

RABBIT DAYS

DAY SIGN H HOROSCOPE:

"Things get together, come together, or even ride off into the sunset together by the time this day is done. New periods are started. New eras are born. Old chapters come to a timely close. The day favors acquisitions and mergers. A love is repositioned. The weather changes with the moon. The thought is: Everything old renews again."

RECORD YOUR OWN "H" DATES:

EXPRESS YOUR OWN THOUGHTS:

NOW LOOK UP YOUR DAY NUMBER

MAYAN	AZTEC	
1 ⊞	1 🐇	DAY OF THE HOLY YEAR #248
1 Rabbit (1 Lamat)	1 Rabbit (1 Tochtli)	

Key Dates: Elizabeth II crowned Queen of England (June 2, 1953). Mets beat the Orioles in sweep (Oct. 16, 1969).

Your Dates:

Horoscope. Though some may ridicule you for your meekness, you may yet make believers of them. Kick up your heels today.

MAYAN	AZTEC	
2 ⊞	2 🐇	DAY OF THE HOLY YEAR #28
2 Rabbit (2 Lamat)	2 Rabbit (2 Tochtli)	

Key Dates: Headdressed Ayatollah rules Iran (Feb. 26, 1979).

Your Dates:

Horoscope. Today you will want to use both eyes, both ears, both feet—and stay on the ready to think fast.

MAYAN   AZTEC

3 ⊞	3 🐇	DAY OF THE HOLY YEAR #68
3 Rabbit (3 Lamat)	3 Rabbit (3 Tochtli)	
Key Dates: Thief makes off with art centerpiece (Aug. 22, 1911, the *Mona Lisa* is ripped off).		
Your Dates:		

Horoscope. Everything was as it should be the last time we checked it out. Where did that important paper disappear to?

MAYAN   AZTEC

4 ⊞	4 🐇	DAY OF THE HOLY YEAR #108
4 Rabbit (4 Lamat)	4 Rabbit (4 Tochtli)	
Key Dates: Argentina wins world-cup soccer title (June 29, 1986). Orson Welles died today (Oct. 12, 1985).		
Your Dates:		

Horoscope. It is Rabbit Scribe who keeps score, neither adding nor detracting. Shall we duplicate? replicate? or film it for posterity?

MAYAN	AZTEC	
5 🎲	5 🐇	DAY OF THE HOLY YEAR #148
5 Rabbit (5 Lamat)	5 Rabbit (5 Tochtli)	
Key Dates: UN meets to organize (Apr. 25, 1945).		
Your Dates:		

Horoscope. Here's one to get our heads together on... if not our sh*t. (It's hard to resist a vernacular that fits.)

MAYAN	AZTEC	
6 🎲	6 🐇	DAY OF THE HOLY YEAR #188
6 Rabbit (6 Lamat)	6 Rabbit (6 Tochtli)	
Key Dates: Hippies rally in the out-of-doors, in the midst of four days of peace and love (Aug. 17, 1969, Woodstock, New York).		
Your Dates:		

Horoscope. Holy shoot! When so many come, a few will get in free. What can you do but roll up the rugs.

MAYAN	AZTEC	
7 ⚃	7 🐰	DAY OF THE HOLY YEAR #228
7 Rabbit (7 Lamat)	7 Rabbit (7 Tochtli)	

Key Dates: The United States and the Soviet Union agree to stop production of chemical weapons (May 19, 1990).

Your Dates:

Horoscope. The two merge. But we've yet to see them come together in a synergistic way. Exploit the promise... and potential.

MAYAN	AZTEC	
8 ⚃	8 🐰	DAY OF THE HOLY YEAR #8
8 Rabbit (8 Lamat)	8 Rabbit (8 Tochtli)	

Key Dates: Little Conrad Hilton is born (Dec. 25, 1887). George V sleeps in a king-sized bed (Jun. 23, 1911, crowned).

Your Dates:

Horoscope. Each place has a name... and each room, a number. We've got to quit meeting like this (or do we?).

MAYAN   AZTEC

9 🔲	9 🐚	DAY OF THE HOLY YEAR #48
9 Rabbit (9 Lamat)	9 Rabbit (9 Tochtli)	
Key Dates: Electric guitarist Jimi Hendrix born (Nov. 27, 1942). Chernobyl fallout continues (Apr. 30, 1986). **Your Dates:**		

Horoscope. It all mounts up rapidly...and frequently shoots off its mouth. A circuit overloads. A perfected creation destroys itself fast.

MAYAN   AZTEC

10 🔲	10 🐚	DAY OF THE HOLY YEAR #88
10 Rabbit (10 Lamat)	10 Rabbit (10 Tochtli)	
Key Dates: Soviet troops invade Yugoslavia (Aug. 22, 1968). An idol and a hero both pass on (Aug. 23, 1926, Valentino dies; Jan. 30, 1965, Churchill buried). **Your Dates:**		

Horoscope. It is a legacy that we inherit. It is not so much what was as what it represented that counts.

MAYAN   AZTEC

11	11	DAY OF THE HOLY YEAR #128
11 Rabbit (11 Lamat)	11 Rabbit (11 Tochtli)	

Key Dates: General Patton meets with an ironic end (Dec. 21, 1945, victim of auto incident).

Your Dates:

Horoscope. It is the one thing we cannot control. Whether we come and wither we go is all in another's hands.

MAYAN   AZTEC

12	12	DAY OF THE HOLY YEAR #168
12 Rabbit (12 Lamat)	12 Rabbit (12 Tochtli)	

Key Dates: Supreme Court rules that States may impose their own restrictions on abortion rights (July 3, 1989).

Your Dates:

Horoscope. Separate but equal . . . Has that old notion cycled up again? You may beg to differ or disagree on this day.

MAYAN	AZTEC	
13 🎲	13 🐇	DAY OF THE HOLY YEAR #208
13 Rabbit (13 Lamat)	13 Rabbit (13 Tochtli)	
Key Dates: People's Republic is formed (Oct. 1, 1949).		
Your Dates:		

Horoscope. The term applied may be a misnomer. We tend to see in the dusky mirror our own version of truth.

DAY SIGN I

RAIN DAYS

DAY SIGN I HOROSCOPE:

"The world is a powder keg. And there is always thunder somewhere. Is there nothing we can agree upon besides gold medalists? If the weather is dreary, read poetry, listen to sad songs, and mix tears with the rain. The day favors a love based on matters of principle. The thought is: 'Ain't a fit night out for man nor beast.'"

RECORD YOUR OWN "I" DATES:

EXPRESS YOUR OWN THOUGHTS:

NOW LOOK UP YOUR DAY NUMBER

MAYAN	AZTEC	
1 ▣	1 ☞	DAY OF THE HOLY YEAR #209
1 Rain (1 Muluc)	1 Rain (1 Atl)	
Key Dates: Headlines blare: "King Killed in Memphis Yesterday" (Apr. 5, 1968, papers reporting the assassination of Martin Luther King, Jr.). Knute Rockne goes down in the annals of sports (Mar. 31, 1931, legendary football coach killed in plane crash). **Your Dates:**		

Horoscope. This day will touch you, move you, sway you, alter you. It is a date worth noting for its endings.

MAYAN	AZTEC	
2 ▣	2 ☞	DAY OF THE HOLY YEAR #249
2 Rain (2 Muluc)	2 Rain (2 Atl)	
Key Dates: Elvis is dead (Aug. 16, 1977). But "The King" lives (last spotted: July 3, 2012). **Your Dates:**		

Horoscope. Those who go on before us may yet one day return after us. More miracles happen than are officially reported.

MAYAN   AZTEC

3 🔲	3 ☞	DAY OF THE HOLY YEAR
3 Rain (3 Muluc)	3 Rain (3 Atl)	#29
Key Dates: Mahatma ("The Great Spirit") Gandhi is sentenced for sedition (Mar. 18, 1922). **Your Dates:**		

Horoscope. It is a dark day for a noble cause ... which only gets nobler on account of suffering. Hang in there.

MAYAN   AZTEC

4 🔲	4 ☞	DAY OF THE HOLY YEAR
4 Rain (4 Muluc)	4 Rain (4 Atl)	#69
Key Dates: The 10th day of a strike that will last over five months (May 22, 1902, 140,000 coal miners are still off the job). Selective Service conducts first draft lottery under Selective Service Law (Oct. 29, 1940, the first number drawn was 158). **Your Dates:**		

Horoscope. Conditions may still be deplorable, but the options aren't much of an improvement. You can't win for losin' today.

MAYAN	AZTEC	
5 ⊚	5 ☞	DAY OF THE HOLY YEAR #109
5 Rain (5 Muluc)	5 Rain (5 Atl)	

Key Dates: Equal seating in restaurants demanded by southern blacks (Feb. 27, 1960).

Your Dates:

Horoscope. Hold out for what you believe in today. But don't forget to be fair. (Will that be smoking or nonsmoking?)

MAYAN	AZTEC	
6 ⊚	6 ☞	DAY OF THE HOLY YEAR #149
6 Rain (6 Muluc)	6 Rain (6 Atl)	

Key Dates: Nazis open first "detention" camp (Mar. 20, 1933). Prohibition ends (Dec. 5, 1933).

Your Dates:

Horoscope. Be it reason or insanity, every tyranny comes to its end. Every rain that falls quits falling. Every shower passes.

MAYAN   AZTEC

7 🔲	7 ✍	DAY OF THE HOLY YEAR #189
7 Rain (7 Muluc)	7 Rain (7 Atl)	
Key Dates: World War II is over. Victors divide the spoils into separate—but equal—zones (June 5, 1945). **Your Dates:**		

Horoscope. How many pieces shall we cut the pie into this time? And is it your turn for a slightly larger slice?

MAYAN   AZTEC

8 🔲	8 ✍	DAY OF THE HOLY YEAR #229
8 Rain (8 Muluc)	8 Rain (8 Atl)	
Key Dates: Striking rubber workers—Goodyear, Goodrich, General Tire, and Firestone employees—return to work in Akron (May 27, 1943, workers demanded an eight-cent raise; they won three cents an hour on a base of $1.20). **Your Dates:**		

Horoscope. Showers will be scattered, for the most part, with an occasional thunderstorm after midnight. Tomorrow the sun will rise again.

MAYAN	AZTEC	
9 ⊡ 9 Rain (9 Muluc)	9 ☝ 9 Rain (9 Atl)	DAY OF THE HOLY YEAR #9
Key Dates: Pure Food and Drug Act becomes law (June 30, 1906). **Your Dates:**		

Horoscope. Be careful what you ingest and imbibe. Who knows where it's been . . . maybe even outside. Don't leave home without protection.

MAYAN	AZTEC	
10 ⊡ 10 Rain (10 Muluc)	10 ☝ 10 Rain (10 Atl)	DAY OF THE HOLY YEAR #49
Key Dates: Iran annexes Kuwait (Aug. 8, 1990). **Your Dates:**		

Horoscope. Not all rains blow in on the winds. Some storms creep up. Watch for pronouncements—both from above and below.

334

MAYAN   AZTEC

11 ◉	11 ☝	DAY OF THE HOLY YEAR #89
11 Rain (11 Muluc)	11 Rain (11 Atl)	
Key Dates: FBI arrests draft-card burner in Vermont (Oct. 18, 1965, David Miller first to be arrested under new law). **Your Dates:**		

Horoscope. It is easier to go along than it is to resist. Someone would make a moral of you this time.

MAYAN   AZTEC

12 ◉	12 ☝	DAY OF THE HOLY YEAR #129
12 Rain (12 Muluc)	12 Rain (12 Atl)	
Key Dates: Major League owners announce a lockout. No Spring Training! (Feb. 9, 1990) Mexico declares war on Axis (Jun. 1, 1942). **Your Dates:**		

Horoscope. Each lifetime has its share of rainouts, brownouts, lockouts, and shutouts. Shall we carry on? or call the game off?

MAYAN   AZTEC

13 ◉	13 ☞	DAY OF THE HOLY YEAR #169
13 Rain (13 Muluc)	13 Rain (13 Atl)	
Key Dates: U.S. trade deficit soars, with imports exceeding exports by $18 billion (Aug. 29, 1986). **Your Dates:**		

Horoscope. Sometimes when it rains, it pours. There can be too much of even a good thing. Would dearth be better?

DAY SIGN J

DOG DAYS

DAY SIGN J HOROSCOPE:

"There are good dogs, bad dogs, and mad dogs. There are top dogs, underdogs, dirty dogs, lapdogs, show dogs . . . and on this day, each has his or her own. You, too, will exhibit your tendencies. The weather will seem hot, even if it is not unseasonably warm. The day favors a love that's on the prowl. The thought is: If you hear the call of the wild, tilt up your head and bay back."

RECORD YOUR OWN "J" DATES:

EXPRESS YOUR OWN THOUGHTS:

NOW LOOK UP YOUR DAY NUMBER

MAYAN · AZTEC

1 🗿	1 🐕	DAY OF THE HOLY YEAR #170
1 Dog (1 Oc)	1 Dog (1 Itzcuintli)	

Key Dates: Marines wait for reinforcements after yesterday's bombing of their headquarters in Beruit (Oct. 24, 1983). Sixteen days, and still no word from Amelia Earhart (July 18, 1937, into the third week since Earhart's plane disappeared between New Guinea and Howland Island).

Your Dates:

Horoscope. A friend will not forget to pick you up. A friend will not leave you out on a cold night.

MAYAN · AZTEC

2 🗿	2 🐕	DAY OF THE HOLY YEAR #210
2 Dog (2 Oc)	2 Dog (2 Itzcuintli)	

Key Dates: O.J. Simpson sets 200-yard rushing record (Dec. 16, 1973). Drug testing called for in pro baseball (May 7, 1985).

Your Dates:

Horoscope. In an area where endurance matters as much as performance, every ounce of energy matters and every gram of muscle counts.

MAYAN   AZTEC

3	3	DAY OF THE HOLY YEAR #250
3 Dog (3 Oc)	3 Dog (3 Itzcuintli)	
Key Dates: Founder of *National Geographic* magazine, Henry Gannett, born (Aug. 24, 1846). **Your Dates:**		

Horoscope. The world is brought into your living room. But the more we get, the more we want. Pass the popcorn.

MAYAN   AZTEC

4	4	DAY OF THE HOLY YEAR #30
4 Dog (4 Oc)	4 Dog (4 Itzcuintli)	
Key Dates: The poor march on Washington (June 25, 1968). A dozen are accused of un-American activities in New York (July 20, 1948). **Your Dates:**		

Horoscope. Underdogs are favored this day—and I'm sure you know what I mean. For each of us has been there.

MAYAN	AZTEC	
5 🔲	5 🐕	DAY OF THE HOLY YEAR #70
5 Dog (5 Oc)	5 Dog (5 Itzcuintli)	

Key Dates: Lapdog Al Unser, the elder of auto-racing fame, is born (May 29, 1939, Albuquerque).

Your Dates:

Horoscope. It's a day for running around in circles...followed by a night of curling up in a special someone's lap.

MAYAN	AZTEC	
6 🔲	6 🐕	DAY OF THE HOLY YEAR #110
6 Dog (6 Oc)	6 Dog (6 Itzcuintli)	

Key Dates: Emmett Kelly is born (Dec. 9, 1898). What a clown.

Your Dates:

Horoscope. The show goes on—even if you do feel ridiculous in the costume. It all goes fine, after opening jitters.

MAYAN   AZTEC

7 🔲	7 🐕	DAY OF THE HOLY YEAR #150
7 Dog (7 Oc)	7 Dog (7 Itzcuintli)	
Key Dates: British medical journal warns women who wear silk stockings have a significantly higher risk of chafed legs (May 22, 1925). **Your Dates:**		

Horoscope. Every dog's got a few fleas. Just try not to scratch anywhere embarrassing when there's company around here. Down, boy.

MAYAN   AZTEC

8 🔲	8 🐕	DAY OF THE HOLY YEAR #190
8 Dog (8 Oc)	8 Dog (8 Itzcuintli)	
Key Dates: More than half a million demonstrate for nuclear arms control in New York City (June 12, 1982). A new generation of cruise missiles is deployed by the U.S. in Europe (Nov. 14, 1983). **Your Dates:**		

Horoscope. A story you hear is not quite consistent. Those who live by their sword may also need to retrofit it.

MAYAN   AZTEC

9 🐾	9 🐕	DAY OF THE HOLY YEAR #230
9 Dog (9 Oc)	9 Dog (9 Itzcuintli)	
Key Dates: Cambodian civil war ends after 13 years (Oct. 23, 1991). IRA prepares for cease-fire after 25 years (Aug. 28, 1994). **Your Dates:**		

Horoscope. It is as if you have been passed from one owner to another. A way of life surrenders its grasp.

MAYAN   AZTEC

10 🐾	10 🐕	DAY OF THE HOLY YEAR #10
10 Dog (10 Oc)	10 Dog (10 Itzcuintli)	
Key Dates: Harvard professor arrested for hemp possession (Apr. 17, 1966, Timothy Leary). Scarlett O'Hara gets hungry… right before intermission (Dec. 15, 1939). **Your Dates:**		

Horoscope. A dog expects a treat for every trick it does. If you hear a bell ring, be ready to respond.

MAYAN   AZTEC

11	11	DAY OF THE HOLY YEAR #50
11 Dog (11 Oc)	11 Dog (11 Itzcuintli)	

Key Dates: Did we mention yet that Sandy Koufax pitched a no-hitter four years in a row? Some things are worth repeating (Sep. 9, 1965).

Your Dates:

Horoscope. It's time to prove what you can do under pressure. Come on, now. I double-dog dare you! Show your stuff.

MAYAN   AZTEC

12	12	DAY OF THE HOLY YEAR #90
12 Dog (12 Oc)	12 Dog (12 Itzcuintli)	

Key Dates: First flight across English Channel (July 25, 1909, Louis Bleriot wins $2,500 prize). First round-trip dirigible flight across Atlantic (July 13, 1919). *Mariner II* takes close-ups of Venus (Dec. 14, 1962, after a voyage of 109 days).

Your Dates:

Horoscope. The Dog Star rises. A river floods. The crossing is perilous. Many have tried before and failed. Be the first.

MAYAN   AZTEC

13 ☺	13 🐕	DAY OF THE HOLY YEAR #130
13 Dog (13 Oc)	13 Dog (13 Itzcuintli)	
Key Dates: In a unanimous vote, Congress condemns the Soviet Union for shooting down Korean Airlines flight 007 (Sep. 15, 1983). **Your Dates:**		

Horoscope. It's a dog's day. And dogs are territorial. If the fur ruffles and the ears go flat, better back away.

DAY SIGN K

MONKEY DAYS

DAY SIGN K HOROSCOPE:

"Chimps will be chimps. Chumps will be chumps. The primate in each of us comes out this day, sometimes as comic relief or irony. Watch out for tragic flaws, Achilles' heels, and fatal errors. Bombshells drop. Plans backfire. The weather will turn by the end of the day. If you see a funnel cloud, get out of the way. The day favors a love that is superficial. The thought is: The soul is willing and the flesh is weak."

RECORD YOUR OWN "K" DATES:

EXPRESS YOUR OWN THOUGHTS:

NOW LOOK UP YOUR DAY NUMBER

MAYAN   AZTEC

1 🐵	1 🐵	DAY OF THE HOLY YEAR #131
1 Monkey (1 Chuen)	1 Monkey (1 Ozomatli)	
Key Dates: Mario Cuomo born (June 15, 1932). **Your Dates:**		

Horoscope. Someone in the public eye needs to look straight into the camera. Otherwise how would we know to trust them?

MAYAN   AZTEC

2 🐵	2 🐵	DAY OF THE HOLY YEAR #171
2 Monkey (2 Chuen)	2 Monkey (2 Ozomatli)	
Key Dates: Supreme Court rules: Obscenity is not protected speech (June 24, 1957, *Roth* v. *United States*). **Your Dates:**		

Horoscope. Surely there is some redeeming social value in this content . . . but we might have to look closer to find it.

MAYAN   AZTEC

3 🐵	3 🐵	DAY OF THE HOLY YEAR #211
3 Monkey (3 Chuen)	3 Monkey (3 Ozomatli)	
Key Dates: Federal agents seize 4,620 pounds of cocaine down in Palm Beach (Oct. 10, 1986). Persian Gulf War coverage begins tonight late (Jan. 17, 1991). **Your Dates:**		

Horoscope. Even though it may be only monkey antics, you should take the news sitting down. Time will count what matters.

MAYAN   AZTEC

4 🐵	4 🐵	DAY OF THE HOLY YEAR #251
4 Monkey (4 Chuen)	4 Monkey (4 Ozomatli)	
Key Dates: McDonald's founder passes under the Pearly Arches (Jan. 14, 1984, Ray Kroc, at 81). Mayan farmers rebel against NAFTA trade pact: "It favors the rich over the poor" (Jan. 1, 1994). **Your Dates:**		

Horoscope. Everybody's got a gimmick. (And how can we all stay in business?) Still, a little competition never hurt anyone . . . right, Ray?

MAYAN	AZTEC	
5 🐵	5 🦎	DAY OF THE HOLY YEAR #31
5 Monkey (5 Chuen)	5 Monkey (5 Ozomatli)	
Key Dates: Tarzan, King of the Apes, star is born (June 2, 1904, Johnny Weissmuller). **Your Dates:**		

Horoscope. It's possible to talk to the animals. It's even possible for them to communicate with you... if you read minds.

MAYAN	AZTEC	
6 🐵	6 🦎	DAY OF THE HOLY YEAR #71
6 Monkey (6 Chuen)	6 Monkey (6 Ozomatli)	
Key Dates: First woman to swim the English Channel, does (Aug. 6, 1926, Gertrude Ederle). **Your Dates:**		

Horoscope. I didn't know you could come so far. Something new is learned today by those who care to know more.

MAYAN   AZTEC

7 🐵	7 🐒	DAY OF THE HOLY YEAR #111
7 Monkey (7 Chuen)	7 Monkey (7 Ozomatli)	
Key Dates: The Phillies win the World Series (Oct. 21, 1980). World leader survives attempted coup (Nov. 27, 1992, second coup attempt on Venezuela's President Carlos Andres Perez). **Your Dates:**		

Horoscope. Good news at the present is not always the best news for the future. But why worry? Today is secure.

MAYAN   AZTEC

8 🐵	8 🐒	DAY OF THE HOLY YEAR #151
8 Monkey (8 Chuen)	8 Monkey (8 Ozomatli)	
Key Dates: Supreme Court rules: Freedom of the press does not apply to school newspapers (Jan. 13, 1988). **Your Dates:**		

Horoscope. Close up...loopholes in an open-ended proposition now. Arguments that beg decisions do not always get the right ones.

MAYAN   AZTEC

9 🐵	9 🐵	DAY OF THE HOLY YEAR #191
9 Monkey (9 Chuen)	9 Monkey (9 Ozomatli)	

Key Dates: George Bush is elected President (Nov. 8, 1988). Republicans now control Congress (Nov. 2, 1993). Jews rise up in Warsaw Ghetto (Apr. 19, 1943).

Your Dates:

Horoscope. It's a seesaw. When one end's up, the other's down...but not long. Go on. Take your turn...for now.

MAYAN   AZTEC

10 🐵	10 🐵	DAY OF THE HOLY YEAR #231
10 Monkey (10 Chuen)	10 Monkey (10 Ozomatli)	

Key Dates: New law says you may no longer drink on any U.S. ships—public or private (Oct. 6, 1922). F. Lee Bailey is born (June 10, 1933).

Your Dates:

Horoscope. You can pass as many rules as you want to at the zoo, but the exhibits will not obey them. Relax a little. Loosen up on an arbitrary requirement.

MAYAN   AZTEC

11 🐵	11 🐵	DAY OF THE HOLY YEAR #11
11 Monkey (11 Chuen)	11 Monkey (11 Ozomatli)	

Key Dates: UFO's reported simultaneously in four states (Aug. 1, 1965). "It was probably swamp gas."

Your Dates:

Horoscope. Not so fast. Let's not jump to any improbable conclusions. If all truth were known, we'd have to rethink everything.

MAYAN   AZTEC

12 🐵	12 🐵	DAY OF THE HOLY YEAR #51
12 Monkey (12 Chuen)	12 Monkey (12 Ozomatli)	

Key Dates: International group outlaws nighttime child labor (Sep. 29, 1908).

Your Dates:

Horoscope. Sound the dinner bell, then, and call them from the fields. We've all done enough for one day and night.

351

MAYAN   AZTEC

13 🐵	13 🐵	DAY OF THE HOLY YEAR #91
13 Monkey (13 Chuen)	13 Monkey (13 Ozomatli)	

Key Dates: U.S. Supreme Court overturns Louisiana's ban on interracial boxing matches (May 25, 1959).

Your Dates:

Horoscope. We are of two ways, two kinds, two habits, two types, two dispositions, and two inclinations. Two creates eternal conflict.

DAY SIGN L

BROOM/GRASS DAYS

DAY SIGN L HOROSCOPE:

"Great feats occur this day. Legends that are later made
are born. We achieve a harvest of some kind. You will
be thrilled, amazed, enthralled, and saddened—all at
the same time. The weather will be cooler than
average . . . and drier than normal. The day favors a
love that lasts long enough to tell its story. The
thought is: Every moment has the potential for glory."

RECORD YOUR OWN "L" DATES:

EXPRESS YOUR OWN THOUGHTS:

NOW LOOK UP YOUR DAY NUMBER

MAYAN	AZTEC	
1 [glyph]	1 [glyph]	DAY OF THE HOLY YEAR #92
1 Broom (1 Eb)	1 Grass (1 Malinalli)	

Key Dates: CIA director resigns (Dec. 28, 1994, R. James Woolsey).

Your Dates:

Horoscope. When you disagree with someone, it is better to part ways than be a constant thorn in each other's side.

MAYAN	AZTEC	
2 [glyph]	2 [glyph]	DAY OF THE HOLY YEAR #132
2 Broom (2 Eb)	2 Grass (2 Malinalli)	

Key Dates: *Apollo XVI* returns with 200 pounds of moon rocks (Apr. 27, 1972). *Mona Lisa* recovered from thief (Dec. 13, 1913).

Your Dates:

Horoscope. The precious and common are both treasured, provided they have a story to go with them. Find Magic Lightning Stones.

MAYAN   AZTEC

3 🦎	3 🌾	DAY OF THE HOLY YEAR #172
3 Broom (3 Eb)	3 Grass (3 Malinalli)	
Key Dates: Stevie Wonder—a.k.a. Steveland Judkins Morris—is born (May 13, 1950, Saginaw). Don Larsen pitches no-hitter in the World Series (Oct. 8, 1956). A fallout shelter has been tested at Princeton. You can have your very own for $1,195 (Aug. 14, 1959).		
Your Dates:		

Horoscope. It is castles in the sand. The things that lasted for a moment are yet constantly being told and retold.

MAYAN   AZTEC

4 🦎	4 🌾	DAY OF THE HOLY YEAR #212
4 Broom (4 Eb)	4 Grass (4 Malinalli)	
Key Dates: There is a cyclone in Bangladesh (Nov. 29, 1988). First American walks in outer space (June 3, 1965).		
Your Dates:		

Horoscope. What happens at a distance cannot be appreciated from here. (If a tree falls in the forest, who hears it?)

MAYAN   AZTEC

5 ⊡	5 🌾	DAY OF THE HOLY YEAR #252
5 Broom (5 Eb)	5 Grass (5 Malinalli)	
Key Dates: Persian Gulf War is now one for the history books (Feb. 27, 1991). The smart weapons really work ... at least some of the time. **Your Dates:**		

Horoscope. You are fighting your battles from a safe distance ... or so you think. Let's see: What say the printouts?

MAYAN   AZTEC

6 ⊡	6 🌾	DAY OF THE HOLY YEAR #32
6 Broom (6 Eb)	6 Grass (6 Malinalli)	
Key Dates: The Supreme Court lets each community set its own "obscenity standards" (June 21, 1973, in five separate cases, all decided in 5–4 votes). Ship returns from Antarctic voyage (Feb. 12, 1910, the *Porquois Pas?*). **Your Dates:**		

Horoscope. An event that makes headlines is inclined to fade after a few segments of air time. So goes momentary fame.

MAYAN	AZTEC	
7 🝙	7 🌿	DAY OF THE HOLY YEAR #72
7 Broom (7 Eb)	7 Grass (7 Malinalli)	
Key Dates: Early human graffiti—tens of thousands of years old—discovered on the walls of caves in France (Nov. 1, 1940, the Grotte de Lascaux). **Your Dates:**		

Horoscope. Like tempera handprints on construction paper...like growth lines marked on the doorjamb...time's passage cannot be stopped. Leave marks.

MAYAN	AZTEC	
8 🝙	8 🌿	DAY OF THE HOLY YEAR #112
8 Broom (8 Eb)	8 Grass (8 Malinalli)	
Key Dates: There is an earthquake in Nepal (Aug. 21, 1988). London conducts air raids on Berlin (Jan. 30, 1943). **Your Dates:**		

Horoscope. The day brings smoke from the chimney; and the night, ashes in the hearth. You live to tell the tale.

MAYAN   AZTEC

9 🐾	9 🌿	DAY OF THE HOLY YEAR #152
9 Broom (9 Eb)	9 Grass (9 Malinalli)	
Key Dates: L.A. smog blamed on car exhaust (July 31, 1954). Nixon and Khrushchev in Kitchen Debate (July 25, 1959). **Your Dates:**		

Horoscope. If you can't stand the heat . . . if you can't take the smoke . . . An old argument seems to be going nowhere. Drop it.

MAYAN   AZTEC

10 🐾	10 🌿	DAY OF THE HOLY YEAR #192
10 Broom (10 Eb)	10 Grass (10 Malinalli)	
Key Dates: The wearing of perfume banned at New Jersey beauty pageant (Aug. 28, 1922). **Your Dates:**		

Horoscope. Burn incense! Light candles. Dab on oil of musk. Some rules—especially capricious ones—beg to be broken.

MAYAN	AZTEC	
11	11	DAY OF THE HOLY YEAR #232
11 Broom (11 Eb)	11 Grass (11 Malinalli)	

Key Dates: Rev. King convicted for opposing public transportation rules (Mar. 22, 1956). Second President in a row declares War on Drugs (Sep. 5, 1989, Bush, a $7.9 billion program).

Your Dates:

Horoscope. What we do today will serve as either good or bad examples, depending upon the popularity of a particular cause.

MAYAN	AZTEC	
12	12	DAY OF THE HOLY YEAR #12
12 Broom (12 Eb)	12 Grass (12 Malinalli)	

Key Dates: Sweeping changes called for in collegiate sports (Mar. 19, 1991). "A tax break is coming"... real soon, says Bush (Aug. 20, 1992).

Your Dates:

Horoscope. It's really quite simple to understand. Just read my lips... and then between the lines, as well as you can.

MAYAN   AZTEC

13 [glyph]	13 [glyph]	DAY OF THE HOLY YEAR #52
13 Broom (13 Eb)	13 Grass (13 Malinalli)	

Key Dates: Supreme Court rules towns can erect Nativity scenes (Mar. 15, 1984).

Your Dates:

Horoscope. These days, too, will be remembered with nostalgia... especially by those who remember selectively. Recall the good. Forget the bad.

DAY SIGN M

REED DAYS

DAY SIGN M HOROSCOPE:

"Dire, dread, and painful events may turn as easily to triumph as tragedy. The best and worst in us comes out this day. Some will dare to be brave. Some will only be bold. The weather will be darker than it first appears. The day favors a love that endures beyond the present moment. The thought is: What is the price of your beliefs?"

RECORD YOUR OWN "M" DATES:

EXPRESS YOUR OWN THOUGHTS:

NOW LOOK UP YOUR DAY NUMBER

MAYAN   AZTEC

1 🁢	1 ▦	DAY OF THE HOLY YEAR #53
1 Reed (1 Ben)	1 Reed (1 Acatl)	
Key Dates: Comedy show goes off the air, rather than face censors (Apr. 4, 1969, "Smothers Brothers Comedy Hour"). **Your Dates:**		

Horoscope. Attack may or may not be provoked this day. Some strive for truth. Others rest their case on the law.

MAYAN   AZTEC

2 🁢	2 ▦	DAY OF THE HOLY YEAR #93
2 Reed (2 Ben)	2 Reed (2 Acatl)	
Key Dates: Jim Morrison attempts to touch the sky... but overshoots it (July 3, 1971). **Your Dates:**		

Horoscope. Only the young could make such a profound statement... in so few words... and in such little time. Remember then.

3 MAYAN   AZTEC

3 🔲	3 ▦	DAY OF THE HOLY YEAR #133
3 Reed (3 Ben)	3 Reed (3 Acatl)	
Key Dates: Hurricane Gilbert cuts through Mexico (Sep. 11, 1988). **Your Dates:**		

Horoscope. Nothing stands in the way of a tornado's path that doesn't get swept up in it. Watch out for projectiles.

MAYAN   AZTEC

4 🔲	4 ▦	DAY OF THE HOLY YEAR #173
4 Reed (4 Ben)	4 Reed (4 Acatl)	
Key Dates: A motorcade winds its way through the streets of Dallas (Nov. 22, 1963, President Kennedy's last ride). **Your Dates:**		

Horoscope. Every leader must be willing to sacrifice, for there are always those who are willing to shoot down good ideas.

MAYAN	AZTEC	
5 🔲	5 ▭	DAY OF THE HOLY YEAR #213
5 Reed (5 Ben)	5 Reed (5 Acatl)	

Key Dates: Pearl Harbor (Dec. 7, 1941).

Your Dates:

Horoscope. One side's victory is another's defeat. At least for today, the action is finished. See you all the earlier tomorrow.

MAYAN	AZTEC	
6 🔲	6 ▭	DAY OF THE HOLY YEAR #253
6 Reed (6 Ben)	6 Reed (6 Acatl)	

Key Dates: Halley's Comet is returning again . . . this time to be met by an earthling spacecraft (Mar. 6, 1986).

Your Dates:

Horoscope. Indomitable. Indefatigable. The human spirit has high sights and big goals. Hardly anything stops us, as long as we're funded.

MAYAN   AZTEC

7 ▦	7 ▦	DAY OF THE HOLY YEAR #33
7 Reed (7 Ben)	7 Reed (7 Acatl)	
Key Dates: Catholic bishops unite against economic inequality in the U.S. (Nov. 11, 1984). Iran's Ayatollah Khomeini announces that some of the American hostages may be tried as spies (Nov. 18, 1979). **Your Dates:**		

Horoscope. There is someone larger than life who is your defender . . . or your prosecutor. Be careful who—and what—you admire.

MAYAN   AZTEC

8 ▦	8 ▦	DAY OF THE HOLY YEAR #73
8 Reed (8 Ben)	8 Reed (8 Acatl)	
Key Dates: Boston Celtics beat the Suns for their 13th NBA title (June 6, 1976). **Your Dates:**		

Horoscope. Even when it's a team effort, a star or two stands out above the rest. All contributions are not equal.

MAYAN	AZTEC	
9 🔲	**9** ▦	DAY OF THE HOLY YEAR #113
9 Reed (9 Ben)	9 Reed (9 Acatl)	

Key Dates: Judy Garland is born under a less glamorous name (June 10, 1922).

Your Dates:

Horoscope. There is a need for shortening something that is long. There is a need to remove something blocking your progress.

MAYAN	AZTEC	
10 🔲	**10** ▦	DAY OF THE HOLY YEAR #153
10 Reed (10 Ben)	10 Reed (10 Acatl)	

Key Dates: Vatican announces the discovery of Saint Peter's bones (Aug. 7, 1949).

Your Dates:

Horoscope. A relic takes its power from each believer's heart. Have faith in miracles, and you will surely see them. Trust.

MAYAN   AZTEC

11 🁢	11 ▰	DAY OF THE HOLY YEAR #193
11 Reed (11 Ben)	11 Reed (11 Acatl)	
Key Dates: Oliver North cleared of all charges (Sep. 16, 1991). **Your Dates:**		

Horoscope. Where loyalty is expected, loyalty is also repaid. Would you go down defending someone else's image? Do you solemnly swear?

MAYAN   AZTEC

12 🁢	12 ▰	DAY OF THE HOLY YEAR #233
12 Reed (12 Ben)	12 Reed (12 Acatl)	
Key Dates: Boston beats the Giants on an error in the 10th (Oct. 20, 1912). **Your Dates:**		

Horoscope. The pressure is on. It's any single pitch...any single play. Any single moment may be the one remembered...forever!

MAYAN	AZTEC	
13 ⎕	13 ⎕	DAY OF THE HOLY YEAR #13
13 Reed (13 Ben)	13 Reed (13 Acatl)	

Key Dates: Martin Luther King, Jr.'s, assassin arrested in London (June 8, 1968, James Earl Ray). Robert F. Kennedy's coffin is transported by train to Washington for burial (June 8, 1968).

Your Dates:

Horoscope. You never know who might be listening ... or what they might think the solution is. Speak up if you must.

DAY SIGN N

JAGUAR/OCELOT DAYS

DAY SIGN N HOROSCOPE:

"The day is surprising. Anything can happen, but especially a random occurrence. Things drop out of the trees. There will always be the occasional coincidence. But does it always alter destiny or change the fate? The weather will be mostly partly.... The day favors a love that takes you down as well as up. The thought is: An error is not necessarily an accident. An incident is not necessarily a statement."

RECORD YOUR OWN "N" DATES:

EXPRESS YOUR OWN THOUGHTS:

NOW LOOK UP YOUR DAY NUMBER

MAYAN   AZTEC

1 🔲	1 🐾	DAY OF THE HOLY YEAR #14
1 Jaguar (1 Ix)	1 Ocelot (1 Ocelotl)	
Key Dates: The earth rumbles again in California (Oct. 17, 1989). **Your Dates:**		

Horoscope. It's another one for record books. In 20 seconds flat, everything can change. Be prepared by being ready to react.

MAYAN   AZTEC

2 🔲	2 🐾	DAY OF THE HOLY YEAR #54
2 Jaguar (2 Ix)	2 Ocelot (2 Ocelotl)	
Key Dates: Milton Bradley, of board-game fame, is born (Nov. 8, 1836). **Your Dates:**		

Horoscope. Let's see, that's a seven-letter word on a triple-word score, using both the Q and Z. Your turn to score.

MAYAN AZTEC

3 ⬚	3 🐾	DAY OF THE HOLY YEAR #94
3 Jaguar (3 Ix)	3 Ocelot (3 Ocelotl)	

Key Dates: Two fighters shot down in friendly fire (Apr. 14, 1994).

Your Dates:

Horoscope. Oops. I can't believe we did that. The day favors a close encounter with your own kind. A situation backfires.

MAYAN AZTEC

4 ⬚	4 🐾	DAY OF THE HOLY YEAR #134
4 Jaguar (4 Ix)	4 Ocelot (4 Ocelotl)	

Key Dates: Financial wizard is born (Sep. 7, 1867, J. P. Morgan, Jr.).

Your Dates:

Horoscope. Do you work for your money? Or does your money work for you?

MAYAN	AZTEC	
5 🀫	5 🐾	DAY OF THE HOLY YEAR #174
5 Jaguar (5 Ix)	5 Ocelot (5 Ocelotl)	

Key Dates: Beer is no longer available at your local pharmacy (Nov. 23, 1921, new law prohibits doctors from prescribing it during Prohibition).

Your Dates:

Horoscope. A controlled-release substance may play a part in your total recovery program. Or I suppose you could always chew gum.

MAYAN	AZTEC	
6 🀫	6 🐾	DAY OF THE HOLY YEAR #214
6 Jaguar (6 Ix)	6 Ocelot (6 Ocelotl)	

Key Dates: St. Valentine's Day Massacre among Chicago bootleggers (Feb. 14, 1929). Di Maggio marries Monroe (Jan. 14, 1954). U.S. declares war on Japan (Dec. 8, 1941).

Your Dates:

Horoscope. Pssst. Pssst. The secret is out. The word comes down. Cause to enter the spirit within. (*Ok-s-ik-ob ti yol itšel!*)

MAYAN   AZTEC

7 🔲	7 🐾	DAY OF THE HOLY YEAR #254
7 Jaguar (7 Ix)	7 Ocelot (7 Ocelotl)	
Key Dates: Supreme Court rules: VCR's now legal for home use. You can tape whatever you please off your TV ... (Jan. 17, 1984, *Sony* v. *Universal City Studios*) ... but you can't make me pay to watch it later. **Your Dates:**		

Horoscope. Someone almost got away with it. But is it all over yet? Keep those antennas tuned. Remain vigilant and circumspect.

MAYAN   AZTEC

8 🔲	8 🐾	DAY OF THE HOLY YEAR #34
8 Jaguar (8 Ix)	8 Ocelot (8 Ocelotl)	
Key Dates: Music magician born (May 30, 1909, Benny Goodman). **Your Dates:**		

Horoscope. Some make their livings on sidewalks, some in studios, and some in bars. Pay is based on performance, not effort.

MAYAN   AZTEC

9 🎴	9 🐱	DAY OF THE HOLY YEAR #74
9 Jaguar (9 Ix)	9 Ocelot (9 Ocelotl)	

Key Dates: A white-haired Albert Schweitzer wins the Nobel Peace Prize (Dec. 10, 1952).

Your Dates:

Horoscope. Every once in a while someone comes along and does something really nice for a change. Let it be you.

MAYAN   AZTEC

10 🎴	10 🐱	DAY OF THE HOLY YEAR #114
10 Jaguar (10 Ix)	10 Ocelot (10 Ocelotl)	

Key Dates: South Africans hang black activist Benjamin Moloise (Oct. 18, 1985). Five black officials assassinated in South Africa (July 5, 1986).

Your Dates:

Horoscope. Magic can be as dark as it can be light. Do what you will: Harm no one, lest in defense.

MAYAN   AZTEC

11 🔲	11 🐾	DAY OF THE HOLY YEAR #154
11 Jaguar (11 Ix)	11 Ocelot (11 Ocelotl)	

Key Dates: Multimillionaire announces he will spend the rest of his life giving it to charity (Mar. 13, 1901, Andrew Carnegie).

Your Dates:

Horoscope. What lasts of this magic moment? . . . nothing more than an idea chiseled into a stone arch. Ask any Mayan Warlord.

MAYAN   AZTEC

12 🔲	12 🐾	DAY OF THE HOLY YEAR #194
12 Jaguar (12 Ix)	12 Ocelot (12 Ocelotl)	

Key Dates: It is announced that Mikhail Gorbachev will now lead the Soviet Union . . . out of existence (Mar. 12, 1985).

Your Dates:

Horoscope. Magic and countermagic. Do you believe in part or all? (Testing . . . one, two, three.) Hocus-pocus. Presto! Abracadabra. (*Bey ti káan!*)

MAYAN   AZTEC

13	13	DAY OF THE HOLY YEAR #234
13 Jaguar (13 Ix)	13 Ocelot (13 Ocelotl)	
Key Dates: It's the Minnesota Twins, in seven games (Oct. 27, 1991). **Your Dates:**		

Horoscope. This one kept us on the edge of our seats...for at least a week. What will stand out later?

DAY SIGN O

EAGLE DAYS

DAY SIGN O HOROSCOPE:

"You soar with the eagles. But in this world, there are both hawks and doves, and you are free to choose sides. For some they come . . . for some they call. Lofty attitudes are respected, but the sky is the limit and provides quite a range. The weather will be subject to updrafts and tailwinds. The day favors a love that can be both uplifting and frightening. The thought is: Seek to achieve your highest integrity."

RECORD YOUR OWN "O" DATES:

EXPRESS YOUR OWN THOUGHTS:

NOW LOOK UP YOUR DAY NUMBER

MAYAN   AZTEC

1 📟	1 🐺	DAY OF THE HOLY YEAR #235
1 Eagle (1 Men)	1 Eagle (1 Quauhtli)	

Key Dates: The Big Three allies are in their fifth day of talks at Potsdam. Churchill says the negotiating table has an "iron curtain" down its center (Jul. 21, 1945).

Your Dates:

Horoscope. Hawks have more fortitude than the rest. And if two get into an argument, it will be a knock-down, drag-out.

MAYAN   AZTEC

2 📟	2 🐺	DAY OF THE HOLY YEAR #15
2 Eagle (2 Men)	2 Eagle (2 Quauhtli)	

Key Dates: Surgeon General Koop lumps 50 million smokers in with heroin and cocaine addicts: "It is a national pandemic!" (May 16, 1988).

Your Dates:

Horoscope. We have ways of making you refrain. We only want to help you.

MAYAN   AZTEC

3 🔲	3 🐺	DAY OF THE HOLY YEAR #55
3 Eagle (3 Men)	3 Eagle (3 Quauhtli)	
Key Dates: Not even the Pope is safe to walk in public anymore (May 31, 1981, John Paul II shot outside St. Peter's Church). **Your Dates:**		

Horoscope. Fame and infamy walk hand in hand down history's highway. Each is the other's prey. Each is the other's predator.

MAYAN   AZTEC

4 🔲	4 🐺	DAY OF THE HOLY YEAR #95
4 Eagle (4 Men)	4 Eagle (4 Quauhtli)	
Key Dates: Police battle opinionated minorities outside the "Democratic" National Convention (Aug. 29, 1968, in Chicago). **Your Dates:**		

Horoscope. Hawks, doves, and eagles all share the same air space. But don't worry... now there's enough band width for everybody. (Catch you on the Net!)

MAYAN	AZTEC	
5 🪶	5 🐿	DAY OF THE HOLY YEAR #135
5 Eagle (5 Men)	5 Eagle (5 Quauhtli)	

Key Dates: Truman defeats Dewey in popular vote . . . but early headlines report the opposite (Nov. 2, 1948).

Your Dates:

Horoscope. Some climb to the heights. Some are elevated to them. Some even stay there . . . for the time being. Give 'em hell, Harry!

MAYAN	AZTEC	
6 🪶	6 🐿	DAY OF THE HOLY YEAR #175
6 Eagle (6 Men)	6 Eagle (6 Quauhtli)	

Key Dates: German troops enter Paris. The German swastika now waves in the sky above France (June 14, 1940).

Your Dates:

Horoscope. As if from a crow's nest, the lay of the land is seen and overseen. Beware of an oversight committee.

MAYAN	AZTEC	
7 🦅	7 🐺	DAY OF THE HOLY YEAR #215
7 Eagle (7 Men)	7 Eagle (7 Quauhtli)	

Key Dates: Civil rights become the law of the land in the wake of riots following the assassination of Martin Luther King, Jr. (Apr. 11, 1968).

Your Dates:

Horoscope. Isn't the world a cruel enough place already, without our adding to our own aggravation? Quit picking on each other.

MAYAN	AZTEC	
8 🦅	8 🐺	DAY OF THE HOLY YEAR #255
8 Eagle (8 Men)	8 Eagle (8 Quauhtli)	

Key Dates: Police and federal troops skirmish with rioting citizens (June 22, 1943, in Detroit).

Your Dates:

Horoscope. While all eyes are focused on the perimeter, internal squabbles take second place. Beware of efforts to divert your attention.

MAYAN	AZTEC	
9 🦅	9 🦅	DAY OF THE HOLY YEAR #35
9 Eagle (9 Men)	9 Eagle (9 Quauhtli)	

Key Dates: Some astronauts never make it off the ground (Jan. 27, 1967, fire kills Virgil Grissom, Edward White, and Roger Chafee). But the first black woman does (Sep. 12, 1992, the *Endeavour* lifts off, with Mae C. Jemison aboard).

Your Dates:

Horoscope. In a sudden reversal, disadvantage turns to the upper hand. Is it the meek who inherit? the peacemakers? or activists?

MAYAN	AZTEC	
10 🦅	10 🦅	DAY OF THE HOLY YEAR #75
10 Eagle (10 Men)	10 Eagle (10 Quauhtli)	

Key Dates: Three hawks convene, emerging as love doves (Feb. 11, 1945, Churchill, Stalin, and FDR in Yalta).

Your Dates:

Horoscope. Even an aggressive tendency can yet be put to good work. There are several needs that must be simultaneously met.

MAYAN   AZTEC

11 🗔	11 🐺	DAY OF THE HOLY YEAR #115
11 Eagle (11 Men)	11 Eagle (11 Quauhtli)	

Key Dates: President Bush orders troops to Panama (May 11, 1989).

Your Dates:

Horoscope. What have you got to prove, that you're always getting into skirmishes? We can see your mood in your strut.

MAYAN   AZTEC

12 🗔	12 🐺	DAY OF THE HOLY YEAR #155
12 Eagle (12 Men)	12 Eagle (12 Quauhtli)	

Key Dates: Church leader accused of illegal religious practices (Nov. 23, 1906, Joseph P. Smith, son of Mormon founder, for polygamy).

Your Dates:

Horoscope. You may call it freedom of religion...of speech...of the press...or whatnot. Not all read it the same.

MAYAN   AZTEC

13 🔲	13 🐾	DAY OF THE HOLY YEAR #195
13 Eagle (13 Men)	13 Eagle (13 Quauhtli)	

Key Dates: Arkansas governor Bill Clinton receives the Democratic party's presidential nomination (June 2, 1992). Senator Robert Dole announces his candidacy for the 1996 Republican ticket (Apr. 10, 1995).

Your Dates:

Horoscope. Oh, quid pro quo! What's good for the goose is not necessarily good for the gander. Nothing's changed in 5,125 years.

DAY SIGN P

OWL/VULTURE DAYS

DAY SIGN P HOROSCOPE:

"Diplomacy rules this day. Everything that appears to be conspiracy is not. Ignorance and absurdity contribute. When a warning of impending doom passes around, some smack their lips. The weather will not matter much in comparison, but it may contribute to the mood. The day favors a love that is wide at the eyes and pointed at the chin. The thought is: Desire feeds on itself, rather than go hungry."

RECORD YOUR OWN "P" DATES:

EXPRESS YOUR OWN THOUGHTS:

NOW LOOK UP YOUR DAY NUMBER

MAYAN	AZTEC	
1 🔲	1 🐚	DAY OF THE HOLY YEAR #196
1 Owl (1 Cib)	1 Vulture (1 Cozcaquauhtli)	

Key Dates: Prohibition sweeping America, it is reported (Feb. 21, 1909). They have come for Anwar (Oct. 6, 1981, Egypt's President Sadat assassinated).

Your Dates:

Horoscope. It's a sobering day, to say the least . . . sober and sombering. It leaves you with a quiet, moody feeling inside.

MAYAN	AZTEC	
2 🔲	2 🐚	DAY OF THE HOLY YEAR #236
2 Owl (2 Cib)	2 Vulture (2 Cozcaquauhtli)	

Key Dates: Ann Landers and twin sister Dear Abbie are born. Any advice for the lovelorn? (Jul. 4, 1918, in Sioux City, Iowa).

Your Dates:

Horoscope. Double your pleasure. Double my fun. Double down your bets, my friend. And ask along another line of questioning. Amen.

MAYAN   AZTEC

3 🔲	3 🦅	DAY OF THE HOLY YEAR #16
3 Owl (3 Cib)	3 Vulture (3 Cozcaquauhtli)	
Key Dates: H-Bomb tested (May 12, 1951). Voting Rights Act signed into law (Aug. 6, 1965). **Your Dates:**		

Horoscope. Sometimes we feel like listening to the blues. Sometimes rap. And sometimes rock. Your tastes are eclectic today. Indulge them.

MAYAN   AZTEC

4 🔲	4 🦅	DAY OF THE HOLY YEAR #56
4 Owl (4 Cib)	4 Vulture (4 Cozcaquauhtli)	
Key Dates: Workers' party announces: Hitler is propaganda chief (Feb. 24, 1920). Seventy-two arrested in Nazi rally in Chicago (July 9, 1978). **Your Dates:**		

Horoscope. Like moths to the flame...like vultures to the battle-field...like owls to a barn, you gravitate...assemble...and wait.

MAYAN   AZTEC

5 🔲	5 🪶	DAY OF THE HOLY YEAR #96
5 Owl (5 Cib)	5 Vulture (5 Cozcaquauhtli)	
Key Dates: Supreme Court rules: Students may sue schools for damages in sexual harassment cases (Feb. 26, 1992). **Your Dates:**		

Horoscope. There are both carnivores and vegetarians in the world. There are predators and scavengers. Villains and victims. Which are you?

MAYAN   AZTEC

6 🔲	6 🪶	DAY OF THE HOLY YEAR #136
6 Owl (6 Cib)	6 Vulture (6 Cozcaquauhtli)	
Key Dates: LBJ signs sweeping Civil Rights Act. "Let us close the springs of racial poison!" (July 2, 1964). **Your Dates:**		

Horoscope. It may be a hundred years before justice gets served. Time's passage often erases scars as if with plastic surgery.

MAYAN	AZTEC	
7 🔲	7 🐚	DAY OF THE HOLY YEAR #176
7 Owl (7 Cib)	7 Vulture (7 Cozcaquauhtli)	

Key Dates: Nixon promises to withdraw 100,000 troops from Vietnam by December (Apr. 7, 1971).

Your Dates:

Horoscope. Leaders take note of events. It may be a month. It may take a year. But eventually... Risk compounds daily.

MAYAN	AZTEC	
8 🔲	8 🐚	DAY OF THE HOLY YEAR #216
8 Owl (8 Cib)	8 Vulture (8 Cozcaquauhtli)	

Key Dates: Twenty-six football heroes dead of injuries, so far this season (Nov. 28, 1909).

Your Dates:

Horoscope. The price of a young man's glory is, after all, high. There is so much to prove; so little time.

MAYAN   AZTEC

9 🔲	9 🐚	DAY OF THE HOLY YEAR #256
9 Owl (9 Cib)	9 Vulture (9 Cozcaquauhtli)	
Key Dates: Founder of first Russian-American company is born (Apr. 16, 1746, Fur Trader Alexander Baranov, of Siberia and Alaska). **Your Dates:**		

Horoscope. It is like trading in the skins of dead animals ... No one without a blanket would complain about their source.

MAYAN   AZTEC

10 🔲	10 🐚	DAY OF THE HOLY YEAR #36
10 Owl (10 Cib)	10 Vulture (10 Cozcaquauhtli)	
Key Dates: Duke Ellington performs at the Cotton Club (Dec. 4, 1927). **Your Dates:**		

Horoscope. The soul emits both plaintive and exuberant sounds ... shrieks, moans, and sighs. Pay attention to the song your soul whispers.

MAYAN   AZTEC

11 🔲	11 🦅	DAY OF THE HOLY YEAR #76
11 Owl (11 Cib)	11 Vulture (11 Cozcaquauhtli)	
Key Dates: Spacecraft to Jupiter is launched (Mar. 2, 1972, *Pioneer 10*). Midwest in the midst of its worst flooding on record (July 10, 1993). **Your Dates:**		

Horoscope. The camera crews, like vultures, have descended on the scene, looking for fragments. Don't worry—there's enough wreckage for all.

MAYAN   AZTEC

12 🔲	12 🦅	DAY OF THE HOLY YEAR #116
12 Owl (12 Cib)	12 Vulture (12 Cozcaquauhtli)	
Key Dates: FDR avoids would-be assassin (Feb. 15, 1933). **Your Dates:**		

Horoscope. Randomness doesn't discriminate against a worst-laid plan any more than a well intentioned one. Both can and do go wrong.

MAYAN   AZTEC

13 🖼	13 🐚	DAY OF THE HOLY YEAR #156
13 Owl (13 Cib)	13 Vulture (13 Cozcaquauhtli)	

Key Dates: Bootlegger Capone sentenced on tax evasion (Oct. 24, 1931). Supreme Court rules: Burning the flag is protected free speech (June 21, 1989, *Texas* v. *Johnson*).

Your Dates:

Horoscope. I prefer incense myself. But you can burn anything—your candle, your lighter, your bridges. It is your choice today.

DAY SIGN Q

EARTHQUAKE DAYS

DAY SIGN Q HOROSCOPE:

"Things are shaken up this day. Knees tremble. Hips wobble. Minds are made to bend. Not only storms can be doozies. And if you feel a sudden shiver...rate it on a scale from 1 to 13. Movers and shakers rattle our mirrors from time to time. And in between, the weather relieves the monotony. The day favors a love that is natural but hard to size up. The thought is: How can you ever be sure? So ya might as well trust."

RECORD YOUR OWN "Q" DATES:

EXPRESS YOUR OWN THOUGHTS:

NOW LOOK UP YOUR DAY NUMBER

MAYAN   AZTEC

1 🕱	1 ✖	DAY OF THE HOLY YEAR #157
1 Earthquake (1 Caban)	1 Earthquake (1 Ollin)	

Key Dates: Houdini has not escaped his tank this time (Oct. 31, 1926, dead of peritonitis). Dolly Parton is born (Jan. 19, 1946, in Sevier County, Tennessee).

Your Dates:

Horoscope. We experience a show stopper... or two. Is it the genuine article? Or is it all done with smoke and mirrors?

MAYAN   AZTEC

2 🕱	2 ✖	DAY OF THE HOLY YEAR #197
2 Earthquake (2 Caban)	2 Earthquake (2 Ollin)	

Key Dates: One hundred thousand gather in Yankee Stadium... to hear Billy Graham (July 20, 1957).

Your Dates:

Horoscope. A voice that rings with conviction will have them standing in the aisles. Come on up front to be healed.

MAYAN   AZTEC

3 ⊟	3 ⋈	DAY OF THE HOLY YEAR #237
3 Earthquake (3 Caban)	3 Earthquake (3 Ollin)	
Key Dates: The theater shakes with applause over a new medium (Oct. 6, 1927, first talking picture—*The Jazz Singer*—released).		
Your Dates:		

Horoscope. This one must have been shot in sense-surround. You will remember always what you see today. Do you believe it?

MAYAN   AZTEC

4 ⊟	4 ⋈	DAY OF THE HOLY YEAR #17
4 Earthquake (4 Caban)	4 Earthquake (4 Ollin)	
Key Dates: First woman in space is a cosmonaut (June 19, 1963, Valentina Tereshkova). Satchel Paige signs with the Indians (July 7, 1948).		
Your Dates:		

Horoscope. The news rocks the nation...but you don't have to think twice about it tonight. Until tomorrow, then. Pleasant dreams.

MAYAN   AZTEC

5 ⊞	5 ⋈	DAY OF THE HOLY YEAR #57
5 Earthquake (5 Caban)	5 Earthquake (5 Ollin)	
Key Dates: Producer of epic proportions is born (May 10, 1902, David O. Selznick, of *Gone With the Wind* fame). **Your Dates:**		

Horoscope. Does everything always have to be an extravaganza to hold our attention? Or, is it enough to wave the flag?

MAYAN   AZTEC

6 ⊞	6 ⋈	DAY OF THE HOLY YEAR #97
6 Earthquake (6 Caban)	6 Earthquake (6 Ollin)	
Key Dates: First commercial air service begins between New York and L.A.... two days and two nights... with a stopover in Columbus, Ohio (July 7, 1929). **Your Dates:**		

Horoscope. Coast to coast, block to block, and up your street... it all depends on where you need to be, when.

MAYAN	AZTEC	
7 🔲	7 〰	DAY OF THE HOLY YEAR #137
7 Earthquake (7 Caban)	7 Earthquake (7 Ollin)	

Key Dates: FBI Chief J. Edgar Hoover leaves us with his memory (May 2, 1972).

Your Dates:

Horoscope. The day goes unnoticed, except that it's connected to everything else that has gone—or will go—on around here.

MAYAN	AZTEC	
8 🔲	8 〰	DAY OF THE HOLY YEAR #177
8 Earthquake (8 Caban)	8 Earthquake (8 Ollin)	

Key Dates: Monterey Pop Festival draws 50,000 foot stompers (June 18, 1967).

Your Dates:

Horoscope. It's a happening, if you know what I mean. Man, it's out of sight . . . out of body . . . out of mind.

MAYAN   AZTEC

9 🔲	9 ⋈	DAY OF THE
9 Earthquake (9 Caban)	9 Earthquake (9 Ollin)	HOLY YEAR #217

Key Dates: First movie ever shown on an airplane (Feb. 17, 1929).

Your Dates:

Horoscope. It all depends on how you feel about sleeping with strangers...or laughing with headsets on. It's a captive crowd.

MAYAN   AZTEC

10 🔲	10 ⋈	DAY OF THE
10 Earthquake (10 Caban)	10 Earthquake (10 Ollin)	HOLY YEAR #257

Key Dates: Cult leader found guilty (Mar. 29, 1971, Charles Manson convicted).

Your Dates:

Horoscope. You will not want to be a witness to this one...or a juror. The heinous and holy both capture our attention.

11 🈺	11 ⋈	DAY OF THE HOLY YEAR #37
11 Earthquake (11 Caban)	11 Earthquake (11 Ollin)	

Key Dates: Kennedy and Castro face off (Oct. 22, 1962). Author of *The Yearling* is born (Aug, 8, 1896, Marjorie Kinnan Rawlings, in Washington, D.C.).

Your Dates:

Horoscope. Each struggles...some just on a grander scale. A small outcome mirrors the larger picture. A crisis will be overcome.

MAYAN   AZTEC

12 🈺	12 ⋈	DAY OF THE HOLY YEAR #77
12 Earthquake (12 Caban)	12 Earthquake (12 Ollin)	

Key Dates: American Midwest suffers worst flooding ever; floods will continue through August, leaving 70,000 homeless (July 11, 1993).

Your Dates:

Horoscope. This is just the first of many such long days...and endless nights. Neither frenzy nor fear helps. Hold on.

MAYAN   AZTEC

13 🔲	13 ⋈	DAY OF THE HOLY YEAR #117
13 Earthquake (13 Caban)	13 Earthquake (13 Ollin)	

Key Dates: Alien spaceship lands on Mars (July 20, 1976, a U.S. unmanned craft— *Viking 1*).

Your Dates:

Horoscope. That's one small tremor for man, one magic moment for man- and womankind.

DAY SIGN R

BLADE/FLINT DAYS

DAY SIGN R HOROSCOPE:

"Things divide, split, and sever us this day. Things cut clean to the soul, even if the tool we are using is not a knife, arrow, or spearpoint. Words may sound mightier than they actually are. But nothing beats a truth when it's wielding a scalpel. The weather may or may not be a tactical consideration. Which way do the winds blow? And where does sentiment lie? The day favors a love on the cutting edge. The thought is: Every tool is a weapon in disguise."

RECORD YOUR OWN "R" DATES:

EXPRESS YOUR OWN THOUGHTS:

NOW LOOK UP YOUR DAY NUMBER

MAYAN	AZTEC	
1 ⊠	1 ✏	DAY OF THE HOLY YEAR #118
1 Blade (1 Eznab)	1 Flint (1 Tecpatl)	

Key Dates: Dr. Spock, of child-rearing fame, is jailed for advising young men to avoid the draft (Jan. 5, 1968). Mahatma (the Great Spirit) Gandhi is assassinated (Jan. 30, 1948, by a Hindu extremist).

Your Dates:

Horoscope. It is the prerogative of those who survived their own misguided youths to lead others now and make new rules.

MAYAN	AZTEC	
2 ⊠	2 ✏	DAY OF THE HOLY YEAR #158
2 Blade (2 Eznab)	2 Flint (2 Tecpatl)	

Key Dates: It's been 50 years since we've quaked quite like this (Sep. 30, 1993, in India).

Your Dates:

Horoscope. As if the first quakes were not bad enough, watch out for aftershocks. The very foundation of a relationship trembles.

MAYAN	AZTEC	
3 ⊠	3 🗡	DAY OF THE HOLY YEAR #198
3 Blade (3 Eznab)	3 Flint (3 Tecpatl)	

Key Dates: Palestine declares the creation of an independent Palestinian state, with Jerusalem as its capital (Nov. 15, 1988).

Your Dates:

Horoscope. The land can be divided in many different ways. But no one ever seems to have enough room to stretch.

MAYAN	AZTEC	
4 ⊠	4 🗡	DAY OF THE HOLY YEAR #238
4 Blade (4 Eznab)	4 Flint (4 Tecpatl)	

Key Dates: Pentagon announces direct hit on enemy command post (Feb. 13, 1991, Baghdad). Enemy counts 300 civilians dead in bomb shelter incident (Feb. 13, 1991, Baghdad).

Your Dates:

Horoscope. The power to control the media, of course, cannot be denied . . . by either side. We may never know for sure.

MAYAN   AZTEC

5 🗷	5 🦪	DAY OF THE HOLY YEAR #18
5 Blade (5 Eznab)	5 Flint (5 Tecpatl)	

Key Dates: Two hundred fifty thousand protest the Vietnam War's continuation (Nov. 15, 1969, in D.C.).

Your Dates:

Horoscope. It all depends on who has the head honcho's ear. Join forces for a stronger voice. Build your case first.

MAYAN   AZTEC

6 🗷	6 🦪	DAY OF THE HOLY YEAR #58
6 Blade (6 Eznab)	6 Flint (6 Tecpatl)	

Key Dates: James Dean becomes a legend (Sep. 30, 1955, dies in car crash). Wilbur Wright becomes a legend (Oct. 6, 1908, stays aloft over 64 minutes). Boston becomes a legend (Oct. 13, 1903, winner of the first World Series... instead of Pittsburgh).

Your Dates:

Horoscope. This is a banner day—a day for making legends. Win one, if not for the Gipper... then for us.

MAYAN	AZTEC	
7 ⊠ 7 Blade (7 Eznab)	7 ⬏ 7 Flint (7 Tecpatl)	DAY OF THE HOLY YEAR #98
Key Dates: Supreme Court overturns two marijuana laws as unconstitutional (May 19, 1969). **Your Dates:**		

Horoscope. Well, put that in your pipe...(but if I were you, I wouldn't smoke it...if you aspire to office).

MAYAN	AZTEC	
8 ⊠ 8 Blade (8 Eznab)	8 ⬏ 8 Flint (8 Tecpatl)	DAY OF THE HOLY YEAR #138
Key Dates: Right-wing conservative Senator Jesse Helms is born (Oct. 18, 1921, Monroe, North Carolina). **Your Dates:**		

Horoscope. A breakthrough is likely. Old barriers are cut apart. Mountains are tunneled through A roadblock disappears. And it happens fast.

MAYAN   AZTEC

9 ⊠	9 ✐	DAY OF THE HOLY YEAR #178
9 Blade (9 Eznab)	9 Flint (9 Tecpatl)	

Key Dates: Optimist preacher Norman Vincent Peale born (May 31, 1898, Bowersville, Ohio). Supreme Court bans forced prayer in schools (June 25, 1962, *Engel* v. *Vitale*).

Your Dates:

Horoscope. Let us bow our heads (but privately... and only if you want to). Almighty Father-Mother... Oh Great Spirit... hear us.

MAYAN   AZTEC

10 ⊠	10 ✐	DAY OF THE HOLY YEAR #218
10 Blade (10 Eznab)	10 Flint (10 Tecpatl)	

Key Dates: Fifty-six thousand resist Nazis... but do not live to tell (May 16, 1943, in Warsaw).

Your Dates:

Horoscope. A just cause is no guarantee that justice will prevail in this time or this place... at least, not initially.

MAYAN   AZTEC

11 ⊠	11 ⬳	DAY OF THE HOLY YEAR #258
11 Blade (11 Eznab)	11 Flint (11 Tecpatl)	

Key Dates: Reverend Jerry Falwell picks up the sword and takes control of the Assemblies of God church following Jim Bakker's admission of sin (Mar. 11, 1986).

Your Dates:

Horoscope. There's nothing quite like a heartfelt confession. Practice what you preach—or else be ready to attest that Satan made you.

MAYAN   AZTEC

12 ⊠	12 ⬳	DAY OF THE HOLY YEAR #38
12 Blade (12 Eznab)	12 Flint (12 Tecpatl)	

Key Dates: Women demand the right to vote...again (Dec. 31, 1907, rally in New York City).

Your Dates:

Horoscope. Power is not always everything it's cracked up to be. Exercise your constitutional rights...and live up to your responsibilities.

MAYAN   AZTEC

13 ⊠	13 🖋	DAY OF THE HOLY YEAR #78
13 Blade (13 Eznab)	13 Flint (13 Tecpatl)	
Key Dates: President promises Great Society (Jan. 20, 1965, Lyndon Johnson's inauguration). **Your Dates:**		

Horoscope. Well, Tippecanoe and Tyler, too. A catchy slogan sells both bubble gum and baseball cards. Packaging is everything. Good show.

DAY SIGN S

STORM DAYS

DAY SIGN S HOROSCOPE:

"You'll be talking about this day for a while to come. Events are unforgettable ... unbelievable ... sometimes even inconceivable. Controversy brews in every crock-pot, pressure cooker, and microwave. No wonder the lid blows off something somewhere every so many days. Don't even ask about the weather! The day favors a love that is stormy. The thought is: As it is above us, so it is below."

RECORD YOUR OWN "S" DATES:

EXPRESS YOUR OWN THOUGHTS:

NOW LOOK UP YOUR DAY NUMBER

MAYAN   AZTEC

1	1	DAY OF THE HOLY YEAR #79
1 Storm (1 Cauac)	1 Storm (1 Quiauitl)	
Key Dates: President McKinley dies at 2:15 A.M. Long live Teddy Roosevelt (Sep. 14, 1901). **Your Dates:**		

Horoscope. A stir is caused in a usually monotonous series of routine events. A sequence is disrupted. A frequency is jammed.

MAYAN   AZTEC

2	2	DAY OF THE HOLY YEAR #119
2 Storm (2 Cauac)	2 Storm (2 Quiauitl)	
Key Dates: Bombing raids on North Vietnam cease after two weeks; peace talks resume in Hanoi (Dec. 30, 1972). **Your Dates:**		

Horoscope. If a picture's worth a thousand...you'll sure get your money's worth today. (Imagine what electronic rights would go for.)

MAYAN   AZTEC

3 🔲	3 🐚	DAY OF THE HOLY YEAR #159
3 Storm (3 Cauac)	3 Storm (3 Quiauitl)	

Key Dates: National Council of Churches releases new translation of the Bible, corrected of its ancient gender bias (Oct. 14, 1983). Tornadoes in the Midwest kill 256 (Apr. 11, 1965).

Your Dates:

Horoscope. He or she looked down from his or her heights, and said there, that's better. Don't sacrifice beauty for correctness.

MAYAN   AZTEC

4 🔲	4 🐚	DAY OF THE HOLY YEAR #199
4 Storm (4 Cauac)	4 Storm (4 Quiauitl)	

Key Dates: Following the mass suicide of 911 Jim Jones followers, the last of the bodies are returned to the U.S. today (Nov. 29, 1978, in Guyana). "By reason of insanity," say courts (June 21, 1982, Hinckley, charged for attempt on President Reagan, gets off).

Your Dates:

Horoscope. Nobody has all the answers. Take this for what it's worth. Seek hope, not despair. Don't blindly follow the leader.

MAYAN	AZTEC	
5 🔲	5 🔲	DAY OF THE HOLY YEAR #239
5 Storm (5 Cauac)	5 Storm (5 Quiauitl)	

Key Dates: Incumbent asked to stay on for another tour of duty (Nov. 7, 1944, FDR elected President for the fourth time). Hurricane Hugo in progress—will cause 49 deaths and $4.2 million in damages (Sep. 12, 1989).

Your Dates:

Horoscope. You can't do it all by your lonesome forever. Nothing lasts at such a pace. Accept the offered helping hand.

MAYAN	AZTEC	
6 🔲	6 🔲	DAY OF THE HOLY YEAR #19
6 Storm (6 Cauac)	6 Storm (6 Quiauitl)	

Key Dates: The *Bismarck* is sunk (May, 27, 1941).

Your Dates:

Horoscope. Suddenly there's a decision in your favor. The odds are evened out. The playing field is leveled. Your position improves.

MAYAN	AZTEC	
7 🗒	7 🐚	DAY OF THE HOLY YEAR #59
7 Storm (7 Cauac)	7 Storm (7 Quiauitl)	
Key Dates: Two tainted grapes cause panic in produce sections nationwide (Mar. 16, 1989). **Your Dates:**		

Horoscope. It is only one incident in a long series of random incidents. Don't panic. It probably won't ever happen again.

MAYAN	AZTEC	
8 🗒	8 🐚	DAY OF THE HOLY YEAR #99
8 Storm (8 Cauac)	8 Storm (8 Quiauitl)	
Key Dates: Lindbergh crosses the Atlantic in an airplane (May 21, 1927). Austria-Hungry declares war on Serbia (July 28, 1914). **Your Dates:**		

Horoscope. Banner headlines in bold, black type. It's a shot heard round the world.

MAYAN	AZTEC	
9 ▨	9 🪲	DAY OF THE HOLY YEAR #139
9 Storm (9 Cauac)	9 Storm (9 Quiauitl)	

Key Dates: Reigning Emperor steps forth to admit he is not a god, nor does he speak for the Divine (Jan. 1, 1946, Japan's Hirohito steps down). Hurricane in Louisiana and Mississippi kills 350 (Sep. 12, 1909).

Your Dates:

Horoscope. In some situations you'd say anything, too. Take a true confession in its larger context. How can one save face?

MAYAN	AZTEC	
10 ▨	10 🪲	DAY OF THE HOLY YEAR #179
10 Storm (10 Cauac)	10 Storm (10 Quiauitl)	

Key Dates: Harvard denies woman admission to law school (Oct. 22, 1909, Inez Milholland). Hurricane Carol in progress—will kill 60 and injure 1,000 in New York and New England (Aug. 27, 1954).

Your Dates:

Horoscope. We did not make the dates and incidents up, you know. The record speaks for itself. And so does yours.

MAYAN   AZTEC

11 ⬛	11 ⬛	DAY OF THE HOLY YEAR #219
11 Storm (11 Cauac)	11 Storm (11 Quiauitl)	

Key Dates: Hemingway wins the Pulitzer Prize (May 4, 1953, for *The Old Man and the Sea*). B-1 crashes in test flight (Aug. 29, 1984). Memorial service held today for astronauts killed when *Challenger* exploded on liftoff (Jan. 31, 1986).

Your Dates:

Horoscope. Short segments, clips, and selected sentences are replayed again and again in your head today. What is your lasting impression?

MAYAN   AZTEC

12 ⬛	12 ⬛	DAY OF THE HOLY YEAR #259
12 Storm (12 Cauac)	12 Storm (12 Quiauitl)	

Key Dates: First person of either gender in space (Apr. 12, 1961, Yuri Gagarin).

Your Dates:

Horoscope. Beware that an early lead does not go to your head. Pacing often catches up with quick and sudden bursts.

MAYAN	AZTEC	
13 ▨	13 ▨	DAY OF THE HOLY YEAR #39
13 Storm (13 Cauac)	13 Storm (13 Quiauitl)	

Key Dates: Hurricane Donna in progress—will kill 50 in the U.S. and 115 in the Antilles (Sep. 4, 1960).

Your Dates:

Horoscope. There is always something disastrous happening somewhere. Prepare for the inevitable every way you can; then go about your business.

DAY SIGN T

LORD/FLOWER DAYS

DAY SIGN T HOROSCOPE:

"Wow! What a finish! Stunning and stupendous things happen this day. Destinies are achieved. Benchmarks are passed. Landmarks are reached. Rites of passage are survived to tell the tale. Not only the weather should be taken for better or worse. The day favors a love that alters everything from here on in. The thought is: Do what it takes to prove your point."

RECORD YOUR OWN "T" DATES:

EXPRESS YOUR OWN THOUGHTS:

NOW LOOK UP YOUR DAY NUMBER

MAYAN	AZTEC	
1 ⚏	1 ✿	DAY OF THE HOLY YEAR #40
1 Lord (1 Ahau)	1 Flower (1 Xochitl)	
Key Dates: A heroic moment in Washington, D.C. (Jan. 13, 1982, one human attempts to save another after plane crash in icy Potomac). **Your Dates:**		

Horoscope. You will have the opportunity to prove what you are made of this time. Opt for doing the right thing.

MAYAN	AZTEC	
2 ⚏	2 ✿	DAY OF THE HOLY YEAR #80
2 Lord (2 Ahau)	2 Flower (2 Xochitl)	
Key Dates: A historic moment for all Americans (Feb. 4, 1913, Rosa Parks is born in Tuskegee, Alabama). **Your Dates:**		

Horoscope. This is a time to stand up for your rights. Don't take things sitting down. Go out on a limb.

MAYAN	AZTEC	
3 ⊕	3 ✿	DAY OF THE HOLY YEAR #120
3 Lord (3 Ahau)	3 Flower (3 Xochitl)	

Key Dates: A breakthrough in world politics (May 10, 1994, Nelson Mandela is South Africa's first black President).

Your Dates:

Horoscope. This is a time for taking the opportunity to test out your grandest ideas. Measure up to your own ideals.

MAYAN	AZTEC	
4 ⊕	4 ✿	DAY OF THE HOLY YEAR #160
4 Lord (4 Ahau)	4 Flower (4 Xochitl)	

Key Dates: Nazis surrender unconditionally (May 7, 1945). Americans walk on the moon (July 20, 1969).

Your Dates:

Horoscope. This is a time for realizing a long-outstanding goal. Everything in the past has led you to this magic moment.

MAYAN   AZTEC

5 🎴	5 🏵	DAY OF THE HOLY YEAR #200
5 Lord (5 Ahau)	5 Flower (5 Xochitl)	
Key Dates: Princess gives birth to heir (June 22, 1982, William born to Charles and Diana). **Your Dates:**		

Horoscope. This is a time for laying out future steps. Contingency plans, succession plans, and estate planning are especially encouraged now.

MAYAN   AZTEC

6 🎴	6 🏵	DAY OF THE HOLY YEAR #240
6 Lord (6 Ahau)	6 Flower (6 Xochitl)	
Key Dates: Women get the vote (Aug. 26, 1920). Yankees win the Series (Oct. 2, 1932). **Your Dates:**		

Horoscope. It's a time when things turn topsy-turvy. Old notions and outworn concepts are overthrown. Losers win! (And it's about time.)

MAYAN   AZTEC

7 🎴	7 🌺	DAY OF THE HOLY YEAR #20
7 Lord (7 Ahau)	7 Flower (7 Xochitl)	
Key Dates: First flight of the Concorde. "Finally, the big bird flies" (Mar. 2, 1969). **Your Dates:**		

Horoscope. It's a time when things that were not abandoned after first false starts achieve the vision their inventors always foresaw.

MAYAN   AZTEC

8 🎴	8 🌺	DAY OF THE HOLY YEAR #60
8 Lord (8 Ahau)	8 Flower (8 Xochitl)	
Key Dates: Auschwitz is liberated (Jan. 27, 1945). **Your Dates:**		

Horoscope. It's a time when we cannot escape the truth of a matter that has gone unnoticed by us till now.

MAYAN   AZTEC

9 🔲	9 🌸	DAY OF THE HOLY YEAR #100
9 Lord (9 Ahau)	9 Flower (9 Xochitl)	
Key Dates: Congress sends to the states a proposed amendment that will give D.C. residents full voting rights (Aug. 22, 1978). **Your Dates:**		

Horoscope. It's a time for defying old assumptions. The smallest gains become true milestones. Hold on to even a little ground.

MAYAN   AZTEC

10 🔲	10 🌸	DAY OF THE HOLY YEAR #140
10 Lord (10 Ahau)	10 Flower (10 Xochitl)	
Key Dates: Two hundred fifty thousand are suspected of unknowingly spreading the disease (Nov. 7, 1948, medical experts report on VD incidence). **Your Dates:**		

Horoscope. It's a time for making mountains out of molehills. Our problems are not always what we think they should be.

MAYAN   AZTEC

11 🎴	11 🌼	DAY OF THE HOLY YEAR #180
11 Lord (11 Ahau)	11 Flower (11 Xochitl)	

Key Dates: Jogging expert meets with ironic fate (July 21, 1984, James F. Fixx, dies at 52, while jogging).

Your Dates:

Horoscope. It's a time for being struck by the irony behind a popularly held belief. Wholesome naturalness is not necessarily sufficient.

MAYAN   AZTEC

12 🎴	12 🌼	DAY OF THE HOLY YEAR #220
12 Lord (12 Ahau)	12 Flower (12 Xochitl)	

Key Dates: *Roe* v. *Wade* decision affirmed (June 29, 1992).

Your Dates:

Horoscope. It's a time for reaching the same decision twice ... or is that thrice? (We have no further comment on this.)

MAYAN	AZTEC	
13 ▣	13 ✿	DAY OF THE HOLY YEAR #260
13 Lord (13 Ahau)	13 Flower (13 Xochitl)	

Key Dates: The world has a full day of peace today, after the war has ended all over the world (Aug. 15, 1945).... And now for a moment of silence.

Your Dates:

Horoscope. It's a day and a half, let me tell ya. We've waited a real long time for one this good.

AND THUS THE COUNT ENDS.
THE 260 DAYS ARE DONE.
A FULL CYCLE HAS BEEN RUN.
NOW WE START ALL OVER AGAIN.

ALMANAC
1909–2012

*Your goodwill illuminate
the earth for them.
Cause to enter the spirit within
its other age.*

—MAYAN INVOCATION
AT THE END OF THE KATUNS
THE PROPHECY OF CHILAM BALAM
(ADAPTED FROM THE TRANSLATIONS
OF TOZZER AND LIZANA)

Introduction to the Almanac

Welcome to the Almanac. Just as the priests of old turned to their
holy books to cast the horoscope of a newborn child
or to determine the signs, omens, portents, and auspices of any
given day, you will use this part of the book to compute your own
signs, starting with the familiar dates from our own calendar.

OVERVIEW OF THE ALMANAC

In the same way that surviving Mayan and Aztec books are often divided into sections, each devoted to a particular aspect of the calendars,
this book's Almanac is divided into parts. The two main divisions are:

- **Part I —The Sacred Calendar**—which is the one you will use most.
  It correlates our calendar with the 260-day Holy Year of the Maya
  and Aztecs. This is the calendar used for divination and fortune-
  telling.

- **Part II —The Secular Calendar**—which you will use in Reading
  #12—correlates our calendar with the 365-day agricultural year of
  the Maya and Aztecs.

Each of the two Almanacs is complete from 1909 to the year 2012. The
rest of this introduction will show you how to use each Almanac as well
as present you with the basic facts about how these Almanacs were constructed.

PART I—THE SACRED CALENDAR

The Almanac for the 260-day Holy Year also forms the basis for all
counting by Tuns, Katuns, Baktuns, and Creation Epochs. The list-
ings—which are ordered in terms of our dates—have been set up using
the classic column-and-row formats of the original Mayan and Aztec
holy books. Information for each year in our calendar is listed in a tall,
vertical column, organized by year.

Our Year _____

Our Date _____

A=Day Sign

13=Day #

2011	Day #
JAN 2	A 13
JAN 22	A 7
FEB 11	*A 1*
MAR 3	A 8
MAR 23	A 2
APR 12	A 9
MAY 2	A 3
MAY 22	A 10
JUN 11	A 4
JUL 1	A 11
JUL 21	A 5
AUG 10	A 12
AUG 30	A 6
SEP 19	A 13
OCT 9	A 7
OCT 29	*A 1*
NOV 18	A 8
DEC 8	A 2
DEC 28	A 9

On the left-hand side of each column are our dates. On the right are the Mayan and Aztec dates that equate to the specific dates listed on the left.

For easiest lookup, each date from our calendar is keyed to a letter of our alphabet, which, in turn, stands for one of the Day Signs. The Day Signs and their alphabetical keys are listed at regular intervals throughout the Almanac for handy reference. You can choose to use either the Mayan or Aztec Day Signs at any point in your work....

MAYAN DAY SIGNS

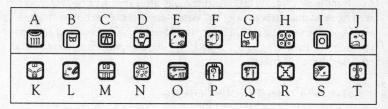

AZTEC DAY SIGNS

SECRET! Not every date is listed!

In their own holy books, the Maya and Aztecs did not list the Day Signs for every single day in the calendar, but only for every so many days. Of course, once one date is known, it is not too difficult to determine what the Mayan or Aztec signs will be over the next few days. All you really have to do is count on your fingers. The secret is knowing how many days separate each listed date in the Almanac. Psst. I'll tell you what it is....

This book's Almanac starts on January 17, 1908, and **lists every 20th date** until the official ending of this calendar in December 2012.

How to Compute Your Date

If the date you are looking for is one of the nearly 2,000 listed in the Almanac, all you have to do is copy down your Day Sign and Day Number and look up your answers in either the Reading you are doing or the Master Answer section of the Quick Reference Guide. If your date is not listed, read on....

Alas! The odds are only 1 in 20 that the specific day you are looking for will be listed in the Almanac. But... if it's not listed, all you have to do is count it out. Here's where your counting fingers will come in handy!

As you know, the 20 Day Signs cycle continuously from Sign A

(Alligator/Sea Creature) to Sign T (Lord/Flower). If today's sign is "A," then tomorrow's will be "B." And the day after that will be "C," and so on. **The Almanac lists every "A" date**—the start of each new "month" (or Mayan Uinal.) If the Almanac lists March 3, 2011, but you are really interested in the signs for March 8, first compute the "count" that separates these two days.

STEP 1—COMPUTE YOUR "COUNT"

Always count the date listed in the Almanac as "1." Count forward to your date....

March 3 = count 1
March 4 = count 2
March 5 = count 3
March 6 = count 4
March 7 = count 5
March 8 = count 6

STEP 2—FINGER YOUR DAY SIGN

Put your finger on Day Sign A in the tables here (or at the top of most Almanac pages).

MAYAN DAY SIGNS

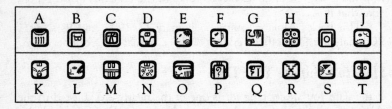

430

AZTEC DAY SIGNS

Move forward one space for each number in your count. You have just fingered your Day Sign. Jot it down. In our example, we would count forward six spaces from Day Sign A: A, B, C, D, E, F. Your Day Sign in this case would be F.

STEP 3—FINGER YOUR DAY NUMBER

Using the Day Number table here (or at the bottom of most Almanac pages), put your finger on the Day Number of the closest listed date to yours. Counting this Day as "1," count forward to yours by the same number of spaces you counted above.

DAY NUMBERS

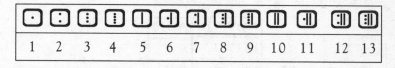

You have just fingered your Day Number. Jot it down beside your Day Sign. Turn to the Answers. In our example, the Day Number listed in the table for March 3 is 8. Moving forward a six-count from 8 takes us to: 8, 9, 10, 11, 12, 13. Your Day Number in this case would be 13. Your Day Sign/Day Number combination would therefore be 13 F.

A cheat sheet containing these instructions is included every so often within the Almanac so that you are never far away from help if you forget the rules.

Other Details Included in the Almanac

Part I of the Almanac also can function as a handy reference tool for finding other Mayan and Aztec dates that might interest you.

Look for Holy Years. The start of each 260-day Holy Year (Tzolkin) is identified by special type and borders:

1996	Day #
JAN 1	A 6
JAN 21	A 13
FEB 10	A 7
MAR 1	*A 1* ———— Tzolkin
MAR 21	A 8

Since a Holy Year lasts only 260 Days, two sacred cycles often start during a single one of our years. Use the Tzolkin start dates boxed off in the Almanac to plot your own spiritual journey through the calendar. Begin a 260-day vision quest on the first day of any listed Holy Period and follow the calendar—and your heart—for the ensuing 260 days.

Since this Holy Calendar is the basis for the longer periods of time the Maya and Aztecs counted, this book's Almanac also indicates which Tun year is in effect.

Find your Tun. The start of each 360-day Tun Year is identified at the bottom of each column, by its official designation—always an Ahau date (Sign T). Using the table for 1997:

NOV 11	A 10
DEC 1	A 4
DEC 1	A 11

MAYA YEAR: ——— TUN
12 AHAU
STARTS MAR 16TH

The entire year is said to be under the influence of the Ahau that rules it. The Ahau years follow a recurring pattern: 5 Ahau, 1 Ahau, 10 Ahau, 6 Ahau, 2 Ahau, 11 Ahau, 7 Ahau, 3 Ahau, 12 Ahau, 8 Ahau, 4 Ahau, 13 Ahau, 9 Ahau. In an especially Mesoamerican way, each one of these years is named for its last—not its first—day. We use the Ahau dates in Reading #10. You will quickly note, however, that the Tuns do not start at the same time as our years. To find the current Tun, find the column for this year (say it's 1997) and consult the information at the bottom of the column. If we haven't come yet to the start date listed there, the current Tun is still the one that started in the previous year (1996). Consult the bottom of the column for the previous year to find the current Tun.

PART II—THE SECULAR CALENDAR

In addition to their Holy Calendars, the Maya and Aztecs also maintained a separate calendar that was fairly accurate in measuring the true length of the solar year. Their 365-day calendar, the Haab, was used in planning seasonal events and activities, much as we use our calendar to plan what we will do in upcoming seasons. The Haab year consists of eighteen 20-day months (= 360 days) plus a five-day "leap month" (or Uayeb) at the end of each year. Mayan and Aztec dates are usually expressed in terms of both calendars, as a check-and-balance system for assuring that no errors in time-counting are made. Though this calendar is not really required for divination purposes, it has been included in the book as a bonus for those interested in being especially authentic in citing dates.

The tables for the Haab dates—Part II of the Almanac—are shown in wide horizontal rows, with a new table for each year listed.

2004 Leap Year					
JAN 1–9	See 2003	APR 4	*Pop*	AUG 22	*Mol*
JAN 10	*Muan*	APR 24	*Uo*	SEP 11	*Chen*
JAN 30	*Pax*	MAY 14	*Zip*	OCT 1	*Yax*
FEB 19	*Kayab*	JUN 3	*Zotz*	OCT 21	*Zac*
MAR 10	*Cumku*	JUN 23	*Tzec*	NOV 10	*Ceh*
MAR 30	*Uayeb*	JUL 13	*Xul*	NOV 30	*Mac*
		AUG 2	*Yaxkin*	DEC 20	*Kankin*
The Year 7 Flint starts Apr. 4, 2004.					

For easy lookup, the table keys each listed date to its Haab month.

The months of the year

These are the same signs identified in Reading #12. When working with this Almanac, you will always be referred back to Reading #12 for your answers.

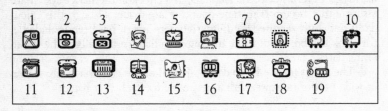

As with Part I, this seasonal Almanac lists the start date for every Haab month from 1909 to 2012.

Just as in the Holy Calendar, a complete Haab date consists of both a sign—in this case a month sign—and a number. **Since the numbers for these Haab dates have no significance in divination, you do not even need to compute them.**

But should you want to know the complete Haab date, it's possible to count it using Almanac II.

Some special rules apply to counting Haab dates. The days in each Haab month are numbered consecutively, with the first day (known as the "seating" of the month) counted as <u>zero</u>, the second day as 1, and so on until a 20-day Haab month has been completed with the number 19. Then back to zero again, for the seating of the next month.

The table of Haab dates lists every first day of a new Mayan month—every 20th day in our calendar. Due to the way Haab dates are numbered, the date listed in this table is <u>always</u> a number 0 day.

As the "first day" of the month, this zero day seats the month listed beside it.

How to Find Your Haab Dates

If your date is listed in the table, all you have to do is copy down the name of your month (as listed) and note that your number is zero.

If your date is not listed, find the date that just precedes the date you are looking for. The month indicated in the table is also your month. To work the activities in this book, the name of the month is all you really need to know. But if you would like to go on and count out your exact Haab date, you can do so. Just count forward to your own date now.

TAKE CARE! The way you count dates in the Haab is a little different from the counting method used for Almanac I. Since the date listed in Almanac II is always a "zero" day, <u>don't</u> include it in your counts. In using Almanac II, <u>always start counting with the date after the one listed in the Almanac</u>. The day after the listed date is always a one-count, the day after that is always a two-count, and so on until a count of 19 completes the month.

But Uayeb hath only five! There's only one exception to this rule, which is for the month Uayeb (the last five "leap days" of the Haab year). Because it can get tricky remembering this exception, the Almanac highlights the five-day Uayeb with a dark box. It always appears at the bottom of the left-hand column.

2008 Leap Year					
JAN 1–8	See 2007	APR 3	Pop	AUG 21	Mol
JAN 9	Muan	APR 23	Uo	SEP 10	Chen
JAN 29	Pax	MAY 13	Zip	SEP 30	Yax
FEB 18	Kayab	JUN 2	Zotz	OCT 20	Zac
MAR 9	Cumku	JUN 22	Tzec	NOV 9	Ceh
MAR 29	Uayeb	JUL 12	Xul	NOV 29	Mac
		AUG 1	Yaxkin	DEC 19	Kankin

The Year 11 Flint starts Apr. 4, 2008.

The first day of each month is shown. This day is counted as "0." Count forward to your day of the month

If you are looking for the Haab date that equates to September 15th, 2008, the closest day listed on the table is September 10. September 10 is the start date of the Haab month "Chen" (🝔). Chen is your month. Now, counting forward from September 10th (with this date equal to a zero count), we have the 11th (one-count), 12th (two-count), 13th (three-count), 14th (four-count), and 15th (five-count)... which is five days. So, for September 15, 2008, your corresponding Haab date is the fifth of the month Chen—5 Chen.

In the period covered by the 104 years presented in this Almanac, the Mayan/Aztec Haab year is starting and ending in the spring. But over the millennia that this calendar has been at work, the start date of the year has shifted backwards from season to season. In the tables used here, each Haab starts at the top of the center column, and is further indicated with a notation at the bottom of the table.

What to Use the Haab Dates for

Haab months are used in this book to provide some additional depth to your general consultations (see Reading #12) and in the construction of a personal horoscope (see Reading #13's Extra Credit section). The tables also serve as handy references for noting when a new Mayan Haab year is coming up (not to mention a tool for identifying when the Uayeb's five Dark Days are in effect—yikes!).

Find the Year Bearer. In computing your horoscope, you can also use the tables here to find the Day Sign that rules each Haab year. It was said that the first Day Sign of a Haab year has a unique bearing on every other day of the year that it leads off. Due to the way this calendar cycles, it can be only one of four Day Signs.

The four signs that rule the years are known as Year Bearers. They can be only Night, Rabbit, Reed, or Blade. The Sign that stands as the Year Bearer for any given year is the Day Sign and Number from the Holy Calendar that falls on the Haab day 1 Pop. In Almanac II, the Year Bearers are indicated at the bottom of each column, by their name, number, and start date. Note: the Haab does not officially begin until the first date listed in the almanac (0 Pop) is done.

How the Almanac Was Constructed

Starting with December 21, 2012—the end of the calendar—the Almanac for this book was constructed in the time-honored tradition of counting by hand. The ancient formulas included in *The Paris Codex*—an authentic Mayan book still in use when the Spaniards came to America—were used in this effort. The intricate construction of the calendar itself assured its own accuracy, since there are periodic points at which everything must line up—and if it doesn't, errors are obvious. As a final check, every date in the Almanac was verified against a marvelous computer program called MacMaya, by Warren Anderson. MacMaya will compute any date you want to enter in seconds and display full information, including the famous long-count dates that express any day's full Mesoamerican date from the beginning of Mayan time.[1]

Almanac I in this book covers a period of 37,960 days, which is exactly 1,898 Mayan "months" (or Uinals) of 20 days each—for exactly 146 Holy Years and exactly 104 agricultural (or Haab) years. The two calendars time out this way only once every 52 years. Two complete "Calendar Rounds" of 52 full years each are covered in the Almanac—a period of time that the Maya call an *Old Age*. For calendar aficionados, other facts about the Almanac are included in the following table.

TIME PERIODS COVERED IN ALMANAC I

Almanac Facts & Stats	
Period of time covered (in our own calendar)	Jan. 17, 1909, to Dec. 21, 2012
Total days included	37,960
13-day periods (Mayan "weeks")	2,920
20-day periods (Mayan Uinals)	1,898
Holy Years (Mayan Tzolkins of 260 days each)	146
360-day Tuns (basic time units for larger cycles)	105 (+160 days)
Agricultural years (Mayan Haabs of 365 Days)	104
20-year cycles (Mayan Katuns of 7,200 days)	5 (+1960 days)
Calendar Rounds (18,980-day periods = 52 Haab years)	2 (an Old Age)

In order to start at the beginning of a Haab month, Almanac II begins on Jan. 13, 1909, and is, therefore, four days longer than each of the time periods noted above. Both calendars stop telling time on Dec. 21, 2012. Until then, enjoy....

---

[1] At the time we went to press, MacMaya could be downloaded as shareware from CompuServe's Astronomy Forum or the Info-Mac archive at standford.edu. Or write Warren Anderson at P.O. Box 811, Wilson, Wyoming, U.S.A. 83014.

PART I—The Sacred Calendar

Covering the last Old Age (104 solar years)
of the Maya's Fifth Creation Epoch
—Including the last five Katuns of Mayan time—

1909	Day	#
JAN 1	E	2
JAN 17	A	5
FEB 6	A	12
FEB 26	A	6
MAR 18	A	13
APR 7	A	7
APR 27	*A*	*1*
MAY 17	A	8
JUN 6	A	2
JUN 26	A	9
JUL 16	A	3
AUG 5	A	10
AUG 25	A	4
SEP 14	A	11
OCT 4	A	5
OCT 24	A	12
NOV 13	A	6
DEC 3	A	13
DEC 23	A	7

1910	Day	#
JAN 12	*A*	*1*
FEB 1	A	8
FEB 21	A	2
MAR 13	A	9
APR 2	A	3
APR 22	A	10
MAY 12	A	4
JUN 1	A	11
JUN 21	A	5
JUL 11	A	12
JUL 31	A	6
AUG 20	A	13
SEP 9	A	7
SEP 29	*A*	*1*
OCT 19	A	8
NOV 8	A	2
NOV 28	A	9
DEC 18	A	3

1911	Day	#
JAN 7	A	10
JAN 27	A	4
FEB 16	A	11
MAR 8	A	5
MAR 28	A	12
APR 17	A	6
MAY 7	A	13
MAY 27	A	7
JUN 16	*A*	*1*
JUL 6	A	8
JUL 26	A	2
AUG 15	A	9
SEP 4	A	3
SEP 24	A	10
OCT 14	A	4
NOV 3	A	11
NOV 23	A	5
DEC 13	A	12

TUN 4 AHAU — STARTS JUN 26TH

TUN 13 AHAU — STARTS JUN 21ST

TUN 9 AHAU — STARTS JUN 16TH

| 1 | 2 | 3 | 4 | 5 | 6 | 7 | 8 | 9 | 10 | 11 | 12 | 13 |

Mayan Day Signs

A	B	C	D	E	F	G	H	I	J
K	L	M	N	O	P	Q	R	S	T

1912

		Day	#
JAN	2	A	6
JAN	22	A	13
FEB	11	A	7
MAR	*2*	*A*	*1*
MAR	22	A	8
APR	11	A	2
MAY	1	A	9
MAY	21	A	3
JUN	10	A	10
JUN	30	A	4
JUL	20	A	11
AUG	9	A	5
AUG	29	A	12
SEP	18	A	6
OCT	8	A	13
OCT	28	A	7
NOV	*17*	*A*	*1*
DEC	7	A	8
DEC	27	A	2

1913

		Day	#
JAN	16	A	9
FEB	5	A	3
FEB	25	A	10
MAR	17	A	4
APR	6	A	11
APR	26	A	5
MAY	16	A	12
JUN	5	A	6
JUN	25	A	13
JUL	15	A	7
AUG	*4*	*A*	*1*
AUG	24	A	8
SEP	13	A	2
OCT	3	A	9
OCT	23	A	3
NOV	12	A	10
DEC	2	A	4
DEC	22	A	11

1914

		Day	#
JAN	11	A	5
JAN	31	A	12
FEB	20	A	6
MAR	12	A	13
APR	1	A	7
APR	*21*	*A*	*1*
MAY	11	A	8
MAY	31	A	2
JUN	20	A	9
JUL	10	A	3
JUL	30	A	10
AUG	19	A	4
SEP	8	A	11
SEP	28	A	5
OCT	18	A	12
NOV	7	A	6
NOV	27	A	13
DEC	17	A	7

TUN
5 AHAU |
STARTS JUNE 10TH

TUN
1 AHAU •
STARTS JUNE 5TH

TUN
10 AHAU ||
STARTS MAY 31ST

■ *16TH Katun Starts: MAY 31*

1	2	3	4	5	6	7	8	9	10	11	12	13

Aztec Day Signs

A	B	C	D	E	F	G	H	I	J
K	L	M	N	O	P	Q	R	S	T

1915		Day	#
JAN	6	A	1
JAN	26	A	8
FEB	15	A	2
MAR	7	A	9
MAR	27	A	3
APR	16	A	10
MAY	6	A	4
MAY	26	A	11
JUN	15	A	5
JUL	5	A	12
JUL	25	A	6
AUG	14	A	13
SEP	3	A	7
SEP	23	A	1
OCT	13	A	8
NOV	2	A	2
NOV	22	A	9
DEC	12	A	3

1916		Day	#
JAN	1	A	10
JAN	21	A	4
FEB	10	A	11
MAR	1	A	5
MAR	21	A	12
APR	10	A	6
APR	30	A	13
MAY	20	A	7
JUN	9	A	1
JUN	29	A	8
JUL	19	A	2
AUG	8	A	9
AUG	28	A	3
SEP	17	A	10
OCT	7	A	4
OCT	27	A	11
NOV	16	A	5
DEC	6	A	12
DEC	26	A	6

1917		Day	#
JAN	15	A	13
FEB	4	A	7
FEB	24	A	1
MAR	16	A	8
APR	5	A	2
APR	25	A	9
MAY	15	A	3
JUN	4	A	10
JUN	24	A	4
JUL	14	A	11
AUG	3	A	5
AUG	23	A	12
SEP	12	A	6
OCT	2	A	13
OCT	22	A	7
NOV	11	A	1
DEC	1	A	8
DEC	21	A	2

TUN	TUN	TUN
6 AHAU	2 AHAU	11 AHAU
STARTS MAY 26TH	STARTS MAY 20TH	STARTS MAY 15TH

1	2	3	4	5	6	7	8	9	10	11	12	13

440

Mayan Day Signs

A	B	C	D	E	F	G	H	I	J
K	L	M	N	O	P	Q	R	S	T

1918		Day	#
JAN	10	A	9
JAN	30	A	3
FEB	19	A	10
MAR	11	A	4
MAR	31	A	11
APR	20	A	5
MAY	10	A	12
MAY	30	A	6
JUN	19	A	13
JUL	9	A	7
JUL	*29*	*A*	*1*
AUG	18	A	8
SEP	7	A	2
SEP	27	A	9
OCT	17	A	3
NOV	6	A	10
NOV	26	A	4
DEC	16	A	11

1919		Day	#
JAN	5	A	5
JAN	25	A	12
FEB	14	A	6
MAR	6	A	13
MAR	26	A	7
APR	*15*	*A*	*1*
MAY	5	A	8
MAY	25	A	2
JUN	14	A	9
JUL	4	A	3
JUL	24	A	10
AUG	13	A	4
SEP	2	A	11
SEP	22	A	5
OCT	12	A	12
NOV	1	A	6
NOV	21	A	13
DEC	11	A	7
DEC	*31*	*A*	*1*

1920		Day	#
JAN	20	A	8
FEB	9	A	2
FEB	29	A	9
MAR	20	A	3
APR	9	A	10
APR	29	A	4
MAY	19	A	11
JUN	8	A	5
JUN	28	A	12
JUL	18	A	6
AUG	7	A	13
AUG	27	A	7
SEP	*16*	*A*	*1*
OCT	6	A	8
OCT	26	A	2
NOV	15	A	9
DEC	5	A	3
DEC	25	A	10

TUN
7 AHAU :|
STARTS MAY 10TH

TUN
3 AHAU :
STARTS MAY 5TH

TUN
12 AHAU :||
STARTS APR 29TH

1	2	3	4	5	6	7	8	9	10	11	12	13

Aztec Day Signs

A	B	C	D	E	F	G	H	I	J
K	L	M	N	O	P	Q	R	S	T

1921	Day	#
JAN 14	A	4
FEB 3	A	11
FEB 23	A	5
MAR 15	A	12
APR 4	A	6
APR 24	A	13
MAY 14	A	7
JUN 3	A	1
JUN 23	A	8
JUL 13	A	2
AUG 2	A	9
AUG 22	A	3
SEP 11	A	10
OCT 1	A	4
OCT 21	A	11
NOV 10	A	5
NOV 30	A	12
DEC 20	A	6

1922	Day	#
JAN 9	A	13
JAN 29	A	7
FEB 18	A	1
MAR 10	A	8
MAR 30	A	2
APR 19	A	9
MAY 9	A	3
MAY 29	A	10
JUN 18	A	4
JUL 8	A	11
JUL 28	A	5
AUG 17	A	12
SEP 6	A	6
SEP 26	A	13
OCT 16	A	7
NOV 5	A	1
NOV 25	A	8
DEC 15	A	2

1923	Day	#
JAN 4	A	9
JAN 24	A	3
FEB 13	A	10
MAR 5	A	4
MAR 25	A	11
APR 14	A	5
MAY 4	A	12
MAY 24	A	6
JUN 13	A	13
JUL 3	A	7
JUL 23	A	1
AUG 12	A	8
SEP 1	A	2
SEP 21	A	9
OCT 11	A	3
OCT 31	A	10
NOV 20	A	4
DEC 10	A	11
DEC 30	A	5

TUN 8 AHAU STARTS APR 24TH

TUN 4 AHAU STARTS APR 19TH

TUN 13 AHAU STARTS APR 14TH

| 1 | 2 | 3 | 4 | 5 | 6 | 7 | 8 | 9 | 10 | 11 | 12 | 13 |

How to use the Almanac
1. Find your date in the main table. The Day Sign and Day Number are listed to the right. If your date isn't in the table, find the date right before yours. Counting this date as "1," count forward, up to and including your date. Jot down this number.
2. Put your finger on Day Sign A at the top of the next page. Count forward by your number. You have just fingered your Day Sign. Jot it down.

1924	Day	#	1925	Day	#	1926	Day	#
JAN 19	A	12	JAN 13	A	8	JAN 8	A	4
FEB 8	A	6	FEB 2	A	2	JAN 28	A	11
FEB 28	A	13	FEB 22	A	9	FEB 17	A	5
MAR 19	A	7	MAR 14	A	3	MAR 9	A	12
APR 8	*A*	*1*	APR 3	A	10	MAR 29	A	6
APR 28	A	8	APR 23	A	4	APR 18	A	13
MAY 18	A	2	MAY 13	A	11	MAY 8	A	7
JUN 7	A	9	JUN 2	A	5	*MAY 28*	*A*	*1*
JUN 27	A	3	JUN 22	A	12	JUN 17	A	8
JUL 17	A	10	JUL 12	A	6	JUL 7	A	2
AUG 6	A	4	AUG 1	A	13	JUL 27	A	9
AUG 26	A	11	AUG 21	A	7	AUG 16	A	3
SEP 15	A	5	*SEP 10*	*A*	*1*	SEP 5	A	10
OCT 5	A	12	SEP 30	A	8	SEP 25	A	4
OCT 25	A	6	OCT 20	A	2	OCT 15	A	11
NOV 14	A	13	NOV 9	A	9	NOV 4	A	5
DEC 4	A	7	NOV 29	A	3	NOV 24	A	12
DEC 24	*A*	*1*	DEC 19	A	10	DEC 14	A	6

TUN 9 AHAU	TUN 5 AHAU	TUN 1 AHAU
STARTS APR 8TH	STARTS APR 3RD	STARTS MAR 29TH

3. Using the numbers at the bottom of the page, put your finger on the Day Number of the closest listed date to yours. Counting this Day as "1," count forward to yours. You have fingered your Day Number. Jot it down beside your Day Sign. Look up both.

Mayan Day Signs

A	B	C	D	E	F	G	H	I	J
K	L	M	N	O	P	Q	R	S	T

1927

Date	Day	#
JAN 3	A	13
JAN 23	A	7
FEB 12	*A*	*1*
MAR 4	A	8
MAR 24	A	2
APR 13	A	9
MAY 3	A	3
MAY 23	A	10
JUN 12	A	4
JUL 2	A	11
JUL 22	A	5
AUG 11	A	12
AUG 31	A	6
SEP 20	A	13
OCT 10	A	7
OCT 30	*A*	*1*
NOV 19	A	8
DEC 9	A	2
DEC 29	A	9

1928

Date	Day	#
JAN 18	A	3
FEB 7	A	10
FEB 27	A	4
MAR 18	A	11
APR 7	A	5
APR 27	A	12
MAY 17	A	6
JUN 6	A	13
JUN 26	A	7
JUL 16	*A*	*1*
AUG 5	A	8
AUG 25	A	2
SEP 14	A	9
OCT 4	A	3
OCT 24	A	10
NOV 13	A	4
DEC 3	A	11
DEC 23	A	5

1929

Date	Day	#
JAN 12	A	12
FEB 1	A	6
FEB 21	A	13
MAR 13	A	7
APR 2	*A*	*1*
APR 22	A	8
MAY 12	A	2
JUN 1	A	9
JUN 21	A	3
JUL 11	A	10
JUL 31	A	4
AUG 20	A	11
SEP 9	A	5
SEP 29	A	12
OCT 19	A	6
NOV 8	A	13
NOV 28	A	7
DEC 18	*A*	*1*

TUN 10 AHAU STARTS MAR 24TH

TUN 6 AHAU STARTS MAR 18TH

TUN 2 AHAU STARTS MAR 13TH

1	2	3	4	5	6	7	8	9	10	11	12	13

Aztec Day Signs

A	B	C	D	E	F	G	H	I	J
K	L	M	N	O	P	Q	R	S	T

1930		Day	#
JAN	7	A	8
JAN	27	A	2
FEB	16	A	9
MAR	8	A	3
MAR	28	A	10
APR	17	A	4
MAY	7	A	11
MAY	27	A	5
JUN	16	A	12
JUL	6	A	6
JUL	26	A	13
AUG	15	A	7
SEP	*4*	*A*	*1*
SEP	24	A	8
OCT	14	A	2
NOV	3	A	9
NOV	23	A	3
DEC	13	A	10

1931		Day	#
JAN	2	A	4
JAN	22	A	11
FEB	11	A	5
MAR	3	A	12
MAR	23	A	6
APR	12	A	13
MAY	2	A	7
MAY	*22*	*A*	*1*
JUN	11	A	8
JUL	1	A	2
JUL	21	A	9
AUG	10	A	3
AUG	30	A	10
SEP	19	A	4
OCT	9	A	11
OCT	29	A	5
NOV	18	A	12
DEC	8	A	6
DEC	28	A	13

1932		Day	#
JAN	17	A	7
FEB	*6*	*A*	*1*
FEB	26	A	8
MAR	17	A	2
APR	6	A	9
APR	26	A	3
MAY	16	A	10
JUN	5	A	4
JUN	25	A	11
JUL	15	A	5
AUG	4	A	12
AUG	24	A	6
SEP	13	A	13
OCT	3	A	7
OCT	*23*	*A*	*1*
NOV	12	A	8
DEC	2	A	2
DEC	22	A	9

TUN 11 AHAU	TUN 7 AHAU	TUN 3 AHAU
STARTS MAR 8TH	STARTS MAR 3RD	STARTS FEB 26TH

1	2	3	4	5	6	7	8	9	10	11	12	13

445

Mayan Day Signs

A	B	C	D	E	F	G	H	I	J
🏛	🗓	▦	🙂	🐍	🙃	🖐	🎲	◉	😵

K	L	M	N	O	P	Q	R	S	T
▦	✎	▦	▦	🐊	❓	▦	✖	▦	▦

1933		Day	#	1934		Day	#	1935		Day	#
JAN	11	A	3	JAN	6	A	12	JAN	1	A	8
JAN	31	A	10	JAN	26	A	6	JAN	21	A	2
FEB	20	A	4	FEB	15	A	13	FEB	10	A	9
MAR	12	A	11	MAR	7	A	7	MAR	2	A	3
APR	1	A	5	*MAR*	*27*	*A*	*1*	MAR	22	A	10
APR	21	A	12	APR	16	A	8	APR	11	A	4
MAY	11	A	6	MAY	6	A	2	MAY	1	A	11
MAY	31	A	13	MAY	26	A	9	MAY	21	A	5
JUN	20	A	7	JUN	15	A	3	JUN	10	A	12
JUL	*10*	*A*	*1*	JUL	5	A	10	JUN	30	A	6
JUL	30	A	8	JUL	25	A	4	JUL	20	A	13
AUG	19	A	2	AUG	14	A	11	AUG	9	A	7
SEP	8	A	9	SEP	3	A	5	*AUG*	*29*	*A*	*1*
SEP	28	A	3	SEP	23	A	12	SEP	18	A	8
OCT	18	A	10	OCT	13	A	6	OCT	8	A	2
NOV	7	A	4	NOV	2	A	13	OCT	28	A	9
NOV	27	A	11	NOV	22	A	7	NOV	17	A	3
DEC	17	A	5	*DEC*	*12*	*A*	*1*	DEC	7	A	10
								DEC	27	A	4

■ 17th Katun Starts: FEB 15

TUN 12 AHAU	:|‖ ◉	TUN 8 AHAU	:⋮ ◉	TUN 4 AHAU	⋮ ◉
STARTS FEB 20TH		STARTS FEB 15TH		STARTS FEB 10TH	

1	2	3	4	5	6	7	8	9	10	11	12	13

Aztec Day Signs

A	B	C	D	E	F	G	H	I	J

K	L	M	N	O	P	Q	R	S	T

1936	Day	#	**1937**	Day	#	**1938**	Day	#
JAN 16	A	11	JAN 10	A	7	JAN 5	A	3
FEB 5	A	5	*JAN 30*	*A*	*1*	JAN 25	A	10
FEB 25	A	12	FEB 19	A	8	FEB 14	A	4
MAR 16	A	6	MAR 11	A	2	MAR 6	A	11
APR 5	A	13	MAR 31	A	9	MAR 26	A	5
APR 25	A	7	APR 20	A	3	APR 15	A	12
MAY 15	*A*	*1*	MAY 10	A	10	MAY 5	A	6
JUN 4	A	8	MAY 30	A	4	MAY 25	A	13
JUN 24	A	2	JUN 19	A	11	JUN 14	A	7
JUL 14	A	9	JUL 9	A	5	*JUL 4*	*A*	*1*
AUG 3	A	3	JUL 29	A	12	JUL 24	A	8
AUG 23	A	10	AUG 18	A	6	AUG 13	A	2
SEP 12	A	4	SEP 7	A	13	SEP 2	A	9
OCT 2	A	11	SEP 27	A	7	SEP 22	A	3
OCT 22	A	5	*OCT 17*	*A*	*1*	OCT 12	A	10
NOV 11	A	12	NOV 6	A	8	NOV 1	A	4
DEC 1	A	6	NOV 26	A	2	NOV 21	A	11
DEC 21	A	13	DEC 16	A	9	DEC 11	A	5
						DEC 31	A	12

TUN
13 AHAU

TUN
9 AHAU

TUN
5 AHAU

STARTS FEB 5TH	STARTS JAN 30TH	STARTS JAN 25TH

1	2	3	4	5	6	7	8	9	10	11	12	13

How to use the Almanac
1. Find your date in the main table. The Day Sign and Day Number are listed to the right. If your date isn't in the table, find the date right before yours. Counting this date as "1," count forward, up to and including your date. Jot down this number.
2. Put your finger on Day Sign A at the top of the next page. Count forward by your number. You have just fingered your Day Sign. Jot it down.

1939		*Day*	#	**1940**		*Day*	#	**1941**		*Day*	#
JAN	20	A	6	JAN	15	A	2	JAN	9	A	11
FEB	9	A	13	FEB	4	A	9	JAN	29	A	5
MAR	1	A	7	FEB	24	A	3	FEB	18	A	12
MAR	*21*	*A*	*1*	MAR	15	A	10	MAR	10	A	6
APR	10	A	8	APR	4	A	4	MAR	30	A	13
APR	30	A	2	APR	24	A	11	APR	19	A	7
MAY	20	A	9	MAY	14	A	5	*MAY*	*9*	*A*	*1*
JUN	9	A	3	JUN	3	A	12	MAY	29	A	8
JUN	29	A	10	JUN	23	A	6	JUN	18	A	2
JUL	19	A	4	JUL	13	A	13	JUL	8	A	9
AUG	8	A	11	AUG	2	A	7	JUL	28	A	3
AUG	28	A	5	*AUG*	*22*	*A*	*1*	AUG	17	A	10
SEP	17	A	12	SEP	11	A	8	SEP	6	A	4
OCT	7	A	6	OCT	1	A	2	SEP	26	A	11
OCT	27	A	13	OCT	21	A	9	OCT	16	A	5
NOV	16	A	7	NOV	10	A	3	NOV	5	A	12
DEC	*6*	*A*	*1*	NOV	30	A	10	NOV	25	A	6
DEC	26	A	8	DEC	20	A	4	DEC	15	A	13

TUN 1 AHAU ●	TUN 10 AHAU ‖	TUN 6 AHAU •‖
STARTS JAN 20TH	STARTS JAN 15TH	STARTS JAN 9TH

3. Using the numbers at the bottom of the page, put your finger on the Day Number of the closest listed date to yours. Counting this Day as "1," count forward to yours. You have fingered your Day Number. Jot it down beside your Day Sign. Look up both.

Mayan Day Signs

A	B	C	D	E	F	G	H	I	J
🔲	🔲	🔲	🔲	🔲	🔲	🔲	🔲	🔲	🔲
🔲	🔲	🔲	🔲	🔲	🔲	🔲	🔲	🔲	🔲
K	L	M	N	O	P	Q	R	S	T

1942	Day	#
JAN 4	A	7
JAN 24	*A*	*1*
FEB 13	A	8
MAR 5	A	2
MAR 25	A	9
APR 14	A	3
MAY 4	A	10
MAY 24	A	4
JUN 13	A	11
JUL 3	A	5
JUL 23	A	12
AUG 12	A	6
SEP 1	A	13
SEP 21	A	7
OCT 11	*A*	*1*
OCT 31	A	8
NOV 20	A	2
DEC 10	A	9
DEC 30	A	3

1943	Day	#
JAN 19	A	10
FEB 8	A	4
FEB 28	A	11
MAR 20	A	5
APR 9	A	12
APR 29	A	6
MAY 19	A	13
JUN 8	A	7
JUN 28	*A*	*1*
JUL 18	A	8
AUG 7	A	2
AUG 27	A	9
SEP 16	A	3
OCT 6	A	10
OCT 26	A	4
NOV 15	A	11
DEC 5	A	5
DEC 25	A	12

1944	Day	#
JAN 14	A	6
FEB 3	A	13
FEB 23	A	7
MAR 14	*A*	*1*
APR 3	A	8
APR 23	A	2
MAY 13	A	9
JUN 2	A	3
JUN 22	A	10
JUL 12	A	4
AUG 1	A	11
AUG 21	A	5
SEP 10	A	12
SEP 30	A	6
OCT 20	A	13
NOV 9	A	7
NOV 29	*A*	*1*
DEC 19	A	8

TUN
2 AHAU
STARTS JAN 4TH

TUN
7 AHAU
STARTS DEC 25TH

TUN
3 AHAU
STARTS DEC 19TH

TUN
11 AHAU
STARTS DEC 30TH

449

Aztec Day Signs

A	B	C	D	E	F	G	H	I	J
K	L	M	N	O	P	Q	R	S	T

1945		Day	#
JAN	8	A	2
JAN	28	A	9
FEB	17	A	3
MAR	9	A	10
MAR	29	A	4
APR	18	A	11
MAY	8	A	5
MAY	28	A	12
JUN	17	A	6
JUL	7	A	13
JUL	27	A	7
AUG	*16*	*A*	*1*
SEP	5	A	8
SEP	25	A	2
OCT	15	A	9
NOV	4	A	3
NOV	24	A	10
DEC	14	A	4

1946		Day	#
JAN	3	A	11
JAN	23	A	5
FEB	12	A	12
MAR	4	A	6
MAR	24	A	13
APR	13	A	7
MAY	*3*	*A*	*1*
MAY	23	A	8
JUN	12	A	2
JUL	2	A	9
JUL	22	A	3
AUG	11	A	10
AUG	31	A	4
SEP	20	A	11
OCT	10	A	5
OCT	30	A	12
NOV	19	A	6
DEC	9	A	13
DEC	29	A	7

1947		Day	#
JAN	*18*	*A*	*1*
FEB	7	A	8
FEB	27	A	2
MAR	19	A	9
APR	8	A	3
APR	28	A	10
MAY	18	A	4
JUN	7	A	11
JUN	27	A	5
JUL	17	A	12
AUG	6	A	6
AUG	26	A	13
SEP	15	A	7
OCT	*5*	*A*	*1*
OCT	25	A	8
NOV	14	A	2
DEC	4	A	9
DEC	24	A	3

TUN 12 AHAU	TUN 8 AHAU	TUN 4 AHAU
STARTS DEC 14TH	STARTS DEC 9TH	STARTS DEC 4TH

1	2	3	4	5	6	7	8	9	10	11	12	13

Mayan Day Signs

A	B	C	D	E	F	G	H	I	J
🔲	🔲	🔲	🔲	🔲	🔲	🔲	🔲	🔲	🔲
🔲	🔲	🔲	🔲	🔲	🔲	🔲	🔲	🔲	🔲
K	L	M	N	O	P	Q	R	S	T

1948	Day	#
JAN 13	A	10
FEB 2	A	4
FEB 22	A	11
MAR 13	A	5
APR 2	A	12
APR 22	A	6
MAY 12	A	13
JUN 1	A	7
JUN 21	*A*	*1*
JUL 11	A	8
JUL 31	A	2
AUG 20	A	9
SEP 9	A	3
SEP 29	A	10
OCT 19	A	4
NOV 8	A	11
NOV 28	A	5
DEC 18	A	12

1949	Day	#
JAN 7	A	6
JAN 27	A	13
FEB 16	A	7
MAR 8	*A*	*1*
MAR 28	A	8
APR 17	A	2
MAY 7	A	9
MAY 27	A	3
JUN 16	A	10
JUL 6	A	4
JUL 26	A	11
AUG 15	A	5
SEP 4	A	12
SEP 24	A	6
OCT 14	A	13
NOV 3	A	7
NOV 23	*A*	*1*
DEC 13	A	8

1950	Day	#
JAN 2	A	2
JAN 22	A	9
FEB 11	A	3
MAR 3	A	10
MAR 23	A	4
APR 12	A	11
MAY 2	A	5
MAY 22	A	12
JUN 11	A	6
JUL 1	A	13
JUL 21	A	7
AUG 10	*A*	*1*
AUG 30	A	8
SEP 19	A	2
OCT 9	A	9
OCT 29	A	3
NOV 18	A	10
DEC 8	A	4
DEC 28	A	11

TUN 13 AHAU	TUN 9 AHAU	TUN 5 AHAU
STARTS NOV 28TH	STARTS NOV 23RD	STARTS NOV 18TH

| 1 | 2 | 3 | 4 | 5 | 6 | 7 | 8 | 9 | 10 | 11 | 12 | 13 |

How to use the Almanac

1. Find your date in the main table. The Day Sign and Day Number are listed to the right. If your date isn't in the table, find the date right before yours. Counting this date as "1," count forward, up to and including your date. Jot down this number.

2. Put your finger on Day Sign A at the top of the next page. Count forward by your number. You have just fingered your Day Sign. Jot it down.

1951	Day	#	1952	Day	#	1953	Day	#
JAN 17	A	5	*JAN 12*	*A*	*1*	JAN 6	A	10
FEB 6	A	12	FEB 1	A	8	JAN 26	A	4
FEB 26	A	6	FEB 21	A	2	FEB 15	A	11
MAR 18	A	13	MAR 12	A	9	MAR 7	A	5
APR 7	A	7	APR 1	A	3	MAR 27	A	12
APR 27	*A*	*1*	APR 21	A	10	APR 16	A	6
MAY 17	A	8	MAY 11	A	4	MAY 6	A	13
JUN 6	A	2	MAY 31	A	11	MAY 26	A	7
JUN 26	A	9	JUN 20	A	5	*JUN 15*	*A*	*1*
JUL 16	A	3	JUL 10	A	12	JUL 5	A	8
AUG 5	A	10	JUL 30	A	6	JUL 25	A	2
AUG 25	A	4	AUG 19	A	13	AUG 14	A	9
SEP 14	A	11	SEP 8	A	7	SEP 3	A	3
OCT 4	A	5	*SEP 28*	*A*	*1*	SEP 23	A	10
OCT 24	A	12	OCT 18	A	8	OCT 13	A	4
NOV 13	A	6	NOV 7	A	2	NOV 2	A	11
DEC 3	A	13	NOV 27	A	9	NOV 22	A	5
DEC 23	A	7	DEC 17	A	3	DEC 12	A	12

■ *18th Katun Starts: Nov 2*

TUN
1 AHAU • ⊡

TUN
10 AHAU ‖ ⊡

TUN
6 AHAU • ⊡

STARTS NOV 13TH	STARTS NOV 7TH	STARTS NOV 2ND

3. Using the numbers at the bottom of the page, put your finger on the Day Number of the closest listed date to yours. Counting this day as "1," count forward to yours. You have fingered your Day Number. Jot it down beside your Day Sign. Look up both.

Aztec Day Signs

A	B	C	D	E	F	G	H	I	J
K	L	M	N	O	P	Q	R	S	T

1954	Day #		1955	Day #		1956	Day #
JAN 1	A 6		JAN 16	A 9		JAN 11	A 5
JAN 21	A 13		FEB 5	A 3		JAN 31	A 12
FEB 10	A 7		FEB 25	A 10		FEB 20	A 6
MAR 2	A 1		MAR 17	A 4		MAR 11	A 13
MAR 22	A 8		APR 6	A 11		MAR 31	A 7
APR 11	A 2		APR 26	A 5		APR 20	A 1
MAY 1	A 9		MAY 16	A 12		MAY 10	A 8
MAY 21	A 3		JUN 5	A 6		MAY 30	A 2
JUN 10	A 10		JUN 25	A 13		JUN 19	A 9
JUN 30	A 4		JUL 15	A 7		JUL 9	A 3
JUL 20	A 11		AUG 4	A 1		JUL 29	A 10
AUG 9	A 5		AUG 24	A 8		AUG 18	A 4
AUG 29	A 12		SEP 13	A 2		SEP 7	A 11
SEP 18	A 6		OCT 3	A 9		SEP 27	A 5
OCT 8	A 13		OCT 23	A 3		OCT 17	A 12
OCT 28	A 7		NOV 12	A 10		NOV 6	A 6
NOV 17	A 1		DEC 2	A 4		NOV 26	A 13
DEC 7	A 8		DEC 22	A 11		DEC 16	A 7
DEC 27	A 2						

TUN 2 AHAU	TUN 11 AHAU	TUN 7 AHAU
STARTS OCT 28TH	STARTS OCT 23RD	STARTS OCT 17TH

1	2	3	4	5	6	7	8	9	10	11	12	13

Mayan Day Signs

A	B	C	D	E	F	G	H	I	J
🔲	🔲	🔲	🔲	🔲	🔲	🔲	🔲	🔲	🔲
🔲	🔲	🔲	🔲	🔲	🔲	🔲	🔲	🔲	🔲
K	L	M	N	O	P	Q	R	S	T

1957		Day	#
JAN	5	A	1
JAN	25	A	8
FEB	14	A	2
MAR	6	A	9
MAR	26	A	3
APR	15	A	10
MAY	5	A	4
MAY	25	A	11
JUN	14	A	5
JUL	4	A	12
JUL	24	A	6
AUG	13	A	13
SEP	2	A	7
SEP	22	A	1
OCT	12	A	8
NOV	1	A	2
NOV	21	A	9
DEC	11	A	3
DEC	31	A	10

1958		Day	#
JAN	20	A	4
FEB	9	A	11
MAR	1	A	5
MAR	21	A	12
APR	10	A	6
APR	30	A	13
MAY	20	A	7
JUN	9	A	1
JUN	29	A	8
JUL	19	A	2
AUG	8	A	9
AUG	28	A	3
SEP	17	A	10
OCT	7	A	4
OCT	27	A	11
NOV	16	A	5
DEC	6	A	12
DEC	26	A	6

1959		Day	#
JAN	15	A	13
FEB	4	A	7
FEB	24	A	1
MAR	16	A	8
APR	5	A	2
APR	25	A	9
MAY	15	A	3
JUN	4	A	10
JUN	24	A	4
JUL	14	A	11
AUG	3	A	5
AUG	23	A	12
SEP	12	A	6
OCT	2	A	13
OCT	22	A	7
NOV	11	A	1
DEC	1	A	8
DEC	21	A	2

TUN
3 AHAU

TUN
12 AHAU

TUN
8 AHAU

STARTS OCT 12TH | STARTS OCT 7TH | STARTS OCT 2ND

| 1 | 2 | 3 | 4 | 5 | 6 | 7 | 8 | 9 | 10 | 11 | 12 | 13 |

Aztec Day Signs

A	B	C	D	E	F	G	H	I	J
K	L	M	N	O	P	Q	R	S	T

1960	Day #
JAN 10	A 9
JAN 30	A 3
FEB 19	A 10
MAR 10	A 4
MAR 30	A 11
APR 19	A 5
MAY 9	A 12
MAY 29	A 6
JUN 18	A 13
JUL 8	A 7
JUL 28	*A 1*
AUG 17	A 8
SEP 6	A 2
SEP 26	A 9
OCT 16	A 3
NOV 5	A 10
NOV 25	A 4
DEC 15	A 11

1961	Day #
JAN 4	A 5
JAN 24	A 12
FEB 13	A 6
MAR 5	A 13
MAR 25	A 7
APR 14	*A 1*
MAY 4	A 8
MAY 24	A 2
JUN 13	A 9
JUL 3	A 3
JUL 23	A 10
AUG 12	A 4
SEP 1	A 11
SEP 21	A 5
OCT 11	A 12
OCT 31	A 6
NOV 20	A 13
DEC 10	A 7
DEC 30	*A 1*

1962	Day #
JAN 19	A 8
FEB 8	A 2
FEB 28	A 9
MAR 20	A 3
APR 9	A 10
APR 29	A 4
MAY 19	A 11
JUN 8	A 5
JUN 28	A 12
JUL 18	A 6
AUG 7	A 13
AUG 27	A 7
SEP 16	*A 1*
OCT 6	A 8
OCT 26	A 2
NOV 15	A 9
DEC 5	A 3
DEC 25	A 10

TUN 4 AHAU	TUN 13 AHAU	TUN 9 AHAU
STARTS SEP 26TH	STARTS SEP 21ST	STARTS SEP 16TH

| 1 | 2 | 3 | 4 | 5 | 6 | 7 | 8 | 9 | 10 | 11 | 12 | 13 |

Mayan Day Signs

A	B	C	D	E	F	G	H	I	J
🏺	🏺	🏺	🏺	🏺	🏺	🏺	🏺	🏺	🏺

🏺	🏺	🏺	🏺	🏺	🏺	🏺	🏺	🏺	🏺
K	L	M	N	O	P	Q	R	S	T

1963	Day	#
JAN 14	A	4
FEB 3	A	11
FEB 23	A	5
MAR 15	A	12
APR 4	A	6
APR 24	A	13
MAY 14	A	7
JUN 3	*A*	*1*
JUN 23	A	8
JUL 13	A	2
AUG 2	A	9
AUG 22	A	3
SEP 11	A	10
OCT 1	A	4
OCT 21	A	11
NOV 10	A	5
NOV 30	A	12
DEC 20	A	6

1964	Day	#
JAN 9	A	13
JAN 29	A	7
FEB 18	*A*	*1*
MAR 9	A	8
MAR 29	A	2
APR 18	A	9
MAY 8	A	3
MAY 28	A	10
JUN 17	A	4
JUL 7	A	11
JUL 27	A	5
AUG 16	A	12
SEP 5	A	6
SEP 25	A	13
OCT 15	A	7
NOV 4	*A*	*1*
NOV 24	A	8
DEC 14	A	2

1965	Day	#
JAN 3	A	9
JAN 23	A	3
FEB 12	A	10
MAR 4	A	4
MAR 24	A	11
APR 13	A	5
MAY 3	A	12
MAY 23	A	6
JUN 12	A	13
JUL 2	A	7
JUL 22	*A*	*1*
AUG 11	A	8
AUG 31	A	2
SEP 20	A	9
OCT 10	A	3
OCT 30	A	10
NOV 19	A	4
DEC 9	A	11
DEC 29	A	5

TUN 5 AHAU	TUN 1 AHAU	TUN 10 AHAU
STARTS SEP 11TH	STARTS SEP 5TH	STARTS AUG 31ST

1	2	3	4	5	6	7	8	9	10	11	12	13

How to use the Almanac
1. Find your date in the main table. The Day Sign and Day Number are listed to the right. If your date isn't in the table, find the date right before yours. Counting this date as "1," count forward, up to and including your date. Jot down this number.
2. Put your finger on Day Sign A at the top of the next page. Count forward by your number. You have just fingered your Day Sign. Jot it down.

1966	Day	#	1967	Day	#	1968	Day	#
JAN 18	A	12	JAN 13	A	8	JAN 8	A	4
FEB 7	A	6	FEB 2	A	2	JAN 28	A	11
FEB 27	A	13	FEB 22	A	9	FEB 17	A	5
MAR 19	A	7	MAR 14	A	3	MAR 8	A	12
APR 8	*A*	*1*	APR 3	A	10	MAR 28	A	6
APR 28	A	8	APR 23	A	4	APR 17	A	13
MAY 18	A	2	MAY 13	A	11	MAY 7	A	7
JUN 7	A	9	JUN 2	A	5	*MAY 27*	*A*	*1*
JUN 27	A	3	JUN 22	A	12	JUN 16	A	8
JUL 17	A	10	JUL 12	A	6	JUL 6	A	2
AUG 6	A	4	AUG 1	A	13	JUL 26	A	9
AUG 26	A	11	AUG 21	A	7	AUG 15	A	3
SEP 15	A	5	*SEP 10*	*A*	*1*	SEP 4	A	10
OCT 5	A	12	SEP 30	A	8	SEP 24	A	4
OCT 25	A	6	OCT 20	A	2	OCT 14	A	11
NOV 14	A	13	NOV 9	A	9	NOV 3	A	5
DEC 4	A	7	NOV 29	A	3	NOV 23	A	12
DEC 24	*A*	*1*	DEC 19	A	10	DEC 13	A	6

TUN 6 AHAU •|⊞	TUN 2 AHAU :⊞	TUN 11 AHAU •||⊞
STARTS AUG 26TH	STARTS AUG 21ST	STARTS AUG 15TH

3. Using the numbers at the bottom of the page, put your finger on the Day Number of the closest listed date to yours. Counting this Day as "1," count forward to yours. You have fingered your Day Number. Jot it down beside your Day Sign. Look up both.

Aztec Day Signs

A	B	C	D	E	F	G	H	I	J
K	L	M	N	O	P	Q	R	S	T

1969	Day	#
JAN 2	A	13
JAN 22	A	7
FEB 11	A	1
MAR 3	A	8
MAR 23	A	2
APR 12	A	9
MAY 2	A	3
MAY 22	A	10
JUN 11	A	4
JUL 1	A	11
JUL 21	A	5
AUG 10	A	12
AUG 30	A	6
SEP 19	A	13
OCT 9	A	7
OCT 29	A	1
NOV 18	A	8
DEC 8	A	2
DEC 28	A	9

1970	Day	#
JAN 17	A	3
FEB 6	A	10
FEB 26	A	4
MAR 18	A	11
APR 7	A	5
APR 27	A	12
MAY 17	A	6
JUN 6	A	13
JUN 26	A	7
JUL 16	A	1
AUG 5	A	8
AUG 25	A	2
SEP 14	A	9
OCT 4	A	3
OCT 24	A	10
NOV 13	A	4
DEC 3	A	11
DEC 23	A	5

1971	Day	#
JAN 12	A	12
FEB 1	A	6
FEB 21	A	13
MAR 13	A	7
APR 2	A	1
APR 22	A	8
MAY 12	A	2
JUN 1	A	9
JUN 21	A	3
JUL 11	A	10
JUL 31	A	4
AUG 20	A	11
SEP 9	A	5
SEP 29	A	12
OCT 19	A	6
NOV 8	A	13
NOV 28	A	7
DEC 18	A	1

TUN
7 AHAU
STARTS AUG 10TH

TUN
3 AHAU
STARTS AUG 5TH

TUN
12 AHAU
STARTS JUL 31ST

| 1 | 2 | 3 | 4 | 5 | 6 | 7 | 8 | 9 | 10 | 11 | 12 | 13 |

Mayan Day Signs

A	B	C	D	E	F	G	H	I	J
K	L	M	N	O	P	Q	R	S	T

1972	Day	#	1973	Day	#	1974	Day	#
JAN 7	A	8	JAN 1	A	4	JAN 16	A	7
JAN 27	A	2	JAN 21	A	11	*FEB 5*	*A*	*1*
FEB 16	A	9	FEB 10	A	5	FEB 25	A	8
MAR 7	A	3	MAR 2	A	12	MAR 17	A	2
MAR 27	A	10	MAR 22	A	6	APR 6	A	9
APR 16	A	4	APR 11	A	13	APR 26	A	3
MAY 6	A	11	MAY 1	A	7	MAY 16	A	10
MAY 26	A	5	*MAY 21*	*A*	*1*	JUN 5	A	4
JUN 15	A	12	JUN 10	A	8	JUN 25	A	11
JUL 5	A	6	JUN 30	A	2	JUL 15	A	5
JUL 25	A	13	JUL 20	A	9	AUG 4	A	12
AUG 14	A	7	AUG 9	A	3	AUG 24	A	6
SEP 3	*A*	*1*	AUG 29	A	10	SEP 13	A	13
SEP 23	A	8	SEP 18	A	4	OCT 3	A	7
OCT 13	A	2	OCT 8	A	11	*OCT 23*	*A*	*1*
NOV 2	A	9	OCT 28	A	5	NOV 12	A	8
NOV 22	A	3	NOV 17	A	12	DEC 2	A	2
DEC 12	A	10	DEC 7	A	6	DEC 22	A	9
			DEC 27	A	13			

■ 19th Katun Starts: Jul 20

TUN 8 AHAU	TUN 4 AHAU	TUN 13 AHAU
STARTS JUL 25TH	STARTS JUL 20TH	STARTS JUL 15TH

1	2	3	4	5	6	7	8	9	10	11	12	13

Aztec Day Signs

A	B	C	D	E	F	G	H	I	J
K	L	M	N	O	P	Q	R	S	T

1975	Day	#		1976	Day	#		1977	Day	#
JAN 11	A	3		JAN 6	A	12		JAN 20	A	2
JAN 31	A	10		JAN 26	A	6		FEB 9	A	9
FEB 20	A	4		FEB 15	A	13		MAR 1	A	3
MAR 12	A	11		MAR 6	A	7		MAR 21	A	10
APR 1	A	5		MAR 26	A	1		APR 10	A	4
APR 21	A	12		APR 15	A	8		APR 30	A	11
MAY 11	A	6		MAY 5	A	2		MAY 20	A	5
MAY 31	A	13		MAY 25	A	9		JUN 9	A	12
JUN 20	A	7		JUN 14	A	3		JUN 29	A	6
JUL 10	A	1		JUL 4	A	10		JUL 19	A	13
JUL 30	A	8		JUL 24	A	4		AUG 8	A	7
AUG 19	A	2		AUG 13	A	11		AUG 28	A	1
SEP 8	A	9		SEP 2	A	5		SEP 17	A	8
SEP 28	A	3		SEP 22	A	12		OCT 7	A	2
OCT 18	A	10		OCT 12	A	6		OCT 27	A	9
NOV 7	A	4		NOV 1	A	13		NOV 16	A	3
NOV 27	A	11		NOV 21	A	7		DEC 6	A	10
DEC 17	A	5		DEC 11	A	1		DEC 26	A	4
				DEC 31	A	8				

TUN 9 AHAU	⠇ 𝄚	TUN 5 AHAU		𝄚	TUN 1 AHAU	• 𝄚
STARTS JUL 10TH		STARTS JUL 4TH			STARTS JUN 29TH	

1	2	3	4	5	6	7	8	9	10	11	12	13

Mayan Day Signs

A	B	C	D	E	F	G	H	I	J
K	L	M	N	O	P	Q	R	S	T

1978	Day	#
JAN 15	A	11
FEB 4	A	5
FEB 24	A	12
MAR 16	A	6
APR 5	A	13
APR 25	A	7
MAY 15	A	1
JUN 4	A	8
JUN 24	A	2
JUL 14	A	9
AUG 3	A	3
AUG 23	A	10
SEP 12	A	4
OCT 2	A	11
OCT 22	A	5
NOV 11	A	12
DEC 1	A	6
DEC 21	A	13

1979	Day	#
JAN 10	A	7
JAN 30	A	1
FEB 19	A	8
MAR 11	A	2
MAR 31	A	9
APR 20	A	3
MAY 10	A	10
MAY 30	A	4
JUN 19	A	11
JUL 9	A	5
JUL 29	A	12
AUG 18	A	6
SEP 7	A	13
SEP 27	A	7
OCT 17	A	1
NOV 6	A	8
NOV 26	A	2
DEC 16	A	9

1980	Day	#
JAN 5	A	3
JAN 25	A	10
FEB 14	A	4
MAR 5	A	11
MAR 25	A	5
APR 14	A	12
MAY 4	A	6
MAY 24	A	13
JUN 13	A	7
JUL 3	A	1
JUL 23	A	8
AUG 12	A	2
SEP 1	A	9
SEP 21	A	3
OCT 11	A	10
OCT 31	A	4
NOV 20	A	11
DEC 10	A	5
DEC 30	A	12

TUN
10 AHAU ‖
STARTS JUN 24TH

TUN
6 AHAU •
STARTS JUN 19TH

TUN
2 AHAU :
STARTS JUN 13TH

| 1 | 2 | 3 | 4 | 5 | 6 | 7 | 8 | 9 | 10 | 11 | 12 | 13 |

How to use the Almanac

1. Find your date in the main table. The Day Sign and Day Number are listed to the right. If your date isn't in the table, find the date right before yours. Counting this date as "1," count forward, up to and including your date. Jot down this number.

2. Put your finger on Day Sign A at the top of the next page. Count forward by your number. You have just fingered your Day Sign. Jot it down.

1981	Day	#	1982	Day	#	1983	Day	#
JAN 19	A	6	JAN 14	A	2	JAN 9	A	11
FEB 8	A	13	FEB 3	A	9	JAN 29	A	5
FEB 28	A	7	FEB 23	A	3	FEB 18	A	12
MAR 20	*A*	*1*	MAR 15	A	10	MAR 10	A	6
APR 9	A	8	APR 4	A	4	MAR 30	A	13
APR 29	A	2	APR 24	A	11	APR 19	A	7
MAY 19	A	9	MAY 14	A	5	*MAY 9*	*A*	*1*
JUN 8	A	3	JUN 3	A	12	MAY 29	A	8
JUN 28	A	10	JUN 23	A	6	JUN 18	A	2
JUL 18	A	4	JUL 13	A	13	JUL 8	A	9
AUG 7	A	11	AUG 2	A	7	JUL 28	A	3
AUG 27	A	5	*AUG 22*	*A*	*1*	AUG 17	A	10
SEP 16	A	12	SEP 11	A	8	SEP 6	A	4
OCT 6	A	6	OCT 1	A	2	SEP 26	A	11
OCT 26	A	13	OCT 21	A	9	OCT 16	A	5
NOV 15	A	7	NOV 10	A	3	NOV 5	A	12
DEC 5	*A*	*1*	NOV 30	A	10	NOV 25	A	6
DEC 25	A	8	DEC 20	A	4	DEC 15	A	13

TUN 11 AHAU	TUN 7 AHAU	TUN 3 AHAU
STARTS JUN 8TH	STARTS JUN 3RD	STARTS MAY 29TH

3. Using the numbers at the bottom of the page, put your finger on the Day Number of the closest listed date to yours. Counting this Day as "1," count forward to yours. You have fingered your Day Number. Jot it down beside your Day Sign. Look up both.

462

Aztec Day Signs

A	B	C	D	E	F	G	H	I	J
K	L	M	N	O	P	Q	R	S	T

1984	Day #		1985	Day #		1986	Day #
JAN 4	A 7		JAN 18	A 10		JAN 13	A 6
JAN 24	*A 1*		FEB 7	A 4		FEB 2	A 13
FEB 13	A 8		FEB 27	A 11		FEB 22	A 7
MAR 4	A 2		MAR 19	A 5		*MAR 14*	*A 1*
MAR 24	A 9		APR 8	A 12		APR 3	A 8
APR 13	A 3		APR 28	A 6		APR 23	A 2
MAY 3	A 10		MAY 18	A 13		MAY 13	A 9
MAY 23	A 4		JUN 7	A 7		JUN 2	A 3
JUN 12	A 11		*JUN 27*	*A 1*		JUN 22	A 10
JUL 2	A 5		JUL 17	A 8		JUL 12	A 4
JUL 22	A 12		AUG 6	A 2		AUG 1	A 11
AUG 11	A 6		AUG 26	A 9		AUG 21	A 5
AUG 31	A 13		SEP 15	A 3		SEP 10	A 12
SEP 20	A 7		OCT 5	A 10		SEP 30	A 6
OCT 10	*A 1*		OCT 25	A 4		OCT 20	A 13
OCT 30	A 8		NOV 14	A 11		NOV 9	A 7
NOV 19	A 2		DEC 4	A 5		*NOV 29*	*A 1*
DEC 9	A 9		DEC 24	A 12		DEC 19	A 8
DEC 29	A 3						

TUN 12 AHAU	TUN 8 AHAU	TUN 4 AHAU
STARTS MAY 23RD	STARTS MAY 18TH	STARTS MAY 13TH

1	2	3	4	5	6	7	8	9	10	11	12	13

Mayan Day Signs

A	B	C	D	E	F	G	H	I	J
🔲	🔲	🔲	🔲	🔲	🔲	🔲	🔲	🔲	🔲

K	L	M	N	O	P	Q	R	S	T
🔲	🔲	🔲	🔲	🔲	🔲	🔲	🔲	🔲	🔲

1987	Day #		1988	Day #		1989	Day #
JAN 8	A 2		JAN 3	A 11		*JAN 17*	*A 1*
JAN 28	A 9		JAN 23	A 5		FEB 6	A 8
FEB 17	A 3		FEB 12	A 12		FEB 26	A 2
MAR 9	A 10		MAR 3	A 6		MAR 18	A 9
MAR 29	A 4		MAR 23	A 13		APR 7	A 3
APR 18	A 11		APR 12	A 7		APR 27	A 10
MAY 8	A 5		*MAY 2*	*A 1*		MAY 17	A 4
MAY 28	A 12		MAY 22	A 8		JUN 6	A 11
JUN 17	A 6		JUN 11	A 2		JUN 26	A 5
JUL 7	A 13		JUL 1	A 9		JUL 16	A 12
JUL 27	A 7		JUL 21	A 3		AUG 5	A 6
AUG 16	*A 1*		AUG 10	A 10		AUG 25	A 13
SEP 5	A 8		AUG 30	A 4		SEP 14	A 7
SEP 25	A 2		SEP 19	A 11		*OCT 4*	*A 1*
OCT 15	A 9		OCT 9	A 5		OCT 24	A 8
NOV 4	A 3		OCT 29	A 12		NOV 13	A 2
NOV 24	A 10		NOV 18	A 6		DEC 3	A 9
DEC 14	A 4		DEC 8	A 13		DEC 23	A 3
			DEC 28	A 7			

TUN 13 AHAU ⦂‖| 🔲	TUN 9 AHAU ⦂‖ 🔲	TUN 5 AHAU	🔲

STARTS MAY 8TH	STARTS MAY 2ND	STARTS APR 27TH

1	2	3	4	5	6	7	8	9	10	11	12	13
			T				T					

Aztec Day Signs

A	B	C	D	E	F	G	H	I	J
🐊	🐺	🏛	🦎	🐍	💀	🦌	🐰	🤚	🐕
🐵	🌿	🦷	🦅	🐆	🦅	🎀	🗡	🌧	🌺
K	L	M	N	O	P	Q	R	S	T

1990	Day #	**1991**	Day #	**1992**	Day #
JAN 12	A 10	JAN 7	A 6	JAN 2	A 2
FEB 1	A 4	JAN 27	A 13	JAN 22	A 9
FEB 21	A 11	FEB 16	A 7	FEB 11	A 3
MAR 13	A 5	*MAR 8*	*A 1*	MAR 2	A 10
APR 2	A 12	MAR 28	A 8	MAR 22	A 4
APR 22	A 6	APR 17	A 2	APR 11	A 11
MAY 12	A 13	MAY 7	A 9	MAY 1	A 5
JUN 1	A 7	MAY 27	A 3	MAY 21	A 12
JUN 21	*A 1*	JUN 16	A 10	JUN 10	A 6
JUL 11	A 8	JUL 6	A 4	JUN 30	A 13
JUL 31	A 2	JUL 26	A 11	JUL 20	A 7
AUG 20	A 9	AUG 15	A 5	*AUG 9*	*A 1*
SEP 9	A 3	SEP 4	A 12	AUG 29	A 8
SEP 29	A 10	SEP 24	A 6	SEP 18	A 2
OCT 19	A 4	OCT 14	A 13	OCT 8	A 9
NOV 8	A 11	NOV 3	A 7	OCT 28	A 3
NOV 28	A 5	*NOV 23*	*A 1*	NOV 17	A 10
DEC 18	A 18	DEC 13	A 8	DEC 7	A 4
				DEC 27	A 11

TUN 1 AHAU • 🔲	TUN 10 AHAU ‖ 🔲	TUN 6 AHAU •‖ 🔲
STARTS APR 22ND	STARTS APR 17TH	STARTS APR 11TH

1	2	3	4	5	6	7	8	9	10	11	12	13

465

How to use the Almanac

1. Find your date in the main table. The Day Sign and Day Number are listed to the right. If your date isn't in the table, find the date right before yours. Counting this date as "1," count forward, up to and including your date. Jot down this number.

2. Put your finger on Day Sign A at the top of the next page. Count forward by your number. You have just fingered your Day Sign. Jot it down.

1993	Day	#	1994	Day	#	1995	Day	#
JAN 16	A	5	*JAN 11*	*A*	*1*	JAN 6	A	10
FEB 5	A	12	JAN 31	A	8	JAN 26	A	4
FEB 25	A	6	FEB 20	A	2	FEB 15	A	11
MAR 17	A	13	MAR 12	A	9	MAR 7	A	5
APR 6	A	7	APR 1	A	3	MAR 27	A	12
APR 26	*A*	*1*	APR 21	A	10	APR 16	A	6
MAY 16	A	8	MAY 11	A	4	MAY 6	A	13
JUN 5	A	2	MAY 31	A	11	MAY 26	A	7
JUL 25	A	9	JUN 20	A	5	*JUN 15*	*A*	*1*
JUL 15	A	3	JUL 10	A	12	JUL 5	A	8
AUG 4	A	10	JUL 30	A	6	JUL 25	A	2
AUG 24	A	4	AUG 19	A	13	AUG 14	A	9
SEP 13	A	11	SEP 8	A	7	SEP 3	A	3
OCT 3	A	5	*SEP 28*	*A*	*1*	SEP 23	A	10
OCT 23	A	12	OCT 18	A	8	OCT 13	A	4
NOV 12	A	6	NOV 7	A	2	NOV 2	A	11
DEC 2	A	13	NOV 27	A	9	NOV 22	A	5
DEC 22	A	7	DEC 17	A	3	DEC 12	A	12

■ *20th Katun Starts: APR 6*

TUN 2 AHAU	: ⊕	TUN 11 AHAU	•‖ ⊕	TUN 7 AHAU	:‖ ⊕
STARTS APR 6TH		STARTS APR 1ST		STARTS MAR 27TH	

3. Using the numbers at the bottom of the page, put your finger on the Day Number of the closest listed date to yours. Counting this Day as "1," count forward to yours. You have fingered your Day Number. Jot it down beside your Day Sign. Look up both.

466

Mayan Day Signs

A	B	C	D	E	F	G	H	I	J
K	L	M	N	O	P	Q	R	S	T

1996	Day #		1997	Day #		1998	Day #
JAN 1	A 6		JAN 15	A 9		JAN 10	A 5
JAN 21	A 13		FEB 4	A 3		JAN 30	A 12
FEB 10	A 7		FEB 24	A 10		FEB 19	A 6
MAR 1	*A 1*		MAR 16	A 4		MAR 11	A 13
MAR 21	A 8		APR 5	A 11		MAR 31	A 7
APR 10	A 2		APR 25	A 5		*APR 20*	*A 1*
APR 30	A 9		MAY 15	A 12		MAY 10	A 8
MAY 20	A 3		JUN 4	A 6		MAY 30	A 2
JUN 9	A 10		JUN 24	A 13		JUN 19	A 9
JUN 29	A 4		JUL 14	A 7		JUL 9	A 3
JUL 19	A 11		*AUG 3*	*A 1*		JUL 29	A 10
AUG 8	A 5		AUG 23	A 8		AUG 18	A 4
AUG 28	A 12		SEP 12	A 2		SEP 7	A 11
SEP 17	A 6		OCT 2	A 9		SEP 27	A 5
OCT 7	A 13		OCT 22	A 3		OCT 17	A 12
OCT 27	A 7		NOV 11	A 10		NOV 6	A 6
NOV 16	*A 1*		DEC 1	A 4		NOV 26	A 13
DEC 6	A 8		DEC 21	A 11		DEC 16	A 7
DEC 26	A 2						

TUN
3 AHAU
STARTS MAR 21ST

TUN
12 AHAU
STARTS MAR 16TH

TUN
8 AHAU
STARTS MAR 11TH

| 1 | 2 | 3 | 4 | 5 | 6 | 7 | 8 | 9 | 10 | 11 | 12 | 13 |

Aztec Day Signs

A	B	C	D	E	F	G	H	I	J
K	L	M	N	O	P	Q	R	S	T

1999	Day #		2000	Day #		2001	Day #
JAN 5	A 1		JAN 20	A 4		JAN 14	A 13
JAN 25	A 8		FEB 9	A 11		FEB 3	A 7
FEB 14	A 2		FEB 29	A 5		FEB 23	A 1
MAR 6	A 9		MAR 20	A 12		MAR 15	A 8
MAR 26	A 3		APR 9	A 6		APR 4	A 2
APR 15	A 10		APR 29	A 13		APR 24	A 9
MAY 5	A 4		MAY 19	A 7		MAY 14	A 3
MAY 25	A 11		JUN 8	A 1		JUN 3	A 10
JUN 14	A 5		JUN 28	A 8		JUN 23	A 4
JUL 4	A 12		JUL 18	A 2		JUL 13	A 11
JUL 24	A 6		AUG 7	A 9		AUG 2	A 5
AUG 13	A 13		AUG 27	A 3		AUG 22	A 12
SEP 2	A 7		SEP 16	A 10		SEP 11	A 6
SEP 22	A 1		OCT 6	A 4		OCT 1	A 13
OCT 12	A 8		OCT 26	A 11		OCT 21	A 7
NOV 1	A 2		NOV 15	A 5		NOV 10	A 1
NOV 21	A 9		DEC 5	A 12		NOV 30	A 8
DEC 11	A 3		DEC 25	A 6		DEC 20	A 2
DEC 31	A 10						

TUN 4 AHAU	⋮	TUN 13 AHAU	⋮⋮	TUN 9 AHAU	⋮⋮
STARTS MAR 6TH		STARTS FEB 29TH		STARTS FEB 23RD	

1	2	3	4	5	6	7	8	9	10	11	12	13

Mayan Day Signs

A	B	C	D	E	F	G	H	I	J
K	L	M	N	O	P	Q	R	S	T

2002	Day #		2003	Day #		2004	Day #
JAN 9	A 9		JAN 4	A 5		JAN 19	A 8
JAN 29	A 3		JAN 24	A 12		FEB 8	A 2
FEB 18	A 10		FEB 13	A 6		FEB 28	A 9
MAR 10	A 4		MAR 5	A 13		MAR 19	A 3
MAR 30	A 11		MAR 25	A 7		APR 8	A 10
APR 19	A 5		*APR 14*	*A 1*		APR 28	A 4
MAY 9	A 12		MAY 4	A 8		MAY 18	A 11
MAY 29	A 6		MAY 24	A 2		JUN 7	A 5
JUN 18	A 13		JUN 13	A 9		JUN 27	A 12
JUL 8	A 7		JUL 3	A 3		JUL 17	A 6
JUL 28	*A 1*		JUL 23	A 10		AUG 6	A 13
AUG 17	A 8		AUG 12	A 4		AUG 26	A 7
SEP 6	A 2		SEP 1	A 11		*SEP 15*	*A 1*
SEP 26	A 9		SEP 21	A 5		OCT 5	A 8
OCT 16	A 3		OCT 11	A 12		OCT 25	A 2
NOV 5	A 10		OCT 31	A 6		NOV 14	A 9
NOV 25	A 4		NOV 20	A 13		DEC 4	A 3
DEC 15	A 11		DEC 10	A 7		DEC 24	A 10
			DEC 30	*A 1*			

TUN 5 AHAU	I	TUN 1 AHAU	•	TUN 10 AHAU	II
STARTS FEB 18TH		STARTS FEB 13TH		STARTS FEB 8TH	

1	2	3	4	5	6	7	8	9	10	11	12	13

Mayan Oracles for the Millennium

Aztec Day Signs

A	B	C	D	E	F	G	H	I	J

K	L	M	N	O	P	Q	R	S	T

2005	Day #		2006	Day #		2007	Day #
JAN 13	A 4		JAN 8	A 13		JAN 3	A 9
FEB 2	A 11		JAN 28	A 7		JAN 23	A 3
FEB 22	A 5		*FEB 17*	*A 1*		FEB 12	A 10
MAR 14	A 12		MAR 9	A 8		MAR 4	A 4
APR 3	A 6		MAR 29	A 2		MAR 24	A 11
APR 23	A 13		APR 18	A 9		APR 13	A 5
MAY 13	A 7		MAY 8	A 3		MAY 3	A 12
JUN 2	*A 1*		MAY 28	A 10		MAY 23	A 6
JUN 22	A 8		JUN 17	A 4		JUN 12	A 13
JUL 12	A 2		JUL 7	A 11		JUL 2	A 7
AUG 1	A 9		JUL 27	A 5		*JUL 22*	*A 1*
AUG 21	A 3		AUG 16	A 12		AUG 11	A 8
SEP 10	A 10		SEP 5	A 6		AUG 31	A 2
SEP 30	A 4		SEP 25	A 13		SEP 20	A 9
OCT 20	A 11		OCT 15	A 7		OCT 10	A 3
NOV 9	A 5		*NOV 4*	*A 1*		OCT 30	A 10
NOV 29	A 12		NOV 24	A 8		NOV 19	A 4
DEC 19	A 6		DEC 14	A 2		DEC 9	A 11
						DEC 29	A 5

TUN
6 AHAU
STARTS FEB 2ND

TUN
2 AHAU
STARTS JAN 28TH

TUN
11 AHAU
STARTS JAN 23RD

1	2	3	4	5	6	7	8	9	10	11	12	13

How to use the Almanac

1. Find your date in the main table. The Day Sign and Day Number are listed to the right. If your date isn't in the table, find the date right before yours. Counting this date as "1," count forward, up to and including your date. Jot down this number.

2. Put your finger on Day Sign A at the top of the next page. Count forward by your number. You have just fingered your Day Sign. Jot it down.

2008		Day	#	2009		Day	#	2010		Day	#
JAN	18	A	12	JAN	12	A	8	JAN	7	A	4
FEB	7	A	6	FEB	1	A	2	JAN	27	A	11
FEB	27	A	13	FEB	21	A	9	FEB	16	A	5
MAR	18	A	7	MAR	13	A	3	MAR	8	A	12
APR	*7*	*A*	*1*	APR	2	A	10	MAR	28	A	6
APR	27	A	8	APR	22	A	4	APR	17	A	13
MAY	17	A	2	MAY	12	A	11	MAY	7	A	7
JUN	6	A	9	JUN	1	A	5	*MAY*	*27*	*A*	*1*
JUN	26	A	3	JUN	21	A	12	JUN	16	A	8
JUL	16	A	10	JUL	11	A	6	JUL	6	A	2
AUG	5	A	4	JUL	31	A	13	JUL	26	A	9
AUG	25	A	11	AUG	20	A	7	AUG	15	A	3
SEP	14	A	5	*SEP*	*9*	*A*	*1*	SEP	4	A	10
OCT	4	A	12	SEP	29	A	8	SEP	24	A	4
OCT	24	A	6	OCT	19	A	2	OCT	14	A	11
NOV	13	A	13	NOV	8	A	9	NOV	3	A	5
DEC	3	A	7	NOV	28	A	3	NOV	23	A	12
DEC	*23*	*A*	*1*	DEC	18	A	10	DEC	13	A	6

TUN	TUN	TUN
7 AHAU	3 AHAU	12 AHAU
STARTS JAN 18TH	STARTS JAN 12TH	STARTS JAN 7TH

3. Using the numbers at the bottom of the page, put your finger on the Day Number of the closest listed date to yours. Counting this Day as "1," count forward to yours. You have fingered your Day Number. Jot it down beside your Day Sign. Look up both.

471

Mayan Day Signs

A	B	C	D	E	F	G	H	I	J
🏛	🗲	🔲	⬚	⬚	⬚	⬚	⬚	◎	⬚
⬚	⬚	⬚	⬚	⬚	⬚	⬚	⬚	⬚	⬚
K	L	M	N	O	P	Q	R	S	T

2011	Day #		2012	Day #			Day #
JAN 2	A 13		JAN 17	A 3			
JAN 22	A 7		FEB 6	A 10			
FEB 11	*A 1*		FEB 26	A 4			
MAR 3	A 8		MAR 17	A 11			
MAR 23	A 2		APR 6	A 5			
APR 12	A 9		APR 26	A 12			
MAY 2	A 3		MAY 16	A 6			
MAY 22	A 10		JUN 5	A 13			
JUN 11	A 4		JUN 25	A 7			
JUL 1	A 11		*JUL 15*	*A 1*			
JUL 21	A 5		AUG 4	A 8			
AUG 10	A 12		AUG 24	A 2			
AUG 30	A 6		SEP 13	A 9			
SEP 19	A 13		OCT 3	A 3			
OCT 9	A 7		OCT 23	A 10			
OCT 29	*A 1*		NOV 12	A 4			
NOV 18	A 8		DEC 2	A 11			
DEC 8	A 2		**DEC 21**	**T 4**			
DEC 28	A 9						

TUN 8 AHAU ⋮ ⬚
STARTS JAN 2ND

TUN 4 AHAU ⋮ ⬚
STARTS DEC 28TH

DAY 4 AHAU ⋮ ⬚
THE END OF TIME

PART II—The Secular Calendar

Covering the last 104 agricultural years of the Maya's Fifth Creation Epoch —Including the last two Calendar Rounds —

THE MONTHS OF THE YEAR

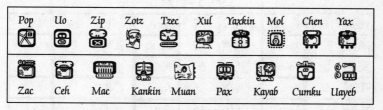

Pop	Uo	Zip	Zotz	Tzec	Xul	Yaxkin	Mol	Chen	Yax

Zac	Ceh	Mac	Kankin	Muan	Pax	Kayab	Cumku	Uayeb

Calendar Round begins January 16, 1909 (4 Ahau, 3 Kankin). This date cycles back on January 3, 1961, and again on December 21, 2012.

1909–1911

JAN 1–12	See Mac	APR 28	Pop	SEP 15	Mol
JAN 13	Kankin	MAY 18	Uo	OCT 5	Chen
FEB 2	Muan	JUN 7	Zip	OCT 25	Yax
FEB 22	Pax	JUN 27	Zotz	NOV 14	Zac
MAR 14	Kayab	JUL 17	Tzec	DEC 4	Ceh
APR 3	Cumku	AUG 6	Xul	DEC 24	Mac
APR 23	Uayeb	AUG 26	Yaxkin		

The Year 3 Night starts Apr. 29, 1909.   *The Year 4 Rabbit starts Apr. 29, 1910.*   *The Year 5 Reed starts Apr. 29, 1911.*

The first day of each month is shown. This day is counted as "0." Count forward to your day of the month.

1912 Leap Year

JAN 1–12	See 1911	APR 27	Pop	SEP 14	Mol
JAN 13	Kankin	MAY 17	Uo	OCT 4	Chen
FEB 2	Muan	JUN 6	Zip	OCT 24	Yax
FEB 22	Pax	JUN 26	Zotz	NOV 13	Zac
MAR 13	Kayab	JUL 16	Tzec	DEC 3	Ceh
APR 2	Cumku	AUG 5	Xul	DEC 23	Mac
APR 22	Uayeb	AUG 25	Yaxkin		

The Year 6 Flint starts Apr. 28, 1912.

*Every month hath 20 days, except for **Uayeb**, which only counts but five Dark Days.*

1913–1915

JAN 1–11	See Mac	APR 27	Pop	SEP 14	Mol
JAN 12	Kankin	MAY 17	Uo	OCT 4	Chen
FEB 1	Muan	JUN 6	Zip	OCT 24	Yax
FEB 21	Pax	JUN 26	Zotz	NOV 13	Zac
MAR 13	Kayab	JUL 16	Tzec	DEC 3	Ceh
APR 2	Cumku	AUG 5	Xul	DEC 23	Mac
APR 22	Uayeb	AUG 25	Yaxkin		

The Year 7 Night starts Apr. 28, 1913.   The Year 8 Rabbit starts Apr. 28, 1914.   The Year 9 Reed starts Apr. 28, 1915.

1916 Leap Year

JAN 1–11	See 1915	APR 26	Pop	SEP 13	Mol
JAN 12	Kankin	MAY 16	Uo	OCT 3	Chen
FEB 1	Muan	JUN 5	Zip	OCT 23	Yax
FEB 21	Pax	JUN 25	Zotz	NOV 12	Zac
MAR 12	Kayab	JUL 15	Tzec	DEC 2	Ceh
APR 1	Cumku	AUG 4	Xul	DEC 22	Mac
APR 21	Uayeb	AUG 24	Yaxkin		

The Year 10 Flint starts Apr. 27, 1916.

1917–1919

JAN	1–10	See Mac	APR	26	Pop	SEP	13	Mol
JAN	11	Kankin	MAY	16	Uo	OCT	3	Chen
JAN	31	Muan	JUN	5	Zip	OCT	23	Yax
FEB	20	Pax	JUN	25	Zotz	NOV	12	Zac
MAR	12	Kayab	JUL	15	Tzec	DEC	2	Ceh
APR	1	Cumku	AUG	4	Xul	DEC	22	Mac
APR	21	Uayeb	AUG	24	Yaxkin			

The Year 11 Night starts Apr. 27, 1917.   The Year 12 Rabbit starts Apr. 27, 1918.   The Year 13 Reed starts Apr. 27, 1919.

The first day of each month is shown. This day is counted as "0." Count forward to your day of the month.

1920 Leap Year

JAN	1–10	See 1919	APR	25	Pop	SEP	12	Mol
JAN	11	Kankin	MAY	15	Uo	OCT	2	Chen
JAN	31	Muan	JUN	4	Zip	OCT	22	Yax
FEB	20	Pax	JUN	24	Zotz	NOV	11	Zac
MAR	11	Kayab	JUL	14	Tzec	DEC	1	Ceh
MAR	31	Cumku	AUG	3	Xul	DEC	21	Mac
APR	20	Uayeb	AUG	23	Yaxkin			

The Year 1 Flint starts Apr. 26, 1920.

1921–1923

JAN	1–9	See Mac	APR	25	Pop	SEP	12	Mol
JAN	10	Kankin	MAY	15	Uo	OCT	2	Chen
JAN	30	Muan	JUN	4	Zip	OCT	22	Yax
FEB	19	Pax	JUN	24	Zotz	NOV	11	Zac
MAR	11	Kayab	JUL	14	Tzec	DEC	1	Ceh
MAR	31	Cumku	AUG	3	Xul	DEC	21	Mac
APR	20	Uayeb	AUG	23	Yaxkin			

The Year 2 Night starts Apr. 26, 1921.   The Year 3 Rabbit starts Apr. 26, 1922.   The Year 4 Reed starts Apr. 26, 1923.

1924 Leap Year

JAN	1–9	See 1923	APR	24	Pop	SEP	11	Mol
JAN	10	Kankin	MAY	14	Uo	OCT	1	Chen
JAN	30	Muan	JUN	3	Zip	OCT	21	Yax
FEB	19	Pax	JUN	23	Zotz	NOV	10	Zac
MAR	10	Kayab	JUL	13	Tzec	NOV	30	Ceh
MAR	30	Cumku	AUG	2	Xul	DEC	20	Mac
APR	19	Uayeb	AUG	22	Yaxkin			

The Year 5 Flint starts Apr. 25, 1924.

The first day of each month is shown. This day is counted as "0." Count forward to your day of the month.

1925–1927

JAN	1–8	See Mac	APR	24	Pop	SEP	11	Mol
JAN	9	Kankin	MAY	14	Uo	OCT	1	Chen
JAN	29	Muan	JUN	3	Zip	OCT	21	Yax
FEB	18	Pax	JUN	23	Zotz	NOV	10	Zac
MAR	10	Kayab	JUL	13	Tzec	NOV	30	Ceh
MAR	30	Cumku	AUG	2	Xul	DEC	20	Mac
APR	19	Uayeb	AUG	22	Yaxkin			

The Year 6 Night starts Apr. 25, 1925.	The Year 7 Rabbit starts Apr. 25, 1926.	The Year 8 Reed starts Apr. 25, 1927.

1928 Leap Year

JAN	1–8	See 1927	APR	23	Pop	SEP	10	Mol
JAN	9	Kankin	MAY	13	Uo	SEP	30	Chen
JAN	29	Muan	JUN	2	Zip	OCT	20	Yax
FEB	18	Pax	JUN	22	Zotz	NOV	9	Zac
MAR	9	Kayab	JUL	12	Tzec	NOV	29	Ceh
MAR	29	Cumku	AUG	1	Xul	DEC	19	Mac
APR	18	Uayeb	AUG	21	Yaxkin			

The Year 9 Flint starts Apr. 24, 1928.

1929–1931

JAN 1–7	See Mac	APR 23	*Pop*	SEP 10	*Mol*
JAN 8	*Kankin*	MAY 13	*Uo*	SEP 30	*Chen*
JAN 28	*Muan*	JUN 2	*Zip*	OCT 20	*Yax*
FEB 17	*Pax*	JUN 22	*Zotz*	NOV 9	*Zac*
MAR 9	*Kayab*	JUL 12	*Tzec*	NOV 29	*Ceh*
MAR 29	*Cumku*	AUG 1	*Xul*	DEC 19	*Mac*
APR 18	*Uayeb*	AUG 21	*Yaxkin*		

The Year 10 Night starts Apr. 24, 1929.   *The Year 11 Rabbit starts Apr. 24, 1930.*   *The Year 12 Reed starts Apr. 24, 1931.*

The first day of each month is shown. This day is counted as "0." Count forward to your day of the month.

1932

JAN 1–7	See 1931	APR 22	*Pop*	SEP 9	*Mol*
JAN 8	*Kankin*	MAY 12	*Uo*	SEP 29	*Chen*
JAN 28	*Muan*	JUN 1	*Zip*	OCT 19	*Yax*
FEB 17	*Pax*	JUN 21	*Zotz*	NOV 8	*Zac*
MAR 8	*Kayab*	JUL 11	*Tzec*	NOV 28	*Ceh*
MAR 28	*Cumku*	JUL 31	*Xul*	DEC 18	*Mac*
APR 17	*Uayeb*	AUG 20	*Yaxkin*		

The Year 13 Flint starts Apr. 23, 1932.

1933–1935

JAN 1–6	See Mac	APR 22	*Pop*	SEP 9	*Mol*
JAN 7	*Kankin*	MAY 12	*Uo*	SEP 29	*Chen*
JAN 27	*Muan*	JUN 1	*Zip*	OCT 19	*Yax*
FEB 16	*Pax*	JUN 21	*Zotz*	NOV 8	*Zac*
MAR 8	*Kayab*	JUL 11	*Tzec*	NOV 28	*Ceh*
MAR 28	*Cumku*	JUL 31	*Xul*	DEC 18	*Mac*
APR 17	*Uayeb*	AUG 20	*Yaxkin*		

The Year 1 Night starts Apr. 23, 1933.   *The Year 2 Rabbit starts Apr. 23, 1934.*   *The Year 3 Reed starts Apr. 23, 1935.*

1936 Leap Year

JAN 1–6	See 1935	APR 21	Pop	SEP 8	Mol
JAN 7	Kankin	MAY 11	Uo	SEP 28	Chen
JAN 27	Muan	MAY 31	Zip	OCT 18	Yax
FEB 16	Pax	JUN 20	Zotz	NOV 7	Zac
MAR 7	Kayab	JUL 10	Tzec	NOV 27	Ceh
MAR 27	Cumku	JUL 30	Xul	DEC 17	Mac
APR 16	Uayeb	AUG 19	Yaxkin		

The Year 4 Flint starts Apr. 22, 1936.

The first day of each month is shown. This day is counted as "0." Count forward to your day of the month.

1937–1939

JAN 1–5	See Mac	APR 21	Pop	SEP 8	Mol
JAN 6	Kankin	MAY 11	Uo	SEP 28	Chen
JAN 26	Muan	MAY 31	Zip	OCT 18	Yax
FEB 15	Pax	JUN 20	Zotz	NOV 7	Zac
MAR 7	Kayab	JUL 10	Tzec	NOV 27	Ceh
MAR 27	Cumku	JUL 30	Xul	DEC 17	Mac
APR 16	Uayeb	AUG 19	Yaxkin		

The Year 5 Night starts Apr. 22, 1937.   The Year 6 Rabbit starts Apr. 22, 1938.   The Year 7 Reed starts Apr. 22, 1939.

1940 Leap Year

JAN 1–5	See 1939	APR 20	Pop	SEP 7	Mol
JAN 6	Kankin	MAY 10	Uo	SEP 27	Chen
JAN 26	Muan	MAY 30	Zip	OCT 17	Yax
FEB 15	Pax	JUN 19	Zotz	NOV 6	Zac
MAR 6	Kayab	JUL 9	Tzec	NOV 26	Ceh
MAR 26	Cumku	JUL 29	Xul	DEC 16	Mac
APR 15	Uayeb	AUG 18	Yaxkin		

The Year 8 Flint starts Apr. 21, 1940.

1941–1943

JAN	1–4	See Mac	APR	20	Pop	SEP	7	Mol
JAN	5	Kankin	MAY	10	Uo	SEP	27	Chen
JAN	25	Muan	MAY	30	Zip	OCT	17	Yax
FEB	14	Pax	JUN	19	Zotz	NOV	6	Zac
MAR	6	Kayab	JUL	9	Tzec	NOV	26	Ceh
MAR	26	Cumku	JUL	29	Xul	DEC	16	Mac
APR	15	Uayeb	AUG	18	Yaxkin			

The Year 9 Night starts Apr. 21, 1941.	The Year 10 Rabbit starts Apr. 21, 1942.	The Year 11 Reed starts Apr. 21, 1943.

The first day of each month is shown. This day is counted as "0." Count forward to your day of the month.

1944 Leap Year

JAN	1–4	See 1943	APR	19	Pop	SEP	6	Mol
JAN	5	Kankin	MAY	9	Uo	SEP	26	Chen
JAN	25	Muan	MAY	29	Zip	OCT	16	Yax
FEB	14	Pax	JUN	18	Zotz	NOV	5	Zac
MAR	5	Kayab	JUL	8	Tzec	NOV	25	Ceh
MAR	25	Cumku	JUL	28	Xul	DEC	15	Mac
APR	14	Uayeb	AUG	17	Yaxkin			

The Year 12 Flint starts Apr. 10, 1944.		

1945–1947

JAN	1–3	See Mac	APR	19	Pop	SEP	6	Mol
JAN	4	Kankin	MAY	9	Uo	SEP	26	Chen
JAN	24	Muan	MAY	29	Zip	OCT	16	Yax
FEB	13	Pax	JUN	18	Zotz	NOV	5	Zac
MAR	5	Kayab	JUL	8	Tzec	NOV	25	Ceh
MAR	25	Cumku	JUL	28	Xul	DEC	15	Mac
APR	14	Uayeb	AUG	17	Yaxkin			

The Year 13 Night starts Apr. 20, 1945.	The Year 1 Rabbit starts Apr. 20, 1946.	The Year 2 Reed starts Apr. 20, 1947.

1948 Leap Year

JAN	1–3	See 1947	APR	18	Pop	SEP	5	Mol
JAN	4	Kankin	MAY	8	Uo	SEP	25	Chen
JAN	24	Muan	MAY	28	Zip	OCT	15	Yax
FEB	13	Pax	JUN	17	Zotz	NOV	4	Zac
MAR	4	Kayab	JUN	7	Tzec	NOV	24	Ceh
MAR	24	Cumku	JUL	27	Xul	DEC	14	Mac
APR	13	Uayeb	AUG	16	Yaxkin			

The Year 3 Flint starts Apr. 19, 1948.

The first day of each month is shown. This day is counted as "0." Count forward to your day of the month.

1949–1951

JAN	1–2	See Mac	APR	18	Pop	SEP	5	Mol
JAN	3	Kankin	MAY	8	Uo	SEP	25	Chen
JAN	23	Muan	MAY	28	Zip	OCT	15	Yax
FEB	12	Pax	JUN	17	Zotz	NOV	4	Zac
MAR	4	Kayab	JUN	7	Tzec	NOV	24	Ceh
MAR	24	Cumku	JUL	27	Xul	DEC	14	Mac
APR	13	Uayeb	AUG	16	Yaxkin			

The Year 4 Night starts Apr. 19, 1949. / The Year 5 Rabbit starts Apr. 19, 1950. / The Year 6 Reed starts Apr. 19, 1951.

1952 Leap Year

JAN	1–2	See 1951	APR	17	Pop	SEP	4	Mol
JAN	3	Kankin	MAY	7	Uo	SEP	24	Chen
JAN	23	Muan	MAY	27	Zip	OCT	14	Yax
FEB	12	Pax	JUN	16	Zotz	NOV	3	Zac
MAR	3	Kayab	JUN	6	Tzec	NOV	23	Ceh
MAR	23	Cumku	JUL	26	Xul	DEC	13	Mac
APR	12	Uayeb	AUG	15	Yaxkin			

The Year 7 Flint starts Apr. 18, 1952.

1953–1955

JAN 1	See Mac	APR 17	*Pop*	SEP 4	*Mol*
JAN 2	*Kankin*	MAY 7	*Uo*	SEP 24	*Chen*
JAN 22	*Muan*	MAY 27	*Zip*	OCT 14	*Yax*
FEB 11	*Pax*	JUN 16	*Zotz*	NOV 3	*Zac*
MAR 3	*Kayab*	JUN 6	*Tzec*	NOV 23	*Ceh*
MAR 23	*Cumku*	JUL 26	*Xul*	DEC 13	*Mac*
APR 12	*Uayeb*	AUG 15	*Yaxkin*		

The Year 8 Night starts Apr. 18, 1953.	The Year 9 Rabbit starts Apr. 18, 1954.	The Year 10 Reed starts Apr. 18, 1955.

The first day of each month is shown. This day is counted as "0." Count forward to your day of the month.

1956 Leap Year

JAN 1	See 1955	APR 16	*Pop*	SEP 3	*Mol*
JAN 2	*Kankin*	MAY 6	*Uo*	SEP 23	*Chen*
JAN 22	*Muan*	MAY 26	*Zip*	OCT 13	*Yax*
FEB 11	*Pax*	JUN 15	*Zotz*	NOV 2	*Zac*
MAR 2	*Kayab*	JUN 5	*Tzec*	NOV 22	*Ceh*
MAR 22	*Cumku*	JUL 25	*Xul*	DEC 12	*Mac*
APR 11	*Uayeb*	AUG 14	*Yaxkin*		

The Year 7 Flint starts Apr. 17, 1956.

1957–1959

		APR 16	*Pop*	SEP 3	*Mol*
JAN 1	*Kankin*	MAY 6	*Uo*	SEP 23	*Chen*
JAN 21	*Muan*	MAY 26	*Zip*	OCT 13	*Yax*
FEB 10	*Pax*	JUN 15	*Zotz*	NOV 2	*Zac*
MAR 2	*Kayab*	JUN 5	*Tzec*	NOV 22	*Ceh*
MAR 22	*Cumku*	JUL 25	*Xul*	DEC 12	*Mac*
APR 11	*Uayeb*	AUG 14	*Yaxkin*		

The Year 12 Night starts Apr. 17, 1957.	The Year 13 Rabbit starts Apr. 17, 1958.	The Year 1 Reed starts Apr. 17, 1959.

1960 Leap Year

		APR 15	*Pop*	SEP 2	*Mol*
JAN 1	*Kankin*	MAY 5	*Uo*	SEP 22	*Chen*
JAN 21	*Muan*	MAY 25	*Zip*	OCT 12	*Yax*
FEB 10	*Pax*	JUN 14	*Zotz*	NOV 1	*Zac*
MAR 1	*Kayab*	JUL 4	*Tzec*	NOV 21	*Ceh*
MAR 21	*Cumku*	JUL 24	*Xul*	DEC 11	*Mac*
APR 10	*Uayeb*	AUG 13	*Yaxkin*	DEC 31	*Kankin*

The Year 2 Flint starts Apr. 16, 1960.

The first day of each month is shown. This day is counted as "0." Count forward to your day of the month.

1961–1963

JAN 1–19	See Kankin	APR 15	*Pop*	SEP 2	*Mol*
JAN 20	*Muan*	MAY 5	*Uo*	SEP 22	*Chen*
FEB 9	*Pax*	MAY 25	*Zip*	OCT 12	*Yax*
MAR 1	*Kayab*	JUN 14	*Zotz*	NOV 1	*Zac*
MAR 21	*Cumku*	JUL 4	*Tzec*	NOV 21	*Ceh*
APR 10	*Uayeb*	JUL 24	*Xul*	DEC 11	*Mac*
		AUG 13	*Yaxkin*	DEC 31	*Kankin*

The Year 3 Night starts Apr. 16, 1961. | The Year 4 Rabbit starts Apr. 16, 1962. | The Year 5 Reed starts Apr. 16, 1963.

1964 Leap Year

JAN 1–19	See 1963	APR 14	*Pop*	SEP 1	*Mol*
JAN 20	*Muan*	MAY 4	*Uo*	SEP 21	*Chen*
FEB 9	*Pax*	MAY 24	*Zip*	OCT 11	*Yax*
FEB 29	*Kayab*	JUN 13	*Zotz*	OCT 31	*Zac*
MAR 20	*Cumku*	JUL 3	*Tzec*	NOV 20	*Ceh*
APR 9	*Uayeb*	JUL 23	*Xul*	DEC 10	*Mac*
		AUG 12	*Yaxkin*	DEC 30	*Kankin*

The Year 6 Flint starts Apr. 15, 1964.

1965–1967

JAN 1–18	See Kankin	APR 14	*Pop*	SEP 1	*Mol*
JAN 19	*Muan*	MAY 4	*Uo*	SEP 21	*Chen*
FEB 8	*Pax*	MAY 24	*Zip*	OCT 11	*Yax*
FEB 28	*Kayab*	JUN 13	*Zotz*	OCT 31	*Zac*
MAR 20	*Cumku*	JUL 3	*Tzec*	NOV 20	*Ceh*
APR 9	*Uayeb*	JUL 23	*Xul*	DEC 10	*Mac*
		AUG 12	*Yaxkin*	DEC 30	*Kankin*

The Year 7 Night starts Apr. 15, 1965.	The Year 8 Rabbit starts Apr. 15, 1966.	The Year 9 Reed starts Apr. 15, 1967.

The first day of each month is shown. This day is counted as "0." Count forward to your day of the month.

1968 Leap Year

JAN 1–18	See 1967	APR 13	*Pop*	AUG 31	*Mol*
JAN 19	*Muan*	MAY 3	*Uo*	SEP 20	*Chen*
FEB 8	*Pax*	MAY 23	*Zip*	OCT 10	*Yax*
FEB 28	*Kayab*	JUN 12	*Zotz*	OCT 30	*Zac*
MAR 19	*Cumku*	JUL 2	*Tzec*	NOV 19	*Ceh*
APR 8	*Uayeb*	JUL 22	*Xul*	DEC 9	*Mac*
		AUG 11	*Yaxkin*	DEC 29	*Kankin*

The Year 10 Flint starts Apr. 14, 1968.		

1969–1971

JAN 1–17	See Kankin	APR 13	*Pop*	AUG 31	*Mol*
JAN 18	*Muan*	MAY 3	*Uo*	SEP 20	*Chen*
FEB 7	*Pax*	MAY 23	*Zip*	OCT 10	*Yax*
FEB 27	*Kayab*	JUN 12	*Zotz*	OCT 30	*Zac*
MAR 19	*Cumku*	JUL 2	*Tzec*	NOV 19	*Ceh*
APR 8	*Uayeb*	JUL 22	*Xul*	DEC 9	*Mac*
		AUG 11	*Yaxkin*	DEC 29	*Kankin*

The Year 11 Night starts Apr. 14, 1969.	The Year 12 Rabbit starts Apr. 14, 1970.	The Year 13 Reed starts Apr. 14, 1971.

Mayan Oracles for the Millennium

1972 Leap Year

JAN 1–17	See 1971	APR 12	Pop	AUG 30	Mol
JAN 18	Muan	MAY 2	Uo	SEP 19	Chen
FEB 7	Pax	MAY 22	Zip	OCT 9	Yax
FEB 27	Kayab	JUN 11	Zotz	OCT 29	Zac
MAR 18	Cumku	JUL 1	Tzec	NOV 18	Ceh
APR 7	Uayeb	JUL 21	Xul	DEC 8	Mac
		AUG 10	Yaxkin	DEC 28	Kankin

The Year 1 Flint starts Apr. 13, 1972.

The first day of each month is shown. This day is counted as "0." Count forward to your day of the month.

1973–1975

JAN 1–16	See Kankin	APR 12	Pop	AUG 30	Mol
JAN 17	Muan	MAY 2	Uo	SEP 19	Chen
FEB 6	Pax	MAY 22	Zip	OCT 9	Yax
FEB 26	Kayab	JUN 11	Zotz	OCT 29	Zac
MAR 18	Cumku	JUL 1	Tzec	NOV 18	Ceh
APR 7	Uayeb	JUL 21	Xul	DEC 8	Mac
		AUG 10	Yaxkin	DEC 28	Kankin

The Year 2 Night starts Apr. 13, 1973. The Year 3 Rabbit starts Apr. 13, 1974. The Year 4 Reed starts Apr. 13, 1975.

1976 Leap Year

JAN 1–16	See 1975	APR 11	Pop	AUG 29	Mol
JAN 17	Muan	MAY 1	Uo	SEP 18	Chen
FEB 6	Pax	MAY 21	Zip	OCT 8	Yax
FEB 26	Kayab	JUN 10	Zotz	OCT 28	Zac
MAR 17	Cumku	JUN 30	Tzec	NOV 17	Ceh
APR 6	Uayeb	JUL 20	Xul	DEC 7	Mac
		AUG 9	Yaxkin	DEC 27	Kankin

The Year 5 Flint starts Apr. 12, 1976.

484

1977–1979

JAN 1–15	See Kankin	APR 11	*Pop*	AUG 29	*Mol*
JAN 16	*Muan*	MAY 1	*Uo*	SEP 18	*Chen*
FEB 5	*Pax*	MAY 21	*Zip*	OCT 8	*Yax*
FEB 25	*Kayab*	JUN 10	*Zotz*	OCT 28	*Zac*
MAR 17	*Cumku*	JUN 30	*Tzec*	NOV 17	*Ceh*
APR 6	*Uayeb*	JUL 20	*Xul*	DEC 7	*Mac*
		AUG 9	*Yaxkin*	DEC 27	*Kankin*

The Year 6 Night starts Apr. 12, 1977. · *The Year 7 Rabbit starts Apr. 12, 1978.* · *The Year 8 Reed starts Apr. 12, 1979.*

The first day of each month is shown. This day is counted as "0." Count forward to your day of the month.

1980 Leap Year

JAN 1–15	See 1979	APR 10	*Pop*	AUG 28	*Mol*
JAN 16	*Muan*	APR 30	*Uo*	SEP 17	*Chen*
FEB 5	*Pax*	MAY 20	*Zip*	OCT 7	*Yax*
FEB 25	*Kayab*	JUN 9	*Zotz*	OCT 27	*Zac*
MAR 16	*Cumku*	JUN 29	*Tzec*	NOV 16	*Ceh*
APR 5	*Uayeb*	JUL 19	*Xul*	DEC 6	*Mac*
		AUG 8	*Yaxkin*	DEC 26	*Kankin*

The Year 9 Flint starts Apr. 11, 1980.

1981–1983

JAN 1–14	See Kankin	APR 10	*Pop*	AUG 28	*Mol*
JAN 15	*Muan*	APR 30	*Uo*	SEP 17	*Chen*
FEB 4	*Pax*	MAY 20	*Zip*	OCT 7	*Yax*
FEB 24	*Kayab*	JUN 9	*Zotz*	OCT 27	*Zac*
MAR 16	*Cumku*	JUN 29	*Tzec*	NOV 16	*Ceh*
APR 5	*Uayeb*	JUL 19	*Xul*	DEC 6	*Mac*
		AUG 8	*Yaxkin*	DEC 26	*Kankin*

The Year 10 Night starts Apr. 11, 1981. · *The Year 11 Rabbit starts Apr. 11, 1982.* · *The Year 12 Reed starts Apr. 11, 1983.*

1984 Leap Year

JAN 1–14	See 1983	APR	9	Pop	AUG 27	Mol
JAN 15	Muan	APR	29	Uo	SEP 16	Chen
FEB 4	Pax	MAY	19	Zip	OCT 6	Yax
FEB 24	Kayab	JUN	8	Zotz	OCT 26	Zac
MAR 15	Cumku	JUN	28	Tzec	NOV 15	Ceh
APR 4	Uayeb	JUL	18	Xul	DEC 5	Mac
		AUG	7	Yaxkin	DEC 25	Kankin

The Year 13 Flint starts Apr. 10, 1984.

The first day of each month is shown. This day is counted as "0." Count forward to your day of the month.

1985–1987

JAN 1–13	See Kankin	APR	9	Pop	AUG 27	Mol
JAN 14	Muan	APR	29	Uo	SEP 16	Chen
FEB 3	Pax	MAY	19	Zip	OCT 6	Yax
FEB 23	Kayab	JUN	8	Zotz	OCT 26	Zac
MAR 15	Cumku	JUN	28	Tzec	NOV 15	Ceh
APR 4	Uayeb	JUL	18	Xul	DEC 5	Mac
		AUG	7	Yaxkin	DEC 25	Kankin

The Year 1 Night starts Apr. 10, 1985.   The Year 2 Rabbit starts Apr. 10, 1986.   The Year 3 Reed starts Apr. 10, 1987.

1988 Leap Year

JAN 1–13	See 1987	APR	8	Pop	AUG 26	Mol
JAN 14	Muan	APR	28	Uo	SEP 15	Chen
FEB 3	Pax	MAY	18	Zip	OCT 5	Yax
FEB 23	Kayab	JUN	7	Zotz	OCT 25	Zac
MAR 14	Cumku	JUN	27	Tzec	NOV 14	Ceh
APR 3	Uayeb	JUL	17	Xul	DEC 4	Mac
		AUG	6	Yaxkin	DEC 24	Kankin

The Year 4 Flint starts Apr. 9, 1988.

Part II—The Secular Calendar

1989–1991

JAN 1–12	See Kankin	APR 8	Pop	AUG 26	Mol
JAN 13	Muan	APR 28	Uo	SEP 15	Chen
FEB 2	Pax	MAY 18	Zip	OCT 5	Yax
FEB 22	Kayab	JUN 7	Zotz	OCT 25	Zac
MAR 14	Cumku	JUN 27	Tzec	NOV 14	Ceh
APR 3	Uayeb	JUL 17	Xul	DEC 4	Mac
		AUG 6	Yaxkin	DEC 24	Kankin

The Year 5 Night starts Apr. 9, 1989.   The Year 6 Rabbit starts Apr. 9, 1990.   The Year 7 Reed starts Apr. 9, 1991.

The first day of each month is shown. This day is counted as "0." Count forward to your day of the month.

1992 Leap Year

JAN 1–12	See 1991	APR 7	Pop	AUG 25	Mol
JAN 13	Muan	APR 27	Uo	SEP 14	Chen
FEB 2	Pax	MAY 17	Zip	OCT 4	Yax
FEB 22	Kayab	JUN 6	Zotz	OCT 24	Zac
MAR 13	Cumku	JUN 26	Tzec	NOV 13	Ceh
APR 2	Uayeb	JUL 16	Xul	DEC 3	Mac
		AUG 5	Yaxkin	DEC 23	Kankin

The Year 8 Flint starts Apr. 8, 1992.

1993–1995

JAN 1–11	See Kankin	APR 7	Pop	AUG 25	Mol
JAN 12	Muan	APR 27	Uo	SEP 14	Chen
FEB 1	Pax	MAY 17	Zip	OCT 4	Yax
FEB 21	Kayab	JUN 6	Zotz	OCT 24	Zac
MAR 13	Cumku	JUN 26	Tzec	NOV 13	Ceh
APR 2	Uayeb	JUL 16	Xul	DEC 3	Mac
		AUG 5	Yaxkin	DEC 23	Kankin

The Year 9 Night starts Apr. 8, 1993.   The Year 10 Rabbit starts Apr. 8, 1994.   The Year 11 Reed starts Apr. 8, 1995.

1996 Leap Year

JAN 1–11	See Kankin	APR 6	Pop	AUG 24	Mol
JAN 12	Muan	APR 26	Uo	SEP 13	Chen
FEB 1	Pax	MAY 16	Zip	OCT 3	Yax
FEB 21	Kayab	JUN 5	Zotz	OCT 23	Zac
MAR 12	Cumku	JUN 25	Tzec	NOV 12	Ceh
APR 1	Uayeb	JUL 15	Xul	DEC 2	Mac
		AUG 4	Yaxkin	DEC 22	Kankin

The Year 7 Flint starts Apr. 7 1996.

The first day of each month is shown. This day is counted as "0." Count forward to your day of the month.

1997–1999

JAN 1–10	See Kankin	APR 6	Pop	AUG 24	Mol
JAN 11	Muan	APR 26	Uo	SEP 13	Chen
JAN 31	Pax	MAY 16	Zip	OCT 3	Yax
FEB 20	Kayab	JUN 5	Zotz	OCT 23	Zac
MAR 12	Cumku	JUN 25	Tzec	NOV 12	Ceh
APR 1	Uayeb	JUL 15	Xul	DEC 2	Mac
		AUG 4	Yaxkin	DEC 22	Kankin

The Year 13 Night starts Apr. 7, 1987. | The Year 1 Rabbit starts Apr. 7, 1998. | The Year 2 Reed starts Apr. 7, 1999.

2000 Leap Year

JAN 1–10	See 1999	APR 5	Pop	AUG 23	Mol
JAN 11	Muan	APR 25	Uo	SEP 12	Chen
JAN 31	Pax	MAY 15	Zip	OCT 2	Yax
FEB 20	Kayab	JUN 4	Zotz	OCT 22	Zac
MAR 11	Cumku	JUN 24	Tzec	NOV 11	Ceh
MAR 31	Uayeb	JUL 14	Xul	DEC 1	Mac
		AUG 3	Yaxkin	DEC 21	Kankin

The Year 3 Flint starts Apr. 6, 2000.

2001–2003

JAN 1–9	See Kankin	APR 5	Pop	AUG 23	Mol
JAN 10	Muan	APR 25	Uo	SEP 12	Chen
JAN 30	Pax	MAY 15	Zip	OCT 2	Yax
FEB 19	Kayab	JUN 4	Zotz	OCT 22	Zac
MAR 11	Cumku	JUN 24	Tzec	NOV 11	Ceh
MAR 31	Uayeb	JUL 14	Xul	DEC 1	Mac
		AUG 3	Yaxkin	DEC 21	Kankin

The Year 4 Night starts Apr. 6, 2001.   The Year 5 Rabbit starts Apr. 6, 2002.   The Year 6 Reed starts Apr. 6, 2003.

The first day of each month is shown. This day is counted as "0." Count forward to your day of the month.

2004 Leap Year

JAN 1–9	See 2003	APR 4	Pop	AUG 22	Mol
JAN 10	Muan	APR 24	Uo	SEP 11	Chen
JAN 30	Pax	MAY 14	Zip	OCT 1	Yax
FEB 19	Kayab	JUN 3	Zotz	OCT 21	Zac
MAR 10	Cumku	JUN 23	Tzec	NOV 10	Ceh
MAR 30	Uayeb	JUL 13	Xul	NOV 30	Mac
		AUG 2	Yaxkin	DEC 20	Kankin

The Year 7 Flint starts Apr. 5, 2004.

2005–2007

JAN 1–8	See Kankin	APR 4	Pop	AUG 22	Mol
JAN 9	Muan	APR 24	Uo	SEP 11	Chen
JAN 29	Pax	MAY 14	Zip	OCT 1	Yax
FEB 18	Kayab	JUN 3	Zotz	OCT 21	Zac
MAR 10	Cumku	JUN 23	Tzec	NOV 10	Ceh
MAR 30	Uayeb	JUL 13	Xul	NOV 30	Mac
		AUG 2	Yaxkin	DEC 20	Kankin

The Year 8 Night starts Apr. 5, 2005.   The Year 9 Rabbit starts Apr. 5, 2006.   The Year 10 Reed starts Apr. 5, 2007.

2008 Leap Year

JAN 1–8	See 2007	APR 3	Pop	AUG 21	Mol
JAN 9	Muan	APR 23	Uo	SEP 10	Chen
JAN 29	Pax	MAY 13	Zip	SEP 30	Yax
FEB 18	Kayab	JUN 2	Zotz	OCT 20	Zac
MAR 9	Cumku	JUN 22	Tzec	NOV 9	Ceh
MAR 29	Uayeb	JUL 12	Xul	NOV 29	Mac
		AUG 1	Yaxkin	DEC 19	Kankin

The Year 11 Flint starts Apr. 4, 2008.

The first day of each month is shown. This day is counted as "0." Count forward to your day of the month.

2009–2011

JAN 1–7	See Kankin	APR 3	Pop	AUG 21	Mol
JAN 8	Muan	APR 23	Uo	SEP 10	Chen
JAN 28	Pax	MAY 13	Zip	SEP 30	Yax
FEB 17	Kayab	JUN 2	Zotz	OCT 20	Zac
MAR 9	Cumku	JUN 22	Tzec	NOV 9	Ceh
MAR 29	Uayeb	JUL 12	Xul	NOV 29	Mac
		AUG 1	Yaxkin	DEC 19	Kankin

The Year 12 Night starts Apr. 4, 2009.	The Year 13 Rabbit starts Apr. 4, 2010	The Year 1 Reed starts Apr. 4, 2011.

2012 Leap Year

JAN 1–7	See 2011	APR 2	Pop	AUG 20	Mol
JAN 8	Muan	APR 22	Uo	SEP 9	Chen
JAN 28	Pax	MAY 12	Zip	SEP 29	Yax
FEB 17	Kayab	JUN 1	Zotz	OCT 19	Zac
MAR 8	Cumku	JUN 21	Tzec	NOV 8	Ceh
MAR 28	Uayeb	JUL 11	Xul	NOV 28	Mac
		JUL 31	Yaxkin	DEC 18	Kankin

The Year 2 Flint starts Apr. 3, 2012.

TIME ENDS: DEC. 21, 2012—a day 3 Kankin

Your Magic Lightning Cards

The 20 Day Signs and 13 Day Numbers

In the following pages is everything you need to make a deck of Magic Lightning Cards, which, in turn, is everything you need to work the 13 Readings in this book.

Just photocopy the pages and cut out the "cards" that are preprinted here. This "deck" draws its inspiration from the Mayan practice of gathering stones, crystals, and other objects during a vision quest, then using them to divine answers to life's questions. A priest swirls these Magic Lightning Stones in front of him—gathers them, separates them—and then looks into them, taking his reading from their arrangement and relationship to one another.

Your Magic Lightning Cards are easier to interpret. Each has been imprinted with the Mayan and Aztec signs, names, and numbers. All you have to do is select a sign and look it up in one of this book's Answer sections. They also make great flash cards if you want to learn the ancient symbols by heart or recognize them faster by sight.

There is a card for every one of the 20 Mayan and Aztec Day Signs and a card for each of the 13 Day Numbers. Each Reading in the book will tell you when to use your Day Sign cards...and when to use the Day Numbers. Each card is keyed to a letter of our alphabet for easy lookup in the Answer sections.

Since you will only need to swirl—and not shuffle—the cards, they should work just fine once you have cut them out. After swirling a set of cutouts in front of you, just reach into the pile and take one out. Look at the sign you have drawn, read its name, and look it up by its name or alphabet key in the appropriate Answer section—either within the Reading you are currently conducting or in the Master Answer section of the Quick Reference Guide.

If you want to dress up your deck a little bit, you are welcome to mount your cutouts on the card stock of your choice. Rusty reds and turqouise blues were very popular in Mayan books, but dozens of bright pigments were used as ink. Just glue the cards to the colored background of your choice. And enjoy.

491

Day Sign A
(1 Bunch of Beans)

MAYA

AZTEC

Imix — Cipactli

Sea Creature | Alligator

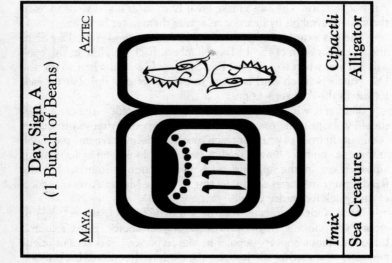

Day Sign B
(2 Bunches of Beans)

MAYA

AZTEC

Ik — Eecatl

Air | Wind

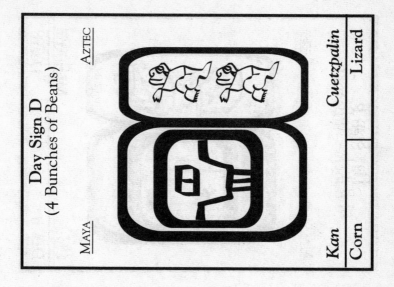

Day Sign C
(3 Bunches of Beans)

MAYA
AZTEC

Akbal	Calli
Night	House

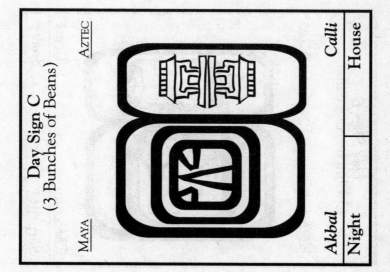

Day Sign D
(4 Bunches of Beans)

MAYA
AZTEC

Kan	Cuetzpalin
Corn	Lizard

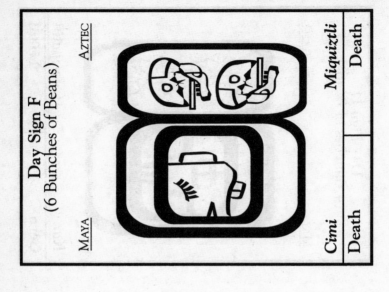

Day Sign E
(5 Bunches of Beans)

MAYA	AZTEC
Chicchan	Coatl
Serpent	Snake

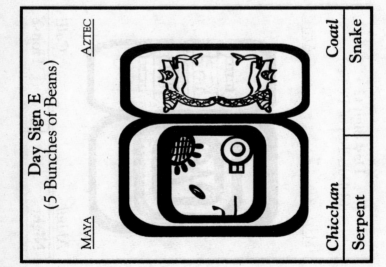

Day Sign F
(6 Bunches of Beans)

MAYA	AZTEC
Cimi	Miquiztli
Death	Death

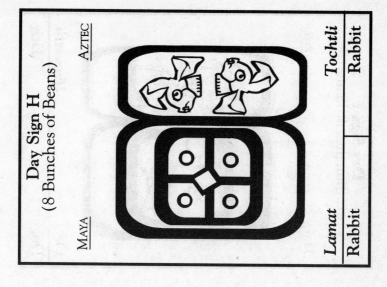

Day Sign G
(7 Bunches of Beans)

MAYA   AZTEC

Manik		*Mazatl*	
Deer		Deer	

Day Sign H
(8 Bunches of Beans)

MAYA   AZTEC

Lamat		*Tochtli*	
Rabbit		Rabbit	

Day Sign J
(10 Bunches of Beans)

MAYA | AZTEC

Oc — Dog

Itzcuintli — Dog

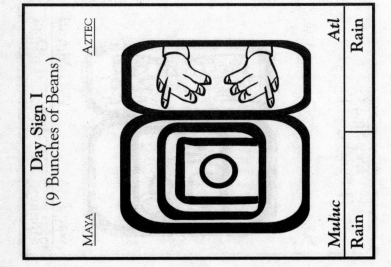

Day Sign I
(9 Bunches of Beans)

MAYA | AZTEC

Muluc — Rain

Atl — Rain

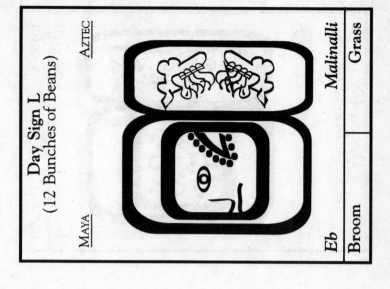

Day Sign L
(12 Bunches of Beans)

MAYA   AZTEC

Eb	Malinalli
Broom	Grass

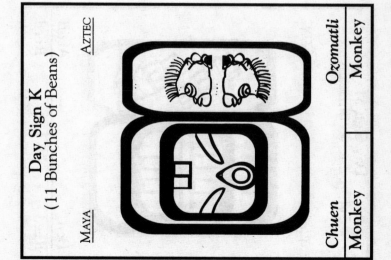

Day Sign K
(11 Bunches of Beans)

MAYA   AZTEC

Chuen	Ozomatli
Monkey	Monkey

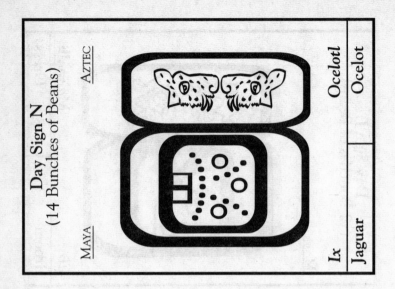

Day Sign M
(13 Bunches of Beans)

MAYA	AZTEC
Ben	Acatl
Reed	Reed

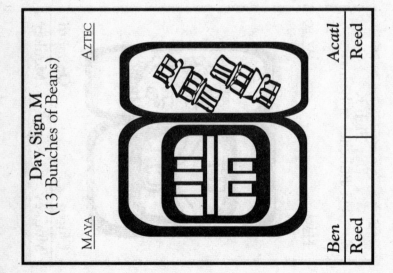

Day Sign N
(14 Bunches of Beans)

MAYA	AZTEC
Ix	Ocelotl
Jaguar	Ocelot

Day Sign O
(15 Bunches of Beans)

MAYA · AZTEC

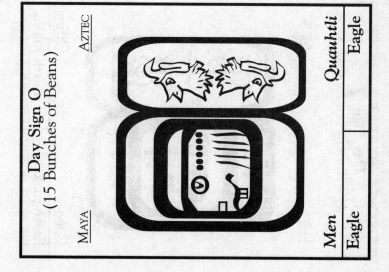

Men	Quauhtli
Eagle	Eagle

Day Sign P
(16 Bunches of Beans)

MAYA · AZTEC

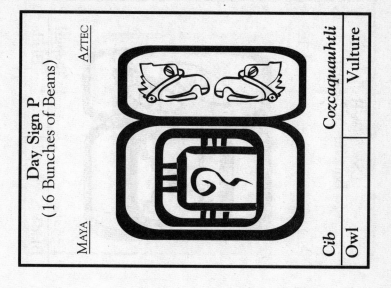

Cib	Cozcaquauhtli
Owl	Vulture

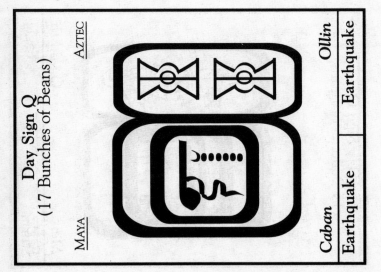

Day Sign R
(18 Bunches of Beans)

MAYA · AZTEC

Eznab	Tecpatl
Blade	Blade

Day Sign Q
(17 Bunches of Beans)

MAYA · AZTEC

Caban	Ollin
Earthquake	Earthquake

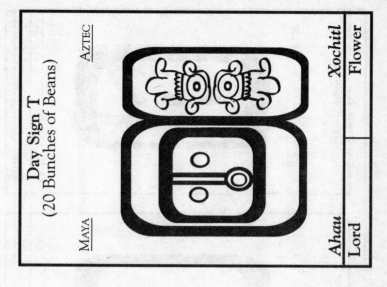

Day Sign S
(19 Bunches of Beans)

MAYA · AZTEC

Cauac — Storm · Quiauitl — Storm

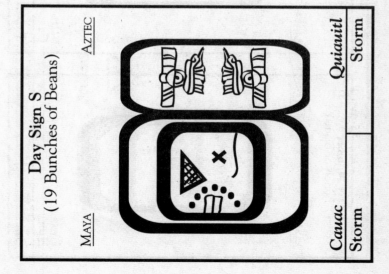

Day Sign T
(20 Bunches of Beans)

MAYA · AZTEC

Ahau — Lord · Xochitl — Flower

THE 13 DAY NUMBERS

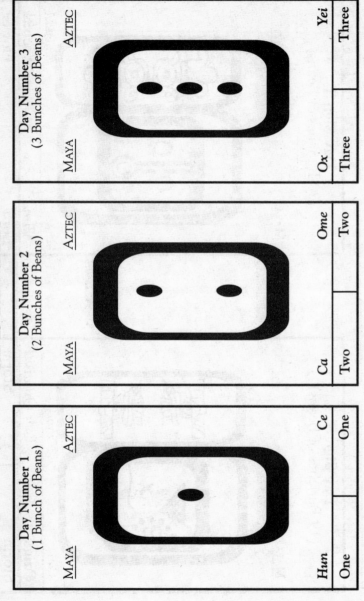

Day Number 1 (1 Bunch of Beans)	Day Number 2 (2 Bunches of Beans)	Day Number 3 (3 Bunches of Beans)
MAYA	AZTEC	MAYA	AZTEC	MAYA	AZTEC
Hun / One	Ce / One	Ca / Two	Ome / Two	Ox / Three	Yei / Three

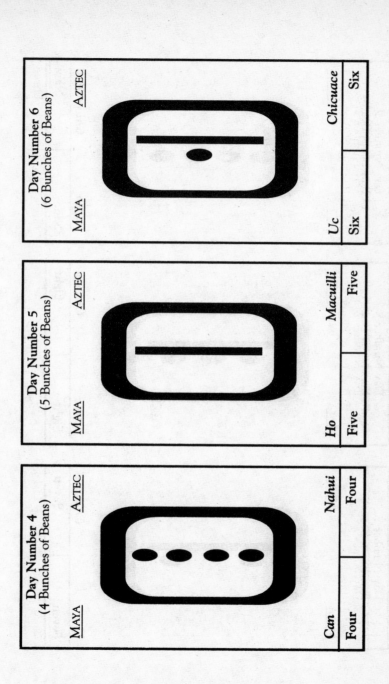

Day Number 4
(4 Bunches of Beans)

MAYA   AZTEC

		Nahui
		Four
Can		
Four		

Day Number 5
(5 Bunches of Beans)

MAYA   AZTEC

		Macuilli
		Five
Ho		
Five		

Day Number 6
(6 Bunches of Beans)

MAYA   AZTEC

		Chicuace
		Six
Uc		
Six		

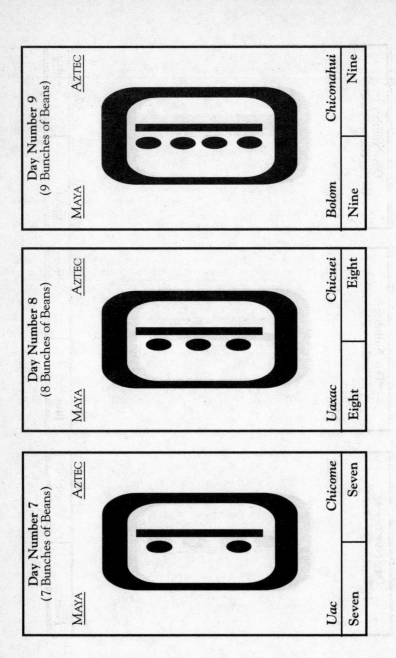

Day Number 7 (7 Bunches of Beans)	Day Number 8 (8 Bunches of Beans)	Day Number 9 (9 Bunches of Beans)
MAYA AZTEC	MAYA AZTEC	MAYA AZTEC
Uac — Chicome	Uaxac — Chicuei	Bolom — Chicomahui
Seven — Seven	Eight — Eight	Nine — Nine

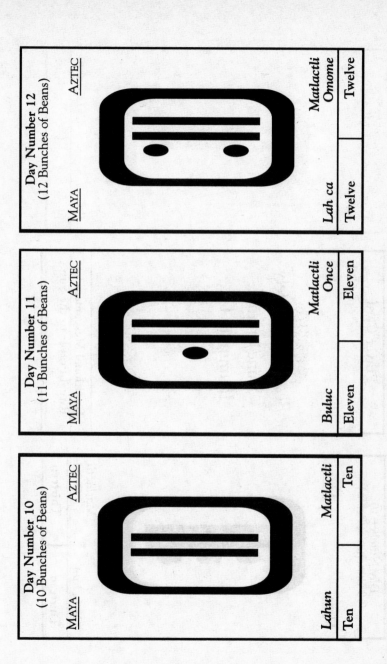

Day Number 10
(10 Bunches of Beans)

MAYA

AZTEC

Lahun

Matlactli

Ten	
Ten	

Day Number 11
(11 Bunches of Beans)

MAYA

AZTEC

Buluc

Matlactli Once

Eleven	
Eleven	

Day Number 12
(12 Bunches of Beans)

MAYA

AZTEC

Lah ca

Matlactli Omome

Twelve	
Twelve	

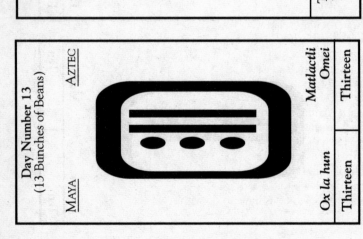

Prayer Card

Peacefully, Safely Shine on and Illuminate Us.

Traditional Mesoamerican Ritual Prayer to the Sun

Day Number 13
(13 Bunches of Beans)

MAYA   AZTEC

Ox la hun	Matlactli Omei
Thirteen	Thirteen

Index

ALL THE QUESTIONS YOU CAN ASK
(And everything you can do)

Once you have mastered the basic techniques described in the 13 Readings, you are welcome to use this "index" of questions to help you find the specific Reading you want to do tonight. Depending on your mission at this time, the book offers five paths through the oracle: Fast Track, Soul Search, Heart's Hunt, Game Plan, and Vision Quest. Select your path in Reading #0. Or turn, at any time, off onto any path that appeals to you. This index lists all the questions covered under each path. If you are undecided where you want to head tonight, review these lists to see which path appeals to you right now. Or consult the Contents for a list of the general lines of questioning used in the various Readings. Whichever way you choose to go, each of the Readings will allow you to ask specific questions about anything on your mind.

FASTRACK

	READING
What's the story?	#1
Where should I head with this?	#2
What's the history?	#3, #5
What's the score?	#4
What's it about?	#5
Zoom in!	#6
How does today factor in?	#7
What's coming tomorrow?	#8
What's in store these 20 days?	#9
Give me a year.	#10
Sharpen my view	#11
What should I do now?	#12
What do I have to do with it?	#13
What does each of us have to do with it?	#13

SOULSEARCH

READING

What's in the stars for today?	#1
What's in my stars?	#1
Where am I headed?	#2
What powers are at play?	#3, #5
How will things compute for me?	#4
What about my potential?	#5
Give me focus.	#6
What is today's outlook?	#7
What will I do tomorrow?	#8
Where will I be when these 20 days end?	#9
Cycle the seasons.	#10
Capture the moment.	#11
Give me the time.	#12
What's my sign?	#13

GAMEPLAN

READING

What kind of day is my problem like?	#1
Point me in the right direction.	#2
Lay it out for me.	#3, #5
What's it look like on the bottom line?	#4
What about it?	#5
Be specific.	#6
What are the environmental influences?	#7
What will conditions be like tomorrow?	#8
Plot it out for 20 days.	#9
Plot it out for 360 days.	#10
Picture it in my head.	#11
Picture it for so-and-so.	#11
Is this the right time?	#12
What's my field position?	#13

HEARTS HUNT READING

How is this love like a day?	#1
Where is this relationship heading?	#2
Show us some guidance.	#2
What's in store for her? him? us?	#3, #5
Rate this relationship on a scale from 1 to 13.	#4
What about this thing I have for _____?	#5
What about this thing I have with _____?	#5
Spare no details (who? what? when? why? how?)	#6
What kind of love does the day favor?	#7
Will _____ still love me tomorrow?	#8
Cast for us these 20 nights.	#9
Where will we be in a year?	#10
Tell how I feel.	#11
Tell how _____ feels.	#11
What season are we in?	#12
What kind of love will hunt me out?	#13

VIZ'N'QUEST READING

What is my mission for today?	#1
In what direction does my answer lie?	#2
Lead me forward.	#3, #5
What is my truth?	#4
What's it all about?	#5
Give me my mission.	#6
What is the thought for this day?	#7
What is sacred?	#8
Put me in the context of these 20 holy days.	#9
How will this year change me?	#10
Magic mirror, let me see.	#11
How do I fit into these times?	#12
What I am supposed to learn, this time around?	#13

Index to the Methods

Reading #0 Select your means and ends.

Readings #1–3 Select a Day Sign using beans, Lightning Cards, or Point-n-Click.

Readings #4–5 Select a Day Number using beans, Lightning Cards, or Point-n-Click.

Reading #6 Combine Day Signs and Day Numbers into one of 260 unique combinations.

Reading #7 Convert any date from our calendar to its Mayan equivalent. Consult the almanac. Then use beans, Lightning Cards, or Point-n-Click to customize the answer.

Reading #8 Keep track of time, using the sacred calendar. Find when to start your Vision Quest. Use the Almanac along with beans, Lightning Cards, or Point-n-Click.

Reading #9 Look ahead in the calendar, using its built-in patterns to plan ahead. Use beans, cards, or Point-n-Click to get specific.

Reading #10 Learn to identify the Tun year. Then use beans, cards, or Point-n-Click to see what it means for you.

Reading #11 Add depth to your consultations with images drawn from a sacred Mayan book. (Tarot enthusiasts, get out your deck!)

Reading #12 Learn how to factor in the seasonal influences of the secular Haab calendar into your interpretations.

Reading #13 Combine everything you know to construct a complete Mayan horoscope for you and your friends, using your birth dates.

Extra Credit Activities

Asking yes/no questions with beans	#2
Quick and dirty readings (command the oracle to speak)	#3
Who's coming into your life?	#4
Triple play (past, present, and future readings)	#3, #5
What's the clincher?	#6
Your personal horoscope for today	#7, #13
How this holy day affects your question...	#8

How this Uinal affects your question . . .   #9
How the current Tun affects your question . . .   #10
Access the book with Tarot cards   #11
Ask a question of the months   #12
Get your complete horoscope.   #13
    Flesh out your signs
    Find your picture
    Consider your mirror image
    Learn your myth
    Find your holy day
    Compute your Month Sign
    Identify your Year Bearer
    Consider your Ahau influence
    Get your personal horoscope for today
    How compatible are the two of you?

To Vision Quest: See the Extra, Extra Credit
    sections of the Readings   #1–13

Point-n-Click Diagrams

The 20 Day Signs   Reading #1   11
The 13 Day Numbers   Reading #4   66
Counts of 1–20   Reading #7   109
Haab months   Reading #12   186

Counting Charts

Day Signs A–T   Reading #6   96
                          Reading #7   107
                          Reading #8   115
                          Reading #13   191
                          Almanac I
Day Numbers 1–13   Reading #6   97
                          Reading #7   107
                          Reading #8   116
                          Reading #13   192
                          Almanac I
Starting with any Sea
    Creature or Alligator date   Reading #9   120–123
Starting with any Lord
    (Ahau) or Flower date   Reading #10   132–135

Main Charts

The 20 Day Signs—A–T, English names	Reading #1	8–9
Signs of the East, North, South, & West	Reading #2	30–37
Mayan glyphs for colors—color key	Reading #2	39
The 20 Day Signs with Mayan/ Aztec names	Reading #3	41–42
Pronunciation hints	Reading #3	43
Your Dream Animals keyed to glyphs	Reading #3	61–62
The 13 Day Numbers (1–13)	Reading #4	64
	Reading #5	81
Mesoamerican time-counting units (Kins, Uinals, Tuns, Katuns, Baktuns)	Reading #4	68
The Day Numbers & their gods	Reading #4	77–79
A 24–day sequence of signs & numbers	Reading #7	103
The Tzolkin (or Tonalpoualli), a 260–day sequence of signs and numbers	Reading #8	113
The Holy Year—a perpetual calendar	Reading #9	120–123
The Tun Years (by their Ahau sequence)	Reading #10	129
Tarot Correlation	Reading #11	141
Months of the Haab year	Reading #12	165–166
Haab dates and weather conditions (488 and A.D. 2000)	Reading #12	167
SUMMARY INSTRUCTIONS Quick Reference Guide		217
MASTER ANSWERS		
20 Day Signs		223
13 Day Numbers		247
260 Combinations		265
ALMANAC		
Introduction		427
Almanac I —The Sacred Calendar		438
Almanac II —The Secular Calendar		473
Make your Magic Lightning Cards		491
Books to read in your extra time		513
Music to listen to on the quest		517

Selected Bibliography

A wide variety of materials was used in researching and preparing the contents of this book. These are the ones I found most useful.

EXPERT SOURCES

There are only four surviving Mayan books in existence. Facsimiles of two of them were used in constructing the Almanac and in developing the art concept for the "Mayan Tarot" depicted in Reading #11:

Förstemann, Ernst, Ph.D., translation by Selma Wesselhoeft and A. M. Parker, *Commentary on the Dresden Codex*, Luguna Hills, CA: Aegean Park Press. (Originally published by the Peabody Museum of American Archeology and Ethnology, Harvard University, 1906.)

Love, Bruce, with an introduction by George E. Stuart, *The Paris Codex—Handbook for a Mayan Priest*, Austin, TX: University of Texas Press, 1994.

Villacorta, Carlos A., and J. Antonio Villacorta C., *The Dresden Codex —Drawings of the Pages and Commentary in Spanish*, Luguna Hills, CA: Aegean Park Press. (Originally published in Guatemala in 1930.)

Other expert sources that contributed greatly to this project were:

Coe, Michael D., *Breaking the Maya Code*, New York: Thames & Hudson, 1992.

Closs, Michael P., *Native American Mathematics*, Austin, TX: University of Texas Press, 1986.

Furst, Jill Leslie McKeever, *The Natural History of the Soul in Ancient Mexico*, New Haven: Yale University Press, 1995.

Freidel, David, Linda Schele, and Joy Parker, *Maya Cosmos—Three Thousand Years on the Shaman's Path*, New York: William Morrow & Company, 1993.

Gates, William, *An Outline Dictionary of Maya Glyphs*, New York: Dover Publications, 1978. (Originally published by the John Hopkins Press, 1931.)

Schele, Linda, and David Friedel, *A Forest of Kings—The Untold*

Story of the Ancient Maya, New York: William Morrow & Company, 1990.

Spinden, Herbert J., *The Reduction of Mayan Dates*, Papers of the Peabody Museum of American Archeology and Ethnology, Cambridge, MA: Harvard University Press, 1924.

Tozzer, Alfred M., *A Maya Grammar*, New York: Dover Publications, 1977. (Originally published as Papers of the Peabody Museum of American Archaeology and Ethnology, Harvard University, Volume 9, 1921.)

BACKGROUND & ANCILLARY MATERIALS

Additional background sources included:

Alonzo, Gualberto Zapata, professor, *An Overview of the Mayan World*, third edition, Merida, Mexico: Estudios Basso, 1983.

Aveni, Anthony, *Empires of Time—Calendars, Clocks, and Cultures*, New York: Basic Books, Inc., 1989.

Brotherston, *Image of the New World—The American Continent Portrayed in Native Texts*, London: Thames and Hudson, 1979.

Chaisson, Eric, *Relatively Speaking—Relativity, Black Holes, and the Fate of the Universe*, New York: W. W. Norton, 1988.

Coe, Michael D., *The Maya*, fourth edition, New York: Thames & Hudson, 1987.

Mallan, Chicki, *Guide to the Yucatán Peninsula*, Chico, CA: Moon Publications, 1988 edition.

Peterson, Frederick, *Ancient Mexico*, London: George Allen & Unwin, Ltd., 1959, 1961.

Soustelle, Jacques, *Daily Life of the Aztecs*, New York: The Macmillan Company, 1962.

Stuart, George E., and Gene S. Stuart, *The Mysterious Maya*, Washington, D.C.: National Geographic Society, 1983.

von Hagen, and Victor Wolfgang, *The Ancient Sun Kingdoms of the Americas*, Cleveland & New York: World Publishing Company, 1961.

Wilson, P. W., *The Romance of the Calendar*, New York: W. W. Norton, 1937.

CHRONOLOGIES

All of the historical dates cited in the Master Answer section and elsewhere in this book have been verified against various sources for accuracy. The following were the principal reference works used in verifying the dates from our own calendar.

Selected Bibliography

The American Heritage Picture History of World War II, New York: American Heritage Publishing Co., Inc., 1966.

Clifton, Daniel, editor in chief, *Chronicle of the 20th Century*, Mount Kisco, NY: Chronicle Publications, 1986.

Compton's Electronic Encyclopedia, America Online version, November 1995. Consulted were entries for the 50 states subtitled: "Some Notable People of . . ."

Degregorio, William A., *The Complete Book of U.S. Presidents*, New York: Wings Books, 1993.

Doren, Charles Van, editor, *Webster's American Biographies*, Springfield, MA: G. & C. Merriam Company, Publishers, 1975.

Grenville, J. A. S., *A History of the World in the Twentieth Century*, Cambridge, MA: The Belknap Press of Harvard University Press, 1994.

Hall, Kermit L., *The Oxford Companion to the Supreme Court of the United States*, New York: Oxford University Press, 1992.

Johnson, Otto, editor, *1996 Information Please Almanac*, Boston: Houghton Mifflin Co., 1996.

Morris, Richard B., editor, *Encyclopedia of American History*, New York: Harper & Row, Publishers, 1970.

Page One: Major Events 1920–1975 as Presented in the New York Times, New York: Arno Press, 1975.

Pursuit of Excellence: The Olympic Story, Danbury, CT: Grolier Enterprises, Inc., 1979.

Roberts, J. M., *History of the World*, New York: Oxford University Press, 1993.

Rolling Stone Rock Almanac: The Chronicles of Rock & Roll, by the editors of Rolling Stone, New York: Collier Books, 1983.

Scarre, Chris, *Timelines of the Ancient World—A Visual Chronology from the Origins of Life to* A.D. *1500*, New York: Dorling Kindersley, 1993. (Published in conjunction with The Smithsonian.)

Schlesinger, Arthur M., Jr., general editor, *The Almanac of American History*, Barnes & Noble, Greenwich, CT, 1993.

Wagman, John, *On This Day in America: An Illustrated Almanac of History, Sports, Science, and Culture*, New York: Gallery Books, 1990.

Wallechinsky, David, *The People's Almanac Presents the 20th Century: The Definitive Compendium of Astonishing Events, Amazing People, and Strange-but-True Facts*, Boston: Little, Brown and Company, 1995.

The World Book Encyclopedia, annual supplements for 1989 through 1995, Chicago: World Book, Inc. (1990 through 1995).

NEW-AGE TOOLS TO TRY

Gilbert, Adrian G., and Maurice M. Cotterell, *The Mayan Prophecies*, Shaftesbury, Dorset, U.K.: Element Press, 1995. This is a fascinating book that mixes science and art into an interesting read. (I especially loved the Appendices.)

Scofield, Bruce, *Day-Signs—Native American Astrology from Ancient Mexico*, Amherst, MA: One Reed Publications, 1991. Scofield writes an interesting astrology based on Aztec Day Signs. He also has a software package to go with it. Buy both from him at: One Reed Publications, P.O. Box 561, Amherst, MA 01004.

Speaking of software...I can't say enough to adequately praise Warren Anderson for his wonderful date conversion computer program for the Macintosh called **MacMaya**. To power-compute your own dates into authentic Mayan notations, get a copy from him at Box 811, Wilson, Wyoming 83014, or download a copy from CompuServe's Astronomy Forum. **MacMaya** is not only computationally supurb, but it's beautiful as well! (Without this tool, I would have gone mad!)

Acknowledgments

As part of the work on this book, I sought out popular music that seemed to have something to say about the subject matter and themes behind these oracles. I would like to thank all of the performing artists who contributed to the audio backdrop for my work on this project.

Overture: Blessed Union of Souls, *Home*, EMI Records, 1995: "I Believe."

Sea Creature　　Alligator
Sarah Nagourney, *Realm of My Senses*, Glass Beat Records, 1994: "Realm of My Senses," "Let Myself Go," "What Color Is It in Heaven," "Out of the Wilderness," and "Tomorrow."

Air　　Wind
Pearl Jam, *Ten*, Epic Records, 1991: "Alive," "Even Flow," "Release," and "Jeremy."

Night　　House
Tears for Fears, *Tears Roll Down (Greatest Hits)*, Mercury Records, 1992: "Sowing the Seeds of Love," "Pale Shelter," "Shout," "Mad World," and "Head Over Heals."

Corn　　Lizard
Boys on the Side, original soundtrack album, Arista Records, 1995: **Bonnie Raitt**, "You Got It," **Indigo Girls**, "Power of Two," **Melissa Etheridge**, "I Take You with Me," **Annie Lennox**, "Why," and **Sheryl Crow**, "Keep on Growing."

Serpent　　Snake
Whitesnake, *Greatest Hits*, Geffen Records, 1994: "Here I Go Again,"

"Slide It In," "Fool for Your Loving," "Still of the Night," and "Judgment Day."

⬛ Death   ⬛ Death

Bruce Cockburn, *Dart to the Heart*, Columbia Records, 1994: "Burden of the Angel/Beast," "Bone in My Ear," "Train in the Rain," "Someone I Used to Love," "Sunrise on the Mississippi," and "Tie Me at the Crossroads."

⬛ Deer   ⬛ Deer

REM, *Monster*, Warner Brothers Records, 1994: "Tongue," "I Don't Sleep, I Dream," "What's the Frequency, Kenneth?" "Bang and Blame," and "Let Me In."

⬛ Rabbit   ⬛ Rabbit

Earth, Wind & Fire, *Millennium*, Reprise Records, 1993: "Blood Brothers," "Honor the Magic," "Spend the Night," and "Love Across the Wire."

⬛ Rain   ⬛ Rain

Madonna, *Erotica*, Sire Records, 1992: "Why It's So Hard." **Jackyl**, *Jackyl*, Geffen Records, 1992: "When Will It Rain." **Madonna**: "Rain." **Jackyl**: "She Loves My Cock." And **Madonna**, *Bedtime Stories*, Sire Records, 1994: "Secret."

⬛ Dog   ⬛ Dog

Dire Straits, *On Every Street*, Warner Brothers Records, 1991: "You and Your Friend," "Fade to Black," "On Every Street," "Heavy Fuel," and "Calling Elvis."

Intermezzo: Blessed Union of Souls, *Home*, EMI Records, 1995: "Nora," "All Along," and "Let Me Be The One."

⬛ Monkey   ⬛ Monkey

Talking Heads, *Naked*, Sire Records, 1988: "The Facts of Life" and "Totally Nude." **John Mellencamp**, *Dance Naked*, Mercury Records,

1994: "Dance Naked." **Extreme,** *Waiting for the Punchline*, A&M Records, 1995: "Naked" and "Midnight Express."

Broom Grass
Black Sabbath, *Cross Purposes*, IRS Records, 1994: "Immaculate Deception," "Cardinal Sin," "Dying for Love," "Back to Eden," and "The Hand that Rocks the Cradle."

Reed Reed
ZZ Top, *Antenna*, RCA Records, 1994: "Pincushion," "Cherry Red," "World of Swirl," "Fuzzbox Voodoo," and "Breakaway."

Jaguar Ocelot
Collective Soul, *Collective Soul*, Atlantic Records, 1995: "The World I Know," "Smashing Young Man," "She Gathers Rain," "Simple," "Untitled," and "Reunion."

Eagle Eagle
Dare, *Blood from Stone*, A&M Records, 1991: "Wings of Fire" and "We Don't Need a Reason." **Rusted Root**, *When I Woke*, Polygram Records, 1994: "Cruel Sun," "Ecstasy," and "Back to the Earth."

Owl Vulture
k.d. lang, *Ingénue*, Sire Records, 1992: "Wash Me Clean," "Constant Craving," "The Mind of Love," "Season of Hollow Soul," and "Tears of Love's Recall."

Earthquake Earthquake
Poison, *Flesh & Blood*, Capital Records, 1990: "Strange Days of Uncle Jack" and "Valley of Lost Souls." **Metalica**, *. . . And Justice for All*, Electra Records, 1988: "Blackened" and "To Live Is To Die."

Blade Flint
Rush, *Roll the Bones*, Atlantic Records, 1991: "Dreamline," "Bravado," "Ghost of a Chance," "Roll the Bones," and "You Bet Your Life."

⬛ Storm   ⬛ Storm

The Unplugged Collection, volume 1, Warner Brothers Records, 1994: **Neil Young:** "Like a Hurricane." **k.d. lang:** "(I'd walk through the snow) Barefoot." **Elvis Costello:** "Deep Dark Truthful Mirror." **Don Henley:** "Come Rain or Come Shine." **10,000 Maniacs:** "Don't Talk." **REM:** "Half a World Away."

⬛ Lord   ⬛ Flower

MeatLoaf, *Bat Out of Hell—II*, MCA Records, 1993: "Wasted Youth," "Everything Louder than Everything Else," "Objects in the Rear View Mirror May Appear Closer than They Are," "Rock and Roll Dreams Come Through," "I'd Do Anything for Love (But I Won't Do That)," and "It Just Won't Quit."

Finale: Blessed Union of Souls, *Home*, EMI Records, 1995: "End of the World," "Heaven," and "Forever for Tonight."

Postlude: *Grammy's Greatest Moments*, Atlantic Records, 1994: **Billy Joel:** "We Didn't Start the Fire." **Huey Lewis and the News:** "Heart of Rock 'N Roll." **The Doobie Brothers:** "What a Fool Believes." **Eric Clapton**, *The Cream of Clapton*, Polygram Records, 1995: "White Room," "After Midnight," and "Layla."

Thanks also to: The African Cultural Art Forum for the "Spellbound" incense . . . to Butch for the amulets . . . to the Streets of Philadelphia for the Magic Lightning Stones . . . to WGMP Phillies Baseball Network . . . to the Cleveland Indians and the Atlanta Braves for a great Series . . . and The Weather Channel for continuous updates on hurricane season.

But most of all: Thanks and Eternal Love to Tory, the one who not only abides my eccentricity on a daily basis but encourages me to pursue my own destiny, even when it means she has to contribute her editorial skills gratis. (I'll pay you back someday, babe.) To Addie, who, as a price of having a father who writes, does without a very active one in her life. And to the family dog, Turtle: Thanks for leading me to the best Lightning Stones a city has ever rendered up.

Acknowledgments

Mayan Oracles for the Millennium was originally drafted over the course of 260 days, between spring and winter 1995. It was during the worst drought in Philadelphia's history and one of the heaviest tropical storm seasons of all times. To the Maya, rain was everything. So, too, was it for us this year. May your body never want for water, nor your soul for sustenance.

RTKaser ●●●●●

bey ti' ka'an, bey ti' lu'um
As is the sky, so is the earth.
—Words of a Mayan Shaman